Myopic Me!

MYOPIC ME!

CAPTURED BY THE FAITH-TIME CONTINUUM

JOHN D LANE JR.

XULON PRESS

Xulon Press
2301 Lucien Way #415
Maitland, FL 32751
407.339.4217
www.xulonpress.com

Printed in the United States of America.

ISBN-13: 978-1-54563-881-1

TABLE OF CONTENTS

PREFACE TO *MYOPIC ME!*

"*Myopic Me!*" is the universal cry and confession of every person on earth at some point in this life. It is Paul the Apostle's query to the universe when he asks the fundamental question: "Who can save *Myopic Me!*"[1] The baby, wet from the womb, effectively articulates, "Hold me, feed me, protect me!" Even the old man rants until his bed is changed, wanting something different to eat, and demanding morphine for the pain! We all want to live in comfort. We crave the praise of men. We seek pleasure at great expense. We work long hours to win this race, to grab this brass ring, to stand on this victor's stage, to win this lottery, or to gain this fleeting freedom. We all want our questions answered, confirming that all the planets actually do revolve around us, just as Alexander the Great and Ptolemy have taught us.

Even the writing of this book implies some kind of superior knowledge concerning the soul's great affliction. The experts describe the symptoms of this universal dis-ease: "When someone has *myopia*, they will experience blurry vision when looking at things that are far away [looking at the needs of others]. Objects that are close [to *Myopic Me!*], however, can be seen clearly."[2] The net result is self-centric acquisition, aberrant self-love, and obsession with ones appearance, perception, and valuation by others. *Myopic Me!* becomes the quintessential hyperbole, and therefore becomes humorous in the extreme case. Acquisition is the foremost attribute of the narcissist, offering the most fragile salvation of all.

"At some point we have to face the certain reality: despite all the good the world seems to offer, true happiness can only be found in one thing: shopping" (Ally McBeal, 1997 as cited in Wagner, 2007). In today's society, shopping is positioned as a major source of happiness and a signal of status and success. Messages in popular media not only condone the excessive acquisition of material possessions but promotes it. Indeed, there is a great deal of pressure to think

---

[1]   Romans 7:24.

[2]   *Myopia*. Despres.

that "we are what we have" . . . Indeed, buying behavior becomes a response to the desire to exert control over one's life.[3]

The multiyear TV series, *The Big Bang Theory,* has presented Sheldon Cooper as the poster boy for this extreme condition of the soul and the eye. His high IQ and "narcissistic droning"[4] provide a memorable portrait of ***Myopic Me!,*** but "Shelly" is not the only embodiment of near-sightedness in this book. When my own story is told, with help from Dorothy, Alice, Solomon, Sheldon, Einstein, and the One who walked among us,[5] you may discover that your own story has great significance. With Mother Teresa at one end of the ***Myopic Continuum,*** and infamous world leaders at the other end, everyone can find their position with the giants of history and fantasy.

Einstein spent his entire life seeking the unifying *Theory of Everything* which would reconcile all the conflicting theories in the world of physics in a single equation. He disliked the big bang theory because of its implicit require-ment that the Word of God alone could speak the essential Genesis Particle into existence in the beginning. The brilliant physicist believed in many invisible things, yet he rejected the One who reconciles all things to Himself, offering the only harmony possible for physicists or fools.[6] Omphaloskeptical, every one of us, we tend to believe what we can see clearly with our nearsighted compre-hension. Focusing on our personal equivalent of this Greek navel, we have all neglected compassion in pursuit of every grandiose priority. We fill our eyes with self-fulfilling dreams, diving into our black pool of melancholy with Narcissus. Our personal Nemesis supernaturally appears with all the easy answers, guiding us to the bridge over our self-reflexive black pond.[7]

Each of us falls into *Oz* from our personal wall cloud. Holding our breath, we slide feet-first with Alice down the rabbit hole into *Wonderland*. We discover Sheldon and Alice sharing a mutual disdain for the dark Queen. Sheldon's arro-gance and rudeness causes the Cal Tech President to declare, "Off with Sheldon's head!" But Sheldon's true Nemesis is Barry Kripke, whose great intellect and Elmer Fudd lisp put him at odds with *Siri* as well as Sheldon. Sheldon's episodes provide the prooftext that arrogance is an affliction, and being wounded is a universal reality. The one wounded, wounds everyone they know; so Sheldon's friends are bound up in his brokenness, in often humorous ways. When the nar-cissist is healed, the others have to be healed as well. Narcissism is a community sport, with casualties to go around.

---

[3] Martinez. *Consumed by Consumption.*

[4] *The Vartabedian Conundrum.* Big Bang Transcripts.

[5] John 1:1-16.

[6] Colossians 1:20; 2 Corinthians 5:19.

[7] *Narcissus.* Wikipedia.

Einstein's *Space-Time* proffers a default religion of materialism that frees **Myopic Me!** from any accountability for brother, sister, neighbor, or friend. While the *Faith-Time Continuum* points continually to abundant life with no end, Space-Time Materialism preaches the melancholy philosophy of "Nothingness," raising up priests for every generation. This religion of the masses preaches that Creation is a random event out of Nothingness, producing life as an accident, with Nothingness returning at death.

This *Theory of Everything* is swallowed whole, and every **Myopic Me!** wants editing privileges. The craving for the visible object which is near, pre-empts the blurry object which is far away. I crave the things of this world I can see with my eye, touch with my fingers, and taste with my tongue. For a long time, I rejected the One who could save me from myself, misconstruing His offer of eternal life which comes with a single necessary and sufficient condition:

"Believe in the Son Whom I have sent!"[8]

My need to be at the Center of Everything started in my crib when my raison d'être was survival. Survival and pleasure prevent me from feeling the pain of the other. I avoided pain, using alcohol to quench any symptoms as soon as they appeared. Masking the external pain, the interior pain increased, blunting any potential for compassion. My checkbook made no mention of the needs of others, and my shelves celebrated my own greatness. Compassion was born when I finally apprehended the messages coming to me through the *Faith-Time Continuum*—when I finally took seriously God's invisible Wind blowing through my life.[9]

Myopic Me! spotlights my own fractured journey through many chapters, as I have searched for my way Home. Lying down in autumn leaves, I searched the wind for its hidden messages.[10] I discovered that my vain efforts could not make me presentable to God during this time when self-destruction had become my wheelhouse. Unmerited favor was unknown to me, and any insinuation of compassion in my life had to come from the pages of Machiavelli's, *The Prince*.

Captured by the Faith-Time Continuum, the subtext of my book, reveals how a benevolent Voice showed me the Way out of *Oz* and *Wonderland*, disarming the dark Queen and silencing the Nonsense of Conformism. The Caterpillar that

---

[8]   John 6:29.

[9]   John 3:7-8.

[10]   Ecclesiastes 1:14.

had nearly enveloped me in its blue smoke yielded to the Transformative Wind.[11] I learned that this *Faith-Time Continuum* begins and ends with two Greek letters, yet He rejects every empty Greek philosophy offering death. *Alpha and Omega* has become the Person speaking encouragement, love, and truth. "The Way, the Truth, and the Life" has neutralized the depressing wind of my own self-interest, the meaningless life. Trustworthy friends, and even neighbors and enemies, now illuminate my path with the favorable Wind sorting every motive of my heart.[12]

In writing this book, I received help and encouragement from John Buchanan, Steven Foley, Jill Moss, Ann Lane, and Christabel Barry. Each one has helped me clarify the autobiographical thread that is the paradox throughout the whole story. Pastor Tim Hatch helped me unlatch the abounding door into Grace, hastening my escape from the cowardly kingdom of **Myopic Me!** He helped me grasp the vast *Good News* which comes through this paradox of the Cross, the Tomb, and the Resurrection from the dead. He helped me more fully articulate an eternal kingdom coming down from heaven,[13] while getting to know the One who reconciles all things to Himself.[14] In this process, I have learned that two Master's degrees do not a writer make. After receiving the Master of Fine Arts degree in creative writing from UNC at Greensboro and the Master of Science in Rhetoric from Rensselaer, I have spent the past four years learning to write!

I assumed it would take a couple of months to finish this project since I had written more than fourteen hundred blogs in the previous eight years. God had different plans, communicating this to me through the *Faith-Time Continuum*. You may be wondering why the Creator of all things would help me with this undertaking. It is because of His lovingkindness. He desires that my brokenness will finally reveal His greatness and His mercy. It is His kindness that has bent down to lift me up, and His wounds have healed me. His Spirit stands guard over my fractured life, and I have no better Hero than Him.

When my wife introduced me to a brand new bookstore nearly four years ago, I was immediately hooked on the atmosphere which has been so beneficial for the writing process. I have received encouragement from many folks at *An Unlikely Story*, Jeff Kinney's masterful *Bookstore and Café* in Plainville USA. When I was served during the first week by Chelsea, she brought free coffee to me in the giant "Edith Ann"[15] leather chair, where she could see that my feet did not touch the floor! The multimillionaire author of the *Wimpy Kid* series of children's books, arrived five minutes later to make sure I was comfortable in

---

[11] John 3:7-8.

[12] Hebrews 4:12-13.

[13] Mark 1:10.

[14] Colossians 1:19-20.

[15] *Edith Ann*. Saturday Night Live.

his brand new store. He offered to order any chair I picked out from the leather furniture catalog! He and I searched the whole first floor of the book store to find a more appropriate chair. Finding one, he carried it over his head to the computer nook near the front window. I've been sitting there nearly every day since. Immersed in this highly supportive atmosphere, my one book has become five books nearing completion.

This beautiful store near Boston remains a minor miracle in the era of instant gratification by way of *Amazon Prime*! Jeff's vision is to creatively encourage children and parents to read together. When children don't get their *Myopic Way!* they resort to one tactic which sometimes gets them what they want. They cry. They scream. They tantrum! But Wisdom shows me daily that the screaming child is an apt metaphor for *Myopic Me!* It is no accident that I have been treated like a king, while I have written this self-centric book. Though adults scream in sophisticated ways, their tantrums can be far more costly, producing the broken marriage, the drug addiction, the homelessness, and a wide variety of suicidal episodes. Suicide, a major footnote in my own story, is so often choreographed over decades. After all, the wages of sin is death.[16]

Not a week has passed, writing at *An Unlikely Story,* that someone has not asked about the progress of my book.

We often talk about the foundations of life and literature, with friends dropping in to sit and talk in the wonderful atmosphere of the visionary store. Drew, Jim, and Ann have been regular visitors who have brought their insights and much encouragement each time they appear in front of my chair. With Drew in China now, and Jim working in Kazakstan, we have to use *Facetime* and *Facebook Messenger*. In no special order, my thanks and appreciation go out to bookstore regulars, Kaitlin, Shaelyn, Kistin, Lynda, Debbie, Glynnis, the Sarahs, Colleen, Duncan, Ari, Amanda, Sandra, Sam, Leo, Karen, Jenna, Bonnie, Mel, and Anna for their friendship and support!

If this story of *Myopic Me!* helps you hear the Voice speaking through the *Faith-Time Continuum*, then I hope you will also read additional books soon to be published. Each one expands on the universal persona of *Myopic Me!* with topics that are relevant for many generations of readers.

- *Time Travel with Solomon and Einstein*
- *Freedom from Religion*
- *Tearing Down the Dividing Walls of Hostility*
- *The False gods of Identity*
- *The Seventh Seal*

---

[16] Romans 6:23.

1.

WORLD AT WAR.

The room was electric in anticipation of the imminent good news. At my age, I didn't know good news from bad, but I could feel the powerful emotions that erupted in that room. I had become the little prince, the antidote for war and familial loss. I was the tiny hero on a rocking horse, standing up on my fat legs before toddlers should be able **to** do that. This was the season when I cracked my head with the hammer's claw while Mama hung clothes on the line, and it was the time when every visitor to our house came straight to me with their wide smiles and hugs of thanksgiving. They were celebrating life during a world war that was finally turning. I was born into this crucible of meaning which no generation since can fully appreciate or imagine. Every family was affected, losing a son or a father. Everyone wore the dark specter of death like a shroud.

Though I was very young, I was one of six family members who had packed the small pine-paneled office to hear the Announcement of all announcements. When the giant radio on Pop's homemade bookshelf crackled with the good news, joy rushed back into the world like oxygen filling a vacuum. Every straining face snapped to full attention—adrenalin leaped like a fire flashing through dry leaves.

Japan Surrenders, End of War!

Screams exploded, as if lightning had struck the radio, frizzing every human hair in that stuffy room. Wild emotions burst forth when peace demanded full eye-contact between all five of my family members who were pressing against each other. Incredulous. Stunned. The faces told five versions of the grown-up reaction, and their looks could have been recorded in historical journals of the day.

The books soon to be written would more than fill Pop's small office, and the tales of courage, horror, and monumental joy could finally be completed. Sharpened pencils whirled, and fresh typewriter ribbons unwound around the world, as final paragraphs were being written with the denouement too good to be true. This was good news so rare that every nation and people group would soon begin to reap the benefits. Even the Germans and Japanese would walk away from the policies of madmen, to find a different economic future.

1

It was the end of World War II, but no one in the room heard the whirring wings of the dirty angels humming their favorite song. "We Steal, we kill, and we destroy, for this is our greedy lot!" No one in the room could imagine the dark philosophies that would soon fill up the vacuum left by Fascism. Stalin's *Gulags* were being expanded while my family screamed for joy. The Soviet Premiere was shifting his stock of workers in Siberia to include all the intellectuals, the writers, the professionals, and the doctors. They were already being rounded up to serve in the hideous work camps to be forgotten in the frozen tundra.[17] Mao Zedong would soon starve forty-five million Chinese farmers and citizens;[18] and no one in Pop's den could have imagined that he would take away their plows, returning blocks of metal as silent sentinels in their unplowed fields.[19]

Without a second thought, Pol Pot was already choreographing his *Killing Fields*,[20] having received his education in all things sexual from the king's concubines. While the strongmen in Africa were beginning to plan their harems, they had no energy left for the starving families. Edie Amin turned his paranoia and narcissistic options to his own advantage. "Amin's rule [would be] characterized by rampant human rights abuses, political repression, ethnic persecution, extra-judicial killings, nepotism, corruption, and gross economic mismanagement."[21] Millions would starve in future time, when rulers like Amin turned their backs on their own citizens.

Returning to my rocking horse in the living room, ***Myopic Me!*** had no idea that these battlefields in Future Time would be virtually invisible on my street, or in my neighborhood. The churches in town were shrinking already, as the good news of peace rushed to fill the ears of the whole world. Churches everywhere had taken on the form of religious institutions, while denying the power of God's living and active Word. Of course, most people were already looking for a new car, a washer, a stove, or the latest convenience from their corner store.

Many Germans nervously cheered the defeat of der Führer, even though they had lived through the hyperinflation in their country in 1923. World War I had come and gone, but the horrors of war left deep scars in the German consciousness. More than a decade before my arrival in the Land of Oz, the world's population had barely healed from the first war where the machine guns had left trenches full of blood. Whirling shrapnel tore the legs from under armies which stumbled through the endless barbed wire strung against any advance of the enemy. It was a stalemate of death and horror before Germany

---

[17] *Gulag*. History.

[18] *Mao Zedong*. Wikipedia.

[19] Fu. *God's Double Agent*.

[20] *Khmer Rouge Killing Fields*. Wikipedia.

[21] Idi Amin. Wikipedia.

2

finally surrendered. Bob Dylan spoke remotely in his Nobel acceptance speech, reflecting on the literature that impacted his own writing. In recounting Erich Maria Remarque's shattering war story, Dylan said World War I became an intense first-personal experience for him.

> "All Quiet on the Western Front was another book that [greatly impacted my soul and my song writing]. All Quiet on the Western Front is a horror story. This is a book where you lose your childhood, your faith in a meaningful world, and your concern for individuals. You're stuck in a nightmare. Sucked up into a mysterious whirlpool of death and pain. You're defending yourself from elimination. You're being wiped off the face of the map. Once upon a time you were an innocent youth with big dreams about being a concert pianist. Once you loved life and the world, and now you're shooting it to pieces."[22]

This terror scape was the setting for Germans crossing over at Christmas time to sing Carols with the Allied soldiers when the Holy Spirit and the powerful traditions of Christianity usurped the exigencies of war. The next day the same soldiers might have killed each other when the battles were renewed. Before this World War I horror-scape from Remarque's pen, Baum had written his wild dance in Oz. Striding through all those wild sets, Dorothy's time-warp encountered Remarque's doppelgänger in the foxhole more than once. She could faintly discern her own family members in this dreamscape from Oz.

After World War I the government of Germany had printed the fantastical hundred-trillion Mark note—worth a mere twenty-four American dollars. The Jews had been blamed by many in Germany in the late-1930s, opening the door for Hitler's rise to power as the anti-Jewish leader of the Nationalist Socialist Worker's Party. He promised to fix the Jewish problem. This twisted misanthrope exploited the millions afflicted by the global Depression which swept the whole world. Adolf Hitler soon gained such power that he mandated public worship of himself. The roar of *Sieg Heil* soon could be heard at all the mass gatherings of his Socialist Party, and many Germans had drifted away from the worship of God. Many had come to embrace religious rituals, forgetting the Cross and the power of God's Spirit. When Hitler removed every Jewish reference from

---

[22] Dylan, Bob. *Bob Dylan–Nobel Lecture*.

the Bible,[23] the masses did not flinch. If Jesus was a Jew, then He was part of the problem.[24]

The upbeat tone in the *Wizard of Oz* had played well in 1936 when L. Frank Baum's prophetic story of diversity erupted with a happy dance after the Wicked Witch of the West was vanquished. While the *Wonderful Wizard of Oz* exposed his many limitations in the Emerald City, Dorothy became the one to confront every evil, finding the good. The world would need this skill at the war's end. The child would lead the nations into peaceful coexistence. But it was Dorothy's serendipity with the burning straw of her new friend that destroyed the Nemesis of Oz. The *Wicked Witch of the West* had to be vanquished before Dorothy and her friends could find their way home again.

With technological, nationalist, and financial incongruities to go around, a spiritual battle boiled over in the heavenly realm while Dorothy confronted good and evil with her innocent authority. Hitler and Hirohito were strange bedfellows directing the ensuing global genocide. In this earthquake of a financial kind, Mussolini had risen to power in Italy, seeking to restore territories lost since the collapse of the Roman Empire. His *brown shirts* used violence to silence every voice speaking against the rise of the Fascist government. Germany was plotting and carrying out early military expansions across Europe. Hitler's generals were employing the blitzkrieg to extend the empire of Germany across the docile continent of Europe.

Their schizophrenic alliance presaged a day when Japanese and Aryan blood would be shed in a final monumental battle to determine the One Ruler of the World. Of course, God had a different plan, for He is the suppressor of nations, placing His fingernail down along the coast of France, while His bright Light flashed along the industrial coast of Japan. He would quickly bring low both idolatrous kingdoms[25] as the Angel of Death took thirty-million soldiers and civilians before the War's end.

My uncle's photograph was hung on the wall that day when the radio speaker crackled with good news. He was proudly holding his big Press camera, flash bulb loaded and ready to fire. He would have flown aerial reconnaissance flights over the battle fields. He never reached the front lines to document the horror of war and the courage of common men. Though I understood nothing then about his untimely death, his ship had gone straight to the bottom of the Mediterranean Sea in 1944.

My sisters were broken hearted, for they loved Uncle Grayson. My mother and grandmother were disconsolate. A German bomb had found the fuel tanks, and Grayson's days as a war correspondent ended before they had begun. Nearly

---

[23] Metaxas. *Bonhoeffer.*

[24] *Hyperinflation.* Wikipedia.

[25] Daniel 2:21

everyone onboard died during this oft-repeated catastrophe. The Germans and Japanese were merciless with their torpedoes from the sky or from the thousands of U-Boats running silent and deep. I have stared years after at that odd portrait of my uncle whom I never knew. He was handsome, manly, confident in those gray tones of the photographs of that era. His large-format camera was his proudest possession.

Dorothy's story in Oz had been delayed for thirty-six years awaiting the *Technicolor* movie-making technology. The *Yellow Brick Road* into the Emerald City had to be in full color. Audiences had been dreaming about a different color for their world, with the rise of the brown shirts in Fascist Italy, and the thuggery in Germany. At the very moment they witnessed Dorothy splashing the Witch with a bucket of wash water, three Witches were rising in Europe. Satan was counseling his Triune Minions in the finer points of world domination when Dorothy put out the fire in the Scarecrow's straw.

The Wicked Witch of the West could not have imagined the evil that had spread across the planet earth while children and their parents were squirming in their theater seats. The dreaded Wicked Witch of Western Europe was dancing with delight when Chamberlain returned to his cowardly abode in London. Like Alice, he had conformed to every undulation of evil he found in Wonderland. Pearl Harbor finally woke up the sleeping giant to help destroy the Japanese scheme to rule the whole world. Millie, Ann, Pop and mom had enjoyed a Sunday lunch when the bombs and torpedoes started falling from the sky at Pearl Harbor. It was hours before they heard the news on the radio or from neighbors or phone calls.

It would be many months before I arrived on the scene, oblivious of all the pain and fear in the world. When General Eisenhower gathered his Allied Commanders together to seek a winning strategy, my oversized body came from my tiny mother. By the time the 156,000 men executed their WWII equivalent of Pickett's Charge on Normandy's beaches, the War seemed nearly out of reach.[26] D-Day resulted in nearly 210,000 Allied casualties, with large numbers running only a few steps before they were cut to pieces. These brave men, hapless men, somehow turned the war for the Allies. Meanwhile, a dozen Jewish scientists at White Sands and Oak Ridge Tennessee were charged with producing a bomb to destroy the world's greatest Jewish adversary.

When ten righteous were finally assembled, all the Jewish physicists washed their hands of the *Manhattan Project*. They shuddered at the harvest from their grim progeny. Einstein himself would get all the credit and the blame, for his equations had captured the atom's wrath. The detonation of *Fat Boy* and *Little Man* in the air above the Mitsubishi torpedo factories killed thirty-five to forty-thousand people instantly. Like the chubby little characters introduced in *Alice in Wonderland* nearly a hundred years before, the nuclear bombs pitched on their

---

[26] *Invasion of Normandy.* Wikipedia.

(fat) fins, killing more than 80,000 people from the initial blast and the nuclear burns and sickness that followed in the months afterward.

A bucket of nuclear wash-water had silenced the hideous screams of the Wicked Witch, splashed from the belly of the B-29 flying high above the munitions factories of Nagasaki and Hiroshima. The fire and brimstones stunned the demigod who had pulled his people into the wringer of a demonic vision. The torpedoes that destroyed the American navy in Pearl Harbor were still being produced when the light from a lump of plutonium baptized the Emperor, reminding him of God's superior fire power. The flash arrived too late to save the millions of Jews and Russian soldiers and civilians who perished in northern Europe and in Germany. Young men from around the world had died to placate every evil appetite of three demigods. Germany and Japan gave up their dark thrones, washed by blood and uranium's blue fire.

The war was nearly over after the second uranium bomb exploded a few days later. Though the devastation in Japan was terrible, it brought an end to the war that slaughtered an average of fourteen thousand people per day. More than 30,000,000 had already died. When Einstein's fantastical E from the chalkboard at Princeton suddenly turned into the worst version of mc^2, green glass littered the landscape. The Energy of the Atom had predictably superheated the silicon that was sucked up into the sky above the Japanese home world.[27]

With the warm glow of the announcement of peace in Pop's den, the terrifying specter of total defeat was quickly forgotten. The catastrophic memory of early losses were forgotten when that good news arrived. Frank Peiffer recalls how close the world came to annihilation.

"These proceedings are closed." Thus, General Douglas MacArthur's words ended the greatest war in history. After Pearl Harbor America was now at war, a truly global war. It was said that Churchill remarked that after hearing the news it led to the best night's sleep he had in some time.

The U.S. was in it. Things did not go well for the U.S. immediately after Pearl Harbor. Wake Island fell after a heroic defense by Marines. The Philippines fell with General MacArthur being evacuated by PT boat on orders from the President of the United States. Command of the Philippines passed to General Wainwright. The largest surrender of U.S. troops in our history took place on the Bataan Peninsula in April 1942. Some 70,000 American and Filipino troops entered

---

[27] Listwa, Dan. *Hiroshima and Nagasaki*.

captivity. Corregidor Island, the guardian of Manila Bay, fell in May 1942. No help came.

The Japanese threatened the great British naval base at Singapore. Two major fleet units, Battle Cruiser Repulse and the new Battleship Prince of Wales were sent to deter the Japanese. Both ships were sunk in about four hours on December 10, 1941 by torpedo planes largely due to the lack of air cover. Admiral Tom Phillips went down with Prince of Wales. This ended the belief that a battleship would not be sunk at sea under way. On February 15, 1942 General Percival surrenders British forces. Some 170,000 local, British, Indian, and Australian troops enter captivity.

A hastily assembled naval force was put together by the Americans, British, Dutch, and Australia (ABDA) to counter Japanese advance on the Dutch Indies (Indonesia) which were the source for rubber and oil. This force suffered a terrible defeat at the Battle of the Java Sea February 1942. Commander of the task force, Dutch Admiral Karel Doorman, went down on the cruiser De Ruyter. U.S.S. Houston and HMAS Perth escaped and made a run for the Indian Ocean. They were sunk two days later in what is known as the Battle of Sunda Strait. [28]

In 1945, the mottled grip of hell released the whole world from darkest vanity. Adolf Hitler, Mussolini, and Emperor Hirohito had played their three trump cards from the hand dealt by demons: Nationalism, Racial Purity, and the Worship of Men as gods. No such alliances could have persisted for long, for racial purity is the darkest goal of men whose hands are full of personal gain. Exploitation of racial enmity is the quickest trick in Machiavelli's book of power. Dark spirits use that book about the *Prince* to manipulate the world order. Machiavelli's story is the playbook for applying evil leverage in a compliant world.

It is no small thing that the Allies supported full economic recovery of two defeated enemies—hated enemies. The leaders and brave armies of the world had "stood firm against all strategies of the devil. For they were not fighting against flesh-and-blood enemies, but against evil rulers and authorities of the unseen world, against mighty powers in this dark world, and against evil spirits

---

[28] Peiffer, *These Proceedings are Closed.*

in the heavenly places."[29] Germany and Japan would soon become two of the great economic powers in the world, for no victors had ever shown greater mercy in the wake of hideous war crimes and the terrible loss of millions of lives. This shifted the world quickly to the manufacture of consumer products.[30] The world would soon realize the value of these necessities around the house.

Consumer goods were nearly unknown when the announcement of the end of war was spoken from the decks of the USS Missouri aircraft carrier in Tokyo Bay. By the time our den radio was turned off, the long line of black cars had already turned chiffon green and robin's egg blue with cream tops and two-tone dreamboat colors from the entire spectrum of the rainbow. It was a shout-out to the Emerald City's multi-colorful display in that first Technicolor movie. While our household shouted hosannah and hooray, dark powers and principalities were seizing their opportunities on every continent.

My youngest uncle was ripped from the world six weeks before my birth. The two events nearly killed my mother. His death at age thirty, painted my birth with a bit of hope in a time when death was ubiquitous. A clay-footed savior at best, I could never redeem what was broken by my family's grief. Neither could I imagine the deep joy when the War ended in our tiny electric den—it ended in the tall oaks of South Carolina and on every continent around the globe. No moment touched more people at the same time as that moment did. Only Christ's return through the clouds will gain more *Twitter* retweets and *Facebook* and *Instagram* reposts.

Six million Jews died in Death Camps all over Europe while they tried everything to make two bombs. Another five-million outcasts from society were exterminated as well by Hitler's cruelty, including homosexuals, gypsies, con-artists, and vagrants. The Jewish scientists became virtual prisoners in their top-secret endeavor to end the War of wars. God sent a Jewish carpenter to save many billions from Satan's schemes. He became a prisoner, whipped, mocked, and crucified for those who had demanded His death. God sent Jews, multiple times, to save an ungrateful world. Antisemitism is the name of the world's response for the Savior God sent. Hitler said that Dietrich Bonhoeffer had prevented him from fulfilling his thousand-year reign in the earth. Bonhoeffer's sacrifice of himself seemed extravagant, but so did the sacrifice of God's Son seem excessive for a bunch of unrighteous sinners.[31]

When the bombs burst in the air, the works of darkness were exposed for the whole world to see. From the splitting of the atom came the light that opened the eyes of the whole world to see the axis of evil brought low. The war was over. Robert Oppenheimer's childhood home in Upper West Side Manhattan provided

---

[29] Ephesians 6:12.

[30] Cohen. *A Consumers' Republic*.

[31] Metaxas. *Bonhoeffer*.

a prophetic backdrop for the codename, "Manhattan Project." He conducted the collaboration of thousands who joined together in absolute secrecy in several facilities in Tennessee, New Mexico, Washington State, and around the world. Canada, and even Great Britain, cooperated in this monumental effort to bring the war to an end. Hirohito watched two terrible flashes in his skies, and his eyes were opened wide with wonder—the demon grinned back at him in his mirror.

> "It is over, Michinomiya Hirohito. You must surrender. Don't delay, for your people will suffer even more if you continue your Narcissistic fantasy tour as the god of Japan. Pearl Harbor's drowning men have finally washed up on your shores, raising the water line to your neck! Surrender, or drown in deep humiliation."

The Light of the World whispered into his one good ear: "Hirohito! Put down your arms. Pull your suicide bombers from their Zeros, and tell your savage warriors to drop their bloody bayonets. The day of the New Heaven and the New Earth is drawing nigh."

> The [New Jerusalem] has no need of sun or moon, for the glory of God illuminates the city, and the Lamb is its light. The nations will walk in its light, and the kings of the world will enter the city in all their glory. Revelation 21:23-24

Robert Oppenheimer reluctantly led his team to transform rare isotopes of Uranium into horrific bombs—the Uranium-based bomb was used on Hiroshima, and the Plutonium-based bomb was used on Nagasaki. These stunning detonations over mainland Japan, turned the kamikaze's smiles upside down. Their fighter planes landed, and they did not return to the war. The unfathomable clicks, when *Fat Man* and *Little Boy* imploded, left nothing behind where the weapons factories vanished beneath the unnatural storm. When I saw the full-sized replicas of Fat Man and Little Boy in Midland Texas at the World War II Museum, I could hardly believe how small they were!

Robert Oppenheimer understood immediately that their calculations had restored peace, but at a great price. When the engineers and metallurgists finished the bombs, they could only watch in horror, shading their eyes with every flash across the White Sands testing grounds. When men make peace, much blood is shed. When God makes peace, His own blood is shed. Untold millions would continue to die around the world during the time when I grew up in the false security of Clemson South Carolina. Though the world war was over, the inertia of spiritual war continued, and the Angel of Death was busier than ever across Africa and Asia.

Like most people, I remained outside of this fray. After all, history is nothing more than a bunch of stories about a time before time. How can you take it seriously when it has no effect on you? Are these people and events not like the stories coming out of *Oz* and *Wonderland?* When the children at my wife's school watched the *Towers* fall on September 11, 2001, they laughed, and even cheered. It was nothing more than a TV show to them. For nothing seems real since those *Tower* workers witnessed the grim faces of the Saudi pilots arriving at 600 miles per hour.

When Mission Commander Neil Armstrong stepped down on that soft soil of the moon in 1969, many Americans were convinced that it was nothing more than a Hollywood production. Even the resurrection of Jesus Christ was staged, some conspiracy theorists believe. They are convinced that His ascension was nothing more than a Hollywood creation like *Gravity*, with the sets built on the backlots or fabricated with CGI. *Myopic Me!* spent the first twenty-four years immersed in this ancient history, and in some of these forgotten stories. I was consumed with my own problems, until the *Lord of Heaven's Armies* stopped me on the Damascus Road with a simple question. "John, why are you persecuting Me?" I fell down on my knees, asking Him, "Who are You, Lord?" Then He led *Myopic Me!* into His beautiful light.

2.

WAR OF THE WORLDS.

I was born during the War of the Worlds, and I look back through this faith-time perspective, to see myself hovering near that front living room window, standing between the gold drapes of my youth. I am nine, and every year passing is a monument to the sacrifices made for me and for my little brother, Grayson. This is not my first memory by any stretch, but I have stumbled into this quiet scene suspended between heaven and earth. Warfare is already a familiar story for me, arriving as I did, when *D-Day* was being secretly planned by General Eisenhower and the Allied Commanders. Victory over Hitler and Hirohito was made possible when thousands of young men gave their lives so that I could stand here by the living room window quietly pondering the meaning of my life.[32]

I see my fragile reflection in the glass panes, with light reflecting softly from the sloping front yard and fieldstone sidewalk down to the street. I also see a waif in a Dickens' novel, a fractured little boy reflected in a long forgotten shop window. I am thin, and my frailty is apparent in this grammar school photo I am holding in my hand. I reluctantly turned the 5x7 and wallet photos over to Mama earlier, though I didn't want her to see them. She said, "The picture is fine. You look so handsome!" I knew she didn't mean it.

Two weeks after that dreadful picture day, the school photo is in my hand. I've got on the horizontally striped long-sleeved shirt with the brown and green colors again. I can see that my smile is thinner than a dollar bill, and my mouth is the size of a dime. My shoulders are narrow as a broom handle, and my eyes are unsure. I am looking reluctantly into the camera lens, as an orphan might— bewildered about my place in the world. This is my first uneasy glimpse into the fragile world of **Myopic Me!** It is not a pretty picture. I will bury every left-over wallet photo I can find in my sock drawer until I can shred them, and flush them down the toilet.

I will hereafter designate picture day at *Edgewood Elementary* as a "sick day." I will stay home until I am sure "picture day" has passed. I am looking again to see the odd expression on that stranger's face in my lame-o photo. I whisper involuntarily into the glass a few inches from my face: "Mouse-boy!"

---

[32] *D-Day*. History.

It is a mean thing to say, but I have loved this striped shirt, before this odd boy wore it without permission. I will never wear this horizontally striped shirt again.

"Who are you?" I ask the photo one more time. "I don't recognize this boy," my parents are wondering, when they climb into bed that night. "What can we do to help this fragile child?" Staring long and hard at my 5x7 photo, they decide to extend a long leash in our small town of Clemson. "He needs to get some confidence doing things on his own." They agree that I need to find my own way, in spite of my obvious mouse-boy status. They want me to be more independent. Pop tells Momma that I need my own Byronic pilgrimage[33] to learn who I am.

Since the town itself seems completely safe to them, they allow me to walk alone to the new *Clemson Theater* on College Avenue. "Downtown" is what we call our business area with six or eight stores. The *Pure* gas station is directly across from the theater, and I love the sign and the white gas I can see through the glass tube. The ad in the newspaper says, "You can be sure with *Pure*." I tell Mama I am going to see the *War of the Worlds* at the 5:30 show. My seven-year-old brother has no desire to go with me to this science-fiction film, so I am going alone. He has no interest in movies yet, and his world and mine don't converge. Our interests are not the same with the two-year difference in our ages.

My much older sisters are away in Decatur, where they are studying at *Agnes Scott College*. My dad will not be home from his classroom or his meetings at *Tillman Hall* until around 7:00. He is a Professor of literature, drama, and journalism. He is also the Faculty Advisor for *The Tiger*, the student newspaper. As the Faculty Athletic Chairman for the football team, Pop and Mama traveled to watch the *Clemson Tigers* beat the *Miami Hurricanes* in the *Orange Bowl* three years ago. I got my feelings hurt at the banquet, and I lost the little trophy they brought me from Miami. I cried openly.

Pop tells me there are only a few good students in his freshman classes. He wants me to be a good student, encouraging me to write stories. He says that writing is a nearly forgotten skill in the education process in high schools. In this post-war era, it is difficult for him to teach students to love poetry. The *Korean Conflict* continues the bloodshed on the other side of the world away from Clemson. The majority of Pop's students come to his freshman writing classes without knowing how to write a clean sentence with correct grammar and spelling. He encourages the best of them to write articles for *The Tiger*, which was founded at *Clemson College* in 1907 when my dad was also nine years old.

His special students learn lines from Shakespeare's plays and poems, and they speak the words into a recorder. He says they can learn to speak without stuttering if they practice. He records their voices on cylinders, so they can hear that they are better than they think they are. When he plays it back, they hear themselves mastering complex lines with perfect diction. He tells me that he has become a "jack-of-all-trades, but a master of none." I think he was bragging, though his voice sounded sad. I am hoping to be a jack-of-all-trades myself

---

[33] *Childe Harold's Pilgrimage*. Wikipedia.

someday. I will try very hard to do everything I see him doing, though I am not sure what he thinks of my striped shirt and my dollar-bill smile.

I am certain he can see that I am the mouse-boy and the mama's boy. I think that Pop wants me to be a hunter like Esau with the hairy arms. Pop hunts with a shotgun, and he brings home dove and quail for supper. I don't eat these wild birds, and my problem with Esau[34] is I don't like to kill animals or birds—or much of anything. I am afraid of spiders, though I love to watch the bats fly in front of the house at twilight when they come out to eat the flying insects.

Pop always looks for ways to drive the mouse-boy out of me. This started when I was six years old. After we felled the pine tree in the woods with a bow-saw and a newly sharpened ax, we looked across the hill at our sixty feet of pine tree on the ground that needed to be sawed for firewood. Pop chose the crosscut saw, with a wooden handle on each end. He said this would be the fastest and most educational way for us to tackle this job. He would teach me teamwork.

The key to the crosscut saw is to let the big teeth and gravity do most of the work, pulling when it is your turn on the wooden handle. The three inch teeth of the saw ripped the wood with each pass through the cut. I got very good at this though I was not very strong at age six. Pop praised me for having very good timing, with the blade sliding freely through the log. The yellow pine sawdust piled up with each cross cut, and the logs rolled down the hill with each one cut free.

When the entire tree was cut up, I wanted to do my part moving the logs to the place where Pop would split them with an ax or wedge. I overdid this lifting task, and later found out that I had injured myself. Lifting heavy logs tore my abdominal wall. At age six, I had a double hernia operation. This painful surgery repaired the damage done by logs weighing as much as I did. I had to prove to Pop that I was strong, but thinking you are something when you are nothing doesn't change anything. This work, and the painful recovery, is stored in my long-term memory.

War of the Worlds has come to town, and I am convinced that I love science fiction stories. I know nothing about this classic story dealing with our primeval fears and the eternal collision between good and evil—alien evil being the worst kind of evil. It is the fear of the unknown that I am plowing into, unawares. It is the archetypal extinction of mankind I am walking into, ill-prepared by age and experience. It is a story about technologically superior Martian invaders who come to harvest humanity as a food source. They come to overwhelm the earth with their invulnerable ships, which even the H-bombs can't touch.

They are horrible creatures, a marauding force coming to annihilate the human population. My Pop would understand it, but I am too young to enter this irreversible thicket of terror. When the Martians arrive with their hideous bodies and seemingly supernatural spaceships, beyond anything human beings

---

[34] Genesis 25:27.

13

can envision, I will stand at that place between heaven and hell, fight or flight, taking a stand or fleeing. New nightmares are already stored up for me in those film canisters snapped securely inside the hermetically sealed shipping cases. When those cases are opened, hell will be released into the world, and no one will be able to put it back inside again.

I push through the spring-loaded kitchen door, oblivious of what is ahead, checking to make sure that I have two quarters in my shorts pocket [fifty-cents is equivalent to nearly fifteen dollars in 2018 buying power]. My mother hates for me to slam this door—the loud "thwack" always marks my passage, and the sound of the strong spring vibrating afterward leaves a nearly inaudible humming sound. The spring always snatches the door from my hand, and then complains with that humming sound for a minute afterward.

"Don't slam that door!" comes down from upstairs. She knows that this door spring has one charter to fulfill: "Keep that big black fly from getting in, to strut around on the butter dish left on the kitchen table." The slamming door serves multiple purposes. It also announces that I have left the building. The Paden's arbor beckons in the hedges at the top of the hill above as I walk through the woods between the houses. That arbor gate always means freedom for me, for there is much fun to be had on the other side. As I walk through the trellis archway in the hedge along the boundary of the Paden's yard, I slide past the porch which I never see them use.

The familiar and strong smell of creosote is pungent in the late afternoon air coming from their exterior planking in the hot afternoon sun. The smell is very unpleasant. It is no wonder they don't use the porch. Walking down their steep driveway, I brake hard with my thin mouse-legs even before I reach the steepest concreted segment. At this point in my mile-long walk, I am ignorant of the horror that awaits me in a Kansas farmhouse. I cannot anticipate the impact this movie will have on my life. Mouse-boy is in for a great shock.

This summer afternoon jaunt to the movies guarantees a nearly empty theater since the military students at Clemson College don't go out on week-nights. There are as many students as there are local residents in Clemson. Pop says their study hall and military exercises keep them occupied in their barracks until the weekend. The freshmen are called "Rats," and their heads are kept shaved through the entire year. They wear tiny orange caps to emphasize their humble status. The Rats call their roommates, "Old ladies." It is a term of affection that describes their bonded relationship as they suffer through the freshman indoctrination in military protocols.

Their full-dress parade is a Friday ritual for all the families in Clemson, with each Cadet Company marching the length of the 1000-foot-long *Bowman Field* for these military reviews. The marching band plays the Souza marches which I love. Everybody hums these tunes which have become deeply scored into our memory—for me, at age nine, I get very inspired every time I hear these patriotic songs swelling. My uncle died in the war, and I never got to meet him.

My sisters cried for days. My mother had lost her brother. My grandmother had lost her "Grayson."

Stars and Stripes Forever is my favorite marching song on Friday's. I wish I could play it here on this page, to show you how exciting the music is with piccolo and brass punctuating the melody, while the tubas and bass drums add a powerful beat. The military college is still popular since World War II has left millions dead, affecting every family. Uncle Grayson died more than nine years ago—one month before I was born. In three more years, a coeducational college will rise from this military heritage in Clemson, opening a brave new world of two-gender classes. Pop tells me this is progress.

He says this change is necessary for a great university to come from the chrysalis of our small South Carolina school founded by John C. Calhoun's son-in-law, Thomas Green Clemson. Clemson attended several Parisian universities before founding an Agricultural and Mechanical College in northwest South Carolina in 1889, nine years before Pop was born. Nine years from now, Pop, nor I, can know that the first black student at Clemson University will enroll in the Graduate School of Architecture [before he becomes the Mayor of Charlotte].[35]

Dorothy's vortex has already carried her out of Kansas, though she has not landed yet in the Clemson Theater. My Technicolor science fiction film will run its terrible course years before her colorful Oz will come to life on our single screen. This title of H. G. Wells book, *The War of the Worlds*, promises terror on a global scale, but I will land through dark skies unawares. This movie will shake me to the core, as the Martians invade Earth with weapons beyond the armies of this world. The extermination of mankind is the dread of everyone who reads the book, and it will become clear that human ingenuity and expertise is powerless against these invaders from a world we have never seen without the aid of a telescope.

Kansas is the focal point in the story, with the remote farmland representing the helplessness of men who face this unknown terror. The farmhouse becomes the final hiding place when tanks and bombs do nothing to push these invaders back to where they came from. While Kansas seems to be the safe place for Dorothy in the Wizard of Oz, this lonely farmhouse is naked to the attacking Martians.[36] Though the tornado ruins Dorothy's wheat fields, the Martians will devour everything in the path of their alien ships. I know nothing about this story as I stride toward the downtown theater. I go on the vague assumption that the movies are there to entertain me and to inspire me. On this night, the Kansas farmer in me will turn, and forever flee, from the eerie lights coming from those alien ships. Little do I know that they are already landing in vacant fields all around me in Clemson South Carolina.

---

[35] *Thomas Green Clemson.* Wikipedia.

[36] Wells. *The War of the Worlds.*

Taking the shortcut through the back yard of St. Andrews Catholic Church on Sloan Street, I am walking down the home stretch. The Catholics never molest me, though their world is strange, and their tiny church building is plenty big enough for the few Catholic students who come from Northeastern parts of the country. Striding closer to town, dark shadows are already being loaded on sprockets in the upper room at the back of the theater. A solitary farmhouse fades into the silence as an alien harvester floats down from the sky—frame-by-frame the images await me in the sinister secrecy of a Martian invasion.

The final hundred yards takes me past Lawrence Starkey's white-columned family home. I can now see *Bowman Field* a half mile away. To the west of town is Newry, where Lawrence Starkey and my two older sisters filmed the 8 mm documentary of the flooding of the Newry Mill. The tiny houses hugging the banks of the river were destroyed by the flood waters. The workers had nowhere to live. Lawrence surely became our first cinematographer, and my sisters loved every acting role in his films. I vividly pictured the rescue of workers after the Newry flood. I pondered these events while thinking of Lawrence and Millie and Ann recreating their tragedy from ancient news accounts and first-hand testimonies.

When Ernest Hemingway published *The Old Man and the Sea* that same year, my father gave me a challenge: "Read the little book, and write the story down in your own words. I will pay you $3.00 (around $50.00 in 2018 money)." Ernest Hemingway has surely made me more earnest about story-telling than I had been before his Nobel Prize winning story.[37] My father knew that Hemingway adapted a journalistic style in all of his writing. Whereas, I use gobs of metaphoric allusions, Ernest used the spare text of the reporter working for the *New York Times,* or the beat writer for the *Atlanta Journal Constitution.*

We are a creative family, and Pop encourages my much older sisters to try their hands at drama. Before going off to college, they used our one-car garage beneath the large screened porch for the staging of their homemade plays. Ann was usually the scriptwriter, and Millie loved every starring role that came her way. Though each of them took multiple roles in these homemade performances, their old-school low-tech staging, employed makeshift curtains and hand-written programs for the hastily gathered guests.

The audience was imported from nearby houses and yards—giving each guest very little advance notice. Minutes before the curtain would rise for Act I, the attendees were seated graciously in the sweaty ambience of our graveled South Carolina driveway. The crunch of the folding chairs in the cinder-strewn track got everyone ready for what was to come. Inside the narrow garage, stage-left was the empty coal bin—with very little coal remaining during these summer months.

The furnace receives coal in the winter through the vertical sliding door holding the coal inside the bin. I shovel coal in winter with a big flat shovel. I

---

[37] *Ernest Hemingway.* Wikipedia.

can barely lift a partial shovel-full. Keeping the stoker filled is hard work, since the augur never stops grinding and popping the flammable chunks of coal into the firebox. The clinkers build up quickly, and they have to be removed each morning. This machinery did not inhibit these young actors from their stories, and they dove in and out of this alcove without injury. If they needed coal dust on their faces for any reason, they had an ample supply from the floor of this coal bin.

Stage right was a little room beneath the back-porch steps. They sprayed DDT into the dank space with a hand-pump sprayer that was covered with rust from the moist atmosphere. They hoped to kill the spiders before each drama was presented. I never went into that tiny "room," though the actors were indifferent to its offensive qualities. Old sheets were hung from the clothesline stretched across the garage door opening. Costume changes and set changes produced frantic flurries of activity when the curtains closed on each scene. Nearly everything was written down before it happened, though they usually improvised, and they always astonished me with their fearlessness. They never had stage-fright, and I couldn't imagine anyone more brilliant than my two older sisters.

Pop teaches drama to his students at the military college. Pop was in Shakespearian plays in off-Broadway productions while attending Columbia University in the 1920s. He lived in Harlem, New York, before taking a teaching job at Clemson College as the Great Depression was about to begin. Drama apparently runs in our family, because Millie is already looking ahead to Iowa State to gain a Master's degree in Drama when she finishes at Agnes Scott College. Ann is on course for Phi Beta Kappa and Magna Cum Laude, majoring in French literature. She is interested in writing short stories. Both of them stay at my great aunt's house in Decatur with my grandmother.

I sometimes think about how the movie was made when I go to the theater— when I am not too frightened by the action. I think about how the actors, sets, and cameras come together according to a script. The director's vision controls the assembling of the story. The film editor decides what film to cut from the movie. Whole scenes are cut. Characters are cut out! A fight or a love scene is excluded when it doesn't meet the goals of the movie. With hours of film, the editor has to cut it to around 2-hours for the theater. So much work is just discarded on the cutting room floor. I am in for a shock, for some terrifying scenes were included in the movie I am going to see.

As I arrive on the sidewalk across the street from the theater, I know nothing about H. G. Wells story about our worst fear—the fear of Martians destroying life on Earth. Hollywood will soon confront my ignorance, rupturing my youthful rituals. I will be swallowed up in an apocalyptic narrative far beyond my years. A voyeur at nine, I will step across the threshold of vague security, arriving inside a vortex of terror. God will have much to say, but I will allow fear to keep me from hearing His encouraging words. I will only hear the first part of His message to me when fear shuts me down. This auditory failure mode will persist in me until the present day, whether caused by fear or some other emotional overload.

17

As I trudge the last fifty yards past the shoe shop, the busy shoemaker inside is rebuilding a pair of leather shoes. Though I can smell that wonderful leather aroma coming through the screen door, my mind is preoccupied with *The War of the Worlds*. The shoemaker will soon paint the glue across the rubber heals. I have watched him produce this aromatic bond several times out of curiosity. I love the smell of the glue he uses. He will then stitch the separated leather parts back together before his customer arrives to pick up his nearly new shoes. The shelves bulge with half-soled cordovans, and high-heels with their new insoles and heals professionally added. I always marvel at the restoration of the well-worn brown boots that will go back to work on a worker's feet very soon.

Judge Keller's General Merchandise, the hardware store, *Revco Drugs* with our *Soda Shop, Kay's Jewelers*, and the *Pure Station* complete the main businesses along this street that is the Clemson business district. The *Clemson Theater* bulges out into the sidewalk with a ticket kiosk beckoning everyone who passes. The *Pure Station*, directly across from the theater, has the glass tube full of clear gasoline. That clear liquid is pumped weekly into our 1950 forest green *Plymouth* four-door. The 1940s *Fords* and a few early 1950s *Chevys* rumble by on the street with an occasional black *Packard, Pontiac,* or *Buick.*

I hardly notice the gray smoke coming from all the tailpipes, filling the air with the smell of gas and oil. That familiar, sweet, rotten egg odor comes with every automobile's passing. With very few cars on the road now at supper time, I am able to trot across to the front window of the Soda Shop where Pete Maravich, a decade later, will win the bet that he could spin a basketball on his finger for more than five minutes while walking back and forth across the street.

In the distance, behind the *YMCA*, Jimmy Howard is sprinting back and forth along the sidelines at the Clemson football practice session that is winding down. He runs from point to point to fetch loose footballs while his dad, the great Frank Howard, is directing the Clemson football team to a dismal 3-5-1 record—the *Tigers* have just tied Boston College at Fenway Park a few days earlier, and there is still hope of a turnaround at this early point in the season.[38] The most ardent fans still cling to the memory of the Clemson team that three years before had beat an undefeated Miami Hurricane team by the score of 15-14 in the *Orange Bowl*. Clemson finished that season with an undefeated record, and were ranked #10 in the national polls.

At this time of day, the whole town is gathering for the evening ritual at the supper table. The smell of *SPAM* and fried chicken is wafting through screen windows from many houses. The *SPAM* meat-treat, inspired by war rations, fills the air with the wonderful smell of frying animal fat. There is no thought of the apocalypse arriving in Clemson tonight. I can see the sun setting over the *Seneca River* to the West, and deep shadows are already rising at the feet of the Blue Ridge Mountains. I will soon be trapped in the basement of a farmhouse under the smothering blankets of night. Strange lights will swell in the surreal gray

---

[38] *1953 Clemson Tigers football team.* Wikipedia.

landscape settling over Kansas like the end of the world. No coal-bin nearby, this dark theater will soon fill up with alien fires. My soul has been choreographed for horror from which there is no escape.

On my skinny nine-year-old legs I arrive in front of the theater where I can now read the big plastic letters on the marquee: "*War of the Worlds* — by H. G. Wells, starring Michael Rennie, Patricia Neal, and Hugh Marlowe." The picture of the alien vessel catches my eye, and I am excited knowing that the movie will start momentarily. "I can't wait!" The cowards of Kansas take their places alongside me in cellulose frames from hell, while the manager, or his minion, is coiling the end of the world around the sprockets in the dark projection room.

Courage will be in short supply soon, and I have learned nothing from the *Now Playing* posters, as my eyes are glowing with excitement in anticipation of the coming conflagration. I have no interest in any of the *Coming Soon* posters as I stride to the ticket kiosk extending into the sidewalk. The Martian ships wait in their queue, lined up on consecutive frames, time marked for terror. The contiguous pictures are vibrating as the 35 mm story is threaded tediously into the giant projector's pulleys.

Now inside, I see the glass eye glinting through the tiny door high above in the rear theater wall. From another world, the Venus flytraps are arriving from Mars inside the terrarium-dome shields. Alien hell is being stuffed into Pandora's Box; and soon H. G. Wells voice will come to open the door into the pitiable Kansas landscape. After a few quick previews for coming attractions, the population of the Earth learns how primitive is the post-war technology. The invulnerable Aliens rise in every city and in every rural clime as the light strikes each frame. There is no bloodshed as my irises shrivel and flash when people and weapons are vaporized by a strange green death ray emanating from a cobra's mouth inside the terrarium domes.

My body shrivels into the deepest crevice in my theater seat. I cannot look away from this dark tunnel full of the unthinkable. Across the street, *Judge Keller's General Merchandise* store is closing its doors for the day, unaware of the aliens arriving a hundred feet away. Blue denim will not stop them. Coveralls or brightly colored pennants and white T-shirts will not distract them. That dark store is padlocked just in time for the long night ahead. Nothing will be the same in the morning.

Filmed a few years after the Allied victories in Germany and the Pacific, the American army is depicted as impotent in this encounter with ships coming out of the vacuum of space, to climb out from their holes deep into the earth's crust. The cobra-like nozzles are shielded by those transparent cylinders, and the eerie stream of light vaporizes every hostile action taken against them. America is suddenly powerless. For the older crowd, these scenes will bring back the impotent feelings during the World War with Hitler's Germany or Hirohito's Japan. With no answer for this Martian assault, the hubris of highly trained military will prove no match for overpowering weapons from another world.

As I sit alone in this withering crossfire ("Why did I come to this movie by myself?"), I am trapped with two others in the basement of a Kansas farmhouse. They seem as terrified as I am. The alien ships move slowly above the fields beyond the small flashing window above my head. It is just a matter of time. I can see the dancing light from the burning cornfields. All of humanity is crouching, trying not to breathe. The man and the woman are squatting together behind the cardboard boxes.

As these ships come closer to our exposed hideout, a burst of light like the sun stuns us. My heart rhythm is ruined. I can hear a drummer pounding an animal skin in my chest. I see their faces as the window breaks above us, glass flying across the concrete floor. An alien presence is moving toward me out of the explosion. Intense fear causes me to flinch, and the alien jerks to move in my direction. I must not throw up. "Oh God!" I say to myself, in a whisper so loud that the man turns a few degrees to look directly at me. The dread in his eyes matches the woman's clenched jaw. Their fear restarts my heart, but I am cauterized by a tornado whirling inside of me.

A one-eyed tentacle appears now, bumping into the boxes, coiling through any visual barrier, looking only for me. This alien entity is trained by the sound of my heart. My heart's crippled drumbeat gives my hiding place away, and my blood thickens, valves fibrillating, shuddering inside my chest. The great eye tracks me, though I have not moved an inch. My eyes refocus to the spine of the book a few inches from me. In bold letters, I can read the non sequitur: "*The War of the Worlds,* by H. G. Wells." I am captured in the cruelest irony, taken to the butcher through space and time, like that pig hanging on as the truck travels the final half-mile to the slaughterhouse.

Night swallows the whole world in deep sorrow as the alien eye stops in front of me. Holding my breath, an axe blade flashes across my field of vision. The eye blinks, and falls away. I am already choosing flight from fighting, as I bolt, hoping no eye is following my tumbling escape onto the dark aisle, stumbling through deep rows of broken-down corn. I almost fall into the unexpected upward incline as the stiff carpet slows me on this Kansas field. I know I will die if I stay in my creaking seat. I know that no human weapon can rescue me now, and no hall pass can free me from this upward climb into hell.

My chest is in severe pain, and I know this horrible scene can never be resolved. Stumbling, I rise to run the rest of the aisle, brushing obstacles aside until the "Exit" glows above me in the dark. I will never know if that couple lives or dies as I burst through double-doors into a blinding room. Where is this? To my right is a large Plexiglas silo, flashing, wildly exploding, white corn piling up into a mountain. The Kansas corn is popping in the fire, and this silo is nearly full. They are preparing for a long nightmare that is coming soon. "Pop, pop, pop-pop, pop-pop-pop-pop!"

I feel vaguely embarrassed when I realize the Martians can't traverse this bright clearing. They hang back in that dark room behind me, paralyzed by the light. Their ships are formidable, but they can't slide through this beautiful interface! More light is slipping under the next row of doors ahead of me, and the demons behind me cannot extinguish this light inside an exploding room. The popping corn will crush the Plexiglas domes and vaporize the cobras. In this new reality, I can finally confess that, "I'm having a heart attack," I tell the adult in front of me. The ships are toppling behind me. One by one they tilt, and the miraculous sidewalk presents me with fierce daylight as the manager guides me to his black car on the street. Am I free? He is taking me to Doctor Brown's office down the street. Will I be the first one to reach his office? Will others wobble from the fire that rages behind this isolated farmhouse?

Unlike Dorothy, who finally parachutes down through a Kansas wall cloud into Oz, I have fallen from my Kansas sky onto *College Avenue*. I am stunned at my new prospects. I am disoriented with this freedom. Behind me, the Flying Monkeys fill the sky as the Wicked Witch torments the whole earth. The spring on the kitchen door has barely stopped vibrating, and I hope now to survive the war engulfing my world. World War II is swallowed by this war, and I am silent in the front seat of the theater manager's car. I have slipped through the eye of the red-hot needle, and the fear of death has been quenched momentarily in the bright sunlight of this hot Mercury automobile. The airflow through the interior is gradually cooling down my overheated world.

3.

WIZARD OF
COLLEGE AVENUE.

As we drive toward Dr. Brown's office, I have no thought of my father or mother or brother, or sisters off at college. It is as if I exist in a world unconnected to anything else. I am truly in the chrysalis of *Myopic Me!* I am an independent actor in a personal drama, squinting, and traveling down this straight street to potential freedom. We roll past the Dixie Store on the left, and I imagine I can smell the rotting blood from the butcher shop in the back rooms of the building. The blood in my heart is moving again, and the pain is completely gone. The sight of Dr. Brown's large white house has healed the pain in my chest, and my embarrassment increases as our distance to his parking lot shrinks. Without a wait, I am heading into Dr. Brown's office. I pull my horizontally striped shirt over my head, and our family doctor places his cold stethoscope on my exposed breastbone.

At the end of his instrument, I can see the eye again, just like the one in the farmhouse. The tubes travel up to his large ears, and he is already listening to the blood in my 60,000 miles of blood vessels—long enough to go around the world twice—one-quarter the distance to the moon. My blood vessels would only reach one percent of the distance to Mars. I feel about 60,000 miles away from that Kansas farmhouse we left behind at the theater. The doctor is listening for any abnormal rhythms or any valve noise that could indicate a problem. The air rushes into an out of his one lung with an alien sound. I feel strange comfort because of his own disfigurement. Lung cancer has taken one of his lungs in this era when smoking is a universal habit. It seems unconnected to the several deadly diseases it is causing in this era when thirteen-hundred will be dying daily from cigarette smoking or second hand smoke.[39]

His probing of my chest finds nothing abnormal. He instructs me to take deep breaths—letting them out. In. Out. In and out. His single lung's alien sound continues in the background: "Hheeerh. hheeerh, hooomph, hheerh, hooomph." With every breath through his left-air-bag full of purple blood, I can hear those alien ships approaching. But I am certain now that I have survived

---

[39] *Blood Vessels*. The Franklin Institute.

the conflagration from Outer Space. I am embarrassed, faintly; and Dr. Brown will find nothing wrong. In a few moments, he informs me of his diagnosis with an encouraging voice.

I have suffered acute indigestion from the popcorn and the Coke I wolfed down before the farmhouse scene. Dr. Brown is transmogrified, becoming the self-conscious Wizard of Oz in his white smock. He points to my Ruby Slippers that are already on my feet, and he tells me they will take me home again. He gives me a cup of antacid liquid to drink down, and he prescribes one thing for my recovery: "Do not return to that theater tonight! Go straight home."

He sends me off to kill the Wicked Witch of the West with nothing more than a paper cup full of water from his cooler. I thank him, and I say very little when I get home from my trip to Kansas, coming too close to Mars, before taking a side-trip to the doctor's office. I say very little to my parents, as if the parental conversation has no relevance for this deeply personal encounter with another civilization. I walk through our foyer as the theater manager's car pulls away from our long fieldstone sidewalk that Pop built two years before I was born.

The light changes in my eyes, and the alien world seems barely connected to home. The Kansas farmhouse hangs in suspended animation, and my psyche is permanently imprinted with a new fear. There is a permanent scar in my soul, and my dreams will forever uncoil with that tentacle slithering into my sleep. Only God can touch this scar, to heal it. That attic room behind my bed has a new phantom to roam the night. It is hiding between the old coats and discarded shirts and dresses that hang from the sawed-off golf club handle that is nailed to the rafters.

My nineteenth century father is wondering why his son is still a coward at age nine, a total mouse-boy, nearly dying in the dark theater. The Hollywood production is so realistic that I thought it was happening to me. Pop did not see the movie with me, so he does not understand that the world faced certain annihilation. It will take me fifty years to understand what happened in H. G. Wells' narrative. My DVD will arrive from the Future to heal my truncated understanding! I will watch the old and the new versions in Future Time, and I will discover God's amazing intervention in the creative fantasy story.[40]

"Checkmate Martians," when God's brilliant countermeasures against extinction were finally revealed to me in 2005. The grand media intervention pierced the membrane between faith-time and space-time to reveal His kindness and foreknowledge.[41] Both of these are demonstrations of Our Father's love and watch-care. The two versions of the movie speak to the prototypical coward within us all. I might have had an interesting conversation with Pop if I had witnessed the denouement on the night when I ran to the bright lights, and

---

[40] *The War of the Worlds* (1953 film). Wikipedia.

[41] *The War of the Worlds* (2005 film). Wikipedia.

climbed into a black sedan; for God said, "I already took care of this threat! My foreknowledge is a profound advantage of My never ending love for you."

Myopic Me! could not take advantage of God's encouragement because of the paralyzing fear that engulfed me during that farmhouse scene. The man's wife, who seemed frozen with fear, ends up on her knees in a church building—but I didn't witness these redemptive scenes at the end of the movie. I fled through the cornfields, fear ruling me, as I yielded to the convincing piccolo shrilling in my ear. Unknown to me on this theater night, the popping corn and the light beneath the exit door were forming into a new parable of deliverance for my soul to devour. Dr. Brown's white coat and single lung breathed new hope into my mind—though I could not process this antithetical message. I had survived God's healing hands, not recognizing His strange disguise. Is it true that, "Perfect love casts out all fear?"[42] How many things in my life will remain unfinished because fear froze me?

Did I know that God speaks to men and boys, women and gals? The answer is "No." In this early encounter with the *Faith-Time Continuum*, the sun had settled into the Seneca River, shining through those rusting iron struts that shiver every time a truck shoots the gap from Clemson to Seneca. The crocodiles settled into the mud along the banks, and the Seminoles unstrung their bows. Their TeePees coughed up the dusk as night arrived. God was speaking to the world about His provision and protection—His intimate involvement in the affairs of men.

Failing to hear Him, I missed this intersection between science and grace in *War of the Worlds,* bringing me to the real issue of life: Will I continue to miss His messages, too frightened to stand still in trust of Him until He can speak? *War of the Worlds* is an exposé of science and technology for those who have ears to hear. H. G. Wells highlights the futility of our best efforts to save ourselves. He is not saying that science is useless, but he points to the finesse of the Omniscient God who covers us with His infinite wings of protection. He exposes the false-god, while demonstrating that the biggest stick doesn't always win the war.

The smallest stick, invisible stick, took down the technological superiority of the "Martians." Wells speaks through the noise of a greater war that is waged in the heavenly realm. Being on the right side of that war is everything. The simple, desperate prayers of those in the church building in the final scenes of the movie purport the great power of prayer for those who have a relationship with the God of heaven and earth. God comes walking in the wilting garden of our own willfulness (choosing death rather than life), and He makes clear to us that relationship is the only safe place in the universe. God's sovereignty is displayed in *The War of the Worlds*[43] as Father, Creator, friend, and defender of man.

---

[42] 1 John 4:18

[43] *The War of the Worlds* (1953 film). Wikipedia.

In this story, the bacteria living in our bodies and in the air are too much for the aliens, slipping under their impenetrable shields and killing them—they drown in their own phlegm. What the Allied Armies are unable to do, God does with these tiny bacteria. Throughout the Scriptures, God sends powerful angels to deliver His people. When He sends Joshua into the Promised Land, He sends a warrior angel ahead of Joshua's army to put fear into the enemy. H. G. Wells portrays His tiny defense system, destroying an entire alien invading force simultaneously. When all hope is gone, the bacteria multiply exponentially as they destroy our enemy from Mars. I would later learn about this deliverance by the intervention of God's invisible micro-army, learning that the meteor barrier and gamma ray belt around the earth, daily combine with the perfect tilt of the earth to keep us from destruction as well.

The creation of our secure environment on earth turns out to be an impossibility, according to theoretical physicists in the twenty-first century.[44] It is impossible that we are here at all. Life is impossible, according to these scientists, some of whom consider themselves to be atheists. The existence of our life-sustaining planet is a super-miraculous event with too many zeros on the negative probability exponent to fit on this page.

Science fiction narratives, including *Star Trek* and *Star Wars,* pretend that nearly every one of their fictional planets are "M-Class," having atmospheres capable of sustaining life. But scientists now say that the existence of M-Class planets is an impossible outcome for a randomly created world.[45] This is powerful medicine for every hopeless observer who finds no hope here on this blue-green-and rust planet.

Wells' story, after all, is not a story about a Martian attack on earthlings. It is a story about the thieves that come to rob us with their noise and their terror and their seductive power. They come to shatter our peace. Wells' denouement comes down to a woman praying in the church on her knees. She is the wife I saw in the farmhouse before I fled the theater. Though she was terrified when the tentacle entered the room, she bravely presented her prayers to God. Moments before the alien ship arrived at the little church, she surrendered all her hopes and fears to God in prayer. The alien invaders toppled over right outside the church where heavenly help had been invoked through the Faith-Time Continuum. These intersections of Space-Time and Faith-Time are always a matter of life and death. They intersect with Science in the mind of God.

If God can place us in the perfect relationship with the yellow Sun and the impossibly large Moon—disproportionately large compared to the size of Earth—then He can handle all of our prayers for deliverance from our enemies. All of these things reinforce for me that God is the God of what we call, "The impossible." What is impossible for men is possible for God. Life on Earth is a

---

[44] *Science has found the Proof.* Fact Reality.

[45] *Star Trek planet classification.* Wikipedia.

miracle rivaling the miracle of His saving us. In spite of our former irreconcilable differences with the Holy God, He found a way.[46] The only way He could have pulled off this impossible feat is to send His Son to die in our place on the Cross. When the alien ships came for us, God sent His only Son to ransom us from hell.

Though we have ridden the rail of entropy a long way from that perfect Garden God made for us, His grace and wisdom guards our safety to the present day. Entropy is a physical chemistry term which addresses the breakdown of all energy to the most fundamental forms. It is the process of decay, and aging, which ends in death. We are alive today because He breathed life into our lungs. This death and decay was preferred by Adam and Eve, our great grandparents.

In order that life can continue to exist on this planet as God intends, He had to set 200 parameters in perfect array on the first day of creation. Is that not a potent message to us in this twenty-first century, telling us that we are dependent upon God for every good thing in our lives? In the age of Science and Evolution, is God's voice not whispering to us through the Faith-Time Continuum? He is revealing to us how much He loves us from the beginning. Some will hear this message loud and clear. Others will scoff, even though it comes to them from the trusted god of Science.

On the second, third, fourth, fifth, and sixth days of the Genesis Creation [God's description given to Moses], every parameter had to be perfect. Millions of planets have failed to meet the 200 parameters required for life to exist in any form. Fewer than five thousand were even candidates for consideration in the last ten years. Each planet has failed for one or more of the 200 mandatory criteria! This is the ultimate And-Gate for creation which the Word of God defined in the beginning. All of the inputs have to be perfect to get an output from this Super-And-Gate called Life! Life comes out the other side when all 200 inputs are absolutely perfect! Scientists have found no other planet than Earth which satisfies every one of these inputs![47]

H. G. Wells and these physicists have arrived at the destination that was coded into our DNA—God has planted eternity in our hearts.[48] He seeds our souls with eternal DNA. We are born to seek Him, looking for our ultimate identity. God's mercy and grace comes through little trials and big ones, to show us the light under the door which leads us to Jesus Christ who connects us eternally to God. His voice is bringing us into the Faith-Time Continuum. He loves us, and desires a relationship with each one of us.

---

[46] Hebrews 10:10.

[47] *Science has found the proof.* YouTube.

[48] Ecclesiastes 3:11.

> Cognitive scientists are becoming increasingly aware that a metaphysical outlook may be so deeply ingrained in human thought processes that it cannot be expunged . . . This line of thought has led to some scientists claiming that, "Atheism is psychologically impossible because of the way humans think," says Graham Lawton, an avowed atheist himself, writing in the New Scientist . . . Humans are pattern-seekers from birth, with a belief in karma, or cosmic justice, as our default setting. "A slew of cognitive traits predisposes us to faith," writes Pascal Boyer in Nature, the science journal, adding that people "are only aware of some of their religious ideas."[49]

Our brains are constructed to seek Him. Distinctively deposited in us, God's Spirit constantly challenges our fear of death, leveraging our searching for answers, to bring us to Himself. He knows that every human being is looking for that pattern in the universe that will save us. We instinctively seek the life raft tossed by the Hero who can lift us from the flood waters above Niagara Falls. It is possible that I discovered, at age nine, His fresh new authority over death, ending some vague notion of immortality within me. For the first time, my little mind became acquainted with peace as a missing parcel in my life's psychic landscape. I became aware of the need of Him in the Solar System that had suddenly become much smaller.

Little did I know, that evening in Kansas, that the existence of the Universe itself is an even more difficult proposition than Life existing on Earth or Mars or anywhere else in the universe! Genesis describes the creation of the 200 quintillion stars through the Word of God's mouth. Somehow, by the will of God, our blue planet spun out of His mind like one of those tops we found in our stockings on Christmas morning. But it seems today, that our blue planet alone is perfectly delineated for life in varied array. Not only did God plant the bacteria to defend us from an imaginary alien enemy, but there are multiple miraculous provisions which scientists now agree on—without which, life would end within hours of the period's arrival at the end of this sentence.

All such provisions came from the Word—for there is no "singularity" that just happened to be floating around, as some scientists have postulated! Imagine presenting that explanation at a big symposium, or in some famous publication to be challenged by every genius and fool. The intellectual dark matter has surely devoured the full absurdity of this singularity—which can only be explained by the Word of God?

The Quark is informative, since it is not visible to the naked eye, nor can it be heard with the good ear. It is not detectable with a microscope or with a virtual reality device. The Quark can only be seen by its effects on its surroundings.

---

[49] Vittachi, *Scientists discover that atheists might not exist.*

27

Like the Wind that blows, rustling the lives of men[50] (certainly not the meteorologists), it speaks from invisibility to those who have eyes to see and ears to hear.[51] The scientists who love the Quarks have encountered this phenomenon, and it was initially difficult for scientists to believe in these Quarks!

> You can't see them directly. They have some unusual properties, and that's why it was difficult for people **to believe in them** at the beginning. And lots of people didn't. Lots of people thought I [Murray Gell-Mann] was crazy. Quarks are permanently trapped inside other particles like neutrons and protons. You can't bring them out individually to study them. So they're a little peculiar in that respect . . . Quarks were permanently confined in the neutron and proton, so you couldn't pull them out to examine them singly . . . Nobody had ever heard of particles being confined permanently inside observable things and not directly attainable.[52]

Einstein found it impossible to believe in the Creator of the Quarks, Who desires a personal relationship with sinners and losers. Though he could see that light is a wave and a particle, He could not see that God reveals Himself in three distinct Persons. Finding it impossible to believe in Jesus Christ in Bethlehem, Judea, and Jerusalem, he could not accept Gods One Door into heaven. He couldn't understand why God would not reveal Himself to the ones created in His Own image, even as he denied the possibility of God's Son risen from the dead, appearing in the upper room with the disciples. He only wanted to ask Him about those equations he could not finish on his Princeton blackboard.

While the Sun continues to warm us from 93,000,000 miles away, very few have ever fried in its heat. Its great light has produced global proliferation of photosynthesis enlivening endless varieties of crucial plants—keeping our microcosm filled with fresh oxygen and the food we need to survive. We remain comfortable, while the thermonuclear fire, a million times the size of Earth, burns and laps at the vacuum of space with its solar flares. If this synchrotron furnace were positioned 1.5% closer or farther from our bodies, we would quickly perish. At 23.5 degrees off-axis, the climate patterns unravel across the Earth's surface in a manner that is ideal for human life. With no tilt in the axis, or a different tilt, we would die. Life on earth would end.

---

[50] John 3:8

[51] John 9:39-41

[52] Kruglinski. *The Man Who Found Quarks.*

The vast magnetic field engulfing our planet protects us from gamma rays and cosmic rays that would end all life. Our atmosphere intercepts meteorites, burning them up before reaching the surface, keeping us safe. Our peculiar mixture of oxygen, nitrogen, and inert gases makes it possible for wild and vibrant life to cover the earth—each plant and animal reproduces itself, according to its kind,[53] in a beautiful and durable harmony. Our best efforts to subdue the Earth have not destroyed this miraculous display—unique within the universe.

The intricate deposit of DNA in every mammal, including man, controls and defines the shapes and sizes and the intelligence of each creature—and every sensitive plant—they lean with some advanced intelligence into the Light that sustains them. They find the light, even as the large-brained human hides from God's Light. Our human brain learns, creates, and searches far beyond our visible tree-line, going out into the universe, hungrily seeking the Theory of Everything—searching for our Creator God, while we still deny the need of Him.

Even the atheist can't ignore this deep voice speaking into his soul—eternity is planted in his DNA and in his foolish and self-serving heart. The Encode project reveals that the DNA in the human genome operates with profound intelligence in defining and producing human life, with mechanisms that are organized like a computer operating system to guide the access and use of the computer functions in the broader world. The Atheist is confronted with the failings of their Materialistic, probabilistic worldview, in which God's imprimatur makes no contribution. The DNA reveals the opposite, with a highly refined functional relationship to everything that happens in the world of humans and animals. God is hands-on. God is in everything, including *The Theory of Everything*.

> As the lead article in *Nature* reported, ENCODE has "enabled us to assign biochemical functions for 80% of the genome in particular outside of the well-studied protein-coding regions." Other research in genomics has shown that, overall, the non-coding regions of the genome function much like the operating system in a computer. Indeed, the noncoding regions of the genome direct the timing and regulate the expression of the data modules or coding regions of the genome, in addition to possessing myriad other functions.[54]

In the final frames of that first *War of the Worlds* movie, the woman from the farmhouse is praying for a miracle in a little church with several others. She is

---

[53] Genesis 1:12,25.

[54] Meyer. *Darwin's Doubt.*

the epicenter of the intimate relationship with the attentive God. He has already put His hand in the face of the alien ships from hell. As the ships close in on the praying remnant in the seemingly vulnerable church pews, God intervenes with a vengeance. The creatures and their ship have arrived at the church property when something dramatic happens.

It is not the magnetic field around the earth that stops them. It is not the human genome, though that genome causes man to seek God. It is not the tilt of the Earth that shields them from destruction. Neither is it the distance from the sun's thermonuclear fire that produces their deliverance. The Martian ships crumple and fall apart all over the world as simple cries for mercy are heard by a powerful and loving God. For an invisible, unappreciated reason, they fall. God afflicts the alien horde with deadly infections.

The creatures inside the ships are afflicted by the common bacteria and viruses on our planet—E. coli or the viruses that give us flu and the common cold. They suffer from the STD they catch from the antisocial intercourse they practice with humankind. From air, blood, and feces, they contract the disease that kills them all. Though they come to steal, kill, and destroy humankind, our own microscopic enemies kill them instead. We can see them, but we can't kill them. They can see us, but they can't kill us. The leveler of the playing field is a molecular-level bug they can't even see coming. While their eyes are focused on our impotent H-bombs popping like a handful of firecrackers, the micro-predator performs its exponential growth in their most vulnerable tissues.

This is a powerful parable. While we look at our visible enemies in this life, the invisible enemies from the dark spiritual realm come against us, leaving the phlegm of fear, lust, greed, ambition, and anger. We don't even see these infections coming upon us, but they take us out. Our invisible enemy feasts on our unforgiveness and our bitterness. As they multiply in exponential ways, they thrive on our cold shoulders and hypersensitivity. In this wonderful parable, prayers hurled against an overwhelming and inexorable enemy find the impossible God just in time: "I will never leave you or forsake you. I will be with you until the end of the age."[55]

God's constant love and kindness rescues a world intent on self-destruction. What is impossible for men is possible for Mighty God. To refer to his actions as a miracle, is ridiculous. It is simply His promise that saves the world. From the beginning He has promised to crush the serpents head—He has promised to destroy the works of the devil. He even sent His Son as the Lamb who would take away the sins of the world. He gives all men who believe, the way, the truth, and the life, so that they will not be devoured by the destroyer, or by their own foolishness.

Later I would understand that Solomon wrote the Proverbs that define the negative space between our irreconcilable lives, before he also fell into the undertow of his own carefully drawn *Fool*. Eighty-three times Solomon

---

[55] Matthew 28:20

describes the Fool in his Proverbs, and every time he is describing his own destination as the fool. The once wise king becomes a fool before he finally returns to hear God's voice at the end of Ecclesiastes. Like the scientist who finally accepts the existence of anti-matter, which he cannot see with his naked eye, we come to see and hear that which is not truly visible to the vanilla eye. The scientists today will permit equations to speak,[56] while they refuse to allow the divine foot to breach any of their hypotheses.[57]

The Theory of Everything is resolved in the mystery and majesty of the Cross of Christ connecting all things together from the divisiveness of death when Adam sinned.[58] Though the scientist will finally believe in the quark, and the anti-quark, he may never believe in the God who came and died a criminal's death. Nobel Prize winning poet, Bob Dylan, speaks from the deep revelation piercing his own life in the late 1970s.

> Sister, lemme tell you about a vision that I saw
> You were drawing water for your husband, you were suffering under the law[59]
> You were telling him about Buddha, you were telling him about Mohammed in the same breath
> You never mentioned one time the Man who came and died a criminal's death.[60]

We speak of the "acts of God" that breach our personal story, arriving in the fury of the storm, in the cruelty of the disease, or in the assault from another world. We forget the night when we climbed the stairs, entered the room, and devoured the fruit of our destruction. We blame Him for every wrong turn in the road from our GPS device. Though our choices are often programmed by the Prince of the Air, we prefer his sinister counsel to the counsel of the One speaking to us through the *Faith-Time Continuum*, showing us the terrible gulf between the tails of the infinite bell curve. Asymptotic mankind can only muster at the lower tail of this faith continuum, while God's Son urges us to hear His words, moving us into the upper regions.

---

[56] Meyer. *Darwin's Doubt.*

[57] Berlinski. *The Devil's Delusion.*

[58] Ephesians 2:14.

[59] John 4:7.

[60] Dylan. *Slow Train Coming.*

For a half-century, I delayed God's wisdom coming from this amazing story of God's deliverance. His Good News from that traumatic context finally pierced my heart when the Tom Cruise version of *War of the Worlds* arrived at Christmas in the form of my stocking gift from my son. My brave son made sure that I didn't miss God's Good News again. He gave me both DVD's—the 1953 version of the story and the 2005 version. When I revisited that original film, peace through God's Son had long since come to live inside of me. Two kingdoms had collided in the intervening years, and the demons of fear and deception had discovered God's firm grip on my heart, soul, mind, and strength. They had shuddered at the mention of His name.

The plot of this world-shattering science fiction story had appeared in book stores in 1898—the same year my father was born. Some fifty years later, the invasion of Clemson had begun. H. G. Wells' worst-kept-fear had surely come to fruition on College Avenue. The same panic I felt, had erupted in 1936 when Orson Welles convinced the nation that the world had been attacked by Martians. He spoke to the fear already existing in tens of thousands who were listening to the popular Mercury Radio broadcast. The "news broadcast" came directly from the pages of H. G. Wells' book. The broadcast was heard by a vast audience who believed the world might come to an end within hours.[61]

The panic led to an estimated six to twenty deaths by the hearers—attributable to the hearing of the terrible news of the invasion from outer-space.[62] The terror I experienced in the Clemson Theater overwhelmed thousands of adults. Orson Welles tapped into the public dread which H. G. Wells fully understood. Hollywood would wait another twenty years until the World War had swept through the European and Pacific theaters culminating in the end of war. Only then could the public be drawn to see a movie about global warfare.

---

[61] Welles. *This is Orson Welles.*

[62] *Real-Life Casualties from "War of the Worlds."*

4.

PARABLE OF DELIVERANCE.

When I returned to this long-delayed parable from *War of the Worlds*, I was thrilled to understand what God had intended for me as early as age nine. As I witnessed His fictional intervention in the affairs of men, I better understood God's voice speaking through the interface of movies—He uses them often in my life as an adjunct of the *Faith-Time Continuum*. I also understood that God has people far flung across the planet who listen closely to His voice. Even a famous writer can enable God to speak into our lives concerning His loving intentions. Wells' book is one of the parables that God has used to reveal His love. Lest you become tangled up with the efficacy of plot details, or even authorial intentions, realize that God can speak through anything to rescue us. This parable reveals His propensity to intervene in our lives. Even though we may behave in terrible ways, God is busy breaking the power of our self-destruction one person at a time.

He will do anything to save us from ourselves or from the assault of enemies coming from outside of us. When the world has nearly convinced us that it has the key for our joy, Solomon reminds us that life is a vain ritual, "A chasing after the wind, meaningless." Jesus puts it even more succinctly, so that we can consider our options with full knowledge of the consequences of this form of religion which denies His power.

> And what do you benefit if you gain the whole world but
> lose your own soul? Is anything worth more than your soul?
> Matthew 16:26

The creatures depicted in the *War of the Worlds* (demonic hordes) die almost simultaneously because of the universal disease infecting the Planet Earth. Their appetite for blood and bodily fluids destroy them when the invisible bacteria in our bodies infiltrate their vulnerabilities. When they abuse us, the bacteria inside of us abuses them. In Wells' story, the bacteria take the role of God's formidable countermeasure to save us.

"Once they had breathed our air, germs, which no longer affect us, began to kill them. The end came swiftly. All over the world, their machines began to stop and fall. After all that men could do had failed, the Martians were destroyed and humanity was saved by the littlest things, which God, in His wisdom, had put upon this Earth..."[63]

But the Martian threat is not the only enemy of humankind, and hydrogen bombs are not the only weapons we have for defending ourselves. From the beginning, Adam and Eve discovered the demonic possibilities, encountering the Serpent in the Garden near the *Tree of the Knowledge of Good and Evil*. The forked tongue of the Serpent was merely the Minion-of-the-Day, posted there by Satan, full of evil venom, exuding friendship while giving bad advice. This seductive spokes-creature for the devil fooled them, and continues to fool us. With this obfuscation from the dark spiritual realms sin was released into the world. Would bacteria save us in the Garden? Would technology wash away our shame? Would our armies protect us from subtle Serpents slithering into our lives?

Since we inherited this great propensity for sin from our Grandparents, what countermeasure could possibly breach this curse upon our families and ourselves from long ago? Will a very good retirement package or a Cadillac medical insurance plan save us? Who will bury us when the time comes? Who will wake us up in our graves when the final judgment comes? Who will heal us when self-love overflows, denying God's existence, promoting our own ascension as gods of love with an overwhelming fear of death? When empathy is no longer relevant, Who will restore our right minds?

---

[63] *The War of the Worlds (1953), Quotes.*

5.

POP'S CLEMSON.

U shered into my father's classroom, I glanced out the window on my left, overlooking the enormous expanse of *Bowman field* below. It was a quick snapshot as I sat down in the large-scaled school desk, for his class was already underway. Every boy in Clemson could count the days until the summertime celebration of all things farming would stretch below on that grand field. A vast, long tent would extend in the hot air from the YMCA, nearly to the Library building at the other end. I turned around to see Pop teaching his all male classroom. I had been ferried from my Calhoun-Clemson Grammar School class by the Principal. The visit on this particular day turned my attention to a long poem by Lord Byron.

This cautionary tale was the autobiographical story from Lord Byron's own life. England's greatest poet followed *Childe Harold's Pilgrimage* through strange lands beyond the familiar countryside and people of Great Britain. The story gripped me, though I was very young. This long poem describes Byron's Romantic hero depicted through this young man (himself). He sets out on a familiar journey to discover the meaning of life. His pilgrimage does not drop him in Oz or Wonderland, where Dorothy or Alice ostensibly find their answers; but Lord Byron intentionally headed into strange cultures to find a meaningful version of himself—unwittingly, he was looking to find his way home.

He discovered in the multicultural world, with all of its advantages and challenges, that His club foot fit right in as he walked along the road. His pet bear seemed reasonable, walking beside him along the way. Byron's short leash on the bear bore no resemblance to the long leash that restrained his own wild lifestyle. Byron lived his early adult life as a kind of virtuoso prostitute of a man, sleeping with family members, male and female lovers, and generally diving into a sensory smorgasbord of pleasure that led to his eventual destruction. He died during the pilgrimage home at the age of thirty-six.[64]

Later, I would understand, Byron ran aground on the same brick wall that the Apostle Paul wrote about in Romans 7. His tragic inability to accomplish the perfection he envisioned for himself, left him tethered to a self-imposed slavery. He was captive to his own brokenness. Diving into the most extreme versions of

---

[64] *Childe Harold's Pilgrimage*. Wikipedia.

Myopic Me! Byron was unable to rescue himself. He was powerless, and in need of a True Hero. He spun out this threadbare romantic hero—more the fool than Solomon ever described in the Proverbs, Byron himself became disillusioned with every sensory illusion. He discovered a bitter irony, seeing clearly his own meaningless life of vanity that Solomon had already described in Ecclesiastes.

> I said to myself, "Look, I am wiser than any of the kings who ruled in Jerusalem before me. I have greater wisdom and knowledge than any of them." So I set out to learn everything from wisdom to madness and folly. But I learned firsthand that pursuing all this is like chasing the wind. The greater my wisdom, the greater my grief. To increase knowledge only increases sorrow."[65]

The romantic hero died on his journey to find Utopia—I use the past tense because the story is not so much about *Childe Harold* as it is about Lord Byron. I would later realize the most shocking thing about the destination, Utopia. The word means Nowhere. At age thirty-six, Lord Byron fell down beside the road, in the middle of Nowhere. His joints were rusted, and the wicked Witch of the West placed her ugly foot on his tin chest. She laughed with that terrible cackle of every witch. She had tripped up another child whom God loved enough to give His life for. Sheep's clothing had disguised every wolf he allowed in his bed, and Lord Byron was too much enamored with sex and drugs to see the wolf-trap grinding on his own club foot.

My Pop had permanent words printed on his blackboard, not to be erased in the evening by the janitor: "A man is always on his honor." These words came from Robert Browning rather than Byron or Solomon the king. Solomon wrote many Proverbs about honor, or being honored. "Honor is no more associated with fools than snow with summer or rain with harvest." I would find Pop reading from Ecclesiastes more than a decade later, during the final weeks of his life.

Pop knew the Proverbs, teaching his students Solomon's warning about the chasing after the wind. He brought me into his classroom to show me a fool, a snowflake in the summer rain. He wanted me to know, in my childhood doldrums, with *Farmer's Week* and Military Parades on Fridays, and Clemson Tiger football games in the fall, that life should never become a chasing after the wind. His methods were circuitous, but his heart was in the right place. Love protects. Love guides to green grass and still waters. Sheep need a lot of shepherding, and no one fully sheds this metaphorical link with these wooly beasts and their propensity for trouble.

---

[65] Ecclesiastes 1:16-18.

I have considered those words on Pop's blackboard all my life, never being able to disregard this exhortation to move beyond the motives of the predator or the victim. He was urging me to become the gentle-man who serves those who have climbed onto that road which leads to death. He was propelling me, against my selfish and cowardly will, to reach into honor that comes from above. He wanted me to find that holy grail of unearthly compassion.

Pop's windows opened up over *Bowman Field*, and I knew that all those long military parades would be held in full dress in the distance on Bowman Field. We were religious in our arrival with our picnic basket and a blanket, seated above the long olive column of the cadet corps below. These soldiers were going off to fight the police action in Korea—Truman's war to avoid another world war. Clemson College was a military college then, and the cadet corps marched in review each week to the famous Sousa Marches. Little did they know that Sousa would not be playing *Stars and Stripes Forever* when they were pinned down near Inchon.[66] This awesome music has since then fallen on hard times as patriotism and military displays of appreciation have ridden the rollercoaster of public opinion.

These military parades and *Farmer's Week* events punctuated our summers for years. The barracks and dorms were not air conditioned, but the visitors happily booked these inexpensive rooms with bunk beds and starched white sheets with a military tuck. The heavy olive-drab canvas tent extended for more than five hundred feet across *Bowman Field*, and there were numerous product areas for fertilizer, insecticides, specialty hardware and technical consulting to help the farmer make a crop while making enough money to pay the bills every year. The sounds of the chain saws chewing through the pine logs made for magnificent mornings at *Farmer's Week*.

I watched the salesmen drop the razor sharp chain on the pine logs with sawdust showering down into piles on the thick grass of *Bowman field*. This symphony of noise and power swept over us every summer. While Pop and I required ten minutes with that crosscut saw to cut through a log that same size, these showmen were slashing three inch wheels of wood in a few seconds. The beautiful glossy tractors, in red and green, red and gray, lined the fields above the big tent with giant rear tire treads attracting our fingers to feel the deep rubber grooves. The power of these gorgeous beasts could be felt in the massive wheel-treads shaped exactly like the patterns they would soon leave in every row of the farmer's field.

These powerful machines made simple farmers into supermen who could plow an acre garden in a half-hour. While we swung our mattocks and pressed our shovels ten thousand times to do the same thing, they would move on to the south-forty. The tread on those tractors was so deep that our hands disappeared in the curving ridges. The rubber was hard and clean with astonishing curving

---

[66] *UN Offensive, 1950.* Wikipedia.

newness. I could see the red clay and topsoil tumbling from those tires as the big *Farmall* tractor pulled a rack of plows through each pass across the fallow field.

Bowman Field was strewn with harrows and harvesters capturing the eye of each rural visitor from hundreds of miles around. *John Deere, Ford,* and *Massey Ferguson* equipment filled every open space with their latest models. The farmers arrived in droves to fill their need for technology and power to get the job done. They needed to sow the seed when the weather was perfect. They had to harvest the crops when the season was ideal. For us kids from Clemson, Central, Pendleton, and Six Mile, *Farmer's Week* was the big entertainment event of the year —excluding the football games in Memorial Stadium where the Tigers played.

That era of *Farmer's Week* is gone today, and the farms that once proliferated in the region have disappeared along with Andy Griffith. Andy saw the handwriting on the walls for farming with his famous recording, *What it Was, Was Football*. Football would be king in the South, while the farms would move to Texas, California, and Dorothy's Kansas. Though Pop was an English and Journalism professor, he became enamored with football while working with his friend Frank Howard, for whom the current 84,000 seat stadium is named. [67]

Dorothy's new friends in Oz had recently been kicked out of their Garden of Eden. They had fallen on hard times in Baum's gentle allegory of the hardships in the American political system. Historical characters are hidden in the details of his portrayals. The backstories, although obscure to most viewers today, expands my understanding of the broken-down world. Oz is no Eden, though there are many reasons to see their multicultural unity as an idyllic alternative to Kansas' bleak outlook in all-gray hues.

Like Lewis Carroll's players in Wonderland, these famous Americans have lost something important along the winding road of public life. Eden has clearly dealt them a curse, and each one is on the road to recovery through the encouraging spirit of Dorothy. Alice's malleability in Wonderland could not transform her London counterparts in the same positive way. The mad Hatter remains mad, watch swinging wildly from his breast pocket. The dark Queen remains a fool, using her playing-card-army in her crochet game.[68]

The Cowardly Lion has lost his roar in real life, and the Scarecrow no longer has a thought in his head after the farmers have been depicted as dolts and half-wits. The farmer's agrarian worldview at the turn of the century is already considering technology and everything modern. These who grow the bread and raise the salads, sorting casseroles in their fields, have little political clout, though they keep the city populations alive with fresh groceries and bread in bags, hot from the oven. No one wants to hear the gory details about the slaughterhouses as these cattle and the pigs arrive on the dining room tables.

---

[67] Griffith. *What it was, was Football*.

[68] *Alice's Adventures*. Wikipedia.

But everyone wants convenience, with prepared meals arriving in a can or bottle or an aluminum tray.[69] Everyone watches in amazement as Dorothy overturns our preconceptions about the farmer's daughter. She changes the profile of the Kansas farmer. Pretty, guileless, this farm girl encourages everyone she meets along the Rues d'Or leading into the Emerald City. She points out the Scarecrow's (the farmer's) knowledge gained through the hours sowing into the furrows, and kneeling in the brown dirt to harvest long afternoons. She is the fresh face of those who are covered with ridicule and shame in the public forum of the nineteenth century.

The intellectuals of Baum's day preferred factory outputs to the grain and produce coming from these farms. The Tin Man had his heart lifted from under his nose in one of those Northeastern factories where multiple modifications and repairs have left him heartless. In Oz, the Wicked Witch cursed him, ultimately removing his heart. L. Frank Baum transposed the Industrial Revolution from positive progress to cursed vortex in *Oz*. The Revolution's assimilation of the rural lifestyle moved the profit margin and materialism to the top of the heap. [70]

The "bottom-line" and the "Curse" converge as the woodsman is moved from the natural forest into the low-rent flats in the dirty city slums. In this revolution, the Tin Man becomes the progeny and victim in this progress. The *Wizard* joins *A Tale of Two Cities* in Dickens' critique of the downside of this revolution touching the whole world. He alludes to the victims of financial prosperity, the rise of the middle class, and the convincing theology of materialism. Pop would have led his students into the dark symbolism of the mineshaft where suffering and death await the workers daily. The mineshaft represents the futility of their lives, functioning daily before the open maw of their private destruction. Pop might have addressed the impotence of the knitting needles toiling in silence while the political convulsions swallowed France in the bloody Revolution. Common life holds on to normalcy in a world gone completely mad. The elephant's melancholy swaying of its trunk reminds the reader that insanity and violence are barely restrained in this ruptured era.[71]

Pop and I sat together instead, in front of the TV, witnessing the impotence of the Woodsman who is powerless in this new-fangled world of Oz. The factory worker learns his new job in an hour, and then repeats the same rote tasks for decades until his heart is removed from his metal chest. The factory worker suffers in silence, while everyone lines up to receive their black T-Model Ford automobile, or their shiny shovel, or their can of beans wrapped in a decorative paper label.

---

[69] Cohen. *A Consumer's Republic*.

[70] Barrett. *From Wonderland to Wasteland*.

[71] Dickens. *A Tale of Two Cities*.

The manufacture of consumer goods in Baum's day addressed every economic problem in America, and the working people give their all to boost the economist's favorite metric in the 1940s—the Gross National Product (GNP). Dorothy was more concerned about happiness, but her farm heritage helped to bring about both ends. In Oz she finds much unhappiness, but the gold streets point to a brighter day ahead in the Emerald City. The Tin Man's heart seems a small thing to sacrifice for GNP and pop-up toasters.[72] That washing machine with the wringer on top cut the drying time of the clothes on the backyard line by 50%. Convenience became the new god, and the ugly face of instant gratification gradually became visible as the backdrop for an ostensible children's story. [73]

The farmer needed the politician's favorable laws. The demand for tractors and plows helped to level-load the industrial hub in the Northeast and beyond. The political Lions depended on the farmers' and the factory workers' votes. The politicians incorporated the democratic ideas birthed in the vast fields of corn and wheat, pointing out that entire continents starve for the lack of this agrarian genius. Their speeches before the Congress benefited from these graceful ideas. The health and welfare of the workers on those 24 x 7 assembly lines provided good rhetoric and a harvest of votes for the Senators and the Judges. Dorothy melted the frozen code for each of those ultra-myopic perspectives, speaking a message of love and unity into the materialistic and political vacuum. Without this healthy vision, there could be no national synergy at the end of the day. The real wizard of Oz was Baum himself, and Dorothy is still his empathetic heroine.[74]

Baum had taken his family for a long visit to Kansas, arriving during the wintertime, but leaving before the spring turned the land green. He believed that Kansas would never be green because of the harsh landscape he found there. He gained a new respect for the hardy souls who ran the agrarian factory-farms which manufactured our grits and cans of beans. He gained greater appreciation for subduing the land and making it bear fruit in season. These farms fed the supply chain of the American supper table. Hers is a hand raised against the pejorative conception of the lonely rural life. Dorothy's pretty persona became the default face for *FarmersOnly.com*.

> Then God blessed them, and God said to them, "Be fruitful and multiply; fill the earth and subdue it; have dominion over the fish of the sea, over the birds of the air, and over every living thing that moves on the earth." Genesis 1:28

---

[72] Fox. *The Economics of Well-Being.*

[73] Cohen. *A Consumer's Republic.*

[74] Baum. *The Wonderful Wizard of Oz.*

She didn't ignore the Tin Man, incapacitated beside the road. Her optimism overwhelms the extensive and terminal rust (tin doesn't rust). She learned quickly who pushed the Tin Man down? The wicked Witch, of course, saw fit to take advantage of his weakness. Baum painted a clear picture of the spiritual war that craves our souls. No longer useful in those factories of the Northeast, the Wicked Witch knocked the Tin Man down beside the road, leaving him to be destroyed by the elements.[75] He no longer had the heart for the battle.

As a boy, I could see my heart, mind, and identity impacted by Dorothy's courage in Kansas. When guys don't step up, the girls will not stand back for long. In my Kansas doldrums, the yellow brick road slowly yielded to the *Faith-Time Continuum* of my future. I would eventually learn that this continuum is a Bell curve. Those who have a very hard time hearing God fall at the left-hand (negative) tail. Those who are average in their sensitivity, fall at the center of the curve. The ones who are hyper-sensitive to God's voice, filled with faith in His attentiveness, will fall in the upper tail of the curve—on the positive end of the continuum. God called me into fruitfulness when I started listening to Him— doing what He said. Early on, I rarely achieved the ability to intercept His tiny neutrino messages arriving from another kingdom.

For Noah, the message included blueprints for a great boat. That design ratio anticipated a great storm coming, when never-before-seen rain would begin falling from the sky. That ratio Noah and his sons adhered to, is still used today for the great oil tankers that travel through ocean storms daily. Rather than shout through a modern smartphone, God the Holy Spirit prefers to expose the motives of our hearts with the whisper of a holy neutrino setting off our deeply buried sensors. A mile and a half underground, my receiver can detect this spiritual frequency. In silence, with arrogance and pride filtered from the signal, I clearly heard Him say: "Be Still and Know that I am God."

The yellow road in Oz is full of subtle messages for those who have ears to hear. The golden way does not compare to the German Autobahn, where I drove a rented Mercedes at more than 240 kilometers per hour. The gold brick highway to the Emerald City offers the hope of financial unassailability. The gold standard is trusted in Europe and beyond through the powerful symbolism of unimpeachable value. Baum fully intended to make his political point with his solid gold metaphor and his silver slippers—ruby in the theaters. But nothing in Oz can bring back confidence in the manner of Dorothy, the pretty young heroine who changed the landscape of children's literature. She altered the locus of Oz, the Wizard, and the Wicked Witch.

Without the unity which followed her everywhere she traveled, there would be no Oz. Dorothy, with her open-mouthed innocence, still leaves everyone smitten in the land of good and evil—wizards and witches trigger the action in nearly every scene. She penetrates the membrane between brown Kansas and the bright colors of Oz. This membrane allowed her a deep glance into another

---

[75] *The Wonderful Wizard of Oz*. Wikipedia.

world, where good overwhelms evil, and deliverance and reconciliation come through unlikely friendships. Dorothy travels through the vortex for us, going into the literary and allegorical Faith-Time Continuum—and all she wants to do in every circumstance is to help us find our true identity. She also, and always, wants to go Home!

The yellow boulevard through Oz leaves a streak of confidence in the minds of those seeing the movie in the 1950s. Just decades earlier they had faced major economic disasters. As they weathered the overconfidence of the *Roaring Twenties* and the psychic after-shocks of the *Great Depression* in the 1930s. They had experienced the shameful whipping behind the barn door, coming out with a red face and eyes, and welts on their behind. The major economic arguments concerned the advantages of silver vs. gold reserves to prevent future economic shocks—this coming after the total collapse of the German economy in the early 1920s. The government storage of pure gold bricks created great confidence in the American dollar.[76]

Dorothy, and her golden footsteps, gave the audience the sense of security they craved. Golden Oz is reassuring in insecure times! The happy tunes coming from the Emerald City provide a welcome balm for the exhausted world population. The myopic fear of financial ruin caused citizens and nations to consider the efficacy of Solomon's collection of golden bars once again. The king's storage rooms were enlarged to house gold bullion arriving annually from the great nations of the world. Gold bricks were stacked high in his vaults and eventually in Fort Knox's storage rooms, and beyond to storage rooms around the world. Tons of gold, guarded by armies, reset the public confidence in the dollar bill—the US Dollar. This confidence-game made the dollar the most trusted currency, and gold glowed again in the Emerald City—and silver became as common as dirt.

---

[76] *The Yellow Brick Road.* A Free Blog about World Events.

6.

BAPTISM INTO FAMILY.

My father was no buffoon, though a clown he could certainly be. While a coterie of older women influenced my early visions of the family reality, he encouraged me to be a man who could look into a hard story to find the good triumphing over evil—or grimacing, to find the tragic reversal of fortunes coming on the man who is seduced by bad company corrupting his good character. Did this spiritual discernment start on the night when I sat in that dark theater to be baptized in fresh terror? Or did it come through grandfathers who died before I was born?

Heredity and Environment certainly collide to make us who we are—but there is much more which we don't discuss or even understand. My eventual encounter with the Faith-Time Continuum would show me that God has programmed His version of identity into my DNA, but He is also actively transforming the synaptic paths of my brain, and guarding my soul for eternity. "And what do you benefit if you gain the whole world but lose your own soul? Is anything worth more than your soul?"[77] Pop asked this question of himself, while challenging everyone he encountered with this same question. "Is anything worth more than your soul?"

My father found himself outnumbered in the jet wash of these women flying in V-formation, sometimes leading his family. He was baptized in the maternal reality as the only man among us. Rud was busy with the CIA, or whatever international developmental role he had been assigned. Momma's brother spent his working years in Tehran, Baghdad, Tokyo, Paris, and Washington DC. In retirement, he moved to Fifth Avenue New York. Pop's family in Clemson knew little about such global matters, being captive to the cultural tsunami of festive family gatherings. He was free to mentor bright students in the pursuit of *Pulitzer Prizes* and advanced college degrees. Journalism was crucial in his day, before the 4th Estate collided with 24-hour entertainment news broadcasts and biased political wings of our factionalized two-party system in America.

It is interesting to look at the history of these four estates to find how anachronistic they really are today. The first estate within the French political system of the 18th and 19th centuries was the clergy. Even the name "clergy"

---

[77] Matthew 16:26.

is anachronistic, having no biblical authority whatsoever, and having diminished importance in the expansive era of self-salvation. The second estate was the nobility, and that category really has never had any distinct influence or power in the American system. The third estate in France and England were the commoners, which we might shoehorn to fit our idea of the "people—we, the people." The fourth estate was the press, with this influential category not being added until 1837 when newspapers gain significant prominence and power in the French political system.[78]

Today, the fourth estate, intended to be the conscience of the government through the daily newspaper has all but disappeared. Pure journalism still has a critical role in communicating accurately the events of the day. Pundits and apologists have replaced the hardcore journalistic documentaries of past decades. It is almost impossible to separate the two today, with factionalism operating in the "news" at the highest intensity of my lifetime.

Pop could easily juggle Shakespeare's metaphoric dialogues and Hemingway's journalistic accounts of the futility of life. Hemingway and Ecclesiastes were close kin, and Solomon might have enjoyed Ernest's dismal company during his later years. In the evenings, Pop coached the staff and editors of *The Tiger* student newspaper, teaching them to put each story in the form and with the power of the journalistic style: He helped them address the Who, What, When, Where, Why, and How of every story.

Nannie, Auntie, and Ella merged from their two automobiles on every special occasion as if they were a single entity. They converged on our driveway simultaneously from Decatur and Spartanburg in perfect choreography. They spilled out the doors of their new Impala sedan or Bel Air, popping the trunks full of packages, table settings, and food still warm or chilled in dry ice from their distant houses. They landed from the heavens as the season prescribed or as the birthday earned its party. We celebrated everything together, sometimes a dozen-strong, with red goblets and gold-rimmed plates on the extended mahogany table in the dining room. We filled our stomachs with barbecued leg of lamb and turkey with ambrosia from the gods.

Ours was a rich heritage, and when everyone died young on Pop's side of the family, the monolithic McIntosh edge of my identity emerged with great fanfare and a diverse history. Auntie was one of the first women to receive a doctorate from the University of Chicago. Ella was one of the first women to be named the Superintendent of Schools in the Spartanburg system of schools. Still, General Lachlan McIntosh seemed the most auspicious of our family line, with his famous boss [Father of his country], and his infamous duel with Button Gwinnett [Declaration of Independence signer] in a field in Savannah Georgia. Imagine putting those two highlights on your resume. "Involved in a formal duel with Button Gwinnett in which this signer of the Declaration of Independence was mortally wounded. Served as a General under George Washington during

---

[78] *Fourth Estate*. Wikipedia.

the Revolutionary War. Raised as an orphan in George Whitefield's Savannah Orphanage (his father, John McIntosh, the former Scottish clan leader, died after imprisonment by the Spanish forces in Florida)."

Pop married into this ancient Scottish heritage. General McIntosh's Peale portrait is on display in Philadelphia with Washington and the other generals, each man wearing the gold uniforms of the day.[79] I never met a male grandparent from either side of my family lineage. My father and my Uncle Rutherford were the only men in my early life! War raged when I was born (WWII), when I visited Pop's classroom (Korean War), with the Revolutionary War marking my mother's line, and the Civil War marking my father's line—Lieutenant Sydney Carter walked from South Carolina to Gettysburg in 1863.

Sydney Carter's name is searchable on Google because my mother wrote the book containing his personal letters to his wife, Bet. *Dear Bet* recounts his journey from South Carolina to the Battle of Gettysburg in Pennsylvania. He is buried in the fields of blood from which a nation rose.[80] He is buried, by chance, with the Connecticut dead at the Gettysburg battlefield. War marked every issue of our lives with Uncle Grayson dying a month before I was born, and with Viet Nam drawing me very close to that terrible war. My Uncle Grayson's best friend growing up, General Westmoreland, is even blamed for the loss of the war in Viet Nam.

My father escaped from his region's economic boom in the tobacco fields of Coastal Carolina. He never again returned to that world which had invited him to give his life to this deadly industry. He would later give his life anyway, with lung cancer taking him decades later. Tobacco spoke his name, but he refused that lucrative invitation. He didn't live long enough to realize that tobacco would become infamous for killing 1200 people a day through myriad deadly diseases which result from smoking or chewing tobacco.

He presciently chose rhetoric and relationships as preferable to the various forms of materialism that beckoned him in that deep smell of tar in the hot drying sheds. He rejected the bundles of tobacco leaves, preferring the bundles of poems and Shakespeare's plays which still speak beyond the pits of London's sixteenth century theaters. His works speak to every age with wisdom and understanding of the vicissitudes of the human condition.

While tobacco soon found its way into every mouth and lung, tobacco's empire fell on hard times, and company executives are still publishing ads confessing their criminal motives to make America's young people into addicts. Until Pop's brother, Sydney, died of cancer, I had rarely heard any names connected with Pop's family. It seemed back then that all my relatives came from my mother's side of the family. I don't know if he was ashamed of them, or that they wanted nothing to do with us.

---

[79] *List of military leaders.* Wikipedia.

[80] Carter. *Dear Bet.*

My father became the Emeritus Professor, and he was never a coward. He went boldly where no man in his family had ever gone before. He went to disarm the Wizard, and he found the good Witch Glenda in Gotham City. She chased his fear of the evil clouds rising like thunderheads, and she raised her wand and everything returned to the happy-dance in a swirling festival of joy. He wrestled literature, creative and journalistic writing, and drama from the hands of the Eastern Witches.

He introduced a southern school to all the possibilities of rhetoric, teaching communication through myriad versions of the same thing. Though his classroom environment was homogeneous in this early time, he had abandoned his rented room in Harlem for a small college town. He had witnessed the cost of diversity in New Amsterdam—the good, the bad, and the ugly. He would take on the constant battle between good and evil after his stay there was interrupted by the ugly black wall of the Great Depression.

Dorothy gained the honors with children and adults alike during Pop's era in the 1920s and 30s—and her first baptismal service, as far as I can see, connected heaven and earth in the diverse Land of Oz. She was being baptized into a different kind of multicultural family, where all are become one in this fantastic story. There is no true unity in Oz, but Dorothy's baptismal accident, and her Ruby Slippers, invoke Christian imagery and reality. She bravely sloshed the wash water on the Scarecrow's flaming straw, and good triumphed over fear in every scene. She thought of others before herself, and the Wicked Witch lost her hold on Oz when she tried to take the powerful ruby slippers from Dorothy. She wanted that power from on high that had been given to her as a potent favor from Glenda.

Evil, which divides by fear and avarice, is broken in Oz by Dorothy's baptismal service. Her good comes from outside to point to the unity of the Body of Christ, the Church (True Church). She touches the good and she brings a victory to everyone she encounters. She discovers family, and unity, of a different kind. The goodness is in the slippers. Don't box with the Bear! His arm is not shortened by the dancing of evil in the day. His goodness protects us from temptation and evil, as the *Our Father* prayer models for us. Greater is He Who is in the believer than him who is in the world. The Prince of the Air suffers the flames when Dorothy's act of love destroys the evil in her pathway. Good triumphs. Courage triumphs in this baptismal parable.

The wash water of God represents (in the earth and in the heavenly realm) the death, burial, and resurrection of Jesus Christ being worked out from the inside out in each believer through faith. It is not a methodology for salvation, but is an action taken by the one who already believes in God's deliverance through the Cross of Jesus Christ. Baptism is for the one living already in the grace of God—no longer seeking salvation through the Law of God. The believer has already been separated from the Curse of the Law which leads to death.

> But those who depend on the law to make them right with
> God are under his curse, for the Scriptures say, "Cursed is
> everyone who does not observe and obey all the commands
> that are written in God's Book of the Law." Galatians 3:10

The Law is a mirror that tells us the Truth—about ourselves and about God.
"No man can help you! You cannot keep the Law, no matter how hard you try!
God has saved you through His demonstrated lovingkindness: " Jesus is not just
your Savior. He is Lord of all. The baptism puts the believer under the Lordship
of Jesus Christ. Jesus first demonstrated His Own submission, as sinless Man
and as God's only Son by obeying fully the will of God the Father. Even Jesus,
at age thirty, submitted to submersion in the baptismal waters of the Jordan River.

> Then Jesus went from Galilee to the Jordan River to be bap-
> tized by John. But John tried to talk him out of it. "I am the
> one who needs to be baptized by you," he said, "so why are
> you coming to me?" But Jesus said, "It should be done, for
> we must carry out all that God requires." So John agreed to
> baptize him. After his baptism, as Jesus came up out of the
> water, the heavens were opened and he saw the Spirit of God
> descending like a dove and settling on him. And a voice from
> heaven said, "This is my dearly loved Son, who brings me
> great joy." Matthew 6:13-17

With Baum's story alluding so explicitly to the Christian baptism, it is
important to understand what that baptism is, and what it is not. Symbolically,
the wash water baptism in Oz symbolizes the great good which comes to the fantasy Land of Oz. By saving the Scarecrow and destroying the Western (wicked)
Witch, Dorothy gains fame throughout the Land of Oz. Her victory over the Evil
One comes entirely through supernatural power which she receives through favor.
She did not bring this power with her from Kansas. Please note that Dorothy's
act was to save the Scarecrow from the fire. She was motivated through love for
others. She desired to protect the Scarecrow from destruction, risking her own
life. By divine favor, she destroyed the evil powers in the land of Oz.

In the narrative of Jesus' baptism in John's Gospel, John the Baptist is bewildered when Jesus comes to him in the Jordan River. Jesus is without sin, while
John is baptizing sinners. John himself is a sinner; therefore, he cannot fathom
the purpose for Jesus' baptism. What would be accomplished by this event in
the presence of many Jews who have come to see what is happening? Jesus tells
John that it is God's will. God demands that it be done, and He has three major
purposes. The sinless Jesus is already under the Lordship of the Father in heaven.

The believer is also submitting to Lordship—Christ's Lordship. The one baptized is made clean through believing in His death on the Cross, the burial in a borrowed tomb, and the resurrection from the dead. These three are demonstrated by Jesus' baptism. Jesus will become Savior in three years when He puts the sins of the world under His Own blood. It is by faith, first demonstrated in Abraham, then demonstrated by God's Own Son in the Jordan River. Faith acts according to the will of God. Lordship is the first issue for the one who walks in faith. Is the lord to be Satan, or is the devil going to be de-winged, his stinger pulled out by Christ's victory? Sin will thus be brought under the Cross of Christ in the baptismal waters of God's Lordship and plans for His adopted sons and daughters.

The believer's past lifestyle of sin and self-interest, even Narcissism, is buried in the baptismal waters. Jesus came up out of the waters, from this symbolic burial, to this symbolic resurrection from the dead. The believer also receives the promise of this resurrection from the dead. While in the tomb, Jesus took the keys to sin and death from the Wicked Witch's grip. Jesus thus demonstrated what He would soon do when He actually rose from the grave to walk the earth in His resurrection body. The waters closed over His entire body, just as the tomb encloses the body of the one who has died. The believer is buried with Christ, and will rise from the dead to be with Christ in heaven.

God's second revelation is this promise of eternal life. In a world that believes in the silence, the blackness, the nothingness of death, Jesus' baptism promises that even death cannot hold the believer in the grave. Resurrection from the dead is a powerful, essential, central promise revealed in the baptism of Jesus. This is a bodily resurrection!

I was more than blessed to be found in a rich family atmosphere in Clemson, but no one can choose their birth family. I loved my Grandmother and Great Aunt and Aunt Ella, not really missing the men who had already died. My uncle, the CIA agent, as I always suspected, was there to remind me that men do big jobs in this world—beyond the simple scope of their upbringings. His years of involvement in government positions in Washington and around the world made me see that education and dedication will lead to service.

We really never knew what he did, though he lived in foreign hotspots and critical capital cities. I remember receiving the triangular stamps from those Middle Eastern countries during my early years. I started my stamp collection because of his travels around the world. He was witnessing the strangeness of the Emerald City during all those years. He was certainly seeing the Wicked Witches first hand. Baptism meant something different for Rud, for he was baptized into macro-politics and nation-building on a scale that I could not imagine then or now. When he was abused during the Confirmation Hearings in DC, I remember the tension in our South Carolina household. My mother's brother had to be beat up, before he could be elevated to that Paris position. He had to declare before men that he would live a new life in Paris for the purposes of the State.

When Jesus informed every witness that He was being consecrated for God's appointment in Jerusalem, He first had to be buried in the Jordan River. Before He could be raised from the dead, He first had to be beat up by the Pharisees and by the soldiers. He would come from death to life through the power of the Spirit, bursting the great stone that sealed His tomb. The third reality in the baptism makes this courage possible—making it possible for a God, who is man, to obey God's instructions to the letter.

When the Dove (the Holy Spirit) landed on Jesus, the Power of God took up residence in Him, just as He does when the new believer is baptized. When we submit to the Lordship of Christ, gaining His resurrection, we come to life with power from on high through His Spirit. The one who is baptized according to Jesus' example is empowered to be a new creation in Christ, full of the Spirit of God, submitting to the Lordship of Jesus, and performing the works that God prepared before the foundations of the world. When we do this by faith, surrendering our lives for His purposes, we also receive God's approbation and love.

This is God's fourth strong message and reality through the baptism according to Jesus' example. When God spoke at Jesus' baptism, He told every witness in a loud voice that He was proud to call Jesus His Son. This is approbation! God's approbation comes to everyone who is baptized into the death, burial, resurrection and Lordship of Christ. God's approbation is a great gift, and those who have submitted to this baptism describe the joy that fills them up when they come from the water. This experience of joy is God's personal approbation and love for each believer. Each one may experience His love. He is proud of them for being obedient, as Christ was obedient. He fills their hearts with joy.

The baptism is not an act leading to salvation, but is an act of worship and obedience by the one who is already saved through grace. That salvation always comes through faith, believing in the One who paid the ultimate price. Salvation is unmerited favor through God's Son. It is a gift which no man can boast about since God the Holy Spirit also brings us to conviction of our sins. Christ's righteousness shields us when we face the final judgment of all men at the end of the age. The Holy Spirit purifies our hearts daily, so that we can more deeply believe in Jesus as Savior, Lord, and Mighty God. We rise up into the new life mission coming out of God's plans for us. He makes us new creatures in Christ, and He adopts us into His family, into the Body of Christ—the True Church. The Church is under the Lordship of Christ Himself.

When I was born, my parents brought me home to Folger Street. They didn't leave me at the hospital. They adopted me as a son, by blood, by the pain of childbirth, and by the will of a human father. They could have put me up for adoption, giving me away to another family; but they chose to keep me as a first son. They brought me home the day that General Eisenhower declared war on the Germans in meetings held in secret. While they planned the onslaught on Utah and Omaha Beaches at Normandy, I was being nursed to strength in the fieldstone house that Pop built. My life of sin, contrary to the opinions of some

49

men, started in those first days on earth. I made my demands known early, and often, though my mother nearly died delivering me.

I needed the baptism from that day forward, but I couldn't be baptized before I believed in Jesus as Savior and Lord. My life could be dedicated by godly parents, but no baptism after Jesus' example could be consummated. Twenty-three years later I would come to believe in His finished work, though I barely understood what He had done. I did not get baptized at that time due to the childhood baptism years before I believed. Another eight years passed before I was obedient to follow Christ's example!

The life of sin was finally buried in the Jordan River waters of the Winston Salem Y-Pool with several others. The flawed works of *Myopic Me!* were surrendered in those chlorinated waters. The water is not holy, but the act of submersion as a believer is made holy, and with eternal ramifications, through the participation of the Holy Spirit Who comes to empower the believer. Baptized in Christ's death, burial, and resurrection, the believer proclaims their new journey according to God's will rather than the will of *Myopic Me!* "Holy" simply means "dedicated or consecrated." It means "set apart, and dedicated, to the mission and purpose of God." The new mission of God is being publicly proclaimed in baptism. The believer comes out of the water, leaving death behind, bursting forth with resurrection power through Christ's Spirit.

The consecration will continue for a life-time, and every unholy pattern from this world will be brought into submission to Christ. Like Jesus, the one baptized will intentionally confront Satan's claims and schemes in the wilderness. After all, Satan became the Prince of the Air when Eve and Adam submitted themselves to his counsel in the Garden of Eden. They turned over to the evil one their rightful place in the world given by God. Jesus righted this wrong when He traveled directly from the baptismal River into the wilderness to face the temptations of Satan.[81]

The believer should expect these same temptations to come his or her way, according to the idolatry consummated before Christ. Eve had surrendered to the beauty of the fruit of the Knowledge of Good and Evil. She chose that bite of fruit as more worthy than obedience to God. She ignored God's warning, wanting to be like God when she ate the beautiful fruit. She went off on her own like a lost sheep becoming tangled in the brambles and pursued by the wolves.

Jesus fasted for forty days, praying for God's kingdom to be advanced fully through His remaining days of life on earth, as man, and as God. Jesus faced three temptations, and gave three responses that are germane to everyone who is baptized. In the first temptation, Jesus confronted the appetites—His deep hunger from fasting made this a strong temptation to resist. Jesus refused to turn the stone into bread to slake His craving for food. He told Satan that the kingdom of God is not food and drink, but is attentiveness to every word that comes from

---

[81] Matthew 4:1-11.

the Father's mouth. For the believer, it is every word that comes from God's mouth—including the words spoken to us through the Son by the Holy Spirit.

The second temptation demanded that He prove His Sonship by getting God to perform supernatural tricks. I would learn that Christians sometimes want God to affirm them through these supernatural tricks. This is contrary to the will of God. It makes the faith into a magic act, demeaning the relationship. Jesus refused to make God His lackey. Satan wanted Jesus to exploit God's goodness and power for vanity. Satan wanted Jesus to prove His special standing with God keeping "His heel from being bruised" when He jumped off the Temple. But Jesus said that this relationship is to accomplish the will of God alone. Our relationship with God is not to support every vain desire of ***Myopic Me!*** This critical relationship is governed by the scripture which says, "You must not test the Lord your God."[82]

In each of the three cases, Jesus referred directly to the Scriptures. He asserted that the believer should be prepared to do the same. The believer has to know what God's Words say in order to do this! But this task is simplified for us, when we realize that Jesus quoted verses from two books of the Bible only: Deuteronomy 6 and Psalm 91. The Word of God is powerful, and we don't have to be intellectual geniuses to know how to defend ourselves.

The third temptation comes from familiar territory. Satan tempted Jesus with worldly fame and money. He offered Him the whole world—which world, Jesus created with the Word of His mouth. Satan offered Jesus the whole world if He would worship him above God. Satan wanted the ultimate victory over the Son of God. Jesus wanted me to see that Pride is always embedded in this third temptation. He wanted me to see that Satan is the very personification of Pride. Pride got him kicked out of heaven—Lucifer was thrown down with his coterie of dark angels which Jesus refers to as demons. Jesus' use of the scriptures as His Sword in this fight with Satan, drives home the full authority of God's Words. Jesus will not worship Satan or any other false god, and He will worship God only.

Jesus is stating that the love of the world and fame is a version of our submission to the lordship of Satan. He rejects this lifestyle on the basis of God's command: "You shall have no other god before Me!" This reveals the Lordship of Christ succinctly. He is the God of gods, Lord of lords, and King of kings. He pioneered our faith through baptism, declaring his commitment to worship God alone. He demonstrated it in three steps: 1 Symbolically burying the life of sin in the waters of the Jordan River—leaving the patterns of this world behind. 2. Being empowered for the Will of God through the Holy Spirit. 3. Then, walking in the reality as a new creature, submissive to God's will, in actions and in words.

---

[82] Ibid.

God will judge every action and every word on the final day.[83] Jesus started His new life as Savior and Lord by learning obedience through what He suffered under God's Lordship. He declared that there is no other god He will worship beside God the Father. He demonstrated to Satan that He would not submit to the evil triad of temptations. He proved that He was sealed, set like flint, according to the Father's will.[84]

In another key biblical example of the baptism, the Treasurer from Ethiopia (a eunuch) believes in Christ after Philip explains the words from Isaiah 53 which describe the suffering of Christ. The Eunuch is a picture of fallen man whose outward nature has to be modified before he can be trusted. With corrupted character, the man is neutered to reduce the risk of sexual sin in the process of serving his master. Jesus said it would be better that your hand be removed, than to live eternally in hell.

The Queen in Ethiopia had his manhood removed, so that he would not be motivated by his sexual drives—the problem of the endocrine had been removed. As a castrated man, some of the sin patterns common to men, were neutralized. It was not unusual for this castration to be performed, making the Eunuch a highly trusted and influential treasurer in Ethiopia. The Treasurer was baffled by the prophetic promise he had been studying on the road. "But he was pierced for our rebellion, crushed for our sins. He was beaten so we could be whole. He was whipped so we could be healed."[85]

The Eunuch believed in Jesus as the Christ when Philip explained what had happened in Jerusalem with the crucifixion and the resurrection of Jesus from the dead—Philip showed the Treasurer that the One promised to Abraham, Moses, and Isaiah was this Jesus, whom the Jews had whipped, beaten, and pierced. The Eunuch was already a new creation in Christ with the Spirit of God living inside him when he spotted the body of water beside the road a few moments later. He insisted on being baptized immediately. For the Eunuch, there was nothing to gain from delaying this baptism. Philip did not have to instruct him, cajole him, or admonish him about the baptism. The Treasurer wanted to have the Spirit of God empowering his life, showing him how to life for Christ and the will of God. He set the example for all of us. "Aha! There is a body of water beside the road. Let me be baptized. I want to live for Christ, being raised with Him."[86]

"I want to live for Christ, being raised with Him." The Eunuch sums up the new purpose for his life. He does not want to go back to Jerusalem to the Jordan River, or to a Synagogue, or to a YMCA pool, as I did. He wants to bury

---

[83] Ecclesiastes 12:14

[84] John 6:38.

[85] Isaiah 53:5.

[86] Acts 8:36.

his former life in the waters he finds beside the road. For me, the YMCA pool in Winston-Salem was perfect. I wanted to be baptized as Jesus had been, even though my parents had baptized me as a baby with a few drops of water on my forehead.

The Methodist Church follows the Catholic tradition of baptism which sprinkles the child, or the baby, with water. This does not meet the Scriptural model of these two examples above. Jesus was very intentional in His exemplification of the Baptism ordinance. I had no say in that original church ritual of convenience. Having a pool for dunking is an expense which some churches have decided to avoid. It all seems to be a theological deviation. I wanted to follow in the pattern of Jesus and the Eunuch. I did not know Jesus Christ when my parents baptized me. I could not make a commitment to live for Christ, for I was not of the age for believing. The Eunuch, and I, submitted to Christ's ordinance. Lordship is central in this ordinance. Deviating from this model is an insertion of the willfulness of *Myopic Me!*

When the Treasurer arrived home in Egypt, he was already Christ's Ambassador, bringing his personal testimony of the Good News of God's forgiveness and reconciliation through faith. Everyone who heard the Treasurer's story could become a Christian through faith, believing in God's Son who was crucified, died, and was buried, before He rose from the dead. The Treasurer became a potent witness while he served the Queen in Ethiopia and beyond.

Jesus prepared this work for the Treasurer to walk in before the world was formed. Past tense, present tense, and future tense is brought under the Lordship of Jesus. Jesus is the Alpha and the Omega, the beginning and the end. He is the Progenitor of God's economy into eternity. Nothing is wasted, and nothing is lost. Past experiences come under His Lordship. Future events are under His Lordship. This present moment is also under His Lordship!

Pop lived in another time which few today can imagine. He was born in the nineteenth century. He lived his life in the twentieth century. He was born two years before *The Wonderful Wizard of Oz* was published by L. Frank Baum in 1900. He did not live to see the landing on the moon in 1969, having seen the Venus flyby missions, and the hard landing of a rocket during the final year of his life. It was hard to imagine then that Americans would be on the moon eighteen months after his death. It is even more astonishing that the Saturn V moon landings occurred nearly fifty years ago.

Our perception of time is relative, and our minds are subsumed inside the invention we refer to as the Clock—the Apple clock, the Atomic clock, or the sundial Clock. Our perception of time is based on the movement of the earth around the Sun, and our rotation on a tilted axis. We see the rotation with the appearance and disappearance of the Sun each day. We see the cycle of the moon going through its stages each 28-day cycle. We see time in the tides, and in the seasons, and in the flash of spring each year blasting the winter browns and whites with multiple colors.

Some who read the Scriptures are puzzled by the resurrection of the Thief on the cross who is promised Paradise on that very day. He had never been baptized in the manner demonstrated by Jesus. Or had He? I don't know anything more than what appears in Luke's Gospel, but the thief did not appear to have a church life on the side. He was beside Jesus on the adjacent cross; and that was sufficient for him to be saved. How he met the required ordinance of the baptism in water is not clear—but I am sure of one thing. He was saved. He believed, and God saved him on the final day of his life. God so loved the world, that He gave His only begotten Son to die on a cross so that all who believe in him might not die but have everlasting life.[87] Believing normally leads to baptism, but the thief was only baptized in the earthquake that struck the city of Jerusalem.

Likewise, the family of the Jailor in Philippi were baptized without raising their hands in church, or walking down to the altar, or going through confirmation or first Communion. They believed, and they were baptized immediately into Christ's resurrection. It doesn't mention the details, but all of them believed and were baptized. They were in awe of Christ because of the miracle at the jail when the earthquake broke open every cell door, but no one fled. Their father, the jailor, could have been executed had they all left him there holding the keys in his hand. Some have explained that the prisoners saw warrior Angels standing before their open doors, so no one dared to push past them.

When my father stood to sing the solo each week in the choir, the pipe organ produced its beautiful chords from those forty-foot long sound tubes standing behind him. He was my constant standard for the faithful man. When he stood up, I could say, "My dad is a Christian man." I felt safer because of his constancy of purpose. He was the guidon for my march through childhood, though my own faithfulness was wearing very thin. I had very little personal understanding of what he believed, or what he was baptized into. How was he saved? What words did he speak to become a follower of Christ. I wasn't sure of these details, nor did I ever hear him speak on this subject.

Some people then, and now, believe that baptism is required for salvation. That is not what the Bible says. It says that the believer is baptized as soon as they believe. Jesus said that the work of the kingdom is believing in the Son whom the Father sent. Part of the answer for the odd case of the Thief is his behavior on the cross when he believes. He mounted a vocal defense of the Lord right there on the cross. He was immediately baptized into persecution coming from the murderer on the third cross. The Thief rebuked the scoffer next to Jesus. The baptism is a chance to stand before men in your faith, saying, "I am not ashamed of the Gospel of Christ! I will follow Him no matter what."

One of the criminals hanging beside him scoffed, "So you're the Messiah, are you? Prove it by saving yourself—and us,

---

[87] John 3:16.

too, while you're at it!" But the other criminal [the Thief]
protested, "Don't you fear God even when you have been
sentenced to die? We deserve to die for our crimes, but this
man hasn't done anything wrong." Then he said, "Jesus,
remember me when you come into your Kingdom." And Jesus
replied, "I assure you, today you will be with me in paradise."
Luke 23:39-43

At 3:00 p.m. the sky grew dark as night, and the Centurion believed in Jesus.
He could finally make the connection between Jesus' dying and this occlusion
of the sun at mid-afternoon. He had run his spear up through Jesus' side and
through His heart to make sure that He was already dead. Jesus' crucified body
gave up the water and the blood of the One who had suffocated on the cross.
God allowed him to see this proof of death by his own spear through God's side.
Inspired by the Holy Spirit, He declared in a clear voice, "Truly this man was
the Son of God."[88]

Earlier, when Peter said something similar at Caesarea, Jesus pointed out
that his words were inspired by the Holy Spirit, and not by Peter's own intellect. When any man, including the Centurion, believes, he has come under the
influence of the Spirit of Christ. From broken body to blood shed for sin, the
Centurion remembered the Lord at His death. He would soon witness the risen
Lord, rising above the death meted out by sinners and corrupted empires. The
baptism includes this miracle of the resurrection. This baptism rises above the
self-interest and the narcissism of political factions. It rises above the depravity
which is embedded in the DNA of the present world.

Baum's allusion to the Christian baptism in Oz is dramatic, albeit inaccurate
in some details. The Wicked Witch who ruled in the Land of Oz is now struck
down! She is drowned, dissolved, washed away from our lives. The baptism is
a direct assertion of Christ's victory over the Sin-Master, who is Satan. Dorothy
is linked directly to this symbolism, and to this deep reality, as she travels within
the Faith-Time Continuum in Oz.

At each instance of danger, Baum's choreography delivers Dorothy, refer-
encing the beauty of this victory over a defeated enemy—who shrinks slowly to
a dot, and then disappears. "Ding dong the witch is dead!" sing the Munchkins,
Glenda, and Dorothy Gale.[89] This detail is important because Jesus promises that
every disciple who continues in His truth will be set free. Continuing is crucial.
The process is part of God's plan of salvation, revealing more and more of the
true nature of Christ to us. It is the promise of the new creation through Him.

---

[88] Matthew 27:54.

[89] *Ding-Dong! The Witch is Dead*. Wikipedia.

Life is a baptism in suffering, disappointment, and loneliness. This baptism brings us to our need of God our Savior. We need a friend who knows us in our weakness, pouring His Own strength into us when we waver. We need the deep covenant with the One who is ever faithful and ever Good. Pop wavered toward the end of his life, losing hope in a life-well-lived. He told me that all of his efforts to teach and help young men were wasted on people who didn't appreciate him. He believed, for a moment, that the university never cared about his problems or appreciated his contributions. That was not true at all, but the self-pity motif is a potent one in our lives. "My life was wasted, doing the wrong things! No one cared. Nothing was changed for the good."

When I go through this syndrome, God encourages me with His divine voice speaking through the people who love me as He does—with no condemnation toward me. Pop was no different, and the ones who loved him traveled thousands of miles to let him know how grateful they had been to have him in their lives. God showed him, at the end, when the water of this life had seemed to run through his fingers, and his hand seemed to be dry, that his life was not meaningless—as Solomon had insisted. Pop knew that God loved him. He knew that we loved him. The baptism is a preparation for the life to come, which is eternally satisfying.

The wickedness in Oz is a portrait of the wickedness in all men which is broken in us through our believing and receiving God's powerful redemption. The water baptism, including its assertion of the spiritual victory over evil through faith in Jesus Christ, is the declaration to man and to the spiritual kingdoms that a new life is launched through the death, burial, and resurrection of Christ. It is the announcement of a journey underway, a pilgrimage as a servant of the Most High God, the hands and feet of Christ, the light and the salt of the world. This journey is not like the vain pilgrimage of Lord Byron, but is the blessing returned for every cursing that will come—according to the pattern of Christ Himself.

Dorothy's Faith-Time pilgrimage is activated through the imperfect instructions of the Wizard. She gains the ruby slippers, giving her the confidence to find her way Home. Though she travels back to Kansas, Home is really that safe abode with God Himself that lies deep inside our hearts. Everyone who avoids Solomon's windy vortex of vanity, has a chance to find the ruby slippers of God. Even Solomon remembered the way home at the end of Ecclesiastes when he speaks of the only thing that matters. The Spirit of Jesus Christ provides the Ruby Slippers in the Gospel story. When there is no way to be saved, He comes in the Wind that lifts the lost traveler when all hope is lost. By His Spirit, the Wicked Witch is neutralized, and the way home is revealed.

7.

MOVIES, OZ, ALICE, OLD MAN AND THE SEA, AND TOP SECRET *BLACKBIRD*.

In those early *Clemson Theater* days, *War of the Worlds* was the only movie that managed to medevac me to Dr. Brown's office. Like the ubiquitous social media of today, movies became a powerful and pervasive social influence on the post-war generation, and I was no exception. I discovered many new characters inside the darkened theater's tall walls, and new worlds coalesced before my eyes. After Dorothy and Alice dove into their strange worlds in *Oz* and *Wonderland*, a stream of Westerns and post-war movies filled the marquee windows outside the red-brick movie house. Lancelot's stories of jousting and valor in Camelot captured the imagination of boys and girls alike. King Author's Court altered our games in the woods behind the house.

We fashioned swords and jousting poles out of poplar wood using a draw-shave as the tool of choice for reshaping them. My great aunt had given me the draw-shave tool for Christmas when I was about ten years old. I made several wide-blade swords, and we used garbage can lids for shields. They were stout enough to survive many intense battles behind the Catholic House down the street, where the statuary in the back seemed to bring the medieval world to life—the Catholic propensity for everything medieval fit perfectly into our fantasy games. The men inside the house never seemed to take notice of our dangerous afternoons, and they never told us to skedaddle. Maybe they feared our swords and archery skills.

During this era, our little TV with the rabbit ears was all that our professor could afford, though every dollar he earned was worth 20-times what it is today: $10 then = $200+ today. This was during the time when a college education cost about a thousand dollars per year vs. the twenty-thousand dollar price-tag today. The TV set in our houses, curiously, cost nearly as much then as they do today. In those early production runs, Pop's meager salary restricted our purchase to the Black and White TV—around seventy-five dollars. Color did not come to our house during the years I lived there.

Though the silver screen transitioned to color in 1939 with the release of *The Wizard of Oz,* black and white movies about the Old West, intriguing science fiction fantasies and post-war recapitulations, avoided the cost of color films. The same thing happened in the television industry because of associated costs for production and delivery. The big budget Technicolor movies were appearing, reenacting the universal war between good and evil, while applying the biased brushstrokes of the director and producer. Colorful brushes were dipped into the writer's wounded soul to paint the stories that tugged at our hearts. The director's motive for fame and financial remuneration produced various wolves in sheep's clothing according to the perceived appetites of the day.

The actor's ability to become someone else advanced the emotional potential in every film, and their star quality expanded exponentially with every famous character they played on the big screen. The writers and directors could aim their lens at whomever or whatever they wished. They could insert foreboding shadows or bright hopeful lights in every scene. The potential for fame and glory was brutally dealt with, leaving the superfluous frames on the cutting room floor. They measured the lucrative potential on theater screens, rejecting the ideologically flawed, or morally unseemly portions — according to the appetites of every fickle age.

Even before the color films appeared in our small-town, *The Black Hand* had presented six-year-old me with another set of nightmares in full black-and-white — mostly black. The nightmares started when my teenaged sister took me to the YMCA-Theater. She paid the dime for our tickets before we entered the darkness. This drama depicts the secret criminal society in New York City in the first decade of the twentieth century. Gene Kelly plays the role of the son who goes after his father's murderer. It uncovers the ugly underpinnings of the Mafia in one of the darkest stories ever told. I cannot remember any plot details, other than the hole in the floor leading down into blackness. It is no wonder that I hate everything Mafiosi today, having experienced that dark beginning in *The Black Hand.* The YMCA theater, and that granite entranceway, is forever disfigured in me. Those giant doors are remembered as a foreboding mouth leading into a black hole of evil.

Even when we had *Day Camp,* I did not like entering that large staging area for the local kids before we boarded the YMCA bus heading for Oconee State Park. I remembered nothing about that secret society of New York, but that dark hole in the floor looms in my brain as the portal to death or worse. I entered into a nightmarish psychic pit in a fear-provoking scene — and that is the sum-total for me. These menacing memories revert again and again to that black hole — not to the *Black Hand.* While Einstein worried about the event horizon of the black hole from which even light cannot escape, all my concerns were for that event horizon in *The Black Hand* — the great black hole in the floor of my memory. My review of the 1950s film is succinct: "No one under age sixteen is permitted!"[90]

---

[90] Crowther. *The Screen in Review.*

The movie can be purchased on *Amazon* today, and has just now been retooled in the 2018 version with Leonard DiCaprio in the lead. I discovered that *The Black Hand* (Stephan Talty) is also available in *An Unlikely Story Bookstore & Café* in the 2017 hardback account of these historical events. My personal nightmare has come back to the big screen and to the bookstore with great fanfare! I will plan to see it through the perspective of all those years since 1950! The "Y-theater" continued to sell tickets for a nickel, including my last visit to that theater, sitting with Pete Maravich in an empty theater while he bounced his Clemson College practice basketball in the aisle for the entire hour-and-a-half movie. That other-dimensional experience at the theater helped me to put *The Black Hand* nightmares behind me forever.

Those devouring doors, funded partially by John D. Rockefeller, remain as an impressive landmark today in this university town. Over the years, the crowds diminished at the Y, and the majority of people chose the College Avenue theater or the reconstituted theater in the old Dixie Store location. My one trip to see *The Black Hand* nearly broke me of ever going back to the movies. Three years later, of course, I fled the theater with the manager driving me away from my *War of the Worlds*! Dr. Brown, with one lung, patched me up for all the movies yet to come.

Editing together all the pieces from this era, would we find anything that might shock us today? Could anything come close to the flood of X-rated films from the 1970s? *I am Curious Yellow*[91] lurked within the financial motives of every project. Compassion or cynicism vied for attention in the choices by Hollywood's best directors. Should we make *Alice in Wonderland* or *Bridge over the River Kwai*? The producers fashioned each proposition in the most effective way possible, with nearly unlimited budgets, bringing together every hidden agenda with their filtered worldview and the latest schemes for indoctrination of a vast movie-going audience.

They shaped and tracked the cultural preferences and sensibilities of the day to entertain and to manipulate public sentiment and individual proclivities. Having no awareness of this subtle warfare in the heavenly realm, these films advanced Hollywood's business model, while we settled into our favorite seats, diving into Audrey Hepburn in *Breakfast at Tiffany's*. We sat side by side in the dark, holding each other's hearts during *Moon River*'s poignant chords. Afterward, the *Dime Store* wooed us like a magnet across the street, and Hollywood, more than any other industry on earth, cornered the market in our memories.

The hometown theater tapped into our souls for good or evil, and the smartphone had not yet siphoned the creativity from the entire world with its unfiltered-consciousness, its tsunami of information, flooding a world yet unformed. While Bollywood expanded throughout the twentieth century in India, Hollywood was making moguls and empires in Southern California's golden

---

[91] *I am Curious*. The Criterion Collection.

ghetto. Before the *Ed Sullivan Show* and the *Lawrence Welk Show* came into our homes via the black-and-white Zenith 13-inch TV, Hollywood had preserved numerous time-capsules on celluloid. TV advanced the art of the Live show, with all of its potential for sudden catastrophic outcomes. While the cameras hummed, the primitive technology whirled its glib excitement into a matrix of cathode-ray tubes selling us on *Gunsmoke* and *Little Rascals*. The movie moguls spun golden worlds when the *Ten Commandments* (Charlton Heston and Yul Brenner) grossed $131,000,000,[92] and *The Robe* (Jean Simmons, Richard Burton, and Victor Mature) became the first CinemaScope film, grossing $36,000,000.[93]

African Queen, with Humphrey Bogart and Katharine Hepburn, hit the movie screens a year after *War of the Worlds*, and I saw the movie at the Clemson Theater with Mama. We sat on the tenth row from the front. I loved this story, with the leeches, and the eventual reconciliation of the two unlikely conspirators. The movie is on DVD today—it scores a 7.9 on IMDb and a 100% score on *Rotten Tomatoes*. It is the story of an unlikely relationship during WWI, contrasting Bogart, the gin drinking riverboat captain, and Katharine Hepburn, the feisty missionary whose brother has died. She is left all alone when the captain offers to take her down the Nile River and out through the dangerous waters near Uganda in his little steamship. Throughout the movie these two characters are at odds with each other—at war with each other. They finally agree on one thing, collaborating to turn his little ship into a torpedo that sinks the German gunboat.

The neighborhood kids gathered on Saturday mornings to watch Disney's *Mickey Mouse Club* in Richard and Gerry's basement TV room in their expansive ranch-style house. Their 25-inch color console enthralled us, wearing our Mickey Mouse ears as Mickey's gang of young people sang to us as if we were living the dream in Golden California. This show captured the kiddie audience, bringing new heroes and imaginations through Walt Disney's fantastic stories of good and evil. The boys in our Saturday-morning gatherings had their favorite girl to ogle and cheer on. I chose Annette! Annette Funicello was so cute, and her confidence was infectious. She quickly became the favorite on the show, and everyone else realized that she kept the weekly variety show on the air.

This technology was fantastic to us, and we knew that the signals came through the air to our houses from Greenville. We tried hard to see these signals; but no one could. Though we could not see the TV images fly through the air, we still believed in the existence of our favorite shows which we watched. "On-the-air," meant something new for our first Wi-Fi-like experience from a giant "router" that hurled VHF and UHF signals thirty miles against our antennae or rabbit ears—our "whole-house modem" amplified the *Mouseketeers* and the lovely *Lennon Sisters* who somehow were recapitulated from the electromagnetic

---

[92] *The Ten Commandments (1953)*. Wikipedia.

[93] *The Robe*. Wikipedia.

energy emanating from that tall building I had seen in downtown Greenville, near the *S & S Cafeteria.*

Today, *DirectTV* arrives at our disk antenna on the back of our house. It is pointed into the Southern sky where the communication satellites broadcast a thousand shows into our houses. If we have the decoding device from the provider, we can watch the show. *Amazon Prime* TV programming arrives through our wall to our router. It is decoded by the computer in our Smart TV. The resulting amplified signal is sent to the LEDs in the flat screen for our entertainment.

Dorothy and Annette would not care how their faces arrived on our screens, and their feisty personalities lifted the *Wonderful World of Disney* for the whole world to see. These shows came in weekly installments, spinning out the world according to Dorothy, Alice, Annette, and Disney's vast array of characters. Girls gained more and more facetime in all kinds of media, and us boys liked what we were seeing. The potential for female idolatry leaped on Saturday mornings and on Sunday nights when these assertive girls influenced an entire generation. They were helping the world imagine what a woman looks like in a post-war era.

Amazing movies and TV serials became the central locus of our lives, in the same way that social media is the rudder for young people today. Technology became the savior, promising security and convenience—making lives better, easier, and faster. Rote tasks could be accomplished using the advertiser's new washer, refrigerator, and electric stove. The advancements made in refrigeration changed the nature of grocery shopping and meal-planning, since fresh and frozen food could be kept for weeks or months. Technology relieved the young housewife of much drudgery, according to this widespread propaganda. This was the era of the first jet aircraft, and the designs of automobiles were strongly influenced by aviation movies we devoured on the big screen—the sweeping wings of the supersonic aircraft and the sloping vertical stabilizer morphed into the designs of automobiles. Cars were suddenly the size of aircraft carriers, and power steering combined with automatic-shifting transmissions to make it possible to drive one of these behemoths. Air travelers felt safer as radar and accurate weather reporting guided pilots through turbulent skies.

I will never forget those first images showing the flat screen TVs hanging on the wall in every room of the house in the 1950s. Those 1950s illustrations predicted the availability of video phones and automobiles that would drive themselves coming by the 1980s. Computers built into clothing never appeared on those pages as far as I know, and Google's search engine, offering nearly infinite knowledge to the curious could not be imagined by futurists. Without Moore's Law (Moore's Observation?), the fantastical world we live in could not exist. I believe! I believe! We accept miracles today, electronic miracles, which our grandparents could not understand if you showed them! Is it just possible, you doubting Thomases, that God has more in store which is beyond your imagining?

"I tell you, many prophets and kings longed to see what you see, but they didn't see it. And they longed to hear what you hear, but they didn't hear it."[94]

Devices which children take for granted today were the thrilling ideas that I read about in *Popular Science* and *Popular Mechanics* magazines back then. I nearly had an intellectual orgasm every time they would project these futuristic illustrations on those hypnotizing pages. The videophone (smartphone) and the flat screen TV (LED screen) were delayed thirty years beyond the prognosticators best estimates—until Moore's Law reached the proper transistor density per integrated circuit chip. That sweet spot of one billion transistors per circuit would not occur until the first decade of the twenty-first century. Before this sweet spot, there was no critical mass for any of these systems, including the self-driving car and the robotic home or factory.[95]

The half-million-fold increase in transistor density from the first integrated circuit in 1971, propelled the worldwide purchase of microminiaturized cell phones and flat screens. "Videophones," proposed by Bell Labs in the 1950s, had finally become a reality because of the astonishing exponential density advancements in the silicon wafer production in the angstrom realm—in a manufacturing environment—not in a lab. No one understood the obstacles that had to be overcome to achieve the widespread deployment of this kind of technology. The complexity far exceeds the challenges faced by the Saturn moon launch.

The Russians hacked our elections back then as well, but they did so without computers. They set up listening posts, and tapped phone calls. In those days, computers costing millions of dollars straddled whole floors of university buildings, and no one could foresee a stack of even more powerful computer devices lying around unused in our closets. Elon Musk's parents were born in the 1950s when these powerful computers were still dreams in the minds of visionaries. Their son's Tesla electric car was six decades away. Google's self-driving car is still in testing today, with a full production run planned for early next decade—seven decades after the ENIAC computer was being considered by the Air Force for flight training.[96]

These fantastic ideas for inventions took me into the impossibly distant future of the 1970s or 1980s. From my 1950s perch in the *Rexall Drug Store and Soda Shop* in Clemson, I could not imagine a time thirty-years away. Of course, these familiar products of our present technological reality did not arrive for additional decades beyond those forecasts. The 1990s came and went, and it was in the first decade of the twenty-first century before we experienced the widespread advent of the smartphone, the self-driving automobile, the flat-screen TV, and the live stream video connection to nearly anywhere in the world. The

---

[94] Luke 10:24.

[95] *Moore's law.* Wikipedia.

[96] *Project Whirlwind begins.* Computer History.

advent of microminiaturization in the realm of computer technology—the invention of the semiconductor chip itself—opened multiple doors to many amazing new products.

Today, every technological fantasy has arrived in your iPhone X. The number, X, will change, but the revolution is a reality. The capabilities and services that might be loaded into this one device, the size of a woman's compact, is nearly unlimited. The movie, *The Circle*, presents a portion of this potential horror, as privacy is replace by the invasion of the Ultra High Definition lens into our flower pots and our tree limbs. We enter the closet for a change of clothes, and we are live to the world in our birthday suits. We climb from the bathtub and the whole world can see us sagging and slipping on the wet tile. The whole world, from sex to shower to the global stage, boardroom and back room, toilet and romantic walk in the park, is now at the fingertips of the World with a click.[97] Part of this potential for the good, bad, and very ugly reality is listed below:

1. Hands free phone service nearly anywhere you go
2. Media services, including TV and movies, Facebook Live, U-Tube
3. Audio services like Soundcloud, Bandcamp, Audiomack, Clyp.it, Mixcloud, Hearthis.at, RepX, Reverbnation, DatPiff, Yung.Cloud, Soundclick, ORFIUM, and Fanburst
4. Commercial services, including *Amazon Prime,* the hardware store and the auto dealership, Order Status, Delivery information, Drone arrival above your head with a change of clothes coming by the time you finish your run through Central Park, available to every child who has a smartphone.
5. Employment services, and mortgage and banking services
6. Transportation services, with subway, train, and Uber; plus, GPS and maps
7. Social connections and Reality Story Telling services such as Facebook, Snapchat, Pinterest, Google Circles, Facetime, and Skype, bring the whole world to your screen, along with non-stop texting while driving, dodging the curbs, culverts, abutments, and children on bicycles along the way
8. Books and publications, including library access and records archives
9. Publishing capabilities, including Cloud-supported document production
10. Reminders, Email, Ordering on demand with a click
11. Apps for everything from heart-rate and #steps to a meal-on-wheels as you walk to work
12. Advertising, customized to your deepest desires and proximal needs, **Everywhere!**

---

[97] *The Circle*. Wikipedia.

13. Social Isolation Syndrome resulting from constantly looking into a tiny screen without a single real human interaction
14. Church services streamed live on U-Tube, Facebook live, or TV screens, with no need for human relationships at all

Wherever you are, these capabilities are there with you. This has shrunk the world down into a 2.5 x 4.5-inch screen that is a couple of centimeters thick. This is not a one-dimensional world any longer. In the mid-1950s, we put our fore-finger into the number on the dial phone on the table in the front hall and rotated the dial to make a four-digit phone call to reach a friend no more than a few miles away. A long-distance call required a significant fee to complete. Every father reminded us, "Get off the phone! It costs by the minute!" To call long-distance required an operator in a call-center to make a manual connection with cords and jacks to put you on a trunk line to another city or to an operator in a for-eign country. Nothing was carried out by microelectronics in those days. Such devices did not exist. Transistors were not used until Western Electric manufac-tured them for use in telephony. Wider use did not occur until I was in college.

While the transistor was being developed for radios, early versions of the computer, and for telephony, I finally saw the classic Technicolor movie, *The Wizard of Oz*, at our College Avenue movie theater. Movies cost twenty-five cents, and worlds appeared before our eyes in that dark cavern. Recently, I viewed the 65-inch ultra-high definition 3-D TV that is priced for less than two thousand dollars. This is about two-week's pay for a vast number of American families today. Ideas that were proposed in the 1950s have exploded on the scene in the era of the iPhone—nearly sixty-five years since I sat under that tree in Clemson reading the mind-expanding magazine that is still popular today.

The promises of an easy life through technological wonders opened us up to the false hope of a better tomorrow through human ingenuity. Has the self-driving car taken away your depression? What about that new dryer with the steam feature to remove every wrinkle? Has that feature silenced your striving? When you hear, "You are worth it," is your identity bulwarked against every storm that will come? That first washing machine, with the wringer rollers on top, made it easy for mom to keep our jeans clean, drying quickly on the line in the backyard breeze. The pop-up toaster fed us brown toast every morning, with butter and jelly spread, and bacon on that Calrod stovetop. But Oz showed us that our Wizard hides behind the curtain of a fraudulent salvation. We learned by osmosis that there is nothing new under the sun, steam iron not withstanding. When Solomon reminds us that life is nothing more than a chasing after wind, we have no reason to doubt him.

Today, young people try to find their identity and salvation through the incomprehensible media devices they take for granted. They experiment with identity politics, sexual politics, and gender politics, while the malleable clay of their thinking apparatus is still forming. Little do they understand the powerful forces that are at work in their lives. In similar manner, the Wizard tailors his identity according to each visitor who arrives on his Facebook page in the Emerald City. Very much in the mold of Solomon, the Wizard's fame and power stumbles when Dorothy and her friends come close to this imposter.

The bold young heroine from Kansas rides the tornado into a new vision of the future-world—the multicultural world. Her plucky sweet psychic portrait hangs on the walls of every young woman across the world. Her identity is projected for millions of young people for decades in America, and to the present day. The imposter is disarmed by the courageous girl whose honesty offers hope that there really is a way home. Her collaboration with broken heroes, whose best days seem far behind them, offers a new beginning to many who see the film or read the book. She is a partial antidote for ***Myopic Me!***

Today, we see these famous characters from the Golden Way appearing again in our everyday lives. Many have fallen down by the road, and they can't get up. The multicultural milieu promised in the Emerald City has come to fruition. We have *Alice in Wonderland* to warn us about flawed Kings and Queens who will try to lead us astray. The street people Alice encountered have all fallen down in Wonderland with the mushroom's delusions tightly clutched in their experimental hands. The blue smoke of their idolatry takes us all down into Alice's robot-like conformism. Her new religion for the masses is born on our screens, as formless lives shape-shift to fit every social mandate.

We pinch off a piece of her mushroom, and we breathe deeply her blue smoke at the gates of every fantasy. The Alice-Syndrome reached a new formality in the Vietnam era, where morphine flowed from Southeast Asia in the duffle bags of the thriving Underground. Today, the blue worm coil at every gate. Every Alice living today will conform to Wonderland's tunnels, taking a toke, and biting off a bit of the deadly fungus—the script of modern man. Such compliance today is non-conforming with good sense.

Forty years after Alice penetrated Wonderland's tiny foyer, 42,000 young people will die because of morphine-related addictions in America. In 2016, we lost nearly as many Americans as perished in Vietnam during the entire conflict! It is the inevitable destination of cultural compliance which refuses to conform to good sense. Nonsense is devoured when the toke is taken in the hands of children and adults alike. When caterpillars counsel our kids, every new arrival in the city gates will conform to these protocols of self-destruction. When my small group meets in my house, three of the members have lost children to the scourge of heroin and/or fentanyl. At least one of them calls it the murder of their son.

The President recently suggested that we follow the Mexican President's approach for the drug sellers—executing them as murderers. The average drug dealer is profiting off of the addiction of thousands of young people, with many of these ending their lives when their autonomic systems stop functioning. In the Nonsense World, children are allowed to choose between life and death, and mothers are allowed to kill their own young. Conformity to blue smoke and the mushroom's sensible rationales has produced a national tipping point in Wonderland.

8.

PROPHETIC BOOKS ON THE CHILDREN'S BOOKSHELF.

The Wonderful Wizard of Oz, published in 1900, sold more than three million copies by 1956 when it entered the public domain. Dorothy confidently walks across the screens in thousands of theaters around the world up to the present day. Printed since 1865 in hundreds of editions and many languages, the Alice books have never been out of print![98] The competent, bold, and unforgettable young women in these stories have left deep traces in the identities of young girls—and boys—extending now over many generations. Dorothy's affectionate persona, and her attentiveness to the needs of others, beautifully develops the rarely occurring counterpoint for *Myopic Me!*

Myopic Me! is a jagged rudder through this narrative, exposing the futility of the narcissistic life. Narcissism is an elaborate hiding place for a variety of human flaws. It will always bear witness to a fixation with ones own physical appearance, or with the social perception of *Myopic Me!* This syndrome, common to man, combines a god-complex with a sometimes crippling fear of man. It is a spawning pool for false and inflated identities.[99]

In the vain pursuit of my Hero, I changed my identity every time a new movie played on College Avenue during my youth. I tried on the clothes of the victim and the predator, but nothing fit until God covered me with His robes of righteousness. This essential garment comes from the Lamb of God who takes away the sin of the world.[100] This is the antidote for the clothes we have been wearing in Oz or Wonderland where we tried to fit in, sacrificing everything else. We came so close to the real deal in both cases through Baum's and Carroll's insights. Inside the strange and wonderful Emerald City, I found many new possibilities for courageous living. During my own deep-dive into Wonderland, I have seen frightening visions of dark kingdoms which are opposed to the Light.

---

[98] *The Wonderful Wizard of Oz*. Wikipedia.

[99] *Narcissism*. Wikipedia.

[100] John 1:29.

Children's literature, and the many movies during my youth, addressed these foibles and hiding places exposed in the famous stories, continuing to expose our impotence and lack of courage in the face of humiliation and rejection by the world. Dorothy and Alice both confront our desperate search for a cultural salvation, trying to find our fit in a square hole. We visit every Wizard in the hope that the King will discover us before it is too late. We hope that He will rescue us from our meaningless and self-destructive roads—yellow, brick, or otherwise.

When I grew up in Dorothy's world, my home town's population of around five thousand included the temporary student population in those military college days. This tiny outpost at the foot of the Blue Ridge Mountains quietly morphed into a modern university as the demand for a military college yielded to a new era. The once segregated community in Clemson gracefully opened the portals for black students, while adding a vast new opportunity for female students arriving in droves.

Try to imagine the absence of either of these today. I grew up in an all-white world, yet with many changes coming soon in the Land of Oz, there was no cultural mandate for female or black assimilation into our white world in those childhood days. Yes, *To Kill a Mockingbird* would eventually arrive in every small town theater;[101] but we had no inkling when we rode our bicycles past the Calhoun neighborhoods on the road toward Central that dark crimes were afoot in our day. We had no idea that racism had been released from Pandora's Box before our world had been formed. During these years, I never saw a young black man, unless he was wearing a striped uniform in the chain-gang repairing the roads with tar, gravel, and pickax.

When our young entourage left the theater together, a kind of ecumenical church for us, we mounted our 24-inch bicycles for the three-mile ride to the gas station on the highway to Central. We could leave our bikes in front of the theater, and they would still be there when we came out two-hours later. Our summer destination coincided with the baseball season in all the major cities in America. Though the English bike had not yet appeared in our yards, we loved our 24-inch American bikes which we could ride anywhere. The hard 26-inch tires and the 10-speed shifter on the handlebars would not have survived our rugged trails and gravel roads. On these seasonal roundtrips, we wore our ubiquitous Keds basketball shoes, and we pedaled away from *Now Playing* to purchase new *Major League* baseball cards.

That quiet highway to Central drew us like a magnet to our Emerald City during the summer months, with no awareness of any of these things! Were we not members of the kingdom of this world where there is a constant distinction between "male and female, black and white, gay and straight, young and old,

---

[101] *To Kill a Mockingbird*. Wikipedia.

Greek or Jew, slave or free?"[102] Were we not all in need of a Savior? Were we not every one in the grip of the spirit of this world, where the love of money and power infects the rich as well as the poor?

Our Emerald City on those summer rides was just a gas station, freshly stocked with the latest batch of baseball cards. It was not a gas station like the new *Cumberland Farms* cathedral nearing completion on my daily rides today. It was a little flat-roof building with a single pump out front with a few items for sale inside. The baseball cards were in a glass display with an attendant who would dispense the mysterious cards to each one of us. Some famous player's photo was inside, wearing the team uniform with bat or glove. We could not tell who would be inside the unmarked wrappers, each player's picture printed in color, with key statistics, front and back.

Oh, we loved those statistics, memorizing every hit, double, home run, and run batted in. We could tell you the batting average of every player, by the season and lifetime. We loved the rookie cards of the baseball phenoms, Roger Maris, Roberto Clemente, and Henry Hank Aaron. The thrill of discovery drew us back again and again, riding the three miles to open each flat sheet with its *Major League* player and a flat pink sheet of bubblegum cut to fit perfectly inside the wrapper.

These sorties kept us from boredom during the long journey into the wide maw of the next dreaded school year. During this era, Alice also spoke her subtle, seductive, hopeful, and stunning solutions for social isolation and alienation. She found her drugs at the door, her shapeshifting chemistry, to make her a fitting participant in the culture of Wonderland. Her stories introduced us to a brand new world during the monochromatic 1950s and our post-war olive-drab lives. With our black automobiles, black and white motion pictures, and the ancient Silver-Screen vanishing from our theaters, we learned to dive into *The Wonderful World of Color*, as Walt Disney called it.

Just as kids today dumpster-dive into their iPhones making up fake identities daily, we dove into the dramatic and unforgettable world presented weekly in our hometown theater on College Avenue. It was our college and our church. These movies spoke prophetically into a twentieth century reality coming to a neighborhood theater near you. The future leaped to life on our screen with fantasy glimpses of a crazy multicultural possibility, where good could find itself in a lap-dance with evil. Though Solomon's morality plays arrived from three thousand years ago, the wise king exposed us to the potential cultural evil that was already speaking into our lives.

Today, we try to translate the deep meaning of the middle finger, which life produces on schedule when we least expect it. "Is it in them, or is it in *Myopic Me!*" we ask ourselves. If *us,* is really *them;* then how can *I,* be *me*? "What's it all about, Alfie?" *Alfie* would learn that caring for others is really the secret to happiness—*Myopic Me!* is not the sole goal for a happy life after all. *Alfie's*

---

[102] Galatians 3:28.

self-centric existence*[103]* had drilled out all the meaning from his life, and every motive of his heart had been sown in dishonor. His house was enlarged by that experience in a diverse classroom in that ancient time.

> But in a great house there are not only vessels of gold and silver, but also of wood and clay, some for honor and some for dishonor. Therefore if anyone cleanses himself from the latter, he will be a vessel for honor, sanctified and useful for the Master, prepared for every good work. Flee also youthful lusts; but pursue righteousness, faith, love, peace with those who call on the Lord out of a pure heart. 2 Timothy 2:20-22

Were these stories from cinema and Wonderland calling us into, or out from, dishonor? Was it calling racial categories, such as Jews and Gentiles? Was it simply calling all men to join God's family? Were these protagonists calling us out of relationships with those who mock God's good counsel? Were we being called from stubbornness and rebellion, which is really witchcraft in disguise?[104] Did Alice ask us to follow her into clay, or into gold? Is Nonsense superior to kindness? Are witches really evil or good? Can we promote death and ever really live?

When we arrived from the Clemson Theater to our Emerald City on the highway, we bought our version of the scratch ticket that would not be invented for another fifteen years. It was our version of instant gratification. Our baseball card's perfect packaging offered us the unlimited possibilities of the great payoff. We got off our bikes each time to receive the dual rush of adrenalin and sugar from this weekly physical and cultural journey. The powdered pink gum hid the colorful figure of our hero inside. We blew bubbles all the way home. Whatever the price for those cards, it was worth every dime.

Riding to this remote outpost of joy was a trip to our Wonderland—where we had no clue that Mickey Mantle was already an alcoholic, Ty Cobb carried racism on his sleeve, Ted Williams was a war-hero, and Babe Ruth was a bounder who raised hell all night. We knew none of these negative stories as we ripped open the famous cards. That pink brittle bubblegum piled up as we sorted each one, celebrating when a new face appeared in this dime-lottery sweepstakes of our youth. We were perfectly conformed in our pursuit of this boys-only ritual. Conformity has its upside and its dark-side.

The conformity to the Gatekeepers in *Wonderland* modeled drug use as a good thing. It opened every door for *Alice*. How close to "heroine" is

---

[103] *Alfie (1966 film)*. Wikipedia.

[104] 1 Samuel 15:23.

heroin! Should we conform in ways that steal, kill, and destroy in our version of Wonderland? Or should we rescue those who tumble into cowardice, mindlessness, and cruelty? Do we save them, preserving their counterfeit identities; or do we help them down from their crow's nest of self-destruction? It is a choice that Alice considered, not saving a one in Wonderland.

Did L. Frank Baum's popular book about Oz pull broken lives back toward the road that would take them home? Or did Alice incline an entire generation of girls to experiment with drugs as the solution for their fractured identities? Did her conformity to Wonderland's entrance requirements cause the young people of America to dive headfirst into the embrace of death—yielding 40,000+ opium-related deaths in 2016? Alice showed millions that their own irreconcilable differences with authority figures could be solved with the proper chemistry. Did we yield to her Blue Caterpillar in order to survive her big-headed Queen?

Solomon showed us the Rabbit Hole long before Lewis Carroll [Charles Lutwidge Dodgson] told his daughter about the rabbit's fantastical world below London's River Thames. Solomon took me below the surface of the Nile River where drugs and demons waited with open arms. The great king brought peace and prosperity to Israel for decades before he fell prey to this universal wolf-trap of the human soul. With thousands of gods running Pharaoh's Nile Delta underworld, Solomon could not escape their influence for long. When he brought the girls home with him, the demons came as part of a package deal. In our little underworld on the Central highway, the shock of sugar slapped us hard each time we traveled that graveled way. We had very little connection to baseball beyond these trips each week. We did not listen to the games on the radio, and there was little coverage on TV at that time. We might have seen the box scores in the newspaper, but we had no actual experience at ballparks.

Pop had played "sandlot baseball" with some of the greatest players of the day when he was young. He played against the black athletes who were not allowed to play in the Major Leagues. We might have seen the *Anderson Braves* play once, but there was nothing comparable to the connection young people have in New England today with the *PawSox* and the *Red Sox* to cheer for in the ballparks. There was nothing like the non-stop TV coverage that is common in 2018. We were simply seduced by these slick cards and their cunning comparative statistics. The sugar shock came as the price we paid for our pleasure.

Each card seemed to carry the hard facts proving the heroism of each player inside. We learned to discriminate between one player and another on the basis of the numbers next to their names. Those numbers became their identity. They were revered or rejected on the basis of those statistics from the game. We were enamored with their fame and glory. "Look. Jimmy Foxx!" I screamed, holding up my prize to gloat over my good fortune. They barely glanced my way as Jimmy held up his Yogi Berra card in the sunlight. We stumbled around our picnic table on the side of the road as if we were so many black bears fighting over the crumbs. "Yogi!" Jimmy stated matter-of-factly. His card was far more valuable than all the bubble gum we carried home. When we had rifled through every package, sorting the sheets of bubblegum into a different container, we pivoted like a military platoon and headed home full of testosterone and sucrose rising in our pre-teen bodies.

The only sound on these trips, beside our voices chattering proudly about our haul of famous players, was the tugging of our 24-inch rubber tires against the hard gravel pavement. "Wommm, woommm, wommm," we pedaled hard to get up to speed, riding side-by-side toward Calhoun Corners and the train station on the raised track above the highway. Beyond that was the Seneca River which we called the Congo when we played in the woods. It was full of crocodiles and pythons in our imaginations. Walking along its sandy banks was the most vivid venture into another world which we had available to us in those safe days in Oz.

Bursts of laughter rose between heavy breaths of oxygen, as we boasted about our good fortune getting the Mickey card, the Maris, and the Musial, on another successful trip. Little did we comprehend the courage of Jackie Robinson as we took for granted his face on our card. Little did we know the price he paid for the card we brought home so effortlessly. Little did we know the dark side of the moon in America that continued its strange pirouette after WWII. The voices of the Southern slave-owners were still speaking into the American ear. "Those sons and daughters of the slaves are inferior—less than human. Give them an inch, and we lose a mile."

The good, the bad, and the ugly fomented hatred still, with self-righteous blind deaf and dumb fear of the unknown continuing. Many dark wounds were closing, but these irreconcilable differences clashed with the highly popular multicultural children's story in *Oz*. Even the churches wore the blank faces of Pharisees, keeping every door (but the janitor's closet) closed in the faces of these children of God. The churches were the foremost to yield to the cultural milieu of racial isolation. They deleted the verses from their Bibles concerning the Greeks and the Jews, the blacks and the whites, the slaves and the freed citizens, the males and the females, refusing the reality that all are One in Christ. They deleted the verse which said to love your neighbor as yourself. They deleted the verse that said to be gracious to the foreigner in your midst, to give a cup of cold water to the one who is thirsty, a coat to the one who is cold, a visit to the prison of the one who is incarcerated.

Our young legs knew nothing of such things, and we developed endurance with strong motivations driving us toward our next hero's baseball card. We looked for heroes in these flawed vessels. We tried to find the better Hero by looking at the batting average of a man, regardless of race, creed, or color. We were not guilty of blatant complicity in our day, but neither did we have any empathy for the thousands who were isolated and shut out of American society. We clenched our heroes in sweaty hands, not understanding the importance of maintaining the perfect condition for the freshly stamped edges of these cards. Did girls collect cards back then? I don't remember a girl ever holding a card in her hand! Maybe there are differences between boys and girls? And then, I remembered.

I can't imagine a mature Dorothy reading through the stats for Babe Ruth—even on the night he struck out every batter and drove home runs over the center field fence, telling the little child what he would do before he even entered the ballpark that night. Girls steered away from the sugar, no doubt, while we chewed a dozen flat pieces of bubble gum on the way back home. The sugar-shock was a necessary evil on these fantasy rides along the golden way of our youth. We never seemed to understand that what you put into your body has an immediate effect on your body. Sugar, salt, carbs, fat, protein, vitamins, minerals, and water. Each one impacts the body, the frame of mind, the feelings, the health and well-being are immediately changed by what goes in. But we knew very little about such things in the 1950s. It never dawned on us that we could chew a couple of those brittle pink sheets of gum and save the rest for later. There was no "later," for everything was, "now!"

Though we were free in a way that is unknown today, our mothers didn't understand the baseball card phenomenon. While we saved every card in shoe boxes, Mama threw them all away while I was away at college. My valuable cards, worth thousands of dollars, went into the trash. How long before you forgive your mother, Frank? I know. The Jimmy Foxx card paid $31,050 in the year 2000. I loved my Jimmy Foxx cards, having several of them. Oh, mama! I am still working on it, for Mama cleaned the attic while I was at The Citadel. The four of us were the first day-traders, and we didn't even know it. We held tiny bets in our hands, not knowing that Roger Maris and Mickey Mantle were like the deeds to Park Place and Boardwalk. In our top drawers, we held the certificates for Apple Computing and General Electric, Lockheed-Martin and Texas Instruments. We were rich, and our mothers didn't even know it. They thought it was a silly waste of time and money. But more important things were happening during these days.

The first natural color, full length film in 1959 was *The World, the Flesh and the Devil*, a doomsday film (7/10, 4.6 rated today) which dealt with a worker trapped deep in a mineshaft after a total nuclear war had killed all but a handful on earth. We dove many times under our desks during our nuclear war drills in the 1950s. Still, the title baffles me, since it implies a different subject matter. I don't remember the movie coming to our theater, but I was partially insulated from the love of the world, the appetites of the flesh, and even the devil's existence during those early days. Harry Belafonte played the part of the surviving miner. Though I listened to his "Jump down, spin-around, pick a bale of cotton; jump down spin around pick a bale of hay," many times, it never dawned on me how racially stereotypical these songs were.

These songs were out of the wheelhouse of the slave reality that hung over America with a giant shadow. This shadow extended for the brief period from 1860 to 1959 with a potent echo. Harry was celebrating his own heritage, while reminding us of the hard decades for a hundred years with every tough change that was a'coming. Mean men reached back for Colonial days, violently resisting these black interlopers into their harvest fields, hearing the terrible songs of freedom:

> "Oh freedom. Oh freedom. Oh freedom over me! And before
> I'd be a slave. I'll be buried in my grave. And go home to my
> Lord and be free. No more moaning. No more moaning. No
> more moaning over me! And before... There'll be singing...
> There'll be shouting... There'll be praying..."[105]

Belafonte's movie made a million dollars, and I missed this apocalyptic drama. He was one of my favorite singers and actors, having many movies in his portfolio during a long career. While I lived inside the cocoon of that small town—like Dorothy living in Kansas—I had no idea that the dark kingdom swirled in the invisible air above me. Nevertheless, puberty (with much encouragement from the Prince of the Air) led me into the unrated showing of *And God Created Woman* at the Clemson Theater. Strike one. Strike two, would come later. This movie was not rated for my eyes to see. Curiosity killed the cat, and experimentation has blinded many pseudo-scientists. Sneaking into this showing of an adult film put a callous on my young soul.

When I placed my quarter into the coin tray, I tried not to make eye-contact. Making eye contact with Brigitte Bardot, would cause me to avoid eye-contact with everyone else. I stood exposed at that sidewalk ticket window. Barely tall enough to reach the tray, the marquee for the Bridget Bardot and Roger Vadim adult-themed film made me very self-conscious. Every driver passing on the street could read the "Now Playing" sign. The two French actors became famous for their roles in this French movie! Southern French women, I was sure, wore no pants, for I had gained this knowledge from the song which we would sing at recess when no adult could hear us. Anything from France, therefore, seemed off-limits for kids in the 1950s. By contrast, the three flat screens in the average house today will display at least one sexual act while the kids wander around with they're coloring book in one hand, and *Mr. Potato Head* in the other hand.

Not satisfied with this boring incursion into pseudo-adult pornography (I actually remember nothing from that movie—not even a kiss), I extended my scandalous behavior in my Sixth Grade English class. My rambling paper, which I read before the class, produced embarrassment and fear in my young teacher's face as she tried to regain control. When she discovered my subject matter, she seemed distressed. I stood, untouchable, reading, and she squirmed with every clumsy word choice and poorly constructed observation. I used the hackneyed phrase: "The movie was not all it was cracked up to be." Cracked up to be? The

---

[105] *Oh Freedom!* Negro Spirituals.

arrogance of **Myopic Me!** reared its undignified persona. It was official now. I had become the dread Lord Byron on my little pilgrimage into darkness. I had surely run smartly into Solomon's vain wind.

The movie is still sold today in DVD-format on *Amazon*. By the measurement standards currently in vogue, my 2.5 rating out of 5 matches the rating for the DVD published in the year 2000. This makes me wonder: "Maybe I should have become a movie critic?" I certainly suffered the good, the bad, and the ugly, coming out of Hollywood (and Southern France) at a very young age. Of course, today, the sixth graders are hooked on beer and bourbon, smoke pot, and have sex on the school bus to and from school. I shudder to think of my small step into this vast new world of self-destruction. How small a step leads to the grand embrace of the evil day. Is this the return to the days of Noah? Of course not. Maybe? Noah was the only one listening to God in his day.[106]

Today, there are many who claim to listen to God. Of course, few of these have actually built a five-hundred foot long Ark, and none of them have climbed in with the animals for a long voyage. But those challenges long ago cannot be compared to what kids face today. Brigitte's poster in the window of the Clemson Theater is nothing compared to the powerful enticement coming from three-thousand ads-per-day, painting the faces of lonely children as they peer into their tiny social media devices—those ads shape they're understanding of the world, the flesh, and the devil in ways that no one can accurately predict.[107]

There is more horsepower in the marketing engine than there is in the sociological engine today. The love of money is still the root of many evil schemes.[108] There is powerful motivation for enrichment, hiring the top psychologists from the universities to formulate the ideal bait to hook every child's lip as they approach their prime spending years. The love of money is more pernicious, and more marvelous, than anything I could ever recount in my sixth grade classroom during that primitive technological era of my youth.

My low grade on that paper surely dampened my interest in writing for years after that. My father tried to stoke the fires of my interest by paying me three dollars per effort for writing my own version of *The Old Man and the Sea*, Ernest Hemingway's amazing story about the old fisherman from Key west. I should have learned then that writing books does not pay for the thousands of hours spent in planning, writing, editing, rewriting, copy editing, rewriting, editing, rewriting, copyediting and publishing a book. Three dollars was a lot back then, but the average author's book sales will not pay for the coffee he drank writing the book.

---

[106] Genesis 6:9

[107] Caitlin. *Cutting through Advertising Clutter*.

[108] 1 Timothy 6:10.

Hemingway may have arrived at the same conclusion before he blew his own brains out in Key West. His novella helped him to win the Nobel Prize for literature in 1954—the same year that I sat down to rewrite the fisherman's odyssey.[109] His story took me to the hairy edge between civilization and the wildness of the created world—it took me to the terrible realism of the survival of the fittest. It displayed to me two proud predators, colliding in a death-spiral in the womb of the sea. Their battle went the full fifteen rounds, with blood flowing from many wounds. Victory was turned to humiliation, and the pilgrimage of the fisherman ended like a snowflake in a summer storm off the coast of Cuba.

The old fisherman gave his life to bring home the skeleton of a glorious fish that had lived a long life slashing through the ocean depths with no equal. The relationship between the ancient fisherman and the powerful sea has become my own story, for I have battled giants in my own strength as well. I have nothing to show for my vain projects, besides these shocking skeletons. When Hemingway's protagonist arrived again at his storm-worn dock, the skeleton of that great swordfish mocked his entire life purpose. Hemingway understood that he had played the fool of Solomon, sadly holding up Byron's mirror, before he could see his own features in the old fisherman. He was sitting exhausted and disconsolate in his worn out rowboat at the end of his life.

This was the final photo of the man who put the *terse* in his best sentences. When he applied the technology of journalism to tell the old man's story, he found himself signing books that gained him a Nobel Prize. His bittersweet self-portrait gained him that potent honor sought by every theoretical physicist and songwriter. For Ernest could now hold high the Gold Medal of authorship. Yet his soul contained nothing but wind—and there was nothing of value but the skeleton of his wilting glory. His hands were empty on that day in 1961 when he cocked the shotgun and pulled the trigger. His wife said it was an accident, but Hemingway's father had killed himself with a pistol when his health failed. Hemingway's stories frequently danced with suicide, as if it were a courageous act of human will.[110]

Ernest Hemingway likely read Solomon's final conclusion: "Fear God and obey Him." In this final proclamation from Solomon's pen, he had foolishly placed all the pressure on each man to become his own savior. He left Hemingway, and me, with a religion based on keeping the Law—which has never saved anyone. Though Jesus did not do away with the Law, He did fulfill every Law for us, if we will just accept His fishing expedition into our harbors. Solomon left out the references to the One whose clothes were sold off while they nailed a mocking sign above His head. He left out his father's most

---

[109] *Ernest Hemingway*. Wikipedia.

[110] Ibid.

prophetic line written into the Psalms: "They have pierced my hands and feet."[111] He never mentioned one time the Man who died a criminal's death, becoming the Lamb of God who takes away the sin of the world.[112] The Lamb's blood was shed on the Hill of Skulls before Jesus rose again from the grave. He returned to the Sea of Galilee to show Peter that He was the greatest Fisherman to ever land a miraculous catch of fish.[113]

My father's brilliant fishing expedition into my own creative waters, kept me from the widespread obsession with comic books in Wonderland. Pop, the professor, would not be surprised today to find half our movies scripted from those *Marvel Comics*. He cringed at the thought that I would end up in the comic book stores with Sheldon, Leonard, Penny, Howard, Bernadette, Stuart, and Raj.[114] He wanted to keep me out of *Comic-Con's* annual gatherings even before they were invented.

William Shatner was recently on the stage for the *2016 Comic-Con* in Boston. So close, yet so far away, the beautiful Diana Troi (Marina Sirtis) still visits these gatherings. My dad would be horrified to know that a ticket to the 2017 Boston Comic-Con[115] costs $123.00 per nerd, if you are lucky enough to get a ticket at all! With Pop's voice in my ear, I suspended the myopic dives into those fantasy stories—though I have seen one movie too many from the world of *Marvel* since then. I still find the plots intriguing.

My addiction to several familiar franchises in my youth, and a couple of comics that I don't hear about any longer, inspired Pop to shift my focus toward classical literature, away from the marvelous *Wonder Woman in the Amazon*.[116] Her invisible flying machine looked very much like the *SR-71 Blackbird*, with which I later had a real-life encounter.[117] That supersonic spy plane has the same advanced parameters as Wonder Woman's aircraft. The *SR-71* was the first "invisible" aircraft, with stealth characteristics that made it very difficult to detect on the best radar systems.

It is not a great leap from *Bat Man* and *Superman* fantasy comic books to experiencing that very real *SR-71 Blackbird* swooping over me in Georgia. These fantasy stories were already merging with technological realities that

---

[111] Psalm 22:16c.

[112] John 1:29.

[113] John 21:10-11.

[114] *The Big Bang Theory*. Wikipedia.

[115] *Comic-Con 2016*. Arts and Entertainment.

[116] *Wonder Woman & Invisible Jet*. Amazon.

[117] *Lockheed SR-71*. Wikipedia.

captured my imagination in the Land of Oz. These fantasies digressed into a single Brigitte Bardot movie, which must have dampened my father's hopes that I would ever be a creative writer. I remember nothing from that dive into the femme-fatale known as Brigitte Bardot—I don't remember a single scene from that movie—but Dorothy and Alice I cannot forget, when they plummeted down into their new adventures in a world spun from the absurd, and the might-actu-ally-be-coming-soon. They disturbed whole worlds within my imagination, and fashioned indelible characters in my deepest memory.

The WWII movies and a plethora of Westerns arrived in a continuous stream of predictable plots and wonderful characters full of courage. Highly rated movies like *Shane* and *Old Yeller,* stand out for many who grew up in this ascension of the American cinema. That dog-story broke many hearts, and Shane's relationship with that little boy left everyone in tears. Though Shane's character symbolized the end of a lawless, gunslinging era, his final departure on his horse left the young boy to understand the ramifications of a new righteousness that was rising up in his bones.[118] I never watched that *Yeller* dog die on any of the TV reruns—having too many dog stories of my own ending in painful tragedies of an unnatural kind.[119]

I did become enthralled with those ferocious wolves and their nemesis, *Yukon King*, Sergeant Preston's wonder dog. He could stand up to the most ferocious wolves to protect his master from harm. His protection of Sergeant Preston seemed to offer a dog's version of God's protection in that barely legible time, before God visited me with His good advice. After reading the amazing tales of King in the subarctic world of the Yukon, I again took to writing bloody alternative stories in my own words. Just as the characters from *The Big Bang Theory* on TV are sometimes effeminate and nerdy in their fantasies, so my father was concerned about my mousy demeanor in a world unequally yoked to these same attributes.

Apparently there are a lot of nerds out there in TV land today because *The Big Bang Theory* gets 94% positive in 2018. The show must be very profitable, with several of the cast members making around a million dollars per episode. The shift of the revenue stream to television stars is made possible by the stunning quality of the ultra HD sixty-inch flat screens which everyone is buying today.[120] The constant appetite for entertainment in our society produces this weekly demand for something new to watch.

Was I the only one touched, changed, damaged by the meta-screen-realities of the 1950s? I looked up the current reviews for these classics, wanting to see if

---

[118] *Shane (1953 film)*. What Culture.

[119] *Old Yeller (1957 film)*. Wikipedia.

[120] *The Big Bang Theory*. Wikipedia.

the ratings for *And God Created Woman*[121] and *Joe Versus the Volcano* matched my own. These ratings provide a partial confirmation of their influence, if they are still highly rated today. *Joe Versus the Volcano* gets 3-stars by most critics, but the late Roger Ebert agreed with me, scoring 3.5 out of 4 stars for this cult classic.[122] I discover the classic *Oz* with 4 stars, while *Wonderland* gets 7.4 out of 10.[123] Some ratings agencies include classic *Oz* in the top ten movies for all time!

Dorothy appears in the list with *The Godfather, Schindler's List, Lawrence of Arabia,* and *Raging Bull. Oz* is in the list with famous films such as *Casablanca, One Flew over the Cuckoo's Nest, Gone with the Wind,* and *Citizen Kane.*[124] This is elite territory, representing the giant footsteps of storytelling in cinematic history. These famous films are prophetic in their own right, speaking into every generation. Each one speaks with clear eyes, visualizing how things are or how they will be. These films speak into the power of the individual to take a stand, changing the larger history. Each one preaches a faint Christ-figure, who is sacrificial in the face of great evil which can never extinguish their little light aimed into a hailstorm of evil.

In revisiting the story, I asked myself whether Dorothy changed Oz, or whether Oz changed Dorothy? It is pretty safe to say that both occurred. Dorothy shattered the Wicked Witch of the West with a pail of wash water. She picked up the broken birds she found along the way, helping to guide them into positions of influence and power once more—she was in the Identity Business. She became the courageous young woman who understood her own heart, resilient until her homecoming to Kansas. Did "Dorothy," the L. Frank Baum literary invention, change the young girls who experienced the *Wizard of Oz* during the decades since the 1930s?

I know that my wife is very much the healer of broken birds, having great empathy for the wounds she finds in others. She never became a social worker, but she has taught children and adults who have fallen down beside the road, helping them learn to read with highly scripted processes which take account of their degraded ability to decipher syntax. The Broca-region of the brain is often affected, taking away a natural syntactic processing skill which uninjured children possess.

Brain injuries may produce severe dyslexia, reversing the sentences and letters, and even inverting them. The page is wrong-side-outward, and the scripted approach gives them a strategy for assembling the meaning contained there. Sometimes sentences slide completely off the page, as if they were slippery.

---

[121] *And God Created Woman (1956).* IMDb.

[122] *Joe Versus the Volcano.* Roger Ebert.

[123] *Alice in Wonderland (1951).* IMDb.

[124] *20-Best All Time Movies.* Washington Times.

Some of her students have confounding issues such as autism, which produce perseveration—not conducive to linear reading processes. These broken birds cannot apply naturally occurring intuition or logic to the challenge of decoding syntax.

Children normally learn to read with little structured assistance because the Broca-brain-synergy deals with syntax easily; but her wounded birds need special love, patience, and structured skills to help them untangle the symbols.[125] Whether my wife's capacity to rescue these broken birds comes from Dorothy's influence in Oz, I can never know. It is certain that Dorothy's brave and compassionate journey out of Kansas is part of her own understanding of what a female person is supposed to be in a world where big brother gets all the love.

Like Dorothy, my wife has always been looking far ahead to the home which God is preparing for her in heaven. She deeply understands that there may be problems in this present life which cannot be solved. She knows there are riddles which can't be unlocked. She knows that some things can only be reconciled by God in our broken-down world. The potential for altering social identities is profound with Dorothy's influential movie, and some of Dorothy's persistence must have rubbed off on my wife.

Judy Garland revealed the potential for her character in the movie theaters in 1939, nearly two decades after Woman's Suffrage won the right to vote in an American presidential election. Her arrival in Technicolor surely contributed to the advancing social identity of girls, intersecting in the shifting cultural landscape of America—is America not a living breathing organism? The fearlessness of the bold young women from *Oz* and *Wonderland* are interwoven in the shared-memories of many people around the world—especially young girls. These role models still influence girls trying to find their way home to this present day.

President Harding arrived in the Oval Office after the 1920 Presidential election. He gained this catbird seat partly through the woman's vote. This transformation of the American democracy took place during an era of weak Presidents reaching the pinnacle of politics. Dying in office, Harding sadly left behind the worst scandal in American political history. He had several well-known mistresses during his brief tenure. When he was replaced by Calvin Coolidge, the influence of the *Wizard of Oz* had just painted the big screen. Coolidge could have learned a few things from the *Wizard* and from Baum's bold counterpoint, *Dorothy*.

The courage of young people facing tumultuous times at least partly comes to us from Baum's famous heroine. His story speaks into a rapidly changing world, entering the homes of millions of American girls in their formative years. Girls and young women were looking for their brand-new twentieth century identity, when they found her striding into the Emerald City in *Oz*. How should a modern girl act? What should she wear? What will she speak, and how will

---

[125] *Orton-Gillingham*. Wikipedia.

she respond to authority, to stress, and to encounters with evil? Should she be naive or shrewd? Should she be gentle or vengeful?

Many famous literary works appeared within a decade after Baum's publishing date in 1900. Rebecca Gross describes the cultural impact of Dorothy in *Oz and Effect*,[126] in which she explains that Dorothy's adventures in *Oz* literally opened the floodgates for the rise of American children's literature. She describes the profound social transformation which came about through this truly American Dorothy.

> Whether we came to the story through the original 1900 children's book by L. Frank Baum, or through the 1939 film adaption with Judy Garland, The Wizard of Oz has become a part of our shared emotional property. This story is deeply entrenched within our collective personal and cultural psyche. Juxtaposing wonder and danger, friendship and enmity, millions of people have found meaningful and memorable connections with the story. Amplified by the nostalgic lens of childhood, few stories have become so mythologized as Oz.[127]

---

[126] Gross. *Oz and Effect.*

[127] Ibid.

9.

MELANCHOLY SEASONS.

his desire for home hovered above my life as mouse-boy wandered into the autumn woods behind our house. In that steep deep woods, undeveloped for nearly a mile to the North and to the East, I found a soft spot in the sunshine. As I lay there on my back below this quiet storm of wind in the tops of tall trees, the mysterious yearning for eternity vibrated in my soul. The leaves were layered into this steep topography for a hundred yards below the stone house of my youth. The woods inclined quickly, toward the gully below, smeared with the yellow hickory and poplar leaves, and with the darkening red leaves of the oaks rocking to and fro on the great limbs of these 100-foot tall trees.

The bright crimson of the sourwood leaves were my favorites, and we used them as play-money for our games. In this fall season, the squirrels, copperheads, and rabbits were preparing for the coming winter, staying close to their homes in their hundred-acres that crossed two ridges before receding into the swamp behind the Dixie Store. We could walk through the western woods to the Seneca River [Seminole Indians lived there], and we could walk through the northern woods toward Dr. Brown's big white house across the swamp to *College Avenue*. This was Louisiana and Texas in our imaginary system of boundaries. Montana was on the top of the hill behind the Willis' big white house. These highlands were too close to prying eyes to visit very often.

Lying silently on the insulated ground, a dual destination tugged at my heart. My Toto-dog lay docile under my arm, and he and I tried to answer life's great questions: "Who am I? Why am I here? Does God exist?" My twelve-year-old self spoke to the wind as if there really would be an answer. I had no answers, but on this day I felt the urgent pull of death. I could not explain these feelings during this pre-teen time.

In these leaves, flashes of sunlight pierced my private reverie, penetrating my oh-so-vulnerable soul. More than one voice was speaking with mutually exclusive answers to my questions. One of those voices said clearly, "You are doomed. Life is nothing but a chasing after wind—your life is meaningless! Your case is hopeless." This was the voice of Solomon from Egypt and Edom, for I knew only that Solomon was a famous king who was very rich and famous.

"Bengals Tigris-Euphrates Lane," my faithful dog, had lain patiently under my arm, but I had no idea that his name contained part of the explanation for my universal disorder of the soul. By decoding his name, I would eventually be able to decode my fear of death. His name should have reminded me of that day in the Garden of Eden when the Serpent told Eve she would not die when she ate the fruit from the forbidden tree.

He told her she would be like God. The story from Genesis explains where death comes from in the first place. It explains that Eve and Adam chose death, rather than life. It reveals an ancient and powerful pact with the devil, when our foolish pride stripped us of every good gift from God. Bengals Tigris-Euphrates Lane should have been able to help me with that. He carried with him the theological accounting of my fear of death. Sin had brought death at the intersection of God's presence and His perfect provision. The paradise in the Garden ended when the wo-man, Adam's bone and flesh, bit into the forbidden apple. He ate his fill, and both of them understood their nakedness from the new perspective of evil. Where evil is, there is also death. Satan, I would learn, is the progenitor of death, even death of the soul.

They hid themselves, covering up their unseemly parts with leaves. They cowered together at the intersection of God's most perfect geography, and topography. Bengals Tigris-Euphrates Lane carried the clues to this geography on his engraved collar. I had no idea what the Word of God would say to me in Future Times, for I had not understood any of its pages when I tried to read the American Standard Translation. As blank as a board, those pages stared back at me. As lifeless as rotting trees in the woods behind our house, those books withheld their messages.

Finally, I asked the wind my most myopic question of all: "Will this fear of death ever depart from me?" Lying in that warm sun, on that 45-degree incline of the forest floor, I asked the Invisible Being: "Will 'Dread' continue to be my master? Will I ever find my way home from hopelessness?" I was lost and didn't know what "being found" could mean. The best listener for me at that time, was my d-o-g, not G-o-d. I was going through my life without talking to God. Bengals was the only one who would listen to my very personal questions.

I would later discover that dogs are in the Bible a couple of times in stories that are very telling. Samuel prophesied that wicked Jezebel, wife of Ahab the evil King of Israel, would have her brains licked up by dogs. This wicked woman became a feast for feral dogs when she fell to the street from her upper story window. Her brains did splatter, and the dogs did come to lick them up. The woman who had terrified Elijah, the famous prophet, became a meal for the dogs of the street.

Much later, Jesus was speaking to a Samaritan [Gentile] woman who displayed great faith. She referred to herself in the context of these feral dogs that were always looking for a meal. In her story, she transposed herself as one of those dogs. She spoke prophetically, with understanding that Jesus had come to save the whole world, including the Gentiles—the Untouchables in the Jewish world. Even His own disciples did not know this. Jesus was amazed that she grasped the full intention of God to save the Jews and the Gentiles. The Gentile woman alluded to the future time when the *Good News* would be preached by Paul to the sons and daughters of Ishmael [the Gentiles], as well as to the progeny of Isaac [the Jews]. Her words to Jesus spoke to the heart of God's plans. "Even dogs are allowed to eat the scraps that fall beneath their masters' table."[128]

This woman understood what I didn't yet understand. I would later ask a priest if a man could be a Christian while he continued to fix toilets in the homes of his customers. Could a man be a plumber or a poet, a black man or a white man, and still be a Christian? "Should a man continue to function as a policeman or a portrait painter, as he follows Christ?" The priest answered immediately, saying, "Of course, you can be both, but Christ will show you the Way." Jesus has never said, "You can't be a plumber." But He did tell the fishermen at the Sea of Galilee, "Follow Me!"[129]

My missing puzzle piece was Christ, Who becomes through the Spirit of God the answer to every impossible riddle of life. He will in my Future Time become the answer to every unspoken and hidden question in my heart. He did not command Peter to stop his lucrative commercial fishing business, but He did show Peter how to fish for the souls of men. He explained to Peter that nothing is worth more than a man's soul. No fish could ever compete with the soul's great value. Peter learned that the relationship with Christ brought freedom from the fear of poverty and the fear of missing out on the best things life has to offer. It gave him peace about no longer being a wealthy fishermen with a steady income. He learned to trust Jesus completely when He said, "Peter, do you love me? Then feed my sheep."

For me, "Church" in those days, was nothing more than a building that overlooked the old Riggs field where Clemson played their football games until 1941—there I later watched the track meets in the spring months—where the NCAA Soccer Championship was played in 1987. Church was a social encounter, which too often just made me self-conscious. The best part of Church was when I left on my bicycle, rolling down the hill toward *Riggs Field* where the Hall of Fame track star, John Dunkelberg, had so many times rounded that final turn on the 440 or 880-yard dash. My heart was always up in my throat, and I would stand there on that third turn to cheer him on as he strode toward the finish line.

The sound of his breathing combined with the powerful crunching of his cleats in the cinders of the track surface as he flew by me. I was never self-conscious there, bathed in that adrenalin. It was thrilling to watch his long strides, anticipating the explosion of cheers as his time would be announced—breaking another collegiate or Clemson College record.[130] Sports became a god for me in those days. Remaining a spectator, my lack of physical development kept me

---

[128] Matthew 15:27.

[129] Matthew 4:19.

[130] *Riggs Field*. Clemson Wiki.

from any such competition. I understood winning these races, but I didn't understand why God had to give His life for mine on the Cross.

I knew Jesus as the baby at Christmas, but really couldn't fathom the naked man on the Cross at Easter. I knew that Easter was somehow related to colored eggs hidden in the blooming Irises—I had no idea that this ancient tradition served to mask Christ's victory from millions of children. Christmas was Santa Claus—Satan Claws? I loved Christmas! Did I know that Jesus was also the King of kings, and the Lord of lords, born to die as the Lamb of God Who would take away the sins of the world?[131] Why would the King die for his subjects? Why would He be punished for my sins? I had no good answer for these questions. Nothing in all the other religions of the world had to deal with this Non Sequitur. That was the great non sequitur of my pre-teen years which entirely blocked my view of His forgiveness and comfort.

A non sequitur, for those who have no clue, is that thing for which you have no response. It can happen when someone starts talking without mentioning the subject or the context. We say, "I don't know what you are talking about!" That sense of befuddlement is a kind of non sequitur. "Where are you in this conversation?" we say to such a person. Our brain curls around their statement, spitting it back out as meaningless, a rhetorical riddle with no door. We can only conclude that there is nothing of interest. There is nothing sensible to decipher, for the non sequitur arrives without any apparent connection to the situation at hand. It seems completely foreign to the present tense life experience. That God's wisdom might somehow be the missing puzzle piece for my melancholy day in those autumn woods seemed like a childhood version of the unknown non sequitur. "What possible reason would you mention God?" I asked Bengals, "Why?" But he just shook his collar in the wind.

Since then, I have discovered that faith is the puzzle piece. The non sequitur can only be solved by Faith. By faith, we see the connection between seemingly unconnected things. That in itself seems to be another non sequitur, but it isn't. We don't see how faith is working every day in our lives in invisible ways. We don't see the faith that operates in the most mundane ways. We just automatically believe that our gas heater in the basement will keep us warm while we sleep. It never crosses our minds that the pilot could go out and the gas could leak out and kill us.

The terrible possibilities of various failure modes remain hidden from view because of our faith in a furnace maintenance man. Our trust is absolute. I never worried about the coal furnace in our basement killing us with toxic coal smoke backing up into the house while we slept. We had no carbon monoxide detectors back then. Even when we read those tragic stories in the news, we were not fazed because our systems were working fine. "Those poor people!" we said. Unfounded faith had killed them, but we remained confident and unafraid.

[131] John 1:29.

Trusting what God planned before the world was formed seems impossible for any of us trusting folks. We trust our nearly invisible furnace, but can't imagine trusting an invisible God whom we have never seen. Even though He knows the three-trillionth move in the 21-dimension game of chess, we can't imagine a day when He will say, "Checkmate." And Satan can't believe that a day will come when he will be thrown into a lake of fire and then into a bottomless pit. "It never happened before, why would it happen now?" We can't see Satan, so we don't believe in him either. We don't understand that even before the ink was dry on the Creation, God threw Lucifer out of heaven—giving him several new names: Satan, the devil, Beelzebub, Prince of the Air, Lord of the Flies, and Father of Lies.

Since I did not know the scriptures in those childhood woods, it was easy for Satan's fallen angels, his demons, to come and slay my emotions on that fall day. I knew, somewhere deep inside, that God could cure me of this fear, but I could not name the great silence that filled the space between my religion and my faith. I could not penetrate the wall of noise in my head. I didn't even know that it was there. I had no access to vague abstractions like, "Wonderful Counselor, Prince of Peace, and Mighty God." These sounded like Christmastime phrases on pretty wrapping paper. But these Carols, not Sunday School, did more to stir up my hope. These beautiful names remained unwrapped gifts beneath those ancient Christmas trees.

I had discovered no Door, nor had I found a Key for the unknown lock. I felt death living inside of my soul, but I could not put death into words. My little dog's collar contained the answers I needed, but I did not understand Bengal's reference to the ancient Garden. Bengals would sadly die a terrible death by the all-too human disease of cancer, and my frail hugs could not protect him on that painful afternoon. Grayson, Pop, and I buried him in the army blanket after the doctor "put him to sleep"—this was my most miserable experience with that terrible euphemism.

Bengals' death seemed to be the only solution for his terrible pain. He made noises I had never heard before he died. My father watched us bury the dog we had all loved. When the red clay fell from the shovel on that thick olive blanket around Bengals' silent body, each one of us felt the somber presence of the Angel of Death who would soon come for one of us as well. Pop had no idea when we buried Bengals in the red clay near the kitchen door that his hidden cancer would soon metastasize.

When would my final day arrive, I wondered that day in the woods, lying in those indifferent leaves? What street, what bed, what foreign land would find me in that final hour? As the sunlight twinkled down through the dead leaves of fall, the strong gusts and downdrafts brushed me with soft bristles and colorful hues, I sighed in my ignorance. A deep fear of death swept me like a wooden floor worn with the constant passing of a soft broom.

Though dogs only appear twice in the Bible, they appear often in the lives of men and women in the twenty-first century. In my youth, I had another dog to care for and to cry over. He made death more real for me. Frisky was run over downtown because of his habit of walking main street during the day. It was an era of light traffic in Clemson, and anyone could head across the street with fair confidence they would make it to the other side without being hit by a car. On that particular afternoon, an indifferent driver had run him over when Frisky didn't move fast enough to suit him. The report came to us on the screen porch with terrible meaning, "Richie's dead! Richie's dead!"

We strained to understand that our neighbor, "Richie," had died. The voice was actually saying, "Frisky's dead!" When I heard my dog was dead, it felt like a hammer to my chest. Though it was a great tragedy for us to lose our pet dog, it was a relief to know that our close neighbor, Richard, had not died suddenly at age thirteen. Older by several years than I, Richard increasingly had become my hero. I watched him grow and learn, and boldly go where no other neighborhood boy had gone before. Actually, all the boys in our neighborhood did amazing things as men. Richard eventually pole vaulted sixteen feet at Annapolis as a member of the track team, and he flew a hundred sorties off an aircraft carrier before his tour in Vietnam was done in the late 1960s. God would protect him, so that he could give his time and skill as a surgeon forty years later in Nicaragua, serving the poor and the lame.

As a highly skilled orthopedic surgeon, he knew how to repair broken and disfigured bodies. He found hundreds of children and adults in need of his skills in the Nicaraguan city with five-hundred thousand people. He has visited Chinandega scores of times to administer life-saving and life-improving surgeries in the *Amigos* mission where he has established two operating rooms in a mission hospital. Giving aid to the fatherless, the widow, the foreigner, and the unborn, I would later understand, is a hallmark of the God I did not know. This fundamental concern runs through God's story as He interacts with the people who are created in His image. He gives aid and comfort to the powerless, and He never fails to lift the shame from everyone who comes to Him with a contrite heart.

I would learn more about this Person, this Holy God, through any number of Nicaraguan experiences in my life. When I found myself in a rented bus heading for the Pacific coast with Richard and the other volunteers, forty-years had passed since that autumn day in the woods. Many things had changed over the years. God was very much with us as we roared along toward the black lava sand of that ocean waiting at the end of that bright paved road. Richard and I reminisced about the seventy-foot tall treehouse over the swamp in our "Louisiana." We discussed his journal of memories about our wonderful Folger Street days growing up. We also recalled him barely brushing the rice fields with his wings, dumping ordinance in Viet Nam.

Before the week was over, he and I were dodging various theological boobie traps when we spoke again in the mission hacienda. Our conversation revealed our efforts to finish our personal paintings of the face of God. With novice painters, God's face might rise as a caricature when the paint-by-the-numbers approach is followed. This approach reveals very little about the relationship of the believer with his God. Another painter might seek to find God's face by working through the shadows, or by focusing on the negative spaces in their relationship with God. Sitting in the computer area of the amazing Chinandega *Amigos Mission*, he and I wrestled with the negative spaces, looking for a way to translate the theological non sequitur that we found in Richard's still wet painting. His daughter is a brilliant painter in Italy, and she would recognize our conundrum. She would know how to paint the religion out of her large canvas.

Richard and I spoke of the salvation of God which had taken over our lives: The Gospel itself was the context, and the non sequitur was something commonly known as "Purgatory." The theology of Purgatory is really the theology of a kind of last gasp self-salvation. It is really the default human religion, which is to put off heaven and hell until the last possible moment. Purgatory is the ultimate form of this delaying tactic—it comes *after* death. This is really the core premise of every world religion, in which the individual works out his own salvation. With this strategy, the individual overcomes sin and failings through personal improvement strategies—through trying harder and harder. By really buckling down, the sinner finally becomes good!

When we truly grasp the depth of our depravity, we try to do everything to fix it. We will even sleep in the that abysmal heat of Nicaragua to make ourselves presentable to God. But deep inside, we know it does no good! We try to obey the law, giving up our adultery, or our coveting, but our long list of sins—past and present—are unaffected. We will learn that our Purgatory is full of imposters and losers who never left their sins at the foot of the Cross! In Purgatory, they will never find a solution for their brokenness. If our good works performed in a Nicaraguan mission could save us, then there would be no need for the Cross, or the Lamb as the final sacrifice for our Salvation. Our non sequitur was eventually addressed, and the only Door to the sheepfold was revealed as Christ Himself. We would discover that His true intention is to give us a life that is meaningful, and also full of good works.[132]

When we find the Cross, God's miraculous and unmerited favor comes to us, and our striving comes to an end. We know that it is His scandalous grace which saves us.[133] We finally allow God to stretch our canvas when He fills us with His Spirit. Then God makes us His personal masterpiece in that always hot Latin American sun. Richard and I did what friends closer than blood always do. We walked to the restaurant and dined on the local delicacies, recounting the day's events, surgeries, tears, anger, exhaustion, and even joy. We laughed and shared a meal together as brothers and friends. We were so hungry, and so thirsty, for we understood our great need of God.

---

[132] John 10:1-16.

[133] Ephesians 2:4-10.

I found Richard lying in the leaves of his own life with his ear tuned to the sky full of answers. I found him in the beautiful quest for a deeper relationship with the Holy God across the height, and breadth, and width of the *Faith-Time Continuum.* I found him in that bright field of the Apostle Paul's revelation of God's love, when the man who bore the Good News to the Gentiles around the known world waited for the sword in Mamertine Prison in Rome[134]—even in death, Jesus used him to shatter Nero's devilish grip. As Paul's head rolled away from the executioner's perfect stroke, Love won the battle over every evil intention. Paul finally got to go Home! Even the servants of Nero had come to faith in the Christ. Being with Him had become more valuable to Paul than any human accomplishment or earthly suffering.

> And I am convinced that nothing can ever separate us from God's love. Neither death nor life, neither angels nor demons, neither our fears for today nor our worries about tomorrow—not even the powers of hell can separate us from God's love. No power in the sky above or in the earth below—indeed, nothing in all creation will ever be able to separate us from the love of God that is revealed in Christ Jesus our Lord. Romans 8:38-39

Paul's head fell away, but death could no longer hold his soul. He knew that the 3rd heaven awaited him—that indescribable place whose sounds still reverberated in his soul. The forebodings of that prison cell were put behind him, and death had no stinger anymore. There is no way to foresee God's divine deliverance scheduled in the heavenly realm for those who love His Son. How could I foresee the winds blowing tumbleweeds and sand-spurs in my West Texas future? Those dust storms boiling in from the North, with mile-high rolling tsunamis across the plains from Lubbock to Sweetwater, blowing sand through the keyholes of my life?

As the wind tugged at the upper limbs of the tall trees in recent weeks in New England, the autumnal premonitions reminded me of that strange autumn day, when Bengal's wore the cryptic answers on his neck. The deep meaning of forgotten seasons came back to remind me of that archetypical tree at the crossroads of Eden's four rivers. No one can find those four rivers on Google maps today. Their positions have dramatically changed over many centuries, but that biblical Garden could have been centered in the desert regions of Iraq where the Tigris and Euphrates still flow today. That Fall from grace in God's perfect Garden, made every fall seem sad ever since, as Bengals and I vaguely understood.

---

[134] *Mamertine Prison*. Wikipedia.

The Fall of Man killed everything in the Garden of God, and eternity was transmogrified, and even Satan received a timestamp for judgment. Everything became more difficult, with pregnancy and crops in the dry fields becoming more difficult to bring to fruit. God left us even hungrier for a personal relationship and a conversational connection with Himself. He made us more likely to lie down in wild leaves with our hands lifted to the heavens, crying, "Lord, have mercy on me, a sinner!"[135]

He made it more likely that we would have questions that only He could answer—problems that only He could solve. The Prince of the Air took control of the flying leaves and all the dark messaging which I had endured on that melancholy day. Satan's demons were put in charge of fear and dread, frequently raising the specter of death to keep us in bondage to every pain-eraser,[136] every chemical compound, that the world might offer us. The devil hurled his cloud of demons into a highly orchestrated war for the souls of men. His tactics for stealing, killing, and destroying have successfully brought us to the very edge of madness.

We can't see the people standing in their grave-clothes, queued up for miles and miles into the landscape of heaven, awaiting the Lamb's final judgment of every word and deed from the life lived before. We can't imagine a verdict based on knowing God's Son, worshiping Him in Spirit and in Truth. We can't comprehend why His Cross and shed blood alone would redeem us from the kill-shelter of our sinfulness. We can't understand why our syringe is being filled up with the second death because we never believed in the Son of the Father!

Satan has already placed a number on our cage, and the deadly injection has already got our name written on it—we will be put down like dogs into hell. Like our current dog, Jethro, we have waited in our Virginia kill-shelter, where they were busily killing all the mutts alphabetically. "Oreo" kept them both alive long enough for the rescue shelter in Salem to fly him to Boston in the belly of a jet plane. From the same city that burned the witches, our Oreo had come home. "Jethro," his new name, after Jethro Gibbs from the NCIS TV series, is our shepherd-collie and black-Lab mix through adoption. He can't believe how fortunate he is now!

It wasn't cheap adopting a dog! It was unbelievably expensive. Yet, the price for our dog was much less than the price paid for our redemption. When God redeemed us from Satan's kill shelter, Jesus paid the ultimate price. No rich man can afford to pay for this redemption. No international bank can afford to pay off this debt. God has laid down His own life to purchase us from our witch's city. He requires one thing: that we believe in the Son whom He sent. Though many will scoff at God's redemption during their lives, they will stubbornly cling to foolish idols with a "death grip." God will angrily, unhappily, have to

---

[135] Luke 18:13 (NIV).

[136] Sheeran. *Eraser.*

populate His banqueting table with aliens and orphans from every tribe, kin, and nation. He will never force any one of us to receive His salvation. Neither will He be surprised when we snap at Him, if He accidentally grabs our collar without calming us first. He will be forbearing toward us because of what we experienced before, and he will heal our wounds.

When Pop died, I selected and read Ecclesiastes at his funeral. It was all the Scripture that I knew about. I read Solomon's litany of the seasons of life because I had seen Pop reading those very verses from the Bible perched in his bedroom window. I failed to note Solomon's statement that God has planted eternity in every human heart. Eternity and seasons had certainly intersected on this day of finality at his gravesite. Solomon's darkest message about the futility of human effort and self-salvation were speaking directly to me during this surreal season of death. I had no idea then, that Solomon had left out the longest season of all in his own life: the season of idolatry. But the rhythms and sounds of Solomon's beautiful poetry captured me, and spoke into my continuing melancholy that followed me into manhood. It was a constant theme locked up inside of *Myopic Me!*

> *For everything there is a season,*
> *a time for every activity under heaven.*
> *A time to be born and a time to die.*
> *A time to plant and a time to harvest.*
> *A time to kill and a time to heal.*
> *A time to tear down and a time to build up.*
> *A time to cry and a time to laugh.*
> *A time to grieve and a time to dance. Ecclesiastes 3:1-4*

Pop's eyes were so poor in those final months that he had to place the Bible in the north sill of his bedroom window to gain enough light. He read the words on pages long-ago marked with his own hand-written notes. I suspect he knew these verses by heart, though they were barely known to me: "A time to be born and a time to die; a time to grieve and a time to dance; a time to plant and a time to harvest." It broke my heart that his final season had come. I couldn't comprehend anything good that would come from his death.

Pop could see this season rushing toward him out of the North Wind that blows nobody good. His final Wind was trying to sooth his heart's fear coming through those old screens in the house he had built forty-five years before. He had gathered the stones from the fields during that season of planting. "A time to scatter stones and a time to gather stones." Solomon's sad emphasis in Ecclesiastes came from the king's own conclusions that life really is meaningless—a chasing after the wind. This black pool of melancholy had swallowed him as surely as it had swallowed Narcissus and *Myopic Me!*

91

I can still remember my father's face the day the buckshot passed my ear like the hail that fell from the black sky during the Georgia vs. Clemson football game. I remember his face the day he bailed me out of jail at the beach. I remember his disappointment that had no words. I remember my shock when my father stepped over that barbed wire with the hammer still cocked on that sawed-off shotgun. Did he try to kill me, or save me, that strange deafening day in the woods? It was not anger that etched his face as he looked through those bars at me. I remember what Pop said, leaving the earth behind forever in his final bed.

I recall the confessional tone of my mother with her adult son, when she told me how difficult those graduate courses had been for her before she could be hired as an adjunct instructor at Clemson University. With Pop gone, she had to earn a living to keep the house he had left behind for his family. The memory of my father's classroom still lives through many former students, active and alive, with his white chalk letters still clinging to the surfaces of my mind. She and I were the only ones in the house the day they took his body away. I remember the odd thwack of those cans flying away with the morning cold, landing on the other side of day after we had lowered him into the ground. On that day, bright cold day, I stopped trying to be good.

I didn't know then that Solomon's melancholy message in Ecclesiastes is simply a reiteration of the mood born in that Garden-Party-gone-wrong. How could Adam and Eve be upbeat after they fumbled eternal life with a couple of ill-chosen bites? Yes, it was forbidden. Yes, God did say that they would die. In spite of those clear warnings, they carried out the crunch heard "round the world." Bengals Tigris-Euphrates Lane would have barked loud when I finally understood the deep riddle's answer engraved on his collar. But I didn't bark. I finally understood my own complicity.

Evil had flown through the kitchen door, and crawled on the soft butter left out on the linoleum table. The sound of the kitchen door spring is still moaning with those fractured harmonics, as the innocent architecture of the world tripped over that forbidden topography. Evil had disguised itself as good, hiding in glinting scales and flashing tongue of that false prophet in the perfect Garden. Disobedience slipped down around their ankles, and God asked His first non sequitur in their hearing: "Who told you that you were naked?"

"Naked?" What was He talking about? Their answers in the Garden that day were similar to the professional manager who shifts the blame in his board meeting. He immediately blames the customer for all the ridiculous expectations. Or he blames the janitor for the dirty mop left in the cleanroom. The home owner blames the illegal alien whom she hired to mop her second story bedroom floor with a bucket full of wash water—"How did she use up all that water on that medium-sized wooden floor with the cracks between the old boards?" she asks, as she looks up in the dining room ceiling below. She squints her eyes at the gargoyles forming in her perfectly plastered ceiling.

Eve's eyes were opened wide when she saw Adam naked, but Adam knew that her body would haunt him soon. He knew that his ceiling would have stains that he couldn't explain, though he would surely blame God. The lamb Adam and Eve adored in the Garden quivered nearby in the lush grass of the meadow. It leaped into the air, running a few feet before stopping in surprise. For the first time the lamb was afraid of dying. "Bring me the lamb that follows you everywhere in Eden. I will make clothes from its skin to cover your nakedness." God's command to Adam was ominous, eschatological, and unbearable.

Their nakedness had a new meaning now, which was connected with something called death. God's instruction brought a temporary solution for their shame. The lamb would die to cover their sins. Their proclivities had been released, and Satan's demons noted their specific vulnerabilities. "This is going to be so easy!" they sneered. The Prince of the Air had seamlessly usurped their roles to subdue the earth, ruling over it. Now, they would be put in charge of a different role, outside of the Garden. God spoke this new role directly to their son, Cain.

> "You will be accepted if you do what is right. But if you refuse to do what is right, then watch out! Sin is crouching at the door, eager to control you. But you must subdue it and be its master." Genesis 4:7

Suddenly Adam and Eve had skin in the game as they picked up their lamb, still submissive and trusting in their arms. Their Lambie would be the first creature to die since the earth had been formed out of nothing. "What does death feel like?" they must have wondered as they handed their beloved pet over to God. "This is what death looks like," they fearfully whispered to each other for the first time. What they failed to understand was this: God had already choreographed the final Lamb-sacrifice for man's disobedience to God's commands. They experienced the first lamb's death with a pain entirely foreign. It would help them comprehend that final Lamb's sacrifice made for their sins.

Eve shuddered like a mare standing in a cold thunderstorm as God pulled the skin from the lamb and fashioned clothing to cover their nakedness. Adam hid his face from the gathering clouds of the future sky. He could not see that violent storm coming in Future-Time, when the rain would wash the Lamb's blood into the Living Water supply. That blood would be the final blood shed for the salvation of everyone who believes in this Lamb who was slain. Adam, if he strained his eyes, squinting into the faint light from that wormhole into the Future, would have seen the graves open in Jerusalem, with these men of faith walking in the streets.[137] They knew that every ocean would be tinted with that

---

[137] Matthew 27:52.

salvation spreading from the greatest Good News ever published to a lost and dying world.

I knew nothing of this complex Garden Party theology. Neither did I know much about Pandora's Box, the Greek's vision of hell's opening salvo. Ironically, the Greeks built their fine statues, their colossal marble buildings, and their lavish sacrificial altars to celebrate the very hell that swam the world with chaos. Their proud Zeus was famous for the one thing the world has agreed upon — erotic orgies are celebrated on the heights of Olympus. Zeus's erotic escapades brought many questionable offspring to life in the many mythologies from that ancient land.

While the Greeks worshiped their spawn of marble men and women, I barely comprehended the swarm of demons that had been set free when that apple cracked, and that box was opened wide. I knew nothing of these forbidden Trees at the center of the Garden, though my hand poked into those limbs like one of those Greek sculptures. I had never had any teacher connect those four rivers of God to my inner struggles, and these vivid explanations were waiting in Future-Time.

God's expectations are necessarily extreme, for He expects each one of us to believe that something Good has come out of Nazareth. He fully expects us to believe that the death of His Son on the Cross is sufficient to wash away all of our sins — past, present, and future — removing the sting of death from our souls. He expects us to believe that the Lamb was sacrificed in the mind of God before the world was even formed. For our soul's sake, God had scheduled an hour when Jesus Christ would set His face like flint on Jerusalem. He said, "Yes," to the cup of suffering, accepting the final sacrifice of the Lamb. He expects us to believe that this is the only efficacious way to avoid judgement's long queue at the doorway to Woe.

10.

LOOKING HOMEWARD.

W hen my brother and I shared a room at ten or twelve years of age, we signed a pact to come back and build a log cabin in the mountains of North Carolina that we could share and enjoy with our families. I was the builder because that summer I had built a slab fort in the woods behind the house. A pot-bellied stove had been purchased for a few dollars at the furniture store in town. A few lumps of anthracite coal from *Clinkscales* ice and coal company behind the *Pure Station* had provided the fuel for our fire. The burning coal turned the thin cast metal of the stove's belly bright cherry red. The small building, with its attic sleeping area, was warm and toasty on the cold nights. Somehow, we avoided burning the place down, or dying of carbon monoxide poisoning, even though the fort was sealed with cardboard wall coverings throughout. We had the faith for it.

In planning our imaginary cabin, we knew that finding an affordable lot would be a challenge. Would we be able to legally make a driveway right off of a mountain road? Our faith was fragile. The driveway might have to be a long one, and we had no good plan for that. At that time, I had not driven a *Case 1450* front-end loader or a *Caterpillar* bulldozer. I had not yet been approved for a drivable dam around a lake with 10 feet of water in it, or approved to lower a 35-foot chimney through the roof with a crane. At that time, I had not driven a hundred pounds of sheetrock nails to put up a hundred and twenty, twelve-foot drywall sheets to cover the walls and ceilings.

We planned to use trees for our North Carolina house (we got that part right), and we would notch these logs, cut to length, sealing them in between with clay or cement. The thought of it was thrilling. It still is. We had seen enough of these construction projects in the *Daniel Boone* movies, and in the *Westerns* about the settlers moving to the prairies. Getting the money for such a big project seemed inconceivable at age ten and twelve, but we both signed the handwritten agreement. We committed to break ground in 1970, after we finished college. Our faith was no more than a bit of smoke.

We Scotch-taped the childhood covenant inside the closet where it would not be disturbed. My heart was aching because I realized that we would never build it! Life is about faith, and faith is trust of something that is unseen, way off in the distant future. We see it, desire it, and believe it. We know that it will come to pass. But this cabin was not supported by our faith. It was a childhood fantasy, and I knew it. I could see it in Grayson's eyes. He would be the lawyer, with his own firm, and his time would be owed to the Company Store. He would be buried in debt as he defended the defenseless, giving them hope, when there was no hope. Each of us had faith, but for different things. My faith melted in his eyes like a snowflake in front of an open hearth. I wanted something to look forward to, something that would be real. I wanted to build a home. That's a story to be told on another day.

In no time, we had forgotten about these plans, and this dream was gone with our youth. The desire for home still burned inside both of us. Our fantasy cabin was not to be our home. The house I did build in North Carolina on 7.5 acres is beautiful and amazing. But neither is it our home. The house in Texas with the third-story loft was not our true home either. The house in New England is not really our home. All along, we had the right idea, but we offered our human solutions in each case.

The cabin in those lonely trees was not really what our hearts yearned for! We were hungry for eternity, something with significance. Those words from Ecclesiastes were not part of our vocabulary then, but the yearning was as deep in our hearts as that house on a manmade lake or the house with a loft or the house with snow piled three feet deep on the roof and four feet deep in the front yard would ever be. We longed for an eternal dwelling that met every need, every hunger, wiping every tear, and fulfilling every dream. We sought a neighborhood, a kingdom, not conceived by the will of man.

We were not looking for a place prepared for us by the will of our childhood covenant, but we yearned for Agape love to take us over with new meaning, though we did not know that Greek word yet, that word was foremost in our dreaming. That Word was God, and He was there from the beginning. And we longed for the city He was building with Agape love. We did not know yet how to paint the first colored stroke of ourselves on that rich canvas. Solomon envisioned this canvas being painted with happiness; but there would be much more than that in our futures.

> I have seen the burden God has placed on us all. Yet God has made everything beautiful for its own time. He has planted eternity in the human heart, but even so, people cannot see the whole scope of God's work from beginning to end. So I concluded there is nothing better than to be happy and enjoy ourselves as long as we can. Ecclesiastes 3:10-12

At the end of the nineteenth century, the Industrial Revolution had brought jobs and economic well-being to a new middle class in rural America. Baum's story is a fantasy, but it contains the abandoned dream for a true home. It contains the abandoned dream for a True Wizard and Savior who understands the heart of man, not just his pocketbook. The population of America sat uncomfortably in their new prosperous surroundings, and these became Baum's target audience for the *Wonderful Wizard of Oz.* In his story, the Wizard runs the government like a kind of vast Seance. In Dorothy's story about this fantastic place, L. Frank Baum took out his brushes and swiped away at the cultural landscape which had excluded the Munchkins and their happy dance.

For Dorothy, Kansas was her "Cabin in the Mountains" or it was my four-thousand foot house on the lake—but Kansas wasn't really her home. It was all she knew about living, and it contained the best efforts to paint the home her heart yearned for. When she finally returns home, the story ends, and reality begins. Where is Oz II? I don't want to see Oz II, but I think I know what happened when Dorothy moved to Hollywood. Did she make a home in the Hills! Was her yearning fully consummated and fulfilled? When Dorothy died young in London, she had become a faint whisper of our Dorothy in Oz. She got her *Wonderland* home, only to find the witches in her yard and the Blue Caterpillar in her foyer. Why? Her own brokenness followed her home from Oz! She couldn't escape the brokenness of the world she was born into, which gradually consumed her, sealing her tragic life for all to see on the evening news.

The kingdom in Oz is not real, but the underlying energies are real. The struggle between evil and good is entirely authentic. The wash water is a potent representation of the hope that is within us—that yearning for eternity that never will be silent. We are, with Bob Dylan, knock-knock-knocking on heaven's door. We are taking off our badges and burying our guns so that we can find the secrets of heaven in this life.[138] We are seeking a city which has no name, asking a Wizard that does not know the way to the home the True Wizard [there is no good wizard in God's eyes) is preparing for us in heaven. [139]

Baum would really be astonished today, to discover that most of our manufacturing has been exported to offshore factories, too often run by flying monkeys and witches wearing the garb of the Wizard. Baum's post-Civil War era audience would barely recognize the strange cultures in China, Mexico, Sri Lanka, India, and Korea that manufacture everything we need today. We have become the Upper Class Lords and Ladies waiting for our new thing-a-ma-bobs from *Amazon Prime.* Our own multicultural mix is found in Baum's prophetic vision for the Emerald City.

Baum could vaguely see the scientific mega-farms arriving in Kansas, Nebraska, and California which employ the wizardry of DNA-modified crops. He would see the drought-resistant, insect resistant, and rot-resistant crops, coming from that advanced scientific farming today. He might be pleased to discover the factory worker of today having a greater sense of satisfaction in his

---

[138] Dylan. *Knocking on Heaven's Door.*

[139] Hebrews 11:16.

work, sometimes building the entire product, and even collaborating on design and process.

In my pre-teen anonymity in Clemson, I could already identify with Baum's allegory of failures and fools. "If I only had a brain!" I said more than once. The role of the coward, I have performed with Oscar-rivaling accuracy. The imposter is my trademark in any number of endeavors over the year—I know personally that feeling when Toto pulls back the curtains and everyone sees me sweating. I have stood in front of hundreds in Atlanta with nothing useful to say, still speaking for a half an hour. Retaining Dorothy's hope through it all, I am convinced that these Technicolor Confessions are good for the soul of man. If I practice in this book, maybe I can learn to do it in real life with the curtains of the imposter dumped on the floor around me. What a scary thought that is.

Out of the creative mind of Baum, powerful lessons arrive through vivid characters. Under the tutelage of Dorothy, we all confess our desire to go home. We may even emulate her gentleness and sincerity. Baum has shown us that it is okay to fail for a season, if we keep our eyes focused on Home. Home is childhood, and children have wisdom we know not of. They come to their Father saying, "Abba, Papa, Father! Help me!" Baum showed our children that courage, love, creativity, and authenticity are bonuses, but they are not enough to get us home. We need help from our Dorothy, our Ananias,[140] and from the One Who stops us on our Damascus Road—no golden way will lead us home until He puts up His hand to ask us: "Why are you persecuting Me?"

Baum's democratic ideas are still being written on the hearts of Millennials in America and around the world. We still fill our surround-sound theaters every time the "Now Showing" sign arrives in our neighborhood. *Black Hand*, *Bridget Bardot*, the Martian invaders, the *Flesh, the Devil*, and the *Cowardly Lion* still come to every small town theater, bringing *sex, lies, and videotape* to the gullible and to the wise.

The Voice helped me attach the proper significance to these cinematic interventions in my own life. The Comforter and the Counselor showed me the Good News—teaching me what I heard with my ears and what I saw with my eyes. When Jesus walked with the disciples on the road to Emmaus, He opened my mind to understand the beginning and the end of things. He showed me the meaning of His Cross. He showed me the meaning of the resurrection.[141] He showed me that the face of failure is sometimes a necessary step, bringing the truth and the life. The Advocate took me through every barrier between faith-time and space-time—He showed me that the only way through death is to pass

---

[140] Acts 9:17.

[141] Luke 24:13-35

through the Eye of the Needle.[142] No spiritual stronghold could keep Him from speaking life into my chaos.

In my former lost days in the Methodist church as a boy, I never really received His personal comfort or peace. I didn't find His righteousness or understand His judgment applying to every word and deed. Though the Church belongs to Him, He does not reveal Himself to anyone who does not come as a little child. "Be still and know that I am God!" But I was never still in those pre-teen years, and never did I know Him during those early years. As much as I protested, God's plan for my life did not yet fit, while my mind flew, and my soul became tied in knots by a growing idolatry, I could not know Him until I surrendered my will to Him.

Even a little king is a king. Even a weak king is a king still. With all the absurd prerogatives of a king to shape our personal hell, I could only be free when I surrendered. In weakness we find His strength. In our strength, we will quickly fall. Even our surrendering is impossible without the conviction of the Holy Spirit coming to call. He changes our perspective toward sin, so that we can no longer bear it. We need remission from death to happen inside of us.

It is harder for an unsurrendered man, or boy, to enter the kingdom of heaven than for a camel to pass through the eye of a needle. There is no one to blame for these false starts and blind alleys, though I suppose my pride is the most obvious culprit. Nevertheless, God had appointed a perfect time for my soul to sing His Song of Grace. Though I tried as hard as I could to sing in my own strength, I could never hit a pure note. I never understood that real life does not thrive in *Myopic Me!* Without God's peace, life is empty, a chasing after the wind.

I did not understand that He is the Love that the poets stumble over in their darkness, faintly grasping the height, depth, and breadth of Him. On the night that I read my poems to the *Marriage Encounter* small group in our spare living room, I had no deep relief from this vanity of self-actualization. I didn't grasp that the love I was writing about unravels as soon as trouble comes. When I read my little ditties about humanistic and romantic love, I forgot about the preeminence of the One who suffocated and died on a Cross for each person in the room that night. They looked at me as if I had three heads. I did have three heads, but I had a lot to learn about the Head of the Church Who is Christ Himself.

My frivolous sentiments about "love" were little more than the effluent from *Myopic Me!* They were witty, and vain insights, not comprehending God's proven intention to nurture an honest relationship with me and with my wife and with our new acquaintances. He has never demanded that I be good, but He shows me daily that nothing good dwells within me. Jesus said, slightly edited, "Only One is Good—the Father in heaven." He wanted to live inside of me that night when I became the Wizard and the fool.

---

[142] Mark 10:25.

When I finally grasped the stories of the Good News of God's kingdom, the stain of religion in me yielded to the fragrant scent of God's presence. During those eight years out of Atlanta, I would learn to worship Him in Spirit—and in Truth.[143] The filth that I could not wash from my jeans or my oily hair, came entirely under His gentle flood. To the ones who seemed most righteous, He had said, "I never knew you—be gone from Me."[144] That verse terrified me, for I barely **understood** His Truth. I know Him much better today. He breathed life into me. I didn't breathe life into myself.

It is no accident that the Scarecrow in that field has no brain, mutely guarding the harvest. God is the Lord of the harvest field, and He is the intellect. He is the One who restores the right mind. When Uncle Henry's face emerges in Oz, we see the protective father-figure guarding Dorothy's welfare. God watches over my life, protecting me from my own blindness. While the farmer guards the nation's health, like Joseph shielding Egypt from famine and starvation, God continues to provide everything I need.

Though we take our food supply in America for granted, the farmer produces our daily bread in secret. He combines science with technology to fill our plates. In Darfur Africa, 4,000,000 lives hang in the balance during an annual drought. They are cursed by weather and lack of water sources. They are cursed by a lack of knowledge and technology. But God is sending sacks of grain and canisters of water to feed the hungry who are falling down beside the road. The wisdom of scientific farming is completely lost on Darfur and Ethiopia, and the provisions of God are poorly understood. Even the Christian forgets that God gave manna daily to the Israelites in the Saudi deserts of Egypt. Without this daily bread, a million Hebrews would have died.

The Cowardly Lion is a real person, reflecting the character and hardship of many of us who have become cowards when life dealt us a blow. The Cowardly Lion in Oz was William Jennings Bryan, who ran three times for President of the United States, losing each time. Strike three is the most humiliating sound from the Umpire after that ball sinks deep into the catcher's mitt—the Cowardly Lion has to walk back to the dugout looking for someone to blame. The disappointed crowd makes it clear who the coward is. The enthusiastic batboy, whose myopic field of view fails to apprehend that the whole world has just fallen apart, misses the end of a brilliant career right in front of him.

Even in their disguises, the Lion, the Tin Man, and the Scarecrow cannot hide their deformities from the children sitting in the theater, or from those reading the hardback books. The brave lion is demoted to Coward status; the intelligent farmer has become the mindless Scarecrow in the field. The faithful

---

[143] John 4:24.

[144] Matthew 7:23.

Woodsman has abandoned his forest and lost his heart in the monotonous security of the city factory. [145]

Grown up now, millions are still confronting these authentic parables. Dorothy is still their friend. The Tin Man still yearns for the forest, gathering his family together to visit the New Hampshire woods for a camping trip—or visiting the Smokey Mountains trails for the smell of shrubs and spruce filling the open air beneath the stars at night. The Southern worker in the German factory builds the cars for the American autobahn, while she seeks to find her way home. Everything is different. The monkeys fly through the air and the daisies are filled with opium, but Dorothy vaguely remembers the love and the home she has lost.

Some say the gay culture of America took Dorothy as their cult hero because of her fantastical and real-life perseverance through many rejections and much alienation. Rumors spread about her husband being gay. She might have ventured into a few gay bars with friends.[146] But Dorothy is not their savior, as some may imagine; for she is a girl who will, at best, lead us to our own ruby slippers.

Though the gay audience might have enjoyed the symbolism of the beautiful slippers and the multicultural lifestyle, they may be missing the redemptive possibilities in Oz. Only the Holy Spirit can lead the Gay citizen or the Straight citizen into God's good, pleasing, and perfect will.[147] It is a creative arena which produced the whole gorgeous Universe, with life in vast array. Only Christ can produce true multicultural unity which our collective hearts crave—in fact, He makes an explicit point of just that.[148]

> And all who have been united with Christ in baptism have put on Christ, like putting on new clothes. There is **no longer** Jew or Gentile, slave or free, male and female. For you are all one in Christ Jesus. And now that you belong to Christ, you are the true children of Abraham. You are his heirs, and God's promise to Abraham belongs to you. Galatians 3:27-29

This true unity, in love for one another, comes through faith, caring for those who are "no longer" unreconcilable enemies of God. No one can remain the same in this illimitable kingdom. We can thank God for that reality, knowing in the deepest places of our hearts that we need to be set free. Faith brings this

---

[145] *William Jennings Bryan.* Wikipedia.

[146] Katz. *Gay American History.*

[147] Romans 12:2. NLT.

[148] *Judy Garland as Gay Icon.* Wikipedia.

goodness through Lordship. Surrender is essential for Lordship. Trust grows as God's love fulfills the deepest hungers of the human heart. God made us male, and He produced the female from Adam's own flesh. He produced the perfect functional and cultural combination for the advancement of love and family, relational intimacy, and deepening commitment to Him and to one another.

Only Christ can advance this mysterious union in the world, and sexuality is a powerful part of this journey. But the cry of sexual cravings can never define us, or shout down the cry of God from the Cross: "Why have you forsaken Me?" Christ experienced rejection by the whole world; not just a spouse or friend. But His greatest pain of rejection was when God the Father turned His face away from His Son because of our sin. He became sin so that we could become righteousness.

Christ was covered with our sins, abandoned by His Father, misunderstood, misrepresented, and mocked, beside a murderer, as if He had done anything wrong. They sold off His clothing while He hung there naked, waiting for death. His mother, John, and Mary Magdalene stood a few feet away as the hatred of men came to full wrath upon Him. The Cross would soon do its intentional work to suffocate Him. He endured all of this, so that we might be set free. He died so that sinners could be rescued from their disfigurement.

During the post-Civil War era, Baum had seen far too many disfigured soldiers. Their metal legs were strapped onto an amputees' stump. Their hearts were removed when their legs were sawed off like so much fire wood. The Tin Man of our modern age still struggles to find a pulse because of all the rust and sheet metal riveted over his heart. His painkillers are powerful, and his panic is like the sounds from some great human disaster. "I don't feel anything anymore," my friend said beside me at the bookstore. "I just listen to them talking about their troubles, and I shrug. I feel nothing. So what, I ask myself, as I hear them babble on and on?"

Lost in the cold metal legs of religion, young men and old men still wonder if there is something they can perform that will save them. "If I only had a brain," the Scarecrow sings, holding the "rain" of brain for a full measure. "If I only had a leg," the war veteran wonders out loud, "then I could serve God. I could be His friend." But God loves us as we are, legs and brains, not withstanding. He asks only that we believe in the Son Whom He sent. This believing changes everything. This believing renews the mind of man, metal legs and all. God had His legs nailed to a cross so that we might have complete freedom serving His people.

He expects us to look full measure into the scandal on the Hill of Skulls where an innocent man, Son of the Father, was crucified. Jesus' half-brother, James, did not believe in Jesus Christ before His resurrection. Then, James would die for the name of his older brother, who was born of his virgin mother before him. James' believing, and my believing, looks to the blinding light coming from that sealed tomb when Jesus walked out alive with a physical body.

Jesus told them [while He was among them], "This is the only work God wants from you: Believe in the one he has sent." John 6:28

In the midst of my spiritual malaise of a third kind, the familiar characters from Oz come to life on the Technicolor screen, revealing the secret coding of my own frail life-signs—da-thump, da-whack, da-bump. I saw each of those characters gaining his missing identity, finding their true journey, as they bonded together as friends-in-need—and collaborators-in-league. The journey home is different for each individual, but there is only one Wormhole into eternity. Mt. Guyot opened up a fold in the *Faith-Time continuum* that helped me put cowardice in the rearview mirror. Mt. Guyot woke up my pattern seeking heart. I would begin to look for my Hero after that encounter with God on the mountain of cold rain.

11.

MT. GUYOT.

W hen the Associate Minister of our family church invited age-fourteen me, along with my best friend, to make a hiking trip along the Appalachian Trail, my answer had to be "Yes." The Smokey Mountains had long evoked great mystery for me, as our family had driven many times through the moss-covered and fern-splashed walls of stone rising above the switch-back roadway. We had traveled slowly along the feet of great evergreens tipped in the smoke of an ever-present cloud-cover. The Cherokee village in the valley below had been a grand enticement for my brother and me for years, with the cheap tom-toms, beaded belts, and feathered headdresses. It was slow-going along the route, with cars winding for hours as they moved toward Clingmans Dome. When we finally tumbled out into the thin atmosphere to romp and run in the wet green paradise, the intoxicating smell of the ferns always met us in the clouds.

Still, I had no knowledge of the Appalachian Trail itself which runs along the ridges of the Smokey Mountains. Nor did I understand much about the Methodist Church which I had attended my whole life. I really didn't know much about my best friend and his precarious family situation. And the associate minister who invited us to go along on this camping trip was barely more than a stranger to me. But the one I was most illiterate about at fourteen years of age was *Myopic Me!* An untested entity in every respect, my emotional and physical boundaries were still unmapped. My internal trails were poorly marked. The topography of my life had only faintly emerged, with endocrine fall-lines beginning to define my future. By agreeing to go on this outing, I defied the coward coiling inside me.

The use of the word *Myopic* to describe my young self, brings a fusillade of derogatory terms that sound very much like the cowardly political rhetoric of 2017. These words jump out of my Apple-Word database with surprising ferocity when I place the cursor over the word "myopic." Though *myopic* is an ophthalmic term, it takes on horrific negative forebodings when these synonyms are considered. I cannot escape these consequences for this series of books I have written with the main title, *Myopic Me!* These synonyms will apply in extreme cases; but in this early stage of my personal formation, I prefer the synonyms: "insular, provincial, unsophisticated, and short-sighted." Their ugly cousins are: "Bigoted, prejudiced, and intolerant."

For me, these remain opinion words, culture words, that carry no absolute meaning since they arise in the mouths of judges. The judges are other men, whose backs are already broken with self-righteousness. These words are loaded with a foul-smelling cultural power that cannot be quenched once released. The accused is found guilty by simple association with the word's use. There is no court that can refit the damaged reputation once applied; these Pandora's Box words cannot be placed back in the box once they are released. "Bigot! Intolerant!" They hang in an air of their own, where the devils grin with delight.

Bigoted and prejudiced were not part of my lexicon or mental process in that time before we chose to spotlight minorities, gays, and Muslims with our modern freakish attention. In the 1950s, every outlier maintained a stealthy profile, seeking assimilation into a harmonized American melting-pot. They spoke English, and went to work daily. They suffered quietly, as we have learned, trying to fit into the surroundings as best they could. It takes all kinds to make a Republic, then and now; but certain common attributes have held the experiment together from the beginning.

The essential threesome are Virtue, Faith, and Freedom. The founders called these the *Golden Triangle*, without which the Republic will not long survive.[149] Virtue, faith, and freedom will draw many outliers into the fabric of life. America has offered freedom, with notable reservations, while encouraging the expansion of virtue and faith in every byway, alley, and boulevard. Sometimes the faith does not smell Catholic, Protestant, or Jewish, and there's the rub. But freedom is slowly expanding to include every faith in this promise of religious freedom. We have much to condemn (we do love to condemn in America), but there is no government like this in the world. The governments of Germany and Sweden have their own problems with race and distribution of wealth. They have their own problems with self-defense and diversity.

Upon my fourteenth birthday, such ideas about this Golden Triangle had receded into a national forgetfulness—we had entered the Materialism Zone, when everything could be purchased from a Sears Catalog—our primitive version of the Worldwide Web. For a 3-cent stamp and a money-order, you could order the electric Heidelberg Belt or the Sears Motor Buggy. Even that little house with a picket fence could be mailed to your chosen lot on Pleasant Street.[150] After the Sears Catalog's success, the world of commerce tapped into various specialty magazines. Captive clienteles were linked to relevant advertisements full of products and services to satisfy every fantasy. These ads focused on their obvious interest in the home, the garden, or outdoor life. These interests had drawn them to the magazine rack in the drug store in the first place.

Pictures of the perfect home drew one hand directly to this goldmine of advertisements. Another hand reached for *Popular Mechanics*, with various ads

---

[149] Metaxas. *If You Can Keep It.*

[150] *Sears Catalogs from the 1900s.* Google.

in the back for do-it-yourself gadgets, hobbies, plans for birdhouses and storage sheds, homemade automobiles and more. This magazine rack was the low-tech version of Google AdWords tuned to the dreams from Oz and Wonderland. It was the first inkling of Tom Cruise's *Minority Report*, with the video screen ads tuned to his passing by on the streets. His personal wish lists and secret dreams flashed along the way as he walked faster through the shopping zone.[151]

Ads were waiting in the back pages of these magazines with fonts too small to read without glasses. They knew that we would read every one until we found what we were looking for. Our young minister had ordered the tent for our trip from an ad in *Outdoor Life Magazine*. He paid 20-dollars for a 3.2 pound *Ripstock* nylon mountain tent—7 X 7-feet with a floor included. L. H. explained that every pound we carried up the mountain would be multiplied by the steepness of the trail and the distance we walked in a day. Dried food came with this strange territory. A canteen full of cold water quickly turned dried food into lunch or supper. Nuts and raisins, and small crunchy bars, were slipped into our pockets for each day-long hike.

We were prejudiced in this primitive time in the South, but we said very little about our feelings toward those who were different from us. The silence must have been deafening then, permitting no sustained consideration of such unseemly matters as race, poverty, homosexuality, or irreligion. I hardly remember "Myself" from that period, much less the "outliers" who are featured today on every TV screen. Identity, purpose, meaning, and human rights were everywhere, and nowhere in that ostensibly homogenous time. I had no idea that being loved by Him would become my identity. Though I grew up in a "loving family," I had never known the love that forgives, protects, forgets, and never fails[152]—creating unity between the strangest of bedfellows

The Father's love is so all-consuming that it supplants every insecurity and doubt of the former reality. Christ is Truth, and being His friend is all you want to talk about. "Oh, I met Tom Brady," the excited fan boasted. "I had lunch with the President!" the politically minded family member expounds. "I spent time with the King of kings and the Lord of lords! He told me that He loves me!" This is the new identity. This is the new Reality in Christ. "He's a good good Father, that's Who He is," as the song declares. "And I'm loved by Him—that's who I am!"[153] I am defined by His love, rather than the love of the world.

I lived in that bubble of family and neighborhood and town, nearly unaware of pain or struggle, except for the typical inner-outer warfare which teens endure without a word. Having very little materially on Pop's meager salary, we did not think much about rich and poor. When Hubert paid for the ball glove at the

---

[151] *Minority Report*. Wikipedia.

[152] 1 Corinthians 13.

[153] Tomlin. *Good Good Father*.

Five and Dime Store, I realized for the first time that he was poor. He sacrificed his entire wealth on me that day, and I was changed forever in my awareness of the poor among us.

Silently, the young white population of our town suffered through the universal and unspoken vortex of testosterone and estrogen cravings—with shame and acne coming in waves. Sex or heroin, pornography or marijuana were not mentioned while I lived on Folger Street. We had no such terms in our perfect world. Heroin entered no home, and pornography could not be found anywhere. And what would we do with it if it turned up in our bottom drawers or under our mattresses? The shockwaves would be felt for miles in all directions. It would have been the topic of conversation in every hushed discussion at recess behind Edgewood Elementary School.

Today the spotlight is ruthlessly fixed on the strange ones among us, as if strangeness has suddenly gained special value. Long-hidden in the tails of the Bell Curve of our Republic, the lesbians and geniuses now find inexhaustible curiosity and sympathy within our public domain. This 0.15%, at either end of the bell curve preoccupies our politics and national policy. Malcolm Gladwell even wrote an entire book on the upper tail of us, addressing the *Outliers: The Story of Success*.[154] His narrative focuses on where these people live, rather than what they are like. The focus is on the environment which incubates their success, not on the genius himself. Gladwell finds their support group, their family, far more important than their GRE score. He discovers that the encouragement and discipline undergirding the genius is far more important than the quantitative or verbal scores on the GRE. Without the right environment, the genius usually suffers profound frustration and unorganized futility—the formula for an unfruitful life.

Einstein's 160 IQ (Mensa quizzes) seems dwarfed by Sheldon Cooper's 187 on *The Big Bang Theory* TV series, and Walter O'Brien's 197 on TV's *Scorpion*. Their scores are calculated against the perfect score of 200, so there is no direct correlation with Einstein, Hawking, and Wahi. Eleven-year-old Kashmea Wahi recently scored a perfect 162 on the Mensa quizzes in London.[155] Is Kashmea going to surpass the modern-day influence of Dorothy on the world culture? Or will she succeed in ways that Einstein never imagined? Einstein accomplished far more than Sheldon or Walter O'Brien could ever dream, and he and Pop share a March 14 birthday. I suspect that Pop's IQ was lower than the 160+ stratosphere of these geniuses.[156]

Albert and Stephen Hawking scored identical 160s on the test. Sheldon would say that Walter Obrien is nothing more than a really smart engineer, while

---

[154] Gladwell. *Outliers*.

[155] *This 11-year-old girl just beat Einstein*. From the Grapevine.

[156] *Ten famous people who share a birthday*. From the Grapevine.

Einstein had "produced his best work before anyone knew anything." While Sheldon measures success by the Nobel Prizes he hopes to win, Albert considered his own life a failure since he found no "Unifying Theory of Everything."[157] The world is watching to see how a genius acts. Outliers are right to believe that everyone is watching them—the world presents its critique after every deed is consummated.

The present-day spotlighting of outliers increases their agitation and despair. If Einstein was convinced that he was an imposter, imagine what the transgender student at a major university hiding in a Safe Room might be feeling. Every eye is on "him or her," and each one has to do something to prove they are who they say they are. They are broiled by the hot lights that never stop following them. The ascension of *Myopic Me!* is no accident in this artificial atmosphere, where compassion is imposed as a political protocol to gain the most votes. No one likes to be used, and it doesn't take long in *Wonderland* to realize that someone or something else is controlling your body.

We aim the hot lights of near hysteria today on everyone who arrives in these statistical tails of the Bell curve—not able to acknowledge that we are all part of the same fallen race, a collection of wild-things with names psychiatrists have given us. In our hysteria, we have sent these outliers running for cover like the roaches in our South Carolina kitchen in the 1950s—they were searching the crevices looking for their safe place in a world where anything goes. These outliers were dropped down in a world where every difference between us is differentiated by friends and foes alike.

Discrimination abounds today, in the best sense of the word, and bigotry has become synonymous with any attempt to see the difference. The whole subject is "Verboten" in the age of tolerance—which is anything but tolerance. It is intolerance on steroids. The outliers have been shuffled, and the roaches run away without explaining why they were crawling around in the butter dish. Flipping the 100-watt light bulb on them always sent those two-inch long golden cruisers scratching and diving so fast they could not get traction on the linoleum countertops or the enamel surfaces of the stove. They dove into the darkness where their guts would remain in tact. They fed the full horror of the outlier's identity which we had given them. They lived their lives in fear of the light, as they tumbled through the crumbs which had fallen from the ample table of Israel.[158]

Like the Gentiles in ancient Jerusalem, they hoped for the best, surviving, and avoiding the feet of the Average Man. With our modern emphasis on this discrimination of differences, we apply the peanut butter of bigotry in subtle ways. We fail to embrace the Other as one of the sons or daughters from our own broken-down family line. No "safe place" will ever succeed, when reconciliation is irreconcilable in the heavenly realm. In a world without "sin," there

---

[157] *Grand Unified Theory*. Wikipedia.

[158] Matthew 15:27

is only the pointing middle finger of mutual hatred. As long as we continue to sort outliers beneath the hot lights of social scrutiny, our reconciliation will be postponed indefinitely. "Go into your Safe Place! Dive down into your darkness. You'll be safe for now!" Really? Safe from whom? Safe from what? Only God can provide a safe place for a roach or a man.

> *For you are my hiding place; you protect me from trouble. You surround me with songs of victory. Psalm 32:7*

We are still anchored to death. We are still at odds with our Father. We still reject the Son. Instead of Commies being driven out of Dan's Hamburger Restaurant, we direct our hot lights on middle-aged white men who work for the Man. They are the new scapegoat in the classroom or in the workplace. These become the enemies of all good men. Instead of labeling Heroin and Fentanyl sellers as the pariahs of our day, we rage against policemen, wishing all of them dead.

Like the former Vice President, we smolder, declaring, "We can't get rid of all of them!" We can't get rid of those people we hate. We can't kill everybody who has a different view about reality than we do. When Pilate asked Jesus, "What is reality?" it was a rhetorical question. He wasn't a hater, he was a politician. For him there was the reality of Rome which saw everybody resisting Caesar's law. There was the reality of the Pharisee—he saw everyone ignoring the Pharisaic laws. There was, and is, the reality of Jesus—and He clears up every flawed perspective with one simple phrase: "No one is good, only the Father in heaven." He has never touched our sin.

Promiscuity is widely lauded on stage and screen, so that frees up another spotlight to aim at those who speak against certain personal freedoms. Plumbers become heroes, when every belly is bulging. When we shut-down free speech, our slogans demand to be heard. We blame the law for everything wrong in our cities—and it is true that the Law shines a light on our wickedness. While we legalize the trunk full of deadly drugs, our babies' brains are destroyed one toke at a time in the foyers of our rent-subsidized houses.

Enlightenment takes on this new hue, as we turn the same dull eye toward the deconstruction of everything which brought us to this point. Still falling short of God's glory, no one denies the sins of the fathers. But sometimes the mothers do their part in the destruction of the family unit. We can't understand the shocking rise of disease or the decline of our nation, and we no longer see the signs of the times. While the statues are torn down by anarchists, we cheer the destruction of Israel. Since God chose the Jews, in spite of their idolatry, Adam and Eve would have nothing helpful to say to us today. Their first-born son was a murderer, while our sons and daughters slaughter their parents while they sleep.

109

When Eve opened a fruit-stand in Eden, even the goats and lambs ran away. The lamb who was slain for Adam and Eve's first skirt and pants had stood uneasily at a distance when the Good and Evil intentions dripped down from Eve's chin. "Who am I?" Eve found herself in big trouble when she wanted to know everything God knows[159]—in the manner of every theoretical physicist seeking the *Theory of Everything*. She decided that she wanted to be like God. Sad truth is, that she was made in God's image, but not above Him. She ignored Him, listening to the Serpent's voice instead.

When my friend and I turned our eyes toward the mountaintop, this question of identity surely came into focus very quickly for both of us: "Who are we?" We asked that same question before we entered the domain of the unknown. We asked, knowing that we would function apart from parents, home, and familiar soothing objects in our lives. "Can a coward mount the heights of Mt. Guyot and live?" As Adam and Eve could attest, the times, they were a'changing! Little did I realize then, that I might arrive at 7000-feet above sea level in the fetal position in the wet ferns. In truth, that specific embryonic posture would not be an option for us as we lay side-by-side in our seven-foot-square mountain tent.

The phrase, *"Myopic Me!"* did not exist in this ancient time, and Carly Simon had not yet sung her song, "You're So Vain (You probably think this song is about you)."[160] Solomon had long since stocked his bedroom with a thousand young women laid-in like firewood for a cold night. I had just now considered the ramifications of Dorothy's multicultural Oz, and her fame rapidly expanded in my neighborhood back then. Alice's Obsessive-Compulsive journeys into the upside-down world of Wonderland remained to be seen. I understood very little about their personal journeys through the vortices of the Space-Time Continuum, for I had been tumbled in the Kansas farmhouse myself. I knew that worlds were colliding, and there was nothing I could do about it.

Only recently have I revisited these long-buried events from the top of that dark mountain with the unpronounceable name: "Mt. Guyot." God has shown me since then that the poison of vanity weakens my soul. Vanity is the kryptonite which even makes *Superman* take a good look into the mirror. The Newtonian Laws of human interaction have become more comprehensible to me since then, and sharing my toys comes easier now than in that earlier times. When I recalled the details of this nearly forgotten place, the contiguous sensory experiences returned with their emotions, smells, temperatures, and sounds emerging with present-tense significance. Mt. Guyot itself, came to life again within me—as if it had been freeze-dried, only needing water to bring it to life again.

When the three of us ascended the heights to the top of Mt. Guyot, Sheldon Cooper had not yet offended nearly every sacred cow in India; and his Nemesis, the Nobel Selection Committee for Physics had not yet fumbled through their

---

[159] Genesis 3:4-5.

[160] *You're So Vain. Wikipedia.*

rolodex to find Sheldon's number. Einstein's brilliant equations were already shaping everything in my world, but Sheldon had not announced that his equations permitted him to "look at the universe naked." Sheldon Cooper and my friend Bill Hamilton, from my college physics classes, had not yet agreed with my grandfather that the energy inside the atoms could fuel the nations or destroy the cities along the western edge of Japan. His prognostication, forty years before Pearl Harbor in his Clemson College physics lecture, did not imagine the day when we would climb Mt. Guyot in the rain.

On the day that we met to plan our hiking trip, Sister Teresa had only recently heard from God about her spiritual roadmap into poverty and death. Her commute took her through the neighborhoods of the poorest of the poor in Calcutta. She would only come out from those *Untouchables* to receive her Nobel Prize and to visit the dying people of Chernobyl. Mother Teresa would yet stand tall in her generation, avoiding the powerful undertow of Narcissus. It is still impossible to imagine a God Who would walk among us Untouchables with a cup of cool water. His crown of thorns makes no sense to the present day. What could motivate a King to visit the squalor of His poorest subjects, to make them shine like a city set on a hill?

Traveling with my parents on those early family trips set the stage for my coming out from family to be myself for the first time. I left home to find my own way. The six of us had always piled into the green 1950 Plymouth flathead-six, four-door automobile to drive the switch-back curves up to Clingmans Dome. Traveling with a familiar string of overheating automobiles, we could see the cars below and those above us, as we struggled together to the top of the world.

Sweating it out in the back seat, the hot engine always filled the car with steam and the smell of the radiator fluid. We pulled over when we were enveloped in our own cloud and unable to see the road ahead. We piled out to run to a bubbling spring to scoop up a half gallon of water for the empty cooling system. I often got this job, toting the large glass bottle through the wet foliage until I knelt beside the miraculous cold water oozing up from the ground.

Without this drink of water, the little engine could not carry our family any farther in low gear. That mountain spring allowed us to continue our progress to the Clingmans Dome parking lot. It seemed that everybody on earth wanted to go to that same terminus at the end of this mountain road. The steep path to the top always climaxed our journey at the top of the smoky world with the clouds offering us its wet gray air.

I breathed the smoke with great awareness of this miracle at 7000 feet, far from the humidity and heat of Myrtle Beach or Ocean Drive along the far-distant Atlantic shore. I loved those trips to a mysterious landscape in the sky—though I remember my head bobbing through every rendition of the brand-new Cherokee Indian drama, *Unto these Hills*. This drama, presented in the stone theater cut into the side of the mountain, always came after an exhausting day.

We met at L. H. Buff's apartment to plan our twenty-five-mile trek, and I realized for the first time that we would carry our own packs with sleeping bag and dried food—it was my first camping trip! Now, Billy and I were heading to the top of the mountains with exciting names like Thunderbird, Gregory Bald, and Mt. Le Conte. We would soon stand on the trail in the sky, with no Pop or Mom to reassure us. This would surely peel the coward's label from my life, jettisoning me into my own personal Oz on the golden trail from Georgia to Maine. I would learn in that planning session that we would walk trails where the fall-lines sometimes plummeted down into a different state on either side. I instinctively knew that my Cowardly Lion and heartless Tin Man would fall down during that brief journey into night.

At age fourteen, I was heading for the mountains like my hero, Daniel Boone! With no coonskin hat, I would face the unknown like Dorothy and Alice whose trails took them off-road into new worlds. It was a relief to be going outside the ritualized atmosphere of those boring church services doing something dangerous! I admit I was excited to be with a young minister from the church doing something real! Church seemed inconsequential and remote in my life at that time, where a hundred church-goers sat together each week on the same hard pews, singing the same endless hymns, while I yawned and checked out the women's giant hats and stopped-watches on their arms. The sermons might have been inspiring to some of these, but I don't remember a word.

There was such a predictable familiarity in these gatherings, and each person could have stuck a name tag on their own pew. No one would have argued with them because each family had regular seats they sat in any way! The men in those services wore hot suits, and spent the entire sermon pulling on constricting neckties. While they tugged at the sharp edges of starched white collars, the ladies balanced flowering hats that blocked my view.

During the summer heat, the sweat trickled down through the chest hair of the men who sat very still, setting a good example for their children—"No wiggling!" they seemed to be saying. Fixed like statues in their hard seats, they hardly moved for an hour unless to stand and sing seven stanzas from that heavy hardback hymnal. There was not enough air in the whole world to get me through those seven stanzas. They were packed with deep theological content, and every word went straight over my head—and nothing seemed to reach my heart!

Us pre-teen boys finally moved to the balcony (Were we instructed to move up there?), where we held our breath during those long impressionless services. We discovered that we could go without air for more than a minute-twenty seconds. This was our record, until one day when God said to me, "Be still and know that I am God!" I never held my breath again after that day. The breath of God had blown over my face with a gentle Wind, and all those soundless sermons were rolled up into this one mysterious message from God's mouth spoken directly to *Myopic Me!* With an awareness of what He spoke to me personally, I asked myself, "Why did He say this to me? Is He telling me to quit wiggling?"

Little did I know that my wiggling had nothing to do with this. Little did I know that He was talking about a whole Book that could speak to me—as if it were alive and active in my personal reality. I did not even know what the

112

Scriptures were, though I had a Bible—American Standard Translation. No one taught me to search my lifeless red-bound Bible to find that critical verse within the sixty-six books of the two-thousand-plus pages. I did not know that the invention of the Gutenberg Printing Press was the most significant invention in human history—invented for one purpose only: To print the Bible so that it could be distributed to every man on earth.

I didn't know that the Bible was the best-selling book in human history— with more than five billion sold between 1815 and 1975; thirteen hundred translations of the Bible have been printed for global distribution in the languages of people in jungles, deserts, and mountaintops; more than fifty-nine million Bibles were distributed by the Gideons, last year alone.[161] From my balcony seat that morning this verse became part of my personal history. I had encountered, for the first time, the precious serendipity of the Faith-Time Continuum breaking into the mundane and familiar Space-Time Continuum.

"Be still and know that I am God!" I did not know that morning that this message came from David's Psalm 46. What did David mean when he wrote his song? What did God mean, telling me to, "Be still! To Know!" What does it really mean to "*know God*?" How could I ever be still like those adults in white shirts with the sweat dribbling down into their navels? Does *knowing* only come when we are *still*? All I knew for sure back then, was this: "I am not God!" I started wondering if there really is a God who has great expectations for us, and Whose very personal messages might actually be transmitted to me. He had just spoken to me, I was sure. Knowing Him had something to do with understanding what He was saying—even being able to answer Him, or ask Him questions.

At that point, as if there were someone on the other side of my solitary confinement cell speaking to me through the cinderblock, I started my Morse code tapping that day. Who was it on the other side of that wall tapping strange sayings for my consideration? What was he saying with that unclear voice? Was he really talking to me? Or to someone else? Was he a prisoner of war held captive against His will? Or was he a Friend with my best interests in mind? What could God possibly want with ***Myopic Me?*** Being still, quieting my breathing, I listened to hear what he might say beyond those eight words of direct instruction!

> "*Be still, and know that I am God*;
> I will be exalted among the nations
> I will be exalted in the earth."
> The Lord Almighty is with us;
> The God of Jacob is our fortress. Psalm 46:10-11

---

[161] *29 Good Bible Sales Statistics*. Brandon [Gaille].

In David's Psalms, God speaks, and then David speaks, responding to what God said. There is a giving, and a taking. There is a two way conversation. Frequently, David speaks to us, rather than God. It is as if David is saying, "This is important—this is God—listen to what He is saying." I would learn decades later that David was always talking about the *Omniscient God* who loves him as an adopted son. He is not the God of the neighborhood, nor is He sent to speak according to the guidelines of the Methodist Church.

He is not the God of the prison, or even the God of the American population. He is the God of Creation, Time, Entropy, spanning Alpha and Omega, and going far beyond every known boundary of humankind—the illimitable God! He is the preeminent God. In fact, I found out that He is, though David was. Verb tenses fail in His presence. He refers to Himself as the "Great I AM—YAHWEH." He is the God beyond time, Maker of Time, Outside of Time, Inside of Time, Forge of Time, Whose Son stopped the Calendar in its tracks on the day He was born: Every bit of time that went before His miraculous birth became "Before Christ"—the infamous BC. Every bit of time after He was born became Anno Domini—the famous AD.

He had visited our little threesome on the day we departed from Clemson, heading for Cades Cove in L. H. Buff's light blue VW Bug. We never mentioned Him once. We never prayed. I was excited and fearful, not knowing any thing about Him. Not knowing that He was with me on that very day, I had no idea that He was my fortress, the God of Jacob, exalted among the nations. We went in our own strength, without prayer, with no mention of Him that I recall, heading for that Genesis destination at 700 feet above sea level. Did L. H. pray over our trip? I will probably never know the answer to that. I know that we did not during the hardship or the good times.

From Cades Cove, we would head straight up the face of Mt. Guyot the next morning. We were not the first people to make this climb, for the path was well worn, rutted, rooted, and full of rocks and boulders along the way. We met to plan the difficult ascent that awaited us, which would eventually connect us to the Appalachian Trail. We would rise one rutted step at a time to the ridge of Mt. Guyot, the second highest peak in the Smokey Mountain chain. The traumatic and transforming nature of our trip confronted deep feelings and fears buried in me from years before. The fear of death, already lurked in my nightmares and waking moments, and I was not the only one on earth with this fear. But I was convinced that I was completely alone in this.

My uncle died six-weeks before I was born, when his ship was bombed in the Mediterranean Sea. The family wore a death shroud of tears and anguish when I arrived a month later. Death was on all sides, affecting everyone, enveloping the whole earth. The planning for *D-Day* at Normandy, on Omaha, and Utah beaches started on the day I was born. This eventual turning point in the war was executed when I was four months old, when the intricate and monumental plans produced the ultimate killing field. In twenty-four days, 425,000 soldiers on both sides were dead. An average of 18,000 per day died in this strategic battle during the fifth month of my life.[162] Death, death, death was everywhere. Death at home, and death far away, dominated everyone's mind, and the heavenly realm was full of it. The experience of death, and the talk of death enveloped me in my crib, permeating my DNA unawares.

Now, this tornado waited for me where Cades Cove and the Land of Oz intersected in the earthly and heavenly realms. It was no accident that this fear of death returned to haunt me. From Cades Cove, we would carry our packs and camping gear to a ridge 6,000 feet above that warm campground in Tennessee. This pleasant valley, where early settlers built their log cabins, provided no insight into what awaited us at the top. Today, I climb thirty sets of stairs daily for exercise. I do eighty push-ups and stretch, and I think this is a pretty good workout. A few conservative calculations reveal that Mt. Guyot's ridge is 600 "sets of stairs" high above the humid valley and Cades Cove Campground. The fatigue resulting from climbing twenty times as many stair steps on that first day of our climb helps me to put the challenge into proper focus. We climbed the equivalent of a 600-story building in one grueling day!

An innovator and problem preventer from the beginning, I chose to pull a rolling apparatus with my loaded pack strapped to it. This seemed easier to me than carrying the traditional pack on my bony back. My invention quickly presented a problem, as my planning did not anticipate the steepness of the climb and the extreme friction on my bare fingers. Ed Freeman, the industrial engineering professor and neighbor, had fabricated the cart for me using my rough design. We used cheap rebar I had found, to weld together this rolling cart that jumped in the air over every rock and root in the path. It slipped in mud, and bounded over tree roots all day long. My blisters opened where the rebar rested in my fingers. This cheese grater action produced open wounds fairly quickly as we proceeded upward into a driving rain that was not forecast for our location.

The fallacy of bringing this cart became a serious issue as this rain grew into a roaring downpour in the last half of the day. Reaching higher altitudes, our cold clothing started to chill us down. When we finally reached the ridge at the top of the mountain, it was completely dark. Soaked by the rain and exhausted from the demanding climb, we had nothing dry to sleep in that night. We faced failure on the first day, with no plan for surviving the night. Setting up our tent in silence—the way men do when they are going to die—we rolled out our sleeping bags, heavy with the cold water. I didn't look at their faces because I didn't want them to see mine.

The air temperature had dropped into the forties after the rain, and the still-falling rain felt colder than that. We were in big trouble, but no one spoke a word of it. L. H. just focused on the tasks at hand, driving tent pegs in mushy moss-covered ground. We tied the flaps to spruce trees and to rhododendron shrubs. I was afraid to listen closely to his tone of voice, fearing that I might hear his voice breaking.

[162] *D-Day.* History.

12.

EVERYTHING GOOD BEGINS IN DARKNESS.

Everything good in God begins in darkness. I would learn a decade later that Jesus died in complete darkness at 3:00 p.m. In that world-changing darkness, fear was put to death when He breathed His last. I wondered on this dark night if Mt. Guyot would become my death shroud. Jesus' dark night of the soul was no accident, for God planned the choreography before the foundations of the world were laid. It was not fun, that Board Meeting, when Father, Word, and Holy Spirit met to account for our flawed freedom. Flesh would mean feeling, and feeling would mean desire, and desire would mean seduction, and seduction would mean sin. And sin would mean Death.

Love required this remedy for those created in His own image. There was no other way to have a relationship with those who yield to their fleshly desires. Sinners would cover the whole earth, and a flood would come to set the stage for the final Solution: The blood of God's own Son precluded, preempted, prevented, made mutually exclusive, ruled out, obviated, the coexistence of Himself with evil. He kneeled down in the Garden of Gethsemane, but they lifted Him up on the Hill of Skulls on a Cross of wood.

The light of the sun was eclipsed by more than rain, as the earthquake caused the Roman guards to shudder with fear as the foundations of the world were shaken violently and the curtains of the Temple were torn in two. In darkness, His borrowed tomb was closed up with an enormous stone, until the light burst through the Roman seal so brightly that the guards never spoke of it. Jesus, and I, were moving according to the itinerary of God—with His Mission of all missions preceding my hike into the mountains. Though my dark night is not worthy of any comparison with His, something good did enter into my life. My dark night was a function of my sinful life, while His was a function of the Will of God. He chose to bless me, while I chose to live selfishly. But God did not hold that against me, and a strange light entered through my screen door to woo me on this spiritual journey of great significance.

This light exists to the present day, and this memorable struggle with wet matches in the pouring rain, is a metaphor for much of my life. The bright Coleman lantern could only illuminate the futility of our plans. The lamp shattered the black night with a strong message at the top of Mt. Guyot. Shocking images leaped out of darkness as if we were spelunkers in a deep cave. Images appeared for the first time, and our isolation from civilization became starkly evident. We were in the heart of darkness. Our light had been designed for campgrounds and big metal trash cans with carefully positioned tent-stakes next to a parked SUV.

Our wet bags and crumpling tent caused us to sink into the thick moss at the center of a land long forgotten. The light was essential for us to position the seven-foot mountain tent on the ferns and deep moss that oozed with rain. This site had never been marked on any map as a stopping place for man or wild animal. Thirty feet from the vaguely defined trail, the dark night consumed us. We were five miles away from the Appalachian Trail that runs from Georgia to Maine. We were off-map, unmarked, dropped down in deep moss and rainwater, as cold as a winter day.

I couldn't take my eyes off the twitching leaves dripping with chilling rain as our flashlight beam stopped short in the black face of the forest surrounding us. I felt suffocated by this unknown world beyond our feeble light. Though I was fourteen years old, I was feeling more like seventy-five. Exhausted, afraid, wet and cold, my coward took over in my mind while L. H. and Billy climbed into the water-locker of their adjacent sleeping bags. What were we doing? How could they be so uncommunicative? No one said a thing, as if this wet nightmare were planned — was it planned to make me a man? I don't like that, if I am being tested. I want my bed. I want my mom, or Pop, to come and take me home! The deep discouragement of the wet tent and sleeping bags deflated any remaining energy after the all-day climb to the top.

"Don't touch the tent unless you want a stream of water on you," L. H. finally spoke. I couldn't imagine being any wetter if a hose had been turned on inside my three-pound fiberfill bag. The bag likely weighed thirty pounds with all the water! The single-fly tent roof already drip-dripped, and no amount of touching could change the course of our human events. The occasional stream flowed through, and the additional water had no effect at all. We were so cold, and these droplets disappeared into the pool we lay in for the entire long night. I didn't even know the word "hypothermia," but "pneumonia," I knew all too well. My mother had made great emphasis of this word. She grew up in the days before antibiotics, and children died routinely from infections that penicillin would have healed.

All day, I had reached back to the curved handle of the cart I pulled, switching hands, dragging that rolling rebar up the vertical trail. My hands were numb, and my back was exhausted. My design had created new problems which a pack might have avoided. If I had anticipated this rough terrain, and vertical slope, I might have worn the traditional backpack, as L. H. and Billy had done. I feared the pack would topple my 117-pound body, propelling me down the hill. The combination of sleeping bag, dried food, clothes, and other gear felt very heavy when I tried on the pastor's pack during our planning session. Maybe I would have had blisters on my shoulders from the straps, but my brilliant invention produced several secondary problems for this initial day's climb. The trip had been envisioned as a relatively flat trail with an occasional rock or root to negotiate. L. H. had never used this access point to mount the Trail. On the map, it appeared to be a straight line to the top of the mountain.

That non-stop vertical climb to the ridge of the 6600-foot mountain wore out our young legs. The associate pastor's thorough planning failed to account for the steady rain, the cold temperatures, and the steep first-day climb into the mountains. His plans for a sunny day missed the mark; and now, we lay side-by-side in sixty pounds of wet Fiberfil—our three bodies quivered uncontrollably, like reluctant corpses awaiting the mortician. We hoped for sleep in Mother Nature's unsympathetic embrace. We lay like frozen hotdogs in a wet package in the refrigerator as that virgin forest ticked like a crazy clock in the falling rain. No one had ever visited this place—unless Albert Guyot had planted his transit here in 1859 when he mapped this mountain—his work was accurate to within fifteen feet of the actual 6621-foot altitude. Our climb missed by a mile because we had no good idea of what we faced tomorrow if we survived this night of deep darkness.[163]

This area was not a stopping point for families to spread out and cook their meal on a camp stove. Where we camped, there were no roads or toilets or inscriptions of man. This "temperate rain forest" belonged to God, and to the black bear that lost its way. Whereas everything in our daily world is paved by the progress of man, this ridge was in darkness through which only the owls can peer. Our mountain tent sagged with the weight of the rain, and I assumed I would die. I thought, "This is it! There is nothing I can do about it." The Cowardly Lion whimpered inside me, and I prayed fervently for God to save me.

I could not pray out loud, for I assumed that I alone understood what lay ahead. I still wanted to appear brave, though I was very frightened. The three of us had never prayed together! Some Christian threesome—but I would have been uncomfortable praying since I rarely prayed over anything. Prayer seemed a completely personal idea. I knew that God alone understood that the three of us were certainly going to die of exposure before this night ended. I wasn't concerned about L. H. and Billy at all because I knew the weak link in this chain was *Myopic Me!*

My mother trained me well for this cold journey. By age fourteen she had drilled me with never staying in wet clothing! Of course, she spoke of the health-hazard of wet clothes in hot summer weather—not this night, feeling more like winter than summer. I told the invisible God Whom I did not know, that I would serve him for the rest of my life if He would save me from this night on the mountain. The God I did not know, likely said, "Okay. But I will hold you to

---

[163] *Mt. Guyot*. Peakware.

that promise; you can count on it." He hooked His tractor beam to my tiny ship, and I was already on my way to better days in a few years. In a single night, God had become a semi-personal Person, though I had very little data for my profile picture of Him in my mind. He was big, I knew that. He was there when I called—the next day would prove that.

But I told no one about His faithfulness, or His Personhood. I still doubted the veracity of my own story. He had done His part according to His promise made to me—and I would learn much more about the promise I had made to Him, saying I would serve Him all the days of my life! That contract on Mt. Guyot now seemed silly, a child's fantasy. But He called it a deal made in the heavenly realm. It was an eternal contract in His mind, and I would live up to it according to His divine will and purpose for my life.

He is the God of the impossible, and I was doomed by something much more deadly than pneumonia or hypothermia. But He was not yet the God who showed me the Way, the Truth, and the Life. He was not yet the God who said, "Go this way. Be wary of that path! Love your neighbor and honor your parents! Believe in my Son Whom I have sent to save you!" My knowledge was thin as shear ice at Highlands' Mirror Lake in November. My faith was nothing more than a wisp of smoke in the Smokey Mountains. My conversation with Him was as sketchy as a contrail in a high-pressure weather front over Mt. Guyot.

My cry to him at age fourteen was authentic, classic life-raft plea from every story of the cast aways. This Person, this Father, Son, or Holy Spirit, remained a mystery visiting me from far beyond my reach or imagining. "How can a boy know the God of the Universe?" All those Sunday School sessions, and I knew nothing. I don't remember falling asleep in that cold tent on that early June night—That was my first invisible miracle? My eyes could not see His hand of compassion, or His power. Was that my water-into-wine surprise, when I fell asleep in cold water up to my ribs? I knew very little about the Light which comes in the morning after the long dark night of the soul.

The next morning, we rose early and started walking toward *Icewater Spring shelter*—a three-sided shelter on the edge of the mountain. We intentionally hiked to a place that was named after "ice water?" I wanted to visit a hot spring! I couldn't believe that I had survived the night. Our new route on the Appalachian Trail would take us five miles farther to this cold spring and three-sided shelter before we continued on to Clingmans Dome. Our overall destination was Fontana Dam on the North Carolina and Tennessee lines. This was a new route L. H. decided on after our difficulties became clear. On the way there, I found my courage, and would begin to hear the beating of a brand-new heart. *Icewater Spring shelter* turned out to be a memorable interlude in this formative journey.

As we trudged along this trail, we now enjoyed the sound of old rainwater squishing in our boots as the day started to warm with the appearance of the sun in the sky. This was no yellow brick road, but Fontana Dam might just as well have been the Emerald City where the foolish Wizard would show us how to get home. These sights and sounds in the mountains were truly coming at me from another world. While our clothes clung to us like coarse sandpaper, the light rose strong above the ridge. Our hope increased as the sun rose higher, with the ambient air temperature rapidly passing through the 60s into the 70s.

We watched the thermonuclear ball ascend above us as we trudged across Thunderhead, with its spectacular views of the Smokeys. The silence was deafening on that remote trail away from the things of man. The remoteness of our morning walk was other-worldly, knowing that we were cut off from every other human being in this beautiful solitude. The meaning of life leaped from silence into our faces as we stopped to stare at the glory of God.

Since the air was thinner, I got more winded as we struggled up the steeper grades that morning.

But God sent us amazing heat from 93,000,000 miles away. The perfectly positioned yellow orb had already heated our wet clothing. When we arrived at the three-sided shelter, we immediately spread our sleeping bags in the direct sun, placing them on the rocks and limbs and picnic tables. In minutes, we saw our laundry smoking like a blazing forest. Our saturated camping gear dried before our wide eyes in a stunning display of radiant energy. The *Icewater Spring shelter* looked like a city on fire! It was glorious. The clothes gave up gallons of cold rain into the heat of a sovereign sun. Everything had dried by the time the yellow sphere vanished into twilight.

We slept that night in wire-mesh hammocks. Three other hikers had arrived after us, including a nineteen-year-old girl from Stockholm Sweden. She arrived at the shelter late in the afternoon; and of course, I immediately fell in love with this brave older girl. My Swedish heartthrob was by herself on the lonely Appalachian Trail—how irresistible. This Dorothy was three years older than Oz's Judy Garland. I felt protective and predatory at the same time—maybe Freud was right.[164]

At age fourteen, I could see that her innocence had long departed. It seemed to be replaced with an implacable will to "do it her way." She had left her parents behind in Sweden with their perfect house and fractured marriage (I imagined). Was she running away? Did her family even know where she was going? Was she in school in America? Georgetown, Harvard, Duke, or the University of Virginia? Did my family even know where I was? This foreign version of Dorothy passed me on the Trail, and I was greatly affected by her self-reliance and aloof demeanor.

That evening, drama and excitement abounded for our little group of intimate strangers. As I returned from filling the canteens down a very steep path that terminated at the edge of a cliff, I nearly collided with the black bear running full speed down the trail toward me. For a moment, my mind considered all the bad outcomes that awaited me. This unexpected game of chicken, with this giant

---

[164] Webster. *Freud, Satan, Serpent.*

black adrenalized "chicken," left me sighing with relief when the bear blinked, abandoning the well-worn trail above me. She ran off into the unmarked forest.

The same bear returned moments later to the shelter when our neighbor's camp stove vented the powerful smell of chocolate into the mountain air. My black nemesis stood five feet behind me as she picked up the hot kettle of *Ovaltine* drink from the blue-flamed camp stove. Mama bear spilled it on her paw and on the ground before licking every drop from the hot aluminum container. When nothing remained, her teeth crushed the sides together, and she dropped the deformed object to the ground. She whirled and went back into the trees below the shelter.

Inside this classic Smokies unnatural adventure, I quickly forgot that God had rescued me from the hypothermia on Guyot the night before. At age fourteen, I was distracted by my strong attraction for the nineteen-year old Dorothy with a mission. Three years older than Dorothy in Oz, Solomon would have been impressed with her as well. The wise king wrote down his own exploits with numerous nineteen year olds in plain Hebrew for us to read. God was not impressed with all that he did, and He told him so. Solomon forgot about God as soon as he looked into these girls' faces. I too had forgotten about God, just as the Hebrew people forgot Him after Pharaoh was in their rear-view mirror.

The Israelites' forgetfulness about the slavery in Egypt occurred after Moses had vanished for forty days to the top of that Mt. Guyot—the famous Mt. Sinai of the *Ten Commandments* movie. Moses was in a big meeting with the Great I AM to receive the Law and the Covenant between God and the Israelites—a people set apart for His purposes. Moses and God reviewed the ancient history of the world from the Creation to the Flood and beyond, and God printed out two tablets of stone engraved with the Ten Commandments in two parts: Governing the relationship with Himself, and the relationship with our neighbor. He had set the Hebrews free from slavery when He sent ten plagues to shatter the demonic strongholds of Pharaoh's Nile Delta. Likely no place on earth had more false gods and idolatry than Egypt in that time, worshiping thousands of gods.[165] God sent Moses into the stronghold of evil in the ancient world.

Pharaoh's stubborn insistence that he was god, only yielded when his first-born son was taken during the Passover night. His son died when the angel of death came for him during the 10th and final plague. The angel passed over the Hebrew houses, painted with the blood of the lamb. There, at the base of Mt. Sinai, the Israelites sighed and moaned, while Moses eidetic memory [from the Holy Spirit, no doubt] remembered everything that God explained concerning the Ten Commandments: "You shall not make any image of anything in the earth to worship as a god. They were instructed to not worship anything that caught their eye in the created world—building their idols to the sun and moon, to the snakes and birds of the earth.

---

[165] Ezekiel 20:7.

They were instructed not to bear false witness against each other, and to honor their parents—they would gain a long life. They should not take the LORD's name in vain, making "Jesus," or "God," into a swear-word, a coward's addendum to every filthy sentence erupting from his profane tongue.

But God's graciousness toward the Hebrews became a distant memory when their estrogen and testosterone recombined in a night of revelry. Isn't it always the endocrine that wrecks our relationship with God? The tag team of Vision and Endocrine do us in when we least expect it. We are (ironically) blindsided by the lust of the eyes and the love of the worldly games of adultery. It is the heart and the mind which hurl us into darkness. The Orgy is the loveless, filthy, denouement of the flesh. While God instructed Moses about man's propensity for idolatry, the former slaves reverted back to slavery in that valley. They reverted back to the worship of the created things—in this case, the golden calf cast from their melted-down jewelry.[166]

Now, it seemed that I was ready to join that unholy family of the Hebrews in the Wilderness, forgetting my promise to God to serve Him for the rest of my life. I had not considered His deliverance since my clothes warmed up in the sunshine I felt on the trail over Thunderhead Mountain. My childhood cowardice had apparently not been sufficient to stop me on that mountain. Immediately, *Myopic Me!* forgot to thank God or praise Him for rescuing me—I became the one who never mentioned the embarrassing prayer composed in the midst of fear.

I was on a church trip, but I didn't say anything about my desperate prayer? I was with a church group, but I was embarrassed to mention that God had heard my prayer on Mt. Guyot. I ignored the real dread which overwhelmed me on top of that mountain! I concluded that the cowardly lion had overreacted to the cold like any mama's boy would. Instead of thanking God, I tried to hide my cowardly behavior. Instead of thanking God for extricating me from Pharaoh's grip, and the waters of the Red Sea, I felt silly for being so fearful. *Myopic Me!* pretended to be brave and resilient, instead of confessing cowardice and fear.

Now I shifted my attention to the making of a golden calf at *Icewater Spring* shelter. All the gold jewelry was being melted down into this idol in the image of this girl from Stockholm who slept on the screen mesh a few inches above my face the night before. There was nothing stopping our love but a sleeping bag mashed thin between us. The irony of this instant idolatry is too potent to ignore from Future Time. God saved the Israelites from dying in the mud pits in the most idolatrous land on earth, where thousands of gods were worshiped. Then the Israelites reverted to their idolatry as soon as Moses disappeared into the top of the mountain!

Their grunts and groans in the mud pits of Egypt were long forgotten, but their cries were still laced with Hebrew and Egyptian profanity. They didn't know any better. But now they directed their anger against Moses instead of Pharaoh's soldiers. "What were we so afraid of," they wondered? "We're free

---

[166] Exodus 32:2-3.

now. Let's enjoy our new freedom with a celebration! Let's celebrate with that long-postponed orgy we have been dreaming about." They returned to the idol-atry they learned during the several generations as slaves in Egypt for over four hundred years. They didn't know how to live in their new freedom because of the centuries of wrong living. They didn't know how to worship. They had worshiped false gods for so long, idolatry had become their comfort zone, their wheelhouse. When times were good, they craved the pleasures that were taken from them in captivity.

God had rescued them from dying in the cold rain under the hot whips, and they immediately returned, with me, to my fourteen-year-old idolatry—the Stockholm Syndrome. God eventually showed me this pattern in my life. But thankful to be alive, I went on with my purpose-free existence, as if nothing had happened! Meanwhile, God records every conversation and every prayer. He heard me when I said, "Oh, God! Help me!" He is the elephant of heaven, never forgetting any little thing we say to Him. He knows our needs before we even ask Him, and these trivial utterances are important to Him. He forgets our sins when we repent, but He remembers His promises made to us. If God can stop the sun in the sky when a man prays, then he is able to stop me from worshiping the created things. When Joshua prayed during the battle, the sun stood still until the battle was won. God is the Creator of these created things.

> So the sun stood still and the moon stayed in place until the nation of Israel had defeated its enemies. Is this event not recorded in [The Book of Jashar]? The sun stayed in the middle of the sky, and it did not set as on a normal day.
> Joshua 10:13

Moses spoke to God on the mountain. The Israelites waited in the valley below. They had no face-to-face relationship with God as Moses did. The number One barrier to this intimacy is Sin: God cannot look on sin, nor can sin touch Him, for He is Holy. Until we are cleansed, we cannot draw near to him. On Mt. Guyot, I was dirty with sin, and I was committed to the messages that were coming through my eyes. I did know that I was wrong to think of Sigrid, Lova, Luna, or whatever her name was, in that intimate way.

God does not forget any verbal contract we make with Him—any pledge of allegiance is recorded in the heavenly realm. He is serious, and faithful to everything He promises us, not changing in His constancy of purpose. Our unfaithfulness and doubt does not dissuade Him from pursuing us in spite of our fits of rebellion and flights of foolishness. He calls us to live in such a way that we don't bring sorrow to the Holy Spirit. Everything becomes relationship, and this relationship is only possible through the Cross, and through Jesus' blood shed to cleanse the one who believes in Him. Fortunately, my salvation did not depend upon my knowledge at that time, but in His promises. He would save me, and He would show me, and He would send Christ's Spirit to live inside of me.

> And do not bring sorrow to God's Holy Spirit by the way
> you live. Remember, he has identified you as his own, guar-
> anteeing that you will be saved on the day of redemption.
> Ephesians 4:30

That night as we drifted off to sleep in the three-sided shelter, the Swedish girl slept silently above me. She slept in the deep exhaustion of her isolation from family and home, sharing her dreams with strangers in a foreign land. Sleeping beneath her on that concrete floor in my sleeping bag I imagined that I could feel her heat through the wire and sleeping bag. This myopic reverie ended instantly when the black bears tore at the tree where we had slung our packs from a limb twenty feet up. Bears must really like dehydrated food, because they ripped the bark from that tree. Their noisy claws represented God's sovereign power in my life which had the power to destroy me in an instant. His sovereign protection shortly became clear when those frustrated animals wandered into our three-sided bedroom. God was speaking into my life, and I was being forced to listen to His good counsel. Light was breaching my ignorant and foolish heart.

His redirection of my attention seemed vague indeed to me at the time, but He effectively distracted me from thoughts and actions by His wonderful choreography—queue the bears! I discovered these interventions everywhere, as I peered back into the innards of the faith-time manifold. His power appeared again and again to encourage or redirect my choices. Distracted by appetites and idols, He sent the bear inside our shelter—LOL! The new idol from Sweden flew out of my mind as these dark monolithic figures stumbled between our log hammocks looking for food in our bags of clothing. The hulking forms, silhouetted against the night sky, brushed against us in our sleeping bags like drunk roommates looking for their beds after a raucous night out. God cooled my jets and the flames receded above me as she slept through it all in her bag.

My fantasies from foreign Sweden and Solomon's Palace reminded me that I was sleeping at *Icewater Spring shelter* on the edge of a cliff in the Smokey Mountains with bears rummaging all around me. "Lead us not into temptation! But deliver us from evil." As I witnessed the poise and grit of this girl, like Dorothy in Oz and Alice in Wonderland, I knew immediately that the cowardly lion in my mirror was short a medal for valor—before God could lead me into the Faith-Time Continuum of my personal history, this cowardice would have to yield to courage.

The next day, it happened! I got my "badge of valor." L. H. decided that I would be heroic that very day. I would drive the VW Bug to Fontana Dam! This was a change of plans, partly to accommodate my equipment problems. This drive, by myself, would reposition LH's VW Bug at the new terminus for our hike. There is a missing piece in this puzzle from ancient memory which I cannot explain in this paragraph. I don't know how the car got to that parking lot. But I know that at age fourteen, I had extremely limited driving experience alone on any road. Though it was legal to drive in South Carolina at age fourteen with a drivers license, my parents were always beside me to assess my performance. I had driven a couple of times on long trips with them in the car—and these were harrowing adventures, with serious mishaps along the route to Decatur, on the Southeastern edge of Atlanta.

Now, I would pilot the VW alone, driving to a rendezvous point that was a little dot on a roadmap. From Clingmans Dome to Fontana Dam, I would follow a circuitous looping highway for more than seventy miles. It would take me two hours to make the trip, averaging about thirty-five miles per hour. I would rendezvous with my hiking companions in a destination I had never heard of before that plan appeared. I can remember my driver's license stats from that first SC license. I was five-foot, five-inches tall and weighed one-hundred seventeen pounds.

Despite my diminutive statistics, the cowardly lion had been dispatched on the switchback turns along U. S. 129 and 441 the entire way. This gravelly-surfaced two-lane road led me directly to the mysterious dam with its 480-foot deep lake, a flood that filled 10,000 acres along the valleys and low-lands of western North Carolina. Built before I was born, it stood the fourth tallest dam in the world at the time of its construction.[167]

Off to see the Wizard, I was driving to a place I had never seen. I would find an unknown parking lot on this micro-faith journey. Facing my fears, and serving the larger mission, I was excited and full of joy as I headed out on the loud orange-peel paving of the switch-back curves. The highway tracked along the valley until it arrived at the reservoir. It was God's sense of humor to throw me back into the game after I had fumbled my courage on that ridge in a cold puddle of rain. Guyot had ushered me into a whole new world. I had climbed the Swiss explorer's peak before arriving at *Icewater Spring shelter* where the girl from Sweden slept so close I could hear her breathing.

I had stayed very still, heart thumping, when the black bears rifled through my underwear. Now, I would receive this badge of courage at Fontana Dam, where I would return the keys to the associate minister—just like a professional driver. My new, and still unknown God, had been there all along. I had no idea what His goal for me would be. This seems absurd, from the vantage point of the present day, but I had not heard Jesus' unvarnished instructions on the day I pulled the keys from the ignition in that parking lot in North Carolina:

---

[167] *Fontana Dam.* Wikipedia.

> *"You will be My witnesses in Jerusalem, Judea, Samaria, and*
> *to the uttermost corners of the earth." Acts 1:8*

For me, this would come in Smyrna, Atlanta, and Winston Salem, before I landed in the near-desert of West Texas, and in the spiritual desert of North Attleboro Massachusetts. In that symbolic desert where the trees are green, and the rain falls constantly, I would witness the spiritual rebirth of that resistant soil. From Providence to Boston, the tiny spiritual flowers would push up through the rocky land that had become the most resistant to the Gospel message of any cities in America. In the dead land near Plymouth and Cape Cod where the Pilgrims had landed, I would see His amazing Grace come to bloom.

> O Lord, our Lord, your majestic name fills the earth!
> Your glory is higher than the heavens.
> You have taught children and infants
> to tell of your strength,
> silencing your enemies
> and all who oppose you. Psalm 8:1-2

It was still Me and God—remote acquaintances at best. I could not imagine at that time that God would fabricate a new creature from the broken stuff of my life. He chose me, even though I had not really chosen Him. I still had the hope of being "good," firmly in mind since this seemed to be the goal of "going to church." Never once did anyone say that I would be a part of the Church when I believed. "Do good; be good; get better; act right; don't get into trouble; be strong; stay away from evil." These mottos rang in my ears. And I gave myself an F-grade at that time.

Being good is not what God wanted, but I did not know then that He alone is good. God is good, and He alone could produce His goodness in me. When it happens, He is to blame for my goodness. He is not to blame for my failures to be good. Therefore, I still marvel that He cares about my brokenness, to speak to me about His love and Grace.

> When I look at the night sky and see the work of your fingers—
> the moon and the stars you set in place—
> what are mere mortals that you should think about them,
> human beings that you should care for them? Psalm 8:3-4

When God speaks, things happen. Faith happens. When He speaks, things change. When He speaks, worlds are created, and dark realms are destroyed. But I could not grasp this on Mt. Guyot. I learned that God is very patient as we come to embrace and trust His instructions. Jesus Christ really is the Son of God! He really is the God Who speaks now. He speaks into the vacuum of modern life with words that are living and active, bringing hope! He speaks with the ultimate authority, and He knows the end of things. When He spoke to Satan in the wilderness, He rebuked the liar who comes to steal, kill, and destroy.[168] He set the importance of God's Words for the heavens and the earth to comprehend.

"No!" The Scriptures say, 'People do not live by bread alone, but by every word that comes from the mouth of God.'"[169] Lucifer, the highest Angel in heaven, had become Satan, when he rebelled against God. The reason Satan rebelled had to do with worship. This craving becomes the raison d'être of thousands, or even millions of people who will sell their souls for this worship. Jesus answered Satan very simply, quoting from Deuteronomy 6. He told Satan that He would worship no other god before God, His Father.

It is an old story, and only Jesus Christ weathered this storm in the desert, while all the rest of us have failed to resist Satan's offers of pleasure and fame. God's standard is 100, not 99; for failure to keep one part of the law is failure to keep the entire law. This failure is punishable by death. God's justice cannot be violated. Failure to keep the law of adultery or murder or false witness sets into motion much destruction in the world—Pandora's Box is opened right where we stand, arms slack by our sides, and many are swallowed up by the Calf's golden glow.

---

[168] John 10:10.

[169] Matthew 4:4.

13.

TV Dinners.

I sat watching Dorothy in our uncomfortable dining room on that 13-inch black and white TV screen. The formal chairs in that room were pushed tightly under the drop-leafed mahogany table used for special family meals. The kitchen chairs were slid into the room where we learned to eat the delicious *Swanson*-brand "TV-dinners" in the aluminum plates. A separate place for the meat, the vegetables, and the dessert made this treat more inviting. [170]

This was pre-microwave, so the dinners were placed in the oven for a half-hour to heat the frozen food. Those tiny partitions in the foil plate separated the deep sugary delight which kept the young ones calling for more TV dinners. This was the beginning of mass-produced sugar treats—beyond the heavenly lemon and chocolate meringue pies at every birthday in my early years. This happened once or twice per year! Sugar wouldn't find widespread use in America in young people until the production of high-fructose corn syrup in the late-1970s, finding its way into billions and billions of soft-drinks.

Our favorite show would appear on schedule per the TV-Guide or news-paper listing, and our "educated family" arrived to sit bolt-upright watching *Lawrence Welk and the Lovely Lennon Sisters, Gun Smoke, The Lone Ranger,* and the *Ed Sullivan Show. The Price is Right* tapped into our brand new materialism birthed by the vast manufacturing potential of the post-war world. No long making guns and bombs, tanks and airplanes, battleships and aircraft carriers, the horsepower of industry shifted fairly quickly to the production of consumer goods, using TV ads to imprint household brandnames in a few weeks of watching a TV serial. Never has TV advertising been more effective, unless the first *Super Bowl* eclipsed that branding performance.

Our mealtime rituals ignored the best-laid plans of Pop's architect, hired in 1941 to design his new fieldstone home. When his blueprints had dried, there was zero potential for this literary family to end up in the Dining Room watching television three hours per night on a 13-inch black and white screen with aluminum foil and rabbit-ears to capture the VHF signal sent through the air from Greenville. A special room for TV viewing did not exist in homes built in this era, for the TV didn't become widespread until the early 1950s. Yet here we were

---

[170] *TV dinner*. Wikipedia.

(sadly, I suppose), watching our tiny TV screen in this formal room. It would be a few years before the *Wizard of Oz* had us glued every Sunday night to our TV screen. Disney harvested many episodes from the original two-hour movie.

Alka-Seltzer discovered a vast audience for "plop-plop, fizz-fizz, oh what a relief it is." We must have had a lot of indigestion from woofing down those TV dinners. *Wizard of Oz* eventually arrived at the Clemson Theater in full Technicolor, and we discovered the multicultural, multi-colorful world beyond the grey hues of Kansas. We would not really see this fantastical world until the next century arrived. When globe-trotting corporations sent their employees to Thailand, Malaysia, India, Japan, and China, the monkeys earned their wings again, and the Wicked Witches appeared in every new scene.

Every scene in Oz is filled with spiritual skirmishes out of the bigger war. The Woodsman is dismembered, being transformed into a heartless Tin Man. The curse of the Wicked Witch takes away his humanity and fuses his body. The Wizard is spinning his foolish lies in the Emerald City, and the Lion is no longer pointing his pads and claws with courage and confidence. He too is under the influence of the witches spell.

The Scarecrow is finally set on fire by the Wicked Witch. Dorothy is drugged in the field full of opium flowers. When the Wizard dispatches Dorothy on a mission, she is chartered with killing the Wicked Witch of the West. Nothing else is more important than this mission, except for Dorothy's desire to get Home. With her three new cohorts, the battle against evil becomes meticulous. They share the common cause beyond **Myopic Me!** Each one of them is redeemed from a fractured reality filled with the fragile china of vanity. Each one is looking for a new chance to live above the evil curse coming from the heavenly realm.

Each one has a deeper purpose in Oz and beyond. Each one receives their unique heart's desire, while accomplishing what no one has succeeded in doing before in the splendid landscapes of Oz. All the happiness is real, and always under the dread of the Witch's next appearance. Isn't it interesting to see that their mission for others results in their own healing, giving their lives meaning? When they drive out the evil from the land of Oz, they discover the goodness permeating their own lives.

Each one forgoes impotence, eschewing self-gratification, but gaining the deeply desirable new creation from the broken stuff of their former lives. Unity comes to Oz through courage and self-sacrifice. Unity is impossible until the evil empire is torn down in Oz. Excitement and joy arrive with the obliteration of the Wicked Witch, and a new benevolence envelopes the Land of Oz—even the Emerald City finds a new identity where every sooth-sayer has been unmasked.

The city is changed when evil is baptized by this new courage and self-lessness. A new collaborative kingdom rises from the fabled and counterfeit joy in the Emerald City. Only when the city is released from bondage can they truly celebrate. These characters understand their great limitations now, even though they have been woven with a new fabric beyond captivity. The love and service of neighbor, friend, and family unfolds as Dorothy models these unknown principles.

On the macro level, these battles are always fought between good and evil depicted through the pens of Baum and Carroll—but microscopically the battle is between narcissism and the greater good. Understanding pushes something new up through the old asphalt of *Myopic Me!* Good, leverages the Wind of God, Who blows away the darkness of our fragile fantasies. The wonderful children's characters were designed with a child in mind, decoded in a book and movies with many memorable images.

Children and adults have found hope of healing as they traveled along this Golden Way, seeing the trouble with conformity in the Rabbit Hole beneath the streets of London. Meaningless and empty lives are reborn, becoming new creatures in the *Land of Oz* and beyond. They are not simply reconstituted Scarecrows or Lions, but they become new creations through the externally wrought powers which arrive in the *Land of Oz*.

Together these vivid portrayals represent us, for Dorothy is brave and kind, while the Tin Man has fallen down by the road. The witch is heartless and cruel, knocking him on his back. The Tin Man becomes the turtle with his quiet legs waiting for the hawk to come and tear his flesh away, one piece at a time. The Cowardly Lion is afraid to try again, for he has been knocked down so many times. His heart is broken by failure. His will is diminished from rejection.

He is cowering in life, trying to avoid the bully, fending off the vulture of death. The Scarecrow is paralyzed in his own field, for he has no mind to process the coming fires. He is belittled and derided, and his aspirations are rejected by naysayers and narrow-minded critics. Taken together with Dorothy, our new friends bring to life a parable of our own frustrations and deepest fears—the adventures of *Myopic Me!* unfurling from of an irrepressible hubris. Together, these new creations give us hope for a happy tomorrow. But we still don't see the scope of it.

When Jesus arrived in a stable in Bethlehem, His parents were very poor. He was visited by three kings who worshiped him at 2-years of age, but they warned His parents to flee, for Herod wanted to kill the King. Herod feared the prophecy concerning Jesus' birth. He feared this King of kings who would be from the root of Jesse, David's father. He would be first-born to a virgin mother. Herod's trap had been set with no chance of this baby escaping from his noose.

Escaping, by the Spirit of God, Jesus grew up as a refugee in a foreign land waiting for a chance to go home. His home was neither Bethlehem, Nazareth, or even Jerusalem. He would go home to be with the Father in heaven. He had learned to work as a laborer, carpenter, and stone mason when His family finally thought it safe to move to Nazareth. Joseph and Mary hid their Son there from Herod's offspring while Jesus learned to sweat and labor for others. He became a man who knew suffering, pain, and even temptation—but He never sinned. He learned the trade of a stone mason and carpenter, toiling long hours every day but the Sabbath. Six days, He worked, as His Father had done, but on the Seventh Day, He rested from His labors.

When His family took Him each year to Jerusalem for the Passover Celebration, the family was still very poor, only able to afford a dove for their sacrifice. Though He was the Lamb of God, they could not afford to buy a lamb for the forgiveness of their sins. After all, their Son would soon become the final Sacrifice. He would become the Lamb of the New Covenant through His own blood—the better Passover Lamb, Who would die once for all men, taking the sins of every man upon Himself.

Becoming shame, He would take the shame of everyone who is ashamed. Being mocked, He would bear the humiliation of everyone who has been mocked or bullied. For all who have been laughed at, He endured the laughter of self-righteous men who demanded He prove that He was the Christ. He had already faced that temptation in the wilderness with Satan, and He knew full well His identity as the Lamb of God and King of kings. He was wounded for everyone who has suffered a wound in this life; He became Sin, so that us sinners could put His righteousness over our shame and futility. For the addict, He broke the power of bondage which hovered over many in that crowd outside the walls of Jerusalem.

After He rose from the dead, He made Himself known to 500 disciples, teaching them Who He is. He gave them final instructions, promising the power of God before they entered the den of wolves. He promised to send the Comforter Who would administer supernatural gifts and power to anyone who calls on the name of Jesus. He sent the power from on-high, Who is the Spirit of Christ, bringing glory to the Lamb, and convicting the whole world of Sin, Righteousness, and Judgment.

The Ruby Slippers represent the redemptive power which comes from the Faith-Time Continuum—the Comforter, the invisible Wind comes into our lives. Baum's ingenious literary device imbues Dorothy's feet with limitless power. Without the Ruby Slippers, she could not experience common courage and supernatural transcendence—with these slippers she can violate Einstein's speed limit and every restriction of the space-time continuum, whose cold parameters are limited to the dimensions of x, y, z, and time. With the Ruby Slippers, she can operate in the full freedom of the *Faith-Time Continuum*. She can function in the uniting bond of hope that now opens the door for love to travel unhindered. Fear is disarmed as a dreadful thief, and love is released where evil has been vanquished. The enshrouding impotence and shortsightedness of ***Myopic Me!*** subsides, when Love appears through inexplicable favor.

Judy Garland's life seemed to lack that same favor as she discovered the inexhaustible cry of "What have you done for me lately?" While her youth seemed blessed, her latter days inherited the curse. God's love of our souls trumps our love of this world. Did you know that tourists visit the Ruby Slippers more than any other artifact on display in the Smithsonian Museum in Washington DC?

You may also be unaware that someone paid $4.6 million for Dorothy's test dress and a pair of those ruby slippers used on the movie set?[171]

The power of those slippers seems forever to invoke the *good magic* [oxymoron]; but the magic derives its power from the deep yearning within the human heart. The hunger for eternity connects each one of us to the faith-time manifold of God's salvation. Why should I use this scientific analogy for such a fundamentally simple connection to God? The reason is found in the meaning of the word, "Materialistic." Much of Science today claims to have no affinity for God. Scientists refuse to permit a "divine foot in the door"[172] of their endeavors and deliberations. They refuse to base their thinking on the idea of an Intelligent Designer, a Creator God.[173] But our deep yearning for Home opens us up to connect to His marvelous gifts. This yearning inside each one of us transcends every mythical hope stored in the sugary libraries of Man.

This yearning is woven into our vague aspirations—transcending every literary description of heaven or hell. These aspirations for eternal fruit derive from the mercy of the God Who held nothing back from us. His love is never-ending. His yearning for a relationship with us is clearly etched in Jesus' eyes from the Cross. He never stops seeking to save us from sin and death, though He understands not one of us is good. As vaguely as this may be preached in our hearts, the Spirit of God is never silent. He is speaking through the membrane with a still, small voice from a mile and a half below the surface of the world, where I have heard His tiny neutrinos bark their answers to me.

"Be still, and know that I am God.
I will be honored by every nation.
I will be honored throughout the world." Psalm 46:10

While the noise of the world roars in our ears, the whisper of God is calling us into the life he always intended for us. Before the beginning of the world, God has been with us. His Spirit has been seeking to correct our flight path into the Way, Truth, and Life. While we crave the bad news, barely able to listen when good news is presented in the News or the conversation with a friend or neighbor or coworker. We are embarrassed and bored with good news. God's Good News is drowned out by the roar of the crowd and the great intentionality of the social gurus who know us better than we know ourselves. Yet, He knows us before we are formed in our mother's wombs.

---

[171] *Dorothy's Ruby Slippers*. The National Museum.

[172] Berlinski. *The Devil's Delusion*.

[173] Meyers. *Darwin's Doubt*.

"O Lord, you have examined my heart
and know everything about me.
You know when I sit down or stand up.
You know my thoughts even when I'm far away.
You see me when I travel
and when I rest at home.
You know everything I do.
You know what I am going to say
even before I say it, Lord.
You go before me and follow me.
You place your hand of blessing on my head.
Such knowledge is too wonderful for me,
too great for me to understand!" Psalm 139:1-6

14.

BABYSITTING
TRIANGULATION.

As young children, we had played the naked game in our basement, standing there to stare uncomfortably at each other. I don't remember how many were present for this baptism in shadows, but I do remember we said little about the codicils or the missing items. We stored away the information in a room reserved for non sequiturs and bewildering memories, a room marked "forbidden," where we would later file the Health instruction from the fourth grade, warning us to walk on the left side of the road facing oncoming traffic. Adults thought these things were important, but we could not grasp why we had to know such irrelevant things.

There was nothing sexual about our embarrassing game, but it was clearly forbidden. It felt forbidden. Do you know what I mean? This event had been transacted in hiding, in secret, without authorization from the authorities who loved us and watched over us. This was sneaky, putting ourselves at risk. This impromptu gathering occurred without God's permission, and instinctively I knew it was forbidden—in my conscience. My prayers at night were simple children's bedtime prayers, recited in rote—I was fearful of the meaning every time I prayed it: "Now I lay me down to sleep, I pray the Lord my soul to keep, If I should die before I wake, I pray the Lord my soul to take." God could kill me, destroy my soul or preserve it. I did not learn about God's unfailing love from that prayer: "Our Father, Who is in heaven, hallowed is Your name!"

So we had put our clothes back on and said not a word about it to anyone. Into our private realms of puzzled embarrassment we fled. But we never forgot what happened that day, and it left me feeling queasy, as if it would come back to haunt me later. Would it be shouted from the housetops, bringing great shame over my life? Who would tell? I certainly never would. There was no projectile vomiting afterward, and no one hid from their parent's glances, I guessed at the time. As far as I knew, they told their parents as soon as they got home. But more than these concerns, I pondered the incongruities. These adaptations of the anatomy of boys and girls would surely have future implications, though I could not comprehend the implications during my adolescent years. Without testosterone, it was very difficult to imagine the meaning of these observations.

Personal identity was a binary matter for all of us back then. There were boys, and there were girls. We didn't know then that identity is founded in the invisible world of the DNA and chromosomes, the environment, and the inheritance from grandfathers. Our personal identity remained an alien concept, drowned out by the presence of loud and aggressive older boys, and made moot by the exemplary performance of smart and obedient girls. There were dresses for sure, and there were trousers and jeans everywhere. We all had two parents in those days, and we ate supper together every night. Each one of us kids would face discipline if we were rude or rebellious. For the most part, we took our parents' instructions very seriously. I understood that I could never share secret knowledge—knowing there would be consequences in the earth and in the heavens if we did such a thing.

Now we were older, and I had been entrusted with this sacred responsibility. One of those girls from the basement had become my charge on this first and only babysitting eve where I would be trusted with a precious girl who was nearly my age. Since there is one or two years delay for a boy's physical changes, we were closer to the same stage of development than our birthdays would indicate. Initiative was one of those things she possessed which I had not yet discovered. She taught me a game, and for an hour before her bed time, we divided the room into halves. "Is it in this half, or in that half of the room?" she asked me. The room shrank, and my interest increased with every reduction of the artifacts remaining.

Finally, we arrived at that same discrepancy from the basement years before. For a while I imagined that I was the only one who could possibly know the identity of the artifact, but when she guessed that same edited region, I realized my naiveté, choosing such a destination for our game. She knew! How could she know my secret, long forgotten? It seemed embarrassing for me to focus on our ancient shared secret. Of course, our real understanding of the significance had barely advanced during the five years in between. Maybe testosterone and estrogen had intervened to make this unseemly quest more intriguing?

She immediately announced that it was time for her to go to bed when the game ended, and she vanished at a very early hour. I started to wonder what I should do in these circumstances—me not feeling like a babysitter any longer. What are the protocols at her bedtime? Do I just sit here until the parents come home? Do I tuck her in? None of those made sense. Since I had received no instruction, I decided to check the lights in the hall upstairs, to make sure she had gone to bed. The ramifications of this decision were already written into my future with invisible ink which I could not erase.

At fourteen, I was babysitting this twelve-year-old girl according to the generous choreography of parents. This was the night I realized "Good" had nothing to do with *Myopic Me!* The vague pretense of universal goodness became the bug on my windshield, and God already knew the full extent of my depravity. I had missed the first class when God explained that all of us run to evil ["Their feet run to do evil, and they rush to commit murder. They think only about

135

sinning. Misery and destruction always follow them"].[174] He was surely talking about *Myopic Me!* But He was undaunted by my heroin rush into endocrine. Though He did not approve of my deeds that evening, He never condemned me, or pushed me away. While I listened to Satan whispering in my mind, I thought I heard the Serpent say, "Did God really tell you surely not to go and check on her?"[175]

Knowing nothing about the layout of the house, I headed partway up the unfamiliar stairs to check for lights in the rooms above. Looking up and to my right, she was standing straight as a statue. The Greek-sculpture-of-a-girl decorated the blank space above me. I stopped and held my breath. She looked older than twelve as she stood there in the tub. The water dripped from her brown skin into the open drain, and I froze as I had in the farmhouse in *War of the Worlds*. This time, it was not fight or flight. I held the banister tightly with a sweating grip as my eyes took in her full-scale canvas still wet with oily ochre hues dripping down into the titanium dioxide tub. Picasso had painted her there before his Cubist period warped her body into fractals flying in all directions. She was absolutely still, and every brushstroke was true to life. She held her breath so the oils could dry on the tightly stretched canvas.

Then I heard the water rumbling through the floor joists and wall studs directly below the tub above me. This was an actual girl! An endocrine tsunami took me by surprise at 500 miles per hour, sweeping over me as I looked too long into this unexpected scene. How long did I stand there? I had to withdraw, or "I would surely die."[176] I could see the white flesh bursting through the red skin of the Apple as I swallowed its juices, the same juices painting her with curving rivulets as she stood like a lamb before the shearer.

She stared into a distant country, into faraway mountains, like the girls astride the high meadow in Austria singing the songs not yet written for *The Sound of Music*. Verse by familiar verse those songs wound down to the final verse of *Edelweiss*. One by one, as the music faded, they slid away into Switzerland. Their stealthy departure barely avoided the Nazi nightmare filling the vacuum left behind. The demons would hang their bright red flags on every pole, and the hypnotic symbology of the hooked crosses would dance above the anti-Semitic rising of the Aryan race. The hideous motives would pull everything but the kitchen sink into their Capitol.

I knew little about demons at age fourteen, and that World War was now over; but I couldn't take my eyes off this girl standing astride the perfect ridges of her youth. She had one foot in Austria, while another probed the mountains of Switzerland. The river ran between her legs, while the effluent voiced its

---

[174] Isaiah 59:7.

[175] Genesis 3:1

[176] Genesis 3:3.

complex harmonies in the cast iron pipes. The hot drain gurgled with sucking sounds, shouting commands into the empty house. The 1940s-era pipes amplified the silence vibrating in the lowest floors of my youth. A coward no more, I had become a silent interloper standing at the boundary of a world from which I would not soon escape.

Streaks slithered around her as my testosterone rushed to document the sensory landscape. I could hear the bursting Apple's echo inside of **Myopic Me!** Affection combined with an unknown electric communion, and the Trees at the Center of the Garden quivered as the two of us plumbed a new hormonal bonding. Freud, the Pied Piper of Freiburg,[177] had a proper name to describe my furtive glances into Bathsheba's rooftop bath. Though I don't remember how my feet found the bottom five steps East of Eden, I knew I had to return to a time before the Clock started the final Countdown. The fear of death leaped into my eyes; and Sin, the lame duck president, flapped its filthy wings in the shuddering valves of my heart. I could feel the Cherubim's flaming sword flashing behind me as I departed the stairs into the arid desert of my life.

This baptism in shadows left me weak and full of worry. Full of shame, my anxious heart fluttered in horror, standing on the broken boundaries of an unknown slavery which I had never imagined. Nothing was more debilitating than this hiding. No sound was louder than this silence. Was I the only one who ever plucked the fruit from the low-hanging limb? I didn't know the answer, but it seemed that my secret would have to follow me to my grave. "I can never tell anyone. But what if everybody already knows?" She was burned into my mind now, like a naked doll in a glass box on my bookshelf. Everyone would see her there and know what I had done.

From that moment, joy vanished, and there was no escaping those stairs going up and down between heaven and earth. I didn't know then that it would take one final baptism to eliminate the power of the wicked Witch who so craftily counseled me pursuant to a vain and worthless crown. I use this legalese because Satan used legalese to constrain his new prisoner. He demanded the fulfillment of every accidental or intentional contract signed on the fifth-step of my brokenness. Waving his contract in my face, he insisted that it was too late for me. He argued forcefully that I would be found wanting in any court of justice, whether in heaven or in the earth. He was always correct in what he told me, forcefully discounting God's Redemption entirely. He persuaded me to discount it as well. "Too late for you, dirty one! You will never erase this night from your unseemly record."

I had swiftly become the churchianity version of what Paul calls, "God's holy people who are faithful followers of Christ Jesus."[178] I was the counterfeit—the imposter. I went to church and Sunday school weekly, but I had no

---

[177] *Sigmund Freud.* Wikipedia.

[178] Ephesians 1:1

relationship with God's Son. I knew about Him, but I had no experience with Him. I locked my door that night, and I put on a fresh crop of fig leaves—I was naked and afraid in my bed. And God saw that I "lived in sin, just like the rest of the world, obeying the devil—the commander of the powers in the unseen world. He is the spirit at work in the hearts of those who refuse to obey God."[179] Alienation had become my new reality.

Refusing to obey God, I had stepped off the pier into darkness on that night when the lower limb struck me in the face in the Garden. I found myself alone with a woman, with a girl, and the Tree of the Knowledge of Good and Evil found me wanting. The proximity of body heat, scent, and visual messaging invoked a sub-natural affinity with the "forbidden." I would discover that time festers in the fresh wound of the soul. When the seeds from the core of this Apple were sown in hiding, a powerful stronghold resulted. This soul-tie persisted throughout much of my youth in our college town. This innocent place no longer felt safe for me. Dread was not gone, but grew into a multi-winged monster that flapped its wings over my teen years.

During this same timeframe, *Farmer's Week*, of all things, provided a new perspective. I would gain a new understanding of the universal problem arising during puberty. My eyes were opened wider to understand the dangers and the emotional traumas which can come during this fragile sexual season. *Farmer's Week* came each summer in this place called Clemson College, where nothing really happened by accident. Clemson, the town, gained its primary population in support of the college. As a young man, my father had bounced from the tobacco belt of coastal Carolina, to Newberry College, before getting a Masters degree from the University of Virginia. From Charlottesville he moved to Harlem and Columbia University. He became a professor at Clemson just before the dark days of the Great Depression.

He put down roots in northwestern South Carolina where the Blue Ridge Mountains can be seen in the distance on a clear day. The college town was the vision of Thomas Green Clemson,[180] son-in-law to United States Senator, and Vice President, John C. Calhoun.[181] Thomas Clemson had studied in Paris, gaining degrees from several universities, including the *Sorbonne*. Clemson College was founded as a *Mechanical and Agricultural* school in 1889.

In the late 1940s and early 1950s, the state-funded mission mandated a commensurate commitment to the farm-based economy of the entire state. *Farmer's Week* was the event each summer that publicly encouraged this mission, while the various schools within the college privately advanced this mission through research and development. Visitors, including farming families, filled the college

---

[179] Ephesians 2:2

[180] *Thomas Green Clemson*. Wikipedia.

[181] *John C. Calhoun*. United States Senate.

barracks during this popular week each summer. They arrived with duffel bags and electric fans to place in every corner of their hot barracks rooms.

The monumental display of farm machinery outside of the main event tent was exciting for local boys, as well as the actual farmers. The single enormous tent, with its heavy waterproofing odor, stretched more than five hundred feet along the lower part of Bowman Field. Looking back on it, it **was** like a dream. But these were not the only memories that pulled at my heart. I remember one *Farmer's Week* in particular when the local kids in my group were all entering that interregnum known as puberty; the tablets and pencils no longer held the same attraction as before.

I don't know if we were thirteen or fourteen, but it was before we went off to Daniel High. Our eyes had been opened wide during a couple of trips down the long halls of the barracks. Young women were napping on their bunk beds with their doors opened wide. With fans whirring, we made "unnecessary" trips through the hot halls as they rested in their new Sears & Roebuck bras. Even that memory, was not the formative *Farmer's Week* moment which brings me back to that time.

She was very pretty by age thirteen, and when I saw her coming through the dormitory door, her face was distorted by powerful emotions. She swept past me without seeing me, and her face expressed panic, shame, and fear. I felt that I had experienced those same emotions a short time before. They seemed all too familiar during my teen years. Her brunette hair orbited her face like winds around the eye of a hurricane passing Turks and Caicos Islands. Her eyes were large, as if she had just seen the devil and survived to flee from his grip. She was young, but her old eyes filled with tears. Of course, the devil was chasing her. She fled her own fifth-step misadventure, disheveled, heading somewhere, anywhere, while the unfamiliar emotions covered her like a storm.

Was there anything I could do? Had she been raped? I knew her, but I was invisible as she rushed past me. The urgency of her passing made me feel that I could never speak to her about what had happened. I never did, unless this paragraph is speaking. I don't know what happened that evening in the long halls of *Farmer's Week*, but I know that it was life-changing for her. I know that it shaped her future in some way that even she could not fully process. I think she lost her innocence, her youth, and her sense of personal worth, on that *Farmer's Week* night. I think that she may have signed her own version of that contract "pursuant to a vain and worthless crown."

I think she had her personhood wounded, fractured, and undermined. I pray for her. I pray for her broken heart. I pray for the shame which might have shaped her actions. I pray that she can appropriate the gift of love which God offers her with His pierced hands. It is never too late to embrace the One who takes our shame and covers our sin with His robe of righteousness. He is the one who makes our scarlet hearts as white as snow. "His love does not delight in evil but rejoices with the truth. He always protects, always trusts, always hopes, always perseveres. His love never fails."[182]

During this same year, when all these emotions were colliding, my bifurcated heart was experiencing strong feelings, wanting to protect, or to dive headfirst into forbidden pleasures. This was a shadowy season which God alone will decode. Any inadvertent contracts made with invisible lords will require His Giant Eraser in the years ahead. My babysitting experience had not been erased by any means available to me in those years. The damage was done. The toys in Pandora's Box had been taken out, and they could not be put back. My Cowardly Lion had returned from the mountain, and his shadow had weakened every natural relationship.

Years later, we double-dated without ever mentioning our prior silent sentinel history. I dated her friend from her college at their big dance in the spring. Our former soundless communiques were ameliorated greatly in this refreshing social encounter on the campus of her Christian school. She had intentionally chosen this path for her life fully aware of its potential influence in her future life. She could have spent her four years at Clemson University instead. The girl from the Bavarian Alps was no more, and I was so thankful for this shift in the precarious landscape. She had seen me at my worst, and her invitation on this night of fun brought a great sense of reconciliation and relief.

We laughed comfortably together that night, kissing our respective dates in a light-hearted evening of laughter and fun. We perched together on the front and back seats of Pop's 1958 Chevy Delray, and God healed deep wounds with great kindness. We were just like the other college kids out for an evening together. How merciful is our loving God? How gentle is His chastisement when we fear the worst? The thief on the cross beside Jesus understood this gentleness. His worst fears were swept away into the paradise of God.[183]

Were we made for each other? That is unlikely, though God could have changed the course of our lives. Regardless, our social and sexual coding had to be processed for all of its meaning. This processing is a dangerous but necessary business, like working with C-4 explosives. Any little mistake could have blown our lives apart. Once again, fear and testosterone had taken center stage for too much of this time. After that date night, with ships and kisses passing in the night, we burrowed deeply into our remote lives, free to choose our futures. The peril and the pleasure of our straightforward outing left us as we had been before — on distant shores.

Both worlds were real: The normal and the surreal existed side by side. But nothing ever developed from this projection of our passing shadows. Nothing ever joined us across spiritual or physical miles. Though we were inches from touching, not one sensory cell was ever breached during any of these

---

[182] 1 Corinthians 13.

[183] Luke 23:40-41.

encounters—not even a hug or a handshake that I can recall. How strange it seems today, that we never touched. I pray still that her life is rich with unexpected and deeply satisfying things. I pray that she knows the love of God as a balm of joy covering every part of her life. I pray that He touches her with hope and deep encouragement.

15.

THE NARCISSISTIC CONTINUUM.

Psychology Today recently spent an entire issue discussing what they call the "Narcissistic Continuum." This term has been my own terminology from the beginning of this book begun in 2014—this continuum of narcissism helps me understand the depths and the breadth of *Myopic Me!* Narcissism helps to explain the real struggles unfolding behind the Wizard's curtain. The Wizard's inadequacy is unmasked when a small dog pulls the curtain away, exposing the imposter hiding there. The psychologists claim that some level of narcissism is necessary for the healthy human being—to block depression, while permitting healthy human interactions. Be that as it may, extreme narcissism will inhibit the existence of empathy or intimacy in every relationship. With those extremes in mind, we will all land somewhere along this narcissistic continuum.

> "Narcissism is a continuum, and the disorder sits at the very end." Brummelman says. The NPI [Narcissistic Personality Index] can detect a person's level of narcissism, but additional real-life effects are necessary for a diagnosis of NPD."[184]

Melancholy Narcissus is the tragic character from Greek mythology who falls in love with his own image in the black waters beneath the bridge of Nemesis. Narcissus provides us with a parable for the human condition. His appearing in our own story leaves us looking for a countermeasure from the heavenly realm to free us from the destructive potential.

Narcissus is the self-obsessed fool of Solomon's story in Jerusalem. He is the Sheldon character from *The Big Bang Theory* on TV. He looks way too familiar when I see him in my own mirror. Though this Greek version of me is almost a caricature (the extreme NPD), Narcissus reveals my default capacity for self-obsession in little ways and big. I don't have to look to Hollywood or to

---

[184] *Meet the Real Narcissists*. Psychology Today.

the government to find my Narcissus, or my Nemesis. My own fractured relationships have reminded me of those two strange bedfellows. I have stumbled on my own bridge over troubled waters, looking down to see if my reflection materializes in those black waters.

In the modern world, we temporarily satisfy our Narcissus by moving in with that sexual partner. We think we have found our Doppelgänger, and the sex is free, with no strings attached. We insist, from our vast experience that, "Marriage ruins every relationship." We are very knowledgeable, so we ignore the warning signs, and every admonition to marry, to commit, or to make a covenant of our love (or our lust). When our bored partner finally walks out the door for the last time, we remember all the years we have squandered. We carry the wound that will never heal, convinced that our chance for happiness has passed us by. Actually, I have been married for forty-nine years to one woman, but the problem is a universal one.

While God provides the only real solution for our sexual cravings through the covenant of marriage, Narcissus seeks to fulfill these desires through unfocused cravings. These deep feelings, fickle feelings, open him up to his Nemesis who comes to steal, kill and destroy. Every young woman who watches her boyfriend walk out the door for the last time knows this Nemesis who has beguiled her.

Narcissus' antagonist comes walking into his life beneath the limbs of the weeping cherry tree. He has our best interest in mind, but his motives are not focused on our good.[185] God would soon use the weeping cherry tree to shake me, and to break down my self-sufficiency. Before He could save me, He shook me in the air like a little dog—loosening me from my arguments, and objections, one by one. "But I'm all set!" I will insist, in a voice much louder than I had intended. "I. Am. A. Good. Person." But I will discover that He loves me so much that He won't put me back down until I accept His unmerited favor—His free gift.

True surrender is impossible until my false gods are shaken from the limbs of my tree. My Wizards and Witches will have to be unmasked. My hiding places will have to be opened one-by-one, letting Him come in through a deep friendship. Placing everything under His Lordship will be essential, knowing that He alone has the necessary and sufficient Countermeasure that will gain my release from hell. Full Disclosure: God knows how to break a man. The Stone the builders rejected will either cause a man to stumble, or it will cause a man to fall.

> God warned them of this in the Scriptures when he said, "I am placing a stone in Jerusalem that makes people stumble, a rock that makes them fall. But anyone who trusts in him will never be disgraced." Romans 9:33

---

[185] *Narcissus*. Wikipedia.

"Come with me, sad friend," Nemesis instructs Narcissus. "I will show you what your heart is yearning for in the black pond in the upper meadow." Narcissus yields wanly, like Hamlet's Ophelia, obediently following Nemesis' pointing finger. He heads up the dirt road into the dark woods ahead. Nemesis knows just how to lift Narcissus from his dark mood. He has the answer for his melancholy—his unquenchable cravings. Nemesis seems to be the trustworthy counselor who never heals you, but offers a patient ear while you spiral down into despair. Nemesis, the counselor, is a predator; he is the destroyer; and though he appears to be Narcissus' friend, he is really his archenemy.[186]

Arriving at the promised black waters of this beautiful tree-sheltered pond, the leaves of the willow are floating haphazardly across the mirror-finish of the water. Narcissus climbs to the center of the arching bridge where he scans through the limbs of the willow tree looking for answers. Finding none there, he gazes into the mirror-surface below. In that mirror, he discovers the object of his deepest desire. There, he finds the most beautiful face and figure he can imagine. His super-natural gaze leads to adoration. It is preternatural. He falls in love with the reflection of himself—he finds the only one who perfectly embodies his own deepest aesthetic criteria. This search for the perfect love is the other side of the coin of our salvation.

This Doppelgänger in the black water is Narcissus, and it is Solomon. It is also the Lamb of God, offering His never ending love. Though we brush Him away with our hand, He still puts up a wall against every invading force seeking our destruction. He desires that none should be lost. A great paradox is created in this water beneath the bridge. My Nemesis knows well how to fool me with his counterfeits, but God has sealed Nemesis' fate. The paradox is unclear and fuzzy when I substitute *Myopic Me!* in those waters, or when an inordinate love comes into focus there. God is the One who loves me more than all the others, and His faithfulness saves me from the blackest waters. He is the dazzling lover in Solomon's brilliant Song of Songs.

> My lover is dark and dazzling,
> better than ten thousand others!
> His head is finest gold,
> his wavy hair is black as a raven.
> His eyes sparkle like doves
> beside springs of water;
> they are set like jewels
> washed in milk.
> His cheeks are like gardens of spices
> giving off fragrance.
> His lips are like lilies,

[186] Ibid.

perfumed with myrrh.
His arms are like rounded bars of gold,
set with beryl.
His body is like bright ivory,
glowing with lapis lazuli.
His legs are like marble pillars
set in sockets of finest gold.
His posture is stately,
like the noble cedars of Lebanon.
His mouth is sweetness itself;
he is desirable in every way.
Such, O women of Jerusalem,
is my lover, my friend. Song of Solomon 5:10-16

Though this passage is Solomon's description of himself through the eyes of his lover, it is written also as a song to be sung to the Lord—the lover of our souls. In biblical lingo, "knowing" is a sexual intimacy. This song reveals this kind of beautiful intimacy, this deep sexual relationship from which life flows forth. Song of Songs opens the door for us to go into the bedroom of these lovers to find them intertwined in deep affection and adoration. It is beautiful, if not embarrassing to our evil minds.

Were you not wounded in love, or have you never experienced this affection? Song of Songs describes what you have been yearning for, but never finding. Though we may have been taught by Satan to wear this shame like some kind of badge, God desires spiritual intimacy that it is pure and blessed inside the protective chrysalis of the marriage covenant. This is more than a cold legal contract, it includes the joy of the marriage bed. For Solomon, it was his love of Abishag, the Shulamite woman.[187]

Abishag had slept beside Solomon's father for more than a year, providing her heat to an old man who was as cold as death. Now, Solomon whispered to the Shulamite girl who completed him in his youth. She provided heat for his body, making him warm with her warmth and life. Eventually, for insatiable Solomon, the fractal-of-self exploded into a thousand lovers' dark eyes. It is unclear why this fractal took over his life, just as it is unclear to us why our fractal idols slay us. When presidents and kings bring one woman after another to their beds, they are trying to find the Lover of their Souls. They are hungering for the recognition, the bond, the intimacy, and the Oneness of that relationship which can only be fulfilled through Christ the Savior and King of kings!

The Bridegroom alone fulfills every sexual, emotional, and spiritual need. Only Solomon could sing this song for us. Rapturous adoration is something he embraced for his bride, and his Bride to be. How much did Solomon understand

---

[187] 1 Kings 2:22.

of his own prophecy? He was speaking of his beloved Abishag, handmaiden to David; but he was also speaking into the *Faith-Time Continuum* with a multilayered allegory revealing the complex levels of sexual and spiritual love which can only be fulfilled through the relationship with God's Promised One—the beautiful Lover of our souls. Even His names are beautiful. His presence is beautiful. His demonstration of love is visceral and overwhelming.

God's affection for us is fierce, intense, and intimate in ways we will only fully understand in heaven. When Paul speaks of "knowing" Him in His suffering, death, and resurrection,[188] he is speaking of this extraordinary intimacy of love which we may associate with the experience in our flesh through erotic sexual relations. Paul is speaking of a love so faithful that nothing can break its hold. When he writes these words, he is in Mamertine Prison awaiting Nero's execution orders. This bond of love is powerful enough to break the curse of sin which Paul writes about in Romans 7. Once Christ frees us, nothing can separate us from the Bridegroom.

> And I am convinced that nothing can ever separate us from God's love. Neither death nor life, neither angels nor demons, neither our fears for today nor our worries about tomorrow—not even the powers of hell can separate us from God's love. No power in the sky above or in the earth below—indeed, nothing in all creation will ever be able to separate us from the love of God that is revealed in Christ Jesus our Lord. Romans 8:38-39

The Song of Solomon is speaking into every human marriage, but this rendition of God's perfect plan is also bringing into focus the reality of the marriage of the Church to Christ. This is a love consecrated, and eternally joined. It is a pure love set apart for God's glory. "Promise me, O women of Jerusalem, not to awaken love until the time is right." [189]

Solomon awakens love again and again, but unable to consummate that cry of Adam: "Bone of my bones and flesh of my flesh!" The search for Solomon's Doppelgänger leads the foolish young king to stumble into inordinate loves and into a political alliance with an evil empire. His reference is not to the love of the Bride for the Bridegroom, but to the sweet communion he had in the marriage

---

[188] Philippians 3:10.

[189] Song of Solomon 8:4.

to the Shulamite woman. "Shulamite" is the female version of "Solomon"—it means "peaceful."[190]

The reflection in that pond had overwhelmed him the first time he saw her. He saw himself in her, with that echo from Adam's first sighting of Eve. Solomon cried out with excitement when he saw Abishag: "The first time I saw you, I felt like I had seen you before!" There was recognition and passion as the fractal of himself was replicated before his eyes. Adam was reborn in Eve's face and form every time he saw her. Solomon was reborn each time he saw Abishag. His identity mixed with hers, becoming one. After all, Eve's perfect body and beautiful eyes were a reflection of Adam's own, for God took the DNA from his side while he was in the deep sleep of God's fentanyl.

This bone, flesh, and DNA came from his side. When he saw her, he recognized her deep connection to him. She was out of him. She was like him. She was the better half of him, and he said so. I saw this in my wife, and only God can do this. I saw myself in her, "bone of my bones, and flesh of my flesh."[191] The scriptures say simply that we cannot hate our own flesh! "In the same way, husbands ought to love their wives as they love their own bodies. For a man who loves his wife actually shows love for himself."[192] Quoting Solomon's own words: "You have captured my heart, my treasure, my bride. You hold it hostage with one glance of your eyes, with a single jewel of your necklace."[193]

When his marriage bed overflowed the bonds of decency, he tried to recapture his beloved—bringing her ever closer, asymptotic Abishag—the unreachable reality! When Narcissus climbed down on the supporting beams beneath the bridge of Nemesis, every narcissist could nearly touch the face of his Beloved in those perfectly still waters below. Solomon almost found his Beloved, though not yet born in Bethlehem, the Word of God, Who was from the beginning.

As he moved from bride to concubine and back again, a thousand times or more, he never found a fit for his cravings—in the pattern of the many kings who followed in his footsteps, his methods confounded the search for deepest congruence with God. Narcissus' voice faded to black, for David's son was no longer listening to his father. Solomon was no longer listening to Our Father. He fell headlong into obsession, head-over-heals in love with the myriad versions of death he put on like a garment. Nemesis always fashions new clothes for the forlorn and the love sick of this world. Solomon finally drowned in his fractal's

---

[190] *Who was the Shulammite Woman?* Got Questions.

[191] Ibid.

[192] Ephesians 5:28.

[193] Song of Solomon 4:9.

redundant gaze—looking for God's ineffable embrace. "For in him we live and move and exist. As some of your own poets have said, 'We are his offspring.'"[194]

H. G. Wells understood Narcissus' deep fear of death. To get the attention of us narcissists, Wells showed us a single facet of our Deliverer. In our dark theater seats, when all hope was gone, Wells debunks our trust in, reliance upon, and belief in technology and science as the Savior of all Mankind. Though many Hollywood scripts exalt Technology—most will follow in the footsteps of H. G. Wells. Their plots will bash the fragile self-salvation theologies of Evolution—a religion which worships the god-like self-sufficiency of man.

God tells every Solomon, and every Abishag, to subdue the earth, ruling over it. But Wells points to the Elephant in the Room, exposing it for what it is. He gives us the surprise ending, leaving us with our mouths hanging open, showing us the very Salvation we mock. He exposes our futile efforts to raise a human standard against our Nemesis. He extrapolates that God is our Deliverer, Savior, and Provider.

God alone is able to take down the giant that has come against us—who is Satan himself. Whether this enemy is within, or coming from far away, Christ is there with the Shield of His sovereign protection. Much of what He does for us goes unnoticed, invisible, overlooked, and undetected— explained away by Science which has become our god. We don't see the Giant because he is subtle, coming in the clothing of our helper—dressed in the clothes of our friend Nemesis.

The truth is, God planned His Countermeasure before He even set the foundations of the earth. He knew that it would be impossible for us to truly love anyone unless we were first loved by Him. He understood that we had nothing to give away unless our sins had been forgiven, so that we could love ourselves— not vain love like Narcissus, but Agape love, like Jesus. He made provision for righteousness and justice to be perfectly satisfied through the finished work of the Cross. He sent His Son to redeem us from slavery and self-destruction. His Son became the ransom for our release from sin and death. Jesus' death on the Cross was, and is, God's greatest countermeasure. What the lamb in Egypt could not do, only keeping the first born of the Hebrews from death, the Lamb of God succeeded in doing—giving the forgiveness of our sins with eternal life.

Mouse-boy passed through these strange shadows with no intention of giving up his horizontally striped shirt from my schoolboy disguise, but he was in for a "chance-encounter" with the mysteries of Abishag. My childhood expression, thin as a dollar bill, exposed the interloper who was wearing my favorite shirt. But in that time before time, the Sculptor was already working tirelessly on the unformed boy who was clinging to the inside of me. I had no idea that He had His hand on my life through it all. What bond could be so strong,

---

[194] Acts 17:28.

what love so profound, that he could save a wretch like me? God, I would learn later, had to get very dirty to save me. He descended into my sinful little world to redeem me from the pit. Though I was *Untouchable*, He invaded my self-interest with His generosity.

> However, he has given each one of us a special gift through the generosity of Christ. That is why the Scriptures say,

> "When he ascended to the heights,
>   he led a crowd of captives
>   and gave gifts to his people."

> Notice that it says, "he ascended." This clearly means that Christ also descended to our lowly world. And the same one who descended is the one who ascended higher than all the heavens, so that he might fill the entire universe with himself. Ephesians 4:7-10

From the Cross, I would soon realize, Jesus spoke to the heart of every self-satisfied man who stood on the Hill of Skulls to gloat. They were proud of themselves, though they were in sinking sand—quick sand. He rescued *Myopic Me!* from that same blindness and ignorance, placing me on a Solid Foundation, on the Rock. Though those men on Calvary were complicit in the killing of this troublemaker, showing Him who was really in charge in Israel, God still came to that hill to save them. Though they killed this blasphemer, this law-breaker, this rebel, and this imposter with three spikes and a crown of thorns, they did not understand that He was their King. All of their false charges came back to condemn them. They had no idea that He could speak a word and their hearts would become lumps of coagulated blood.

But He chose to forgive them instead.

Even *Myopic Me!* could not ruin His best laid plans. The One who created the DNA said what we never expected to hear. From the Cross, Jesus' first prayer was spoken to the God of heaven: "Father, forgive them for they know not what they do." Though He was in great pain, in shock by medical terminology, He thought of us first. By that great act of love, the sinners around Him would discover their soul's value: "For God loved them so much that He gave His only Son so that anyone who believed in Him would not die but would have everlasting life."[195] Even the destructive Narcissist, leaving many wounded in his wake, could become a new creation in Christ.

Before that new creature could come from the chrysalis of my cowardly life, football arrived for my initial transformation. Football made level my hills, and straight my ways, for the coming of the Lord.[196] That unlikely means for my deliverance helped me through some difficult high school years. As the quarter-back of the football team, I learned quickly to put the team above *Myopic Me!* Discipline, the first stone of discipleship, became a visceral reality in those three years playing football at Daniel High under Coach Singleton's patient tutelage.

---

[195] John 3:16.

[196] John 1:23.

16.

WILD CHERRY.

O n my football recruitment visit to The Citadel—South Carolina's version
of West Point—I discovered that I could be influenced by a carefully choreographed set of enticements. I had wanted badly to play football at Clemson
University, but Coach Frank Howard likely did not think I was ready for *Division
1*. My desire to play college football overruled any common sense. Football was
my salvation during this interregnum through high school and into these college
years, and it never crossed my mind that God might become my rescuer. Football
was imposed on me with its highly disciplined, demanding, exciting, and
team-oriented lifestyle, in order to winch me out of the quagmire of *Myopic Me!*

God was always there, even when I didn't know Him. He knew what I was
getting into, and He knew that none of my high school classes could prepare
me for the enticements of a third kind in Charleston South Carolina. My veneer
of goodness was wafer thin, though my high school coach had observed that I
never used a cuss word in all the time he had known me. I was a sitting duck for
these carefully designed enticements. Though I understood seduction, manipulation, and coercion, this journey to The Citadel in Charleston would find me
ill-equipped to handle the arrival of all three at once.

The first leg of the recruitment itinerary was a very pleasant jaunt aboard
the President's yacht in Charleston Harbor. We ate a fabulous lunch together and
were able to mingle with the coaches and with General Mark Clark, the school's
Commandant. Then, to my ambivalent dismay, we visited some sleazy setups.
Just as Dorothy had found the unseemly and the sublime in the Land of Oz, I
was looking to find the road paved with gold through this season of life. Just
as Alice found insanity and nonsense beneath the Thames River, I discovered
unsettling realities in this underground world beneath the surface of the Ashley
River in Charleston.

This small college environment was hardly the football program that I
wanted, but these enticements were effective in tilting this entire recruiting
class to consent to play football at a military college! What were we thinking?
That prospect had seemed very unlikely to me before this trip. Having grown
up with Clemson's football teams, 240 miles to the Northwest, I knew what it
was like to have an exciting, competitive team to follow. I could still remember
the first undefeated team during my youth, when Clemson was ranked in the

top ten nationally. Now, I was looking at this potential four-year military tour at The Citadel.

The ignominious tilt of this recruiting trip should have repulsed me. Why didn't it? The simple answer is the Enticements. Their scheme worked well, just as they planned it. I wanted to play football! Was that all I cared about? Was it the fine food on the yacht? Was it the forbidden glance into Wild Cherry's world? She showed up after we returned from our luncheon with the coaching staff in Charleston Harbor. Toward the end of our day, an entourage, five-hundred strong, arrived at an outdoor venue where "Wild Cherry" appeared on a large raised stage. This sudden shift in scenery seemed more like a dream, or a nightmare, rather than an actual scheduled event. Did this really happen? Was it accidental?

She seemed to come from nowhere. As soon as this young woman walked to the center of this long three-foot-high platform, the crowd started pressing close to her. She promptly stripped down to her Eve-ning attire (sans fig leaves) directly in front of the student body of upperclassmen. I could see the Spanish moss draped above her like a hairy wreath almost reaching her frail body. I was standing in this red light district which I had not agreed to visit. I had gazed too many seconds five years earlier on those stairs; but this time I was repulsed by what I was seeing.

Though I knew nothing of Hosea the prophet, or his shrine prostitute wife, I was repelled by and attracted to Wild Cherry's performance for the troops—but it seemed more like a tragedy unfolding before my eyes. Though this was the kind of thing that every eighteen-year-old boy dreamed of, I was dismayed at this turn of events. Is it possible that I really learned a lesson that night on the stairs? Hosea the prophet learned the lesson of God's love, when he too fell in love with his shrine prostitute whom God had instructed him to take as his bride. He finally embraced her in the manner of God who had put His arms around wayward Israel in spite of her adulteries.[197]

Hosea's profligate wife returned daily to her job as a temple prostitute where she participated in the unseemly worship rituals to the Baal god of fertility. God had instructed Hosea to marry Gomer as a highly visible demonstration of His own faithful and enduring love for Israel. It was a painful and humiliating experience for Hosea, who eventually embraced Gomer as his beloved bride. My encounter with "Wild Cherry" in Charleston, showed me that God wanted to plant His love into my voyeuristic heart. I knew very little about the love which also protects; for God had not yet revealed this central part of His character to *Myopic Me!*

One of the upper-class cadets stood directly in front of Wild Cherry wearing his dress uniform. He offered her his shiny-brimmed hat like an offering to the goddess standing above him. After the hat had been baptized with her love, the two of them finished this Baal worship to the cheers from this madding crowd. I couldn't take my eyes completely away from these shocking events, for I had

---

[197] Hosea 3:1.

never before seen such things. Though I tried to avert my eyes, the train wreck was unfolding in front of a thousand eyes, including mine.

I stood there staring, as one made-stupid by curiosity—as one whose pretense of naiveté persisted to the very end. I was ashamed to stare, while the star of the show seemed to grow smaller before my naked eyes. She was being thrown down before us like so much fertilizer from a shovel, or a bit of road salt cast down on the ice and snow. She would be easily discarded by these eventual soldiers, like one of Solomon's women devoured in a night, and then spit out into anonymity. But her tiny demeanor remained permanently etched into my memory, even though it happened fifty years ago and thirty-feet away from me.

My tornado out of Kansas had dropped me in a foreign land. As Solomon never seemed to learn, everything foreign is not automatically good. I had fallen down his rabbit hole, sliding down through the Spanish moss and ancient live-oak trees. I had seen the squirrel in the Wild Cherry tree beside Narcissus' black pond. The sights and sounds from our strange visit will never completely leave me. I had landed in Charleston, the town where slaves had been displayed in cages for buyers who came with sacks of money. I was in the town where children were bought and sold, and I had seen children among my contemporaries carrying open containers of alcohol in the streets. There was no age limit for public drinking in this lawless place. Why was I surprised to find the boundaries were redrawn in these gray areas of The Citadel map?

Once school started, I discovered that this teenage girl was working in the school's sandwich and soda shop. From sodas to Salome, she scooped the ice cream into the tall glasses. I saw her every time I went in after classes. I remember the sadness I felt for this girl in her strange shadowy world—she was infamous and she was exploited. She felt loved, but they devoured her with their eyes when they came to her door. She had worn the mad hat too long, and now she was quite mad. Like the Mad Hatter, she had been exposed to too much mercury since she was a young girl, and now she was a wild cherry prostitute in front of hundreds of men on the way to Viet Nam. The twenty-seven-hundred-year old untouchable woman in Hosea's story had mounted the stage erected along the Ashley River. Gomer, or Wild Cherry, or the Bride, had ebbed in the Charleston tide pools to become a fragile child—her body, small and insignificant, on that famous platform before a thousand eyes reminding me of my own frail existence without meaning or purpose.

God loved her as she stood there by herself, with nothing hindering our critical and lascivious eyes. God wanted to put His robes of righteousness over her. He wanted to cover her sins so that no one could see her shame. He defended her in many hearts that day, as He had defended the prostitute who was thrown at His feet in Jerusalem—or that shrine prostitute in Israel—for I knew nothing about those momentous events or those powerful demonstrations of God's intentionality towards us unworthy prostitutes. Anyone who misuses his talents or gifts is a prostitute, and I have spent too much time spending my own gifts on unworthy sorties into idolatry.

As I stood there in that warm air, Jesus stood with her, invisible, deep touching deep, speaking audibly to many who looked on from places of superiority. He stood between her and the rock throwers in that crowd—they were the ones who had kicked the little pig in the petting zoo. They were the ones who had been given everything they wanted from birth, no one ever saying, "No! You have to wait." They were the ones who had been bullies at recess a few years earlier. They were the hyenas, the tearers of flesh, and some of them were accustomed to taking anything they wanted, and spitting out the bones. The Citadel's disciplined life would be good for them.

The self-righteous in this crowd were completely right to throw their stone if they arrived at that bema without sin. But every rock fell in the dust, for none was good—only the Father.[198] I remembered that night on the stairs, and that earlier basement innocence, when we crossed a red line in the shadows as children. Every young man walked away as Jesus wrote our sins clearly in the sand. On that day, *Wild Cherry* might have been ruined by our eyes, but I felt more like those Pharisees, like those religious leaders, clutching my stones of judgment. I found myself broken down in crude prayers—praying for my own sins. "Forgive them, for they know not what they do!"

I can still see her today, but with Jesus' eyes now—loving her without any desire to take anything else from her. If she is still among the living, she has seen more than seventy hot Charleston summers. Her body surely has many tales to tell, and her soul has been pulled in every direction by the enticements of this life. She may have many memoirs to be expurgated from her book.

Dr. Helen Fisher, a neurological anthropologist, has written many books about the body, by way of familiar topics such as romantic love, sexual love, and love which leads to commitment. She investigates the import of these three categories, applying anthropological strategies. She has collaborated with *match.com* and *chemistry.com* because she finds the influences of chemistry to be more measurable by the scientific method than either psychology or theology.[199]

I see through her eyes that endocrine plays a powerful role in "love," attraction, and sexual exploitation alike. Who can argue against that! Endorphins and other hormones fuel the sexual, the romantic, and the relational soup during our wild ride through life. No scientist would deny these potent influences. But Dr. Fisher's conclusions may lead us to that sad dead-end of Materialism—that sad black water of Narcissus. This materialism is not simply focused on the next shipment from *Amazon Prime*, but actually becomes the cold religion of the masses.

Materialism purports that consciousness is a function of material and chemical agencies alone. Dr. Fisher's trust of science as the all-seeing eye attempts to lead Myopic Me! to subscribe to this materialistic determinism as the final

---

[198] Luke 18:19

[199] *Defining the Brain Systems*. Helen E. Fisher.

authority in all things sexual and spiritual. To the hammer, everything else looks like a nail. To the dust, everything else seems wet. To the dead soul of man, everything that feels good is worthy of some sort of praise.

> [Materialistic Determinism reasons] that the moral, cultural, intellectual, vocational choices of man are determined by material factors. Men are not what they are because of their commitment to ideas and faith; they are what they are because something material outside or inside of them makes them be what they are. This is the essence of materialistic determinism.[200]

Endorphins and testosterone? Estrogen and adrenalin? Which one of these landed *Wild Cherry* on that platform? Was deterministic chemistry at work in her life? Was it religion at work, as in the case of Hosea's Gomer? What sequence of chemical reactions led to her participation in these explicit outcomes which I witnessed on that raised platform in the Spanish moss of Charleston? How did this college choose to expose their football prospects to these chemical inducements? Did they follow a simple formula that stimulates young men—offering food and sex? Was this activity pragmatically chosen to address our two main appetites, unleashing powerful endorphins, sealing our fates in this military institution for a season?

The food on the yacht combined with puerile enticements to bring us into the nets. Was their decision triggered by their own endorphins or testosterone in the school's planning offices? Was this "Squirrel," as they called her, dropped from the limb of a live oak branch against her will? Or did she fall through the rabbit hole from an absentee father's worst bedtime story? Was she hopping along the Ashley River in Charleston, arriving just in time for this very important date? Was her giant pocket watch shed on the bema's wooden surface with the rest of her clothes?

Why did I go to that school which exposed me to these temptations—the very same temptations as in Solomon's day? Three-thousand years ago his pupils flared when he saw Pharaoh's daughter in her princess garb? King David's pupils flared when he looked down on the roof to see Bathsheba coming from her bath. Like Solomon, I opened a tiny door to idolatry—a little Wild Cherry naked doll when I did not avert my eyes in Charleston. I saw the good and the evil possibilities under the same forbidden tree. Wild Cherry's body became the momentary object of desire for five-hundred cadets. She stood on the throne of worship for a few brief minutes, and her body was the visual locus for a thousand eyes. When her body was exploited, sin entered the world, turning the Spanish moss

---

[200] Marinov. *The Fallacy of Materialistic Determinism.*

gray in all the live oak trees of the whole world. But God's kindness somehow visited my ambivalent heart.

No doubt, our shallow breathing, that day, was synchronized with the choreography of her clothing falling on that open-air platform—even then, during this imprinting of our souls, God foreshadowed the Bema (the platform) of Judgment for my future mind to understand. This judgment stage will bring us ALL together again at the end of time. We will all be naked before the eyes of the One who has been exalted as the final Judge. Those who are wearing the righteous robes of Christ will receive God's rewards. Those clutching their idols will face judgment.

God brings no bully's cowardice to that final Bema. All who have ever lived will be present for this review by the Lamb Who was slain for us. He will divide the Sheep from the Goats into two queues for Final Judgment.[201] As Solomon points out, God will judge every secret thing we have done or said—whether good or bad during our lives.[202] Expecting punishment, many will receive His great kindness, receiving unexpected rewards for things they did not even know that they had done. Jesus will see the good works, worthy of these rewards, which the believer has done in secret, or even done unawares.

The sinners—Goats—who are far from God, will receive no second chance, no respite in Purgatory, and no chance to go back and warn their families and friends.[203] They will not be reincarnated as butlers or chauffeurs or doctors to see if they might do better the second time, or the thousandth time. Why would we *not* imagine a religion like this, receiving these second chances for six-hundred thousand years? God is the God of second chances—seven times seventy-seven, according to Jesus Himself; but these chances are benefits coming through Friendship with the Savior, through the sealed relationship with Christ, and in no other way.

Judgment Day will therefore fall like a hammer on anyone who has exploited the little ones who could not protect themselves from predators. These predators, who never believed or received the Son Whom the Father sent, will face eternal sentencing. Those who did not come to Christ through authentic and godly sorrow will receive what they deserve. When we demand fairness from life, it will only come to us through the Son—justice, with mercy. This is true justice which comes through the Lamb of God Who suffered and died so that our sins could be washed away as far as the East is from the West. In God's eyes, His blood alone is able to atone for our wrongdoing.[204]

---

[201] Matthew 25:32.

[202] Ecclesiastes 12:14.

[203] Luke 16:24-31.

[204] 1 John 2:2.

God's highest motivation at the Bema Judgment for the Righteous on the final day is to give out "merit badges." Jesus will assign rewards, and place crowns, on everyone who has been faithful to carry out all the will of God assigned to them. It will be so much better than the Boy Scouts or Girl Scouts when the believer receives these rewards in heaven. The rewards for righteous acts will bring glory to the King of kings. It will have nothing to do with anyones salvation, for Christ's blood alone is efficacious, accomplishing this redemption. Our eternal roles in heaven will be decided at this Bema, according to these rewards and crowns.

In the Boy Scouts, Jimmy Dubois and I went toe-to-toe with bony knuckles rifling through the air like little missiles. Our lords at that time were testosterone and saving face. But on the Bema in Charleston, I could not imagine a future time when Wild Cherry or I would stand there on the Bema to receive rewards for our often misspent lives. How wonderful a day it will be—if I find her standing on this Stage of stages receiving crowns and privileges from the King of kings. Oh, happy day!

That this Scandalous Grace might come to her is a joyful thought! That she might be the one receiving those glorious merit badges is a thrilling thought. I know today that God alone can save us wretches, causing us to do great things. Even this Charleston prostitute can be reborn to a life full of joy, courage, and blessings. Even Wild Cherry might find her way through the only Door, arriving on that glorious Bema platform at the end of days. Casting her crowns at the feet of Jesus, she might be the one filled with joy everlasting.

This scandalous grace offended the religious leaders in Jesus' day, and still seems a scandal to hypocrites to the present day. But Jesus came to save the broken things of this world, and to set the captives free.[205] He will give each person a new name, through His soul-piercing eyes. "Wild Cherry," no longer, she may become "Morning's Hope" or "Precious Dancer." The merit badges will not be intended to bring glory to the one who has believed. These crowns acknowledge the fruitfulness which has come through Jesus' death, burial, and resurrection. The crowns will be cast down at His feet, acknowledging His sacrifice and His glory.

His world-changing love is the only leverage for producing eternal rewards on that final day. These things are spiritually perceived, and spiritual things can only be apprehended through the Spirit of God. The flesh rejects spiritual things, not able to understand or to distinguish them.[206] The unspiritual man considers them to be foolishness. When Sheldon makes fun of Penny's belief in horoscopes in *The Big Bang Theory*, he is right to discourage this activity. But Sheldon does not understand that Penny is exposing herself to evil.

---

[205] Isaiah 61.

[206] Mark 6:7.

Tarot Cards and Seances are not silly, for dark spirits inhabit these activities.[207] In Penny's dim understanding, the seance is useful, and is good. She receives help from her daily horoscope which is beneficial in her life. She sees nothing sinister in these activities. Going to a palm reader is a wise thing to do, according to Penny's naïveté. After all, everyone wants to know what will happen in the future. The horoscope gurus love Penny's open-door policy, for they have become wealthy selling their books and their expensive counseling sessions. Such people invest in these gurus and witches, considering the Christian's investment in the kingdom of God as an utter waste.

Even highly educated people in high stations in life, believe in these counselors. Visiting dead family members in a seance is popular in every city and town. Children who lose parents want to connect with dad one more time. Ouija boards and Tarot Cards brings nervous laughter to many social groups, proudly spreading their cards on the coffee tables in the houses of fools. Fools put on slavery without knowing there are negative consequences. They don't know that they are permitting the demons to whisper at the doorway to their souls.[208]

It is similar to the danger we encounter on the internet when we click "yes" on those Malware drop-down menus. We permit, legally permit, those malevolent strings of code to occupy our programs and hard drives. When we believe in the power of the horoscope or the interpretations coming from Tarot Cards, we say, "Yes" to the strings of code Satan plants in our souls. It is the same string of code the Serpent put in Eve when she listened to his corrupted advice about the forbidden fruit in the Garden. Satan takes over all our private information, controlling our futures. He releases His Python into our souls. It is no longer that innocent Serpent counseling us unto death. Satan looses the Python into our souls to strangle the life out of us.

The young woman in Charleston had chosen her slavery in that famous slaver's town. The slaves were taken captive in Africa or in the Caribbean Islands. In chains they were displayed in raised cages from the live oak limbs, draped in Spanish moss. Now she had become a slave to her shame and her desperate need of money. She confused fame and shame. Her indentured status linked her to every prostitute who has ever lived. Economic necessity translated her moral objectives to pay the rent or to pay her daddy. Sin became her invisible chains in her limited, and pejorative, new lexicon. A good income should have covered a multitude of sins, but hers became the moralistic rudder of her youth. Love truly does cover a multitude of sins; and love outlasts the Clock which is winding down before our naked eyes.

---

[207] Deuteronomy 18:14.

[208] Genesis 4:7c.

The end of the world is coming soon. Therefore, be earnest
and disciplined in your prayers. Most important of all, continue to show deep love for each other, for love covers a multitude of sins. 1 Peter 4:7-8

Unfortunately, we confuse love most often with sexual pleasures. The love Peter is writing about is God's love. The Lamb
has already demonstrated a Love which Dr. Fisher did not
address in her article, as far as I can see. This Love is what the
Greeks call Agape. Agape is selfless, self-sacrificial servant-
hood, given freely to the greatest and the least among us. This
Agape protects, believes, trusts, keeping no record of wrongs,
and acting with patience and gentleness—never celebrating
with lascivious eyes when a young woman drops her clothes,
becoming a prostitute on a stage.[209]

Love is patient and kind. Love is not jealous or boastful or
proud or rude. It does not demand its own way. It is not irri-
table, and it keeps no record of being wronged. It does not
rejoice about injustice but rejoices whenever the truth wins
out. Love never gives up, never loses faith, is always hopeful,
and endures through every circumstance. 1 Corinthians 13:4-7

Paul is describing the character and nature of Jesus Christ in his letter to
the Corinthian church. He is detailing what "Love" really looks like. He is
describing God's love, which becomes evident in the life and the character of
the believer over time. This happens, not through the efforts of men, but through
the renewing Spirit of God. No man, through his own effort and human will can
exhibit this Agape love—which demonstrates the good and perfect will of God.

Sin is the antithesis of this Love. Sin is an uncomfortable word we try to
avoid, uncomfortable even when it appears on this page; but with the arrival of
sin, death has already been released into this world. Sin is the breaking of our
bond with God, with neighbor, and with ourselves. No one is exempt from this
rush of Entropy. No one can escape its Gravity. Squarely facing this glacier of
sin and judgment brings the dawn of wisdom and freedom.

Though the rich young ruler believed himself to be a good man, Jesus cor-
rected his understanding, showing him that no one on this earth is exempt from
the death sentence which sin requires. No man is without sin. No man is good.
No one meets God's standard, for it is impossible for flesh to demonstrate the

[209] 1 Corinthians 13:4-7.

selfless love of God. Redemption from sin's deadly grip comes only by faith in Jesus Christ. Through His inexplicable suffering on our behalf, we may inherit this resurrection from the dead.

We might not believe the weather report on the golf course before we were hit by lightning. We might trust the suspension bridge before falling to our death. We might trust the crumbling edge of a cliff, falling a thousand feet into the Colorado River. When we trust the Cross, Jesus grabs our hand and our heart, keeping us from falling headlong. When they removed the spikes and the spear from His dead body, Nicodemus and Joseph placed his badly damaged body into Joseph's family tomb.

The Roman soldiers, like these soldiers-in-the-making at The Citadel, stood guard at Jesus' sealed tomb. But the stone was rolled away before their eyes, and they were transfixed and powerless to stop the Angels who came to minister to the Lord of life. He was raised from death by the Holy God, and the course of history was changed in those few moments. These soldiers stared at the Lamb Who had been slain for their rescue as He walked from the grave. They stared, as if their eyes were captured in the tractor-beam of God's redemption. They gazed on the Lord of heaven and earth Who walked through them as if they were nothing more than a mist.

No one could stop God from the rescue of the Gentiles and the Jews. Jesus' story could not be delayed, and the Angels removed the stone while the soldiers stared in their temporary paralysis. The seal of Rome was broken, the government of God was placed upon Jesus' shoulders. No ruler could stand against God's good and perfect will. Satan stood back, licking his wounds, waiting for his chance to strike Jesus' Bride, the Church. The tomb is symbolic of our captivity in sin, our proclivities, and our hopeless perspective. The seal is symbolic of the impotent wax of Satan, intending to hold us in a counterfeit relationship with various well-worn lifestyles which all lead to destruction. The burst of light coming from inside the Tomb is the resurrection life of God which rescues us from our darkness—from our idolatry.

At The Citadel, the wax seal was applied to my life, but Satan had no real power to hold me when Jesus came to free me from my tomb. Satan applied his rude methods, seeking to take my soul captive. He imagines that he gains some form of revenge when he destroys the soul of the one made in the image of God. His humiliation came in the Tomb when Jesus stood up from the death that could not hold Him beyond three days. Today, Satan baits his hook in the world with the love of money and power. Though endocrine still plays a major role in deceiving me, money is always the goal when Satan designates one of us as his minion. Though we may play the role of the Serpent before He saves us, we will likely never see that forked tongue flashing in our mirror.

I have forgiven The Citadel for what they did to Wild Cherry and to me. I realized that the authorities of the school likely were not aware of this tawdry venue. This is too often the case for athletic programs which offer every enticement they can invent. I remember that the coach for the Freshman team seemed to be cut from this same rotten meat. His tongue produced a nonstop stream of four-letter words in and out of context and meaning. It was simply his native language, his only language; and his face turned red and swollen with many unhealthy emotions when he spoke to us in the practices—failure must have been foremost among his fears.

I remember that his only strategy for the offensive side of the football was the halfback sweep. For long yardage, short yardage, desperate yardage, he would call for the sweep—and he did this somehow within his stream of his four-and-more-letter epithets. I forgive all those who knew not what they were doing in those unintended morality plays during my one year flying around in their schizophrenic hive. As I have already confessed, I didn't manage this pressure very well myself. It is not about comparisons, for my mouth has spewed epithets as well. Not one is good! This greatest lesson comes each time I remember that the Father alone is good. God shows no favoritism, but sees us through that open tomb and our absolute trust of His Son. Because of that trust, I can thank God for the experiences at The Citadel. I needed that season for my seasoning.

Remembering the visual imprinting in Charleston, I learned again the precipitous peril which comes with wide eyes. This experience stands out as formative, in spite of the inordinate discipline flung wide, and flung down, during that unique year in the history of the Military School of South Carolina. Though God made the human topography I stared at beneath the Spanish moss, He bounded every version of this intimacy with covenantal protections. He knows us too well, for the rush of testosterone is devoid of any loving inclination. And He knows that our hearts are deceitful above all things.[210] He never intended that private topographies should be paraded as something consumable or worthless. A woman's body should not be something we buy online or celebrate again and again in a movie or painting. Our world has made nudity palatable and salable, a vain billion dollar industry. The love of nudity is the root of many evils.

When Adam and Eve's unseemly parts were first exposed (misconstruing their function and manipulation for good and for evil purposes),[211] the life in the first lamb was required to pay the wages for their shame. The lamb's small death was the first, and the last, in the perfect Garden of Eden. The Lamb of God, alone, would restore that perfection when He laid down His life willingly. His nakedness in the crucifixion has covered the nakedness of every young woman and every old man who comes to kneel at His Cross.

When the resurrected Jesus spoke to the disciples on the road to Emmaus, He opened their eyes to see the Good intentions of God from the beginning—from the beginning, before Time had been poured into the Clock or the Hourglass. Jesus showed the downcast disciples that His death, burial, and resurrection was planned before the foundations of the world. He revealed to them the love

---

[210] Jeremiah 17:9

[211] Genesis 3:7

God has poured out upon every: 1. Race, 2. Nation, 3. Gender, 4. Economic Classification, 5. Social standing, 6. Tribe, or 7. Geographic Identity.

Sin was not the issue, for He took our sins. Depravity was not the issue, for He took our depravity. Fear was not the issue, for he took our fear when He said, "Yes" to God's will. He showed them that God's Spirit would be poured out on all flesh. He helped them see that the Word of God, the Christ, God's Son, the Lamb of God, is present in every single book of the Bible, from the first Hebrew word in Genesis to John's Revelation of Jesus yet to return.

John himself was carried into heaven so that we might see firsthand the glory of God and the terrible days which still lie ahead, warning us to turn from our Narcissistic lives before our souls become as tough as leather. John died on the Isle of Patmos, the only disciple who did not die violently for the Good News of God's redemption. He had survived their attempt to kill him in a boiling tub of oil. [212]

---

[212] Luke 24:31

17.

LORDS OF DISCIPLINE.

T he syndrome of socially acceptable bullying from high school spilled over into my year at The Citadel. At this Military College of South Carolina, the upperclassmen enjoyed great freedom hazing the incoming plebes, the dumb-heads. Fresh from our high school exploits that had puffed some of us up like bull frogs, the cadet upperclassmen in R-Company beat us down to a humbler level, using an arsenal of extreme hazing instruments. Their intention was to drive the snowflakes away. They wanted nothing to do with nerds. Their idea of an acceptable cadet would determine how far they had to push us before the year was over.

The corporal asked me why I was leaving after the plebe year. "You can haze the incoming freshmen next year! You've earned it!" That made perfect sense to him; he was a corporal, evidence of his mediocre performance at shirt-tucks, hazing, and shoe shines. I couldn't alter his thinking when I said, "I have no interest in hazing the in-coming freshmen." He knew that I rejected his flawed system, but he was partially correct in understanding the important role of military discipline. That sharp scalpel had cut away great chunks of Myopic Me! I knew that no military unit would survive long if narcissism was rampant in every member of the unit.

Hazing and bullying by the sergeants in the Military Service's boot camps brings greater attentiveness to authority. This is essential for survival, and for winning the war. While I was contemptuous of The Citadel's cultish approach to new recruits during that semester, I knew that a war had been stirred in my seemingly compliant heart. I had always been submissive to authority in every encounter for the previous eighteen years—or so I imagined. But God was exposing my rebellious heart during this Citadel year. He would eventually show me that even Nero, the evil Roman Emperor, had been used two thousand years ago to reveal the Agape love of God.[213]

During this unpleasant process at The Citadel, I somehow embraced the bully which I despised. It happened by default, before those two semesters were done. I learned well, somewhere deep in my soul, that I did want to be the one to attack, rather than always being the mouse-boy in the shadows. I wanted to

---

[213] Philippians 4:22

be the alpha-male, the one to be feared. I wanted that nine-year-old boy gone forever from my sight. I can see him perfectly well, still—with enough clarity and detail to paint his picture after all these years.

Cadet Commander Cowan could attest to the need for each plebe to surrender his self-will for the good of the company. But surrendering to the wrong thing is no better than surrendering to no-thing. Commander Cowan achieved his high status at The Citadel by laying down his rights and privileges for the shared goals of the Company and the Cadet Corps. I will admit I admired his cool demeanor, remembering his name and fame. He seemed above the fray, mature, wise as Solomon, and willing to cut the baby in half to discover the truth in a situation. I respected him, and submitted to the military demands imposed on me during those two semesters of Plebe life.

I reported to him for execution of punishment after I had knocked another cadet across the floor of the Mess Hall (good name for the place we ate three meals a day). I found out that having an ice tea glass intentionally dumped on your starched uniform does not give you the right to send a classmate sliding ten feet on his back with a single angry punch. Commander Cowan seemed very calm about it, and the punishment seemed to fit my crime. The twenty Tours came down from Lt. Colonel Thomas N. Courvoisie, when he determined the scope of my offense in the Mess Hall. The Army Colonel basically ran the daily operations of the school from his second level office in the Admin Building. His French name suffered a Charleston modification, becoming, "Cavorsy."[214] He remained shrouded in great mystery during my year there. His assignment of twenty Tours reminded me who really ran The Citadel. He too was nice, respectful, and I felt the love! Crazy, I know.

The Colonel and the Cadet Commander were reprimanded during the second half of the year, from what I heard, when excessive hazing blew up in their faces. It had turned into a cult story which Pat Conroy later made famous in his book, *Lords of Discipline*. The movie, *Lords of Discipline*, depicts the cult which had formed in secret at the school. Conroy had attended immediately after these incidents became infamous within the cadet corps.[215] I wondered how Cadet Cowan handled being demoted when the Major General traveled east from Huntsville to Charleston to retrieve his badly abused son from our company ranks. The General likely rehearsed his concerns before meeting with Major General Mark Clark in his offices. The General likely caught a ride on a C-130 Herky Bird headed for Charleston AFB. In a few hours, he found himself in a discussion of the military college's future. They spoke, as fellow generals, over three-fingers of bourbon and a snifter of ancient cognac from General Clark's finest stock.

Dramatic changes would come from their solemn deliberations. Push-ups became the new hazing instrument for the second half of the year. Doing more

---

[214] *Pat Conroy*. Wikipedia.

[215] Conroy. *Lord's of Discipline*.

pushups was not a problem for me since I was doing thirty pull-ups off the steam pipes in my barracks room and bench-pressing two-hundred and twenty-five pounds fifteen times. I routinely did French curls off the end of a bench using two-hundred forty pound barbells—from the floor, over the head, to the chest, and then back down again, over the head and to the floor behind me. Doing a hundred pushups was not uncommon before making it up the stairs to the room after our two-hour practices in the afternoons and our Mess Hall in the evenings. Playing football made these new physical hardships part of my daily routine during the second half of The Citadel's "Knob Year." The discipline would become important for my future life, and for my eventual encounter with God's authentic deliverance. He would teach me a different kind of discipline which is the very evidence of His divine intervention and love.

18.

ARTERIAL FRATERNITY.

After that season in Charleston on the Ashley River, I transferred to Clemson University in the early 1960s where I majored in Physics, played Quarterback, and served as *Features Editor* for *The Tiger,* the school newspaper. I wrote articles about the construction of the new six story library, with three stories underground. A special area below the earth was designated to hold my father's papers, books, journals, and written artifacts. His time living in Harlem in the 1920s, while attending Columbia University, was of particular interest. His experiences were pre-Clemson, providing intimate details from the times leading up to the *Great Depression* in NYC. If we had ever talked about these years (we didn't), he might have likened this season as his own Byronic pilgrimage.

There was faith aplenty during the 1960s, but it was increasingly a faith in the individual's ability to know what was right to do. Faith in God was under a giant Question Mark. Freedom was in the air already, and sexual freedom was at the top of the list. When the founders of America listed *Freedom*, they did not mention sexual freedom as a specific category; but among the students, this had risen to the top of the list. The founding Fathers would have reminded us students, if we would give them ear, to remember the mutuality of *Virtue* and *Faith* as necessary and sufficient Corner Stones for the Republic's survival and for the health of the individual. Without these, *Freedom* turns into *License*, which is another name for profligacy—another name for sin; and sin is the generic nature of all idolatry.

The Stone Tablets from the mountaintop were thrown down somewhere during those years, when our President was murdered in Dallas, his brother was killed in California, and Martin Luther King was murdered in Arkansas. Death continued to assert its ugly reality everywhere. The shattered pieces of those sacred tablets were stepped over like so much broken pottery. The next great "depression" was coming, and vast numbers of Americans would descend into vaguely defined despair. As for *Virtue*, the definition would migrate according to the new demands made by the college students during this interregnum which spilled over into the streets. Authority was being questioned, and this din would only grow stronger in the next two or three years.

The American population would soon get lost in the *Forest of Sin*,[216] in the Wilderness of Wounded souls. Sexual avarice would reach a new waterline along the shores of America's history, and the institution of Abortion on Demand (Roe vs. Wade) would parallel the rise of various, so-called, sexual freedoms. The voiceless victims during this new political dynasty would not live long enough to ever learn the name of *Planned Parenthood*. This euthanasia—euphemism—would disguise a multitude of sins. Death, again, was in the very air. The jugular of the beast was beating like a drum since June 17, 1970, when a three-judge panel of District Court judges swung the door wide for the fifty-four million babies to die from "legal abortions."[217] Fifty-four million times, the woman decided that she did not want to be the mother of her child. More than 98% of the abortions were elective—having nothing to do with rape or diagnosed medical risks.[218] Sexual freedom was the battlecry. I was oblivious to this deep moral shift in the world around me. Death, for the first time, was orchestrated and funded by the government, affecting the children of a nation. Death, like mustard gas, swirled around our noses as the atmosphere changed.

For the high school and college aged people, the spirit of death would become the most pervasive and destructive. The scourge of purposelessness, and worthlessness, sent suicides dramatically upward from 1970 into the 1980s.[219] The Great Rebellion of the 1960s (I was there, bewildered, but swept along) sowed its wild oats in every farmer's field. Before long, Satan was moving furniture around in the houses, face-to-face in many visions and dreams, replacing lust with fear in the fields growing high with wild weeds. It was the beginning of a tumultuous time in Clemson, with the war in Southeast Asia raging, and every headline filling up with death. Creative writing became a reaction to this for me during this time at Clemson, when I tried to address my own strong feelings about many things. I started well, skirting the *Forest*, but my own garden was filling up with tall weeds.

Writing surfaced these strong feelings, like that debris from the unfortunate U-Boat when the torpedo found it hiding in darkness. While journalism kept me tersely contained by the Who, What, When, Where, and rarely Why of the story, I held on for the bumpy ride. Somewhere during this same season, I was inducted into *Gamma Alpha Mu*, an honorary writer's fraternity, where I was encouraged to pursue all kinds of writing, including journalistic projects with *The Tiger*. One of my articles did a shallow dive into the Fermi-surface research

---

[216] Alighieri. *The Divine Comedy.*

[217] *Roe v. Wade. Wikipedia.*

[218] Johnston. *Reasons given.*

[219] *US Suicide Rates.* NCBI.

in the Physics department, while another investigated the Chemical Engineering processes that collaborated with good bacteria to break down human sewage.

These bacteria declared war on our effluents, making short work of an ugly job which no engineer's slide-rule could accomplish. Like those bacteria in H. G. Wells story, these kept us from vanishing under the rising oceans of our own excrement. Engineers always give the hard work to the blue-collar crews who set the concrete forms and install the piping and steel. But these Chemical Engineers used microbes to do the tasks they couldn't perform. Once again, God designed these little guys for a purpose. These tiny soldiers made short work of the aliens attacking us from Inner Space.

In this mixed atmosphere of educational exigencies, my arterial fraternity party was set. I can't explain it. It can't excuse it. It just happened on one of these really weird, out-of-body nights when emotions took over, and strong feelings became my gods. The good sense displayed in some of those Clemson projects, vanished when the sun went down on that emotionally engineered evening. This timeline is unclear to me, but somewhere in these early college years at Clemson University I headed off to this fraternity party with a mission.

Viewing the nearly forgotten scar on the underside of my wrist, I remember this misadventure far too vividly. For me, the recurrent theme includes a pretty, spunky girl—a Dorothy girl—for whom I have become smitten. Even her name points to good outcomes, and it seemed that she could do everything well. A cheerleader for the Clemson football team, she had a way of speaking which was like real butter on sourdough bread. In my late high school days I had fallen for her, though she seemed to be welded to the arm of her Clemson cheerleader boyfriend. He might have been gay for all I know, but their ostensible alliance made me more desperate for her. I drove to the Fraternity party she would be attending, stopping at the "moonshine" house I had just heard about the night before. I bought a quart of illegal, 100 proof vodka, and half of it ended up in my stomach and blood stream before I even arrived.

Every highway patrolman on duty that night is dead by now, or he might still be willing to incarcerate me if I come inside his jurisdiction. With so much age on my ancient crimes today, they could not prosecute my case—though I should have checked this out before publishing. I certainly am not the victim in this arterial tale from Clemson University, and I never am the victim in any of the sordid tales in this book. I had learned well the manly art of the instant excuse. It is much easier to blame, than to grow up, and change my ways. "I was motivated by unrequited love." I would have explained afterward, I suppose. Yawn. Snore. Even the annals of literature abandoned this genre four-hundred years ago, after calling it, *The Comedy of Errors*. "Comedy of Errors" is a good name for it, though I seemed to learn little from the errors I was making.

Shakespeare used this genre wonderfully, and his best comedy used this exact title. He shaped his dialogue and his plots to entertain the crowds who gathered in the cheap seats—standing room only tickets for the pits in front of the raised stage. His complex metaphoric dialogues completely satisfied the erudite guests who came to sit in the box seats above the stage. His visceral plots captured the imagination of every audience. These Comedies of the Garden Revisited, found Eve blaming the Serpent for her perpetual tragedies. But I have no excuse for my series of errors and many dark comedies that took me to the precipice of death. Mine were tragicomedies, and Satan made me do them all, I am sure; but that excuse has never redeemed a single foolish act, or freed a single slave from the consequences. I am glad my father and mother are not alive to read my confessions in these chapters. I wish you didn't have to read them here, but I have prayed for your edification, not your harm.

When I told my writing consultant about the origin of this particular *Tragicomedy of the Scars*, I put my finger nail just below the actual scar so that she could be convinced of the veracity of my story. "Can you see this scar?" I leaned over the chair arm so she could see. "You have to look closely." She was easily convinced of my tall tale. "See where the tiny stitches were made in the emergency room?" She rocked her head, reassuring me a couple of times that she could see it. I surmised that time had rendered my foolish wounds less foolish. After all, I was a writer now. God had not rejected me, in spite of what I had done to myself and to others.

But this faded scar held the telltale DNA of my temporary insanity from that former time. Though that trauma has faded, and is nearly gone, scars recede, but never really disappear. Is this true for you? The pain is beautifully woven into the threadbare clothes of memory, and gradually, the chains and soul-ties have faded away. "Today," I explained, "I can laugh as if this happened to someone else. I can remember a very foolish young man in love with a girl, peering into the precipice of death." I told her that, "My scar is my TimeMachine. It carries me back into a former time when my emotions were too strong for me to manage, and peace was far from me." I grabbed my left wrist with the other hand, saying,

"You can still see how God grabbed my wrist and shoved the Angel of Death away from me! He used several young men, for whom I held contempt. I was jealous like Cain; and I never knew their names. I have never spoken against fraternities since that night, except for the ones with the mindless hazing rituals. Arterial blood pulsed onto the dance floor that night, like some kind of macabre entertainment, God saved my life in the most peculiar circumstances."

The consultant got what she wanted, for I had described the events in a little more detail. She had read my flat descriptions of episodes in my life, and she had to get me to open up those rooms so that she could peer into the context with her five senses. Unless I revisited these events the same way, it would be impossible for me to tell you my story! She coaxed me to look down into that rabbit hole to see the range of things the earth might spit up from that dark night. I t helped me look down through time into the things that moved me deeply, recreating the sensory atmosphere.

169

Beneath the faint scar, I found a whole world, full of questions and answers—full of mercy and grace—unmerited favor from God and man. Inside my scar I have found a life full of parables and celebrations. Each scar on my wrist, leg, abdomen, elbow, and enumerable scars on my heart, contain the DNA of the average man. We all have scars, with these rooms opening up behind each one. These stories all have entrances and exits. There is insanity aplenty, and there is kindness coming inexplicably through it all.

I could barely finish the sentences, swallowing tears, knowing that this Phi Sigma Chi frat crew had brought me and their motto to life that night—*The Golden Rule*. "Do unto others as you would have them do unto you." They had been the Lamb of God to my foolish Adam. They had stepped between me, shielding me from the stone throwers and the Angel of Death. They had blocked his sickle with their own bodies, driving a bleeding stranger the seven long miles to the Emergency Room. Seven, the number of God—the number of days for the Creation described in Genesis—the Seventh Day was designated as a Day of Rest.[220] It is not the rest that we get from a *MyPillow* under our heads. It is the rest which comes when we know God loves us—when we know God has forgiven all of our sins, speaking to us as adopted sons and daughters. It is the day when God has done everything for us, creating the magnificent universe, and even sending His Son so that we might rest in Him—rest in His completed work on the Cross.[221]

After I arrived at their frat house that night, I was sure that the object of my affection would be dancing somewhere inside those vibrating walls. Moments later, I was shuffling along with her—dancing—and I was already too drunk to complete a primitive sentence. "I'm glad you came," she said, as I tried to stand up straight. "I am too," I slurred, surprised at her first words to me, barely hearing what she meant. She seemed so inexplicably affectionate that it surprised me. The decades have sobered me up enough to decode what happened that night on the dance floor and in that bloody room. Even through the alcohol's blinding effects, I felt her kindness directed to me. She was always kind.

How did I miss that? I remember walking into the open bar in the kitchen and pouring another drink even though I could barely see the plastic cups on the cluttered linoleum countertop. Bottles of liquor, beer, and wine filled the surface as I pushed my cup into a tiny crevice. I placed my vodka bottle there with the others, and I had a vague sense of the rising danger in that surrealistic yet existential moment that was unfolding. I felt very out-of-control, still afraid of appearing foolish. I knew, as drunks alone can understand, that the crazed bull had already burst its stall. I realized that I was clinging now to his arching back for dear life.

---

[220] Genesis 2:2.

[221] Hebrews 4:3.

When I went outside to urinate in the back yard, I discovered my complete lack of balance in the darkness—I had become a pirouette balancing on two rubber legs, not able to see my feet in the dark. The infinite persistence gyroscope failed in this first test, as the vodka took full authority over my autonomic life forces. Behind the propped-open door, I put my left hand up to brace as I stood there in the dark. I was unaware that I was standing in the crosshairs of the valley of the shadow of death. Does anyone ever know, just before the death Angel appears? As my hand pressed on a single pane of glass in front of me, the silicon crystal gave way in a confused instant. The pane splintered into a perfect point—like the tip of a spear. My hand slipped through the hole receiving a sharp prick.

The spear pierced my wrist as my hand slipped through the brand-new opening in the back door. I felt pressure on my wrist, and then a dull, darkening pain. "Uh oh," I thought out loud. I could vaguely see a dark contrail geysering from my wrist. The artery squirted its blood into the darkness as I staggered into the room where they were dancing. I held up my arm with that dark contrail spurting everywhere. This video excerpt from my life is filmed in grays and whites, with no colors. Quite calmly, I requested some advice about what to do next. With a couple of minutes to live, I looked for someone who might tell me what to do with the rest of my life.

The room must have been covered in blood, but I wouldn't know. The fraternity brother who saw me, took my wrist with a ferocious grip. He somehow steered me with that same urgency to a car, and I vaguely remember getting in.

This frat brother had the presence of mind to stop the bleeding and transport me to help! Someone else dove in, and the car lurched away, heading for the Emergency Room to the West in Seneca. My friend, the only one I knew by name, did not go with us as we bounced and jolted away into the night. God's grip grew firmer, as they questioned me about what had happened. "I had to pee—I fell through the glass in the door." I likely spoke these words to them in vodkaese. "You're going to be fine. We'll be there in a few minutes, and the doctor is going to stitch you up. Just hang in there. How are you feeling?" After a few quiet moments, the driver asked, without turning around, "You still okay?" His voice sounded grim with this simple informational request. I said, "I'm fine." I was actually fine.

I felt a drunken version of absolute trust of them, with an incredible amount of gratitude for these strangers whose gathering for a night of fun had been split in half because of my narcissistic shallow dive into their favorite girl. Their general competency gave me confidence that I would actually be fine. My negative feelings about fraternities, and this one in particular, ended that night in a most dramatic way. Their attention to the *Golden Rule* had become the only thing between my living and my dying. Every negative thing I had ever said got ameliorated by these unknown young men whose names I never knew, who were saving my life. Whoever grabbed my wrist, and whoever drove his car while my arterial blood spurted on his floor mats, gave me another day of life. A deep humility came with this collision into the solid brick wall of Myopic Me!

The ER doctor quickly went to work, with nurses helping all around. "How much did you have to drink?" he tried to keep me awake and talking, I suppose. My blood carried the toxic ethanol molecules all through a dehydrated body, slowing my brain's conversation with my diaphragm and lungs. If I went to sleep, I might stop breathing. Lots of dopamine had been released, and I had become a dope not far from death. The ER nurse connected the glucose bottle to the vein in my other hand. The doctor stitched up the artery and closed the wound with thread through the eye of this needle of God's circumstantial architecture.

On this night, I died in that dark back yard—and I am convinced that God instructed Satan and the Angel of Death with words like the ones spoken over Job in the famous Bible story. "You can do anything to him, but you may not take his life."[222] Now, the Angel of death heard God say, "Not time for John to be with Me! He will meet my Son in Atlanta in a couple of years! On Mt. Guyot, the last time he got into trouble, he promised to serve Me, signing an invisible spiritual contract. Though he has forgotten that covenant—it was a binding contract in the earth and in the heavenly realm."

---

[222] Job 2:6.

19.

INNOCENCE?

After I transferred to Clemson University from The Citadel, I ran into a man who graduated from Daniel High a few years before I did. We entered the Daniel High School basketball game together, coming to see the phenom, Pete Maravich. I had briefly played basketball with him in my senior year, and now in his third season at Daniel, he was only fifteen years old. The two of us walked into the game that was already underway, and the crowd was roaring every time Pete touched the ball. They also cheered when Jim Sutherland ripped the nets from the other forward position.

Each of them would star in college, with Pete breaking every collegiate scoring record, still standing after forty years—before the 3-point shot existed. Pistol Pete Maravich would become the first million dollar basketball player in the National Basketball Association with his bust displayed in the NBA Hall of Fame in Springfield Massachusetts. His bust faces the only other NBA player who has beat me at H. O. R. S. E.—the Hall of Fame great, Sam Jones, made short work of me in my driveway in New England. Horse is the game of special shots being made, requiring the other player to shoot the exact same shot, bounce for bounce, distance for distance, angle for angle. Pete could shoot from anywhere, and he did that day in the "Little Gym" in the "Y." Sam had coached Pete in Boston at the end of both of their careers! There I was talking about Pete with him in my driveway, and he was ripping shots from every direction. My neighbor came over the next day to ask me a question: "Was that Sam Jones shooting baskets in your driveway?"

Sam has never met a stranger, but he can tell stories about the challenges of being an *NBA* player in Boston in the early years. Having won ten championships during his playing time, he became famous for his high-scoring bank shots, using the backboard. He was teamed with Bob Cousy and Bill Russel on those great *Boston Celtics* championships in the 1950s and 1960s. Fame brings many things, and some of those things are actually good. Sam is one of those good things—a great man—who had a great mother. Louise gets all the credit for her son, for she faced impossible odds, raising him to be a successful man, and a gentle-man. Her faith and prayers helped to keep our marriage together, for she was more than a mother to my wife. She was her friend.

When Sam coached Pete in his final years in Boston, he had bad knees, plus that same frail body-type. If I had looked at him that night in the Daniel High gym with crystal clear hindsight, I might have been able to see the defect in Pete's heart as he ran by. I might have seen that defect that would finally kill him twenty-seven years later. I could have zoomed in with the 3-D imagining technology from the future to see the missing artery on the exterior of his heart. That defect in his heart was physiological, as well as spiritual. The missing artery would have supplied the blood of Jesus to consecrate his life. Jesus would later be there to fill him with holy oxygen when he died in his brother's arms. The last thing Pete said on earth was, "I feel awesome!" Pete was pale, thin, bony, and fiercely competitive, but his heart was leaking eternal life out into the vacuum of space.

Pete never stopped dribbling, shooting, and spinning the basketball in the air on one finger. He bounced the ball in the theater beside his seat when we watched the Western together. He bounced it when he rode his bike, and bounced it out the car window of Press Maravich's car when his dad took him home from the Clemson College *Field House*. He knew the personality and the bounce of the ball better than any other player. Firing from his chest, behind his back, or between his legs, he could do nearly anything he wanted with a basketball. The game of basketball itself was captured in the eye-of-his-storm, and nothing could dislodge him from this ultimate game since the foundations of the world—on this night, he was utterly dedicated to ripping the nets with a ball that still looked enormous in his fifteen year old hands.

If you looked closely that night, you might have seen the Cross of Christ replacing that bouncing ball and every other idol which Pete would finally worship before he surrendered to the Lord. No idolatry has been more powerful than the one God tore down in his life. It nearly destroyed him. He tried every religion, before Jesus saved him. Jesus hooked his soul when many destructive patterns were dominating his daily routines. If you looked closely that night at Daniel High, you could see a small boy about to become a man in a world that devours its heroes. If you looked closely, you could have seen Bobby and me committing some offense before that crowd gathered in praise of Pete and Jim.

They praised our winning team. They praised Daniel High, where the Lions were roaring, where I had played football, basketball, and ran track, even considering pitching on the baseball team. We all praised Pete, for he was a phenom. Who could look away from his presence impacting our little bump into the Space-Time Continuum? But I always worried, knowing the powerful forces he would encounter, the terrible headwinds of fame and fortune. As foolish as I was, I saw him as a younger brother, braver than all of us. Though he was from Aliquippa, I saw him as a Clemson kid growing up among us. General Lachlan McIntosh, my multi-great grandfather, had built his fort in Pete's back yard near Aliquippa in central Pennsylvania.

Bobby and I must have done something which made the crowd and the authorities angry. We stood for a moment too long on the sidelines watching Pete fly down the court with his socks flopping as he hoisted a 25-foot set shot from his right ear. He was still quite small, and he had learned to use every form of leverage to send the ball into the steel orange rim. He used angular momentum and inertia—Newtons' first, second, and third laws—along with his bony elbows and shoulders. He had become the super-computer-modified Roman catapult flinging the ball through space and time—while on a full-speed dash, with drib-bles programmed into his very soul. Pete flew along our near sideline while the fanatics behind us tried to watch him go by—Bobby and I could have reached out to snatch the ball off his dribble, and Pete would have easily avoided us.

Then he let go of the ball off his right ear, sweeping an arc across the end of the gymnasium, and it sailed cleanly through the nets without disturbing a single cotton fiber. Everyone roared with ecstasy, being able to watch this impossible player perform. Every seat was filled, but we still tried to find an empty slot above us in the bleachers. Apparently the authorities in the crowd saw some-thing they didn't like. I never really understood what had angered them, though they said we created a disturbance. We must have stood there longer than it seemed, for the sheriffs ushered us out of the gym before we could be assimi-lated into the mob. Dramatic things happen in crowds, where the superfluous and the sublime merge as one. Pete was dying, and should have been dead, but no one even noticed!

> "Usually patients like this don't go on for 40 years. They don't make it that long," said Dr. Paul Thompson, a sudden death expert at Brown University in Rhode Island who reviewed the Maravich autopsy file Wednesday. "The problem with the diagnosis," said Dr. Thomas Klitzner, a UCLA specialist in pediatric cardiology and the way heart rhythm disturbances lead to sudden death, "is how did he play basketball for all those years in the NBA?"[223]

While we were disturbing the fan-atics, Pete's doctors were ignoring the missing artery in his heart! While Pete was doing the impossible, Bobby might have done the possible, behind my back. Did he hurl the middle finger of con-tempt at the rude crowd looking down on us? I vaguely sensed that I had entered the gym with "Bobby the Kid," the famous gun slinger from Manhattan who died in New Mexico. There was something about him that ruffled their feathers as we passed through this tiny undulation in the fabric of time—did he drag some prior history behind him like a wrecking ball? I must have been caught up in the jet wash of his trouble-maki8ng reputation, for we were kicked out of the building and told not to come back.

---

[223] Parachini. *Maravich's Heart.*

Did Jesus also stand too long in the public forum, blocking the view of the Pharisees in Jerusalem? How angry they must have been when He stole their crowds and syphoned off their adulation by the common man. If we stood too long in the Daniel High gym, Jesus must have cast a great shadow across their self-aggrandizement. He must have called them a brood of vipers, a white-washed tomb full of dead men's bones!

When He healed the man on the Sabbath, they must have been furious, convinced that it was Satan's power, in direct violation of God's ordinance for the day of rest. Little did they understand God's rest, and many of them would never enter His rest because of their lack of faith. While Bobby and I created some kind of vague kerfuffle in the gym, Jesus, the rebel with a cause, must have also turned over their tables when He found them showing favoritism— still excluding every Gentile person from the Holy of holies. In one week, He would included them, tearing the Curtain in the Temple, permitting all men to draw near to God's throne of grace.

Jesus' lawyer was no better than ours, for Bobby and I would be crucified for our disruption of the worship in the Daniel High gym. Pete was the unintentional priest of a new kingdom that would include him in its Hall of Fame. When the dust cleared in the Lion's Den at Daniel High, the Scapegoats had been chosen, only to be released outside the city's walls. The curtain of the Temple had been torn from top to bottom, exposing the High Priest scurrying about in his Holy Robes. We were baffled as to what had just happened.

The dead had climbed from their graves to walk among their families. The Roman officer with his men had declared that Jesus truly was the Son of God. The earthquake split the world at the moment of His death, and the sky turned dark as night at 3:00 p.m. when Satan's screams could be heard as Judas Iscariot leaped from the tree limb. On Golgotha, the blood of the Scapegoat was washed away in the storm, filling every well across the whole world with God's offer for reconciliation and friendship.

My family hired our lawyer, and I remember him gesticulating and spraying his spittle in all directions in that old dusty courtroom where the air filled up with his spurious arguments, just moments before they fined us $250—the equivalent of about $2500 today. My father had to pay the bill for our disruptive behavior since I was in college with no income. That was a lot of money for a minute of a basketball game—even if Pistol Pete was playing. I remained convinced that the fine had been paid for someone else's crime since I had done nothing.

There was an agenda in the air which I could never fully understand. There was an injustice that I could never comprehend. For one moment, I had stood with a troubled young man who had a chip on his shoulder. Our fragile case unraveled in the courtroom where the law doesn't care about much of anything. We were charged, presumed to be guilty, and there was nothing we could do to clear our names.

The Son of God was grabbed in darkness when Judas betrayed Him with a kiss. In an illegitimate court, paid witnesses were waiting to repeat their lies to keep this troublemaker out of their politics. Their status quo was their god, and they would even kill God's Son to preserve it. They needed a Scapegoat to die for all of them, and they found Him praying late at night in the Garden of Gethsemane. He was praying for them, that He would follow the Father's plan to die on the Cross for the ones who had wrongly accused Him. He was telling God the Father that He would drink the cup of suffering, even for the ones who wanted to kill Him.

I became a scapegoat for the anger and unforgiveness directed toward us from somewhere that my eyes could not comprehend. In that season of Pistol Pete's rise into his great fame, I still did not understand that the Lamb had also been slain for my rebellion. Jesus' great fame had flown across the entire universe, and beyond the universe, but I was unaware of His heroism. I couldn't comprehend His set shot, or His socks high on His ankles as he flew by me while I blocked the view of those who worshiped Him. I did not know that three spikes would kill him, not at age forty, but at age thirty-two. He had become so famous that He made many enemies by the time that spear was run through His side in death. The shadow of Jesus' Cross had become the shield against eternal destruction, but I could not get past that dust and spittle flying in my remote life.

The strength of man, I would finally understand, did not accomplish the good things of this life, for good men will simply kill God's Son sent to save them. God's kindness is the miracle. It is easy to dive into the Garden of Eden where God's kindness and provision were brushed aside by Adam and Eve. When their scapegoat was slaughtered for their shame, their nakedness, they were forced to leave the safety and eternal provision of that paradise they took for granted. Their little lamb died for their disobedience. Jesus would be the final Lamb to cover our shame, when we brushed aside the kindness and provision of God. Therefore, He is worthy of all praise.

> "You are worthy to take the scroll
> and break its seals and open it.
> For you were slaughtered, and your blood has ransomed
> people for God
> from every tribe and language and people and nation.
> And you have caused them to become
> a Kingdom of priests for our God.
> And they will reign on the earth." Revelation 5:9-10

I don't know what happened to my eventual good friend. He seemed to be carrying chains around on his shoulders everywhere he went. The last time I saw him, he was hovering over a friend's wife in the strangest scene of seduction the world has ever known. He was trying to seduce her while he counseled her about her future. She was lying on a table, in the middle of the room, and Bobby stood around her with a couple of others in the darkened room. They were hanging over her with their seductive, drooling, counsel, and there was no question that she was the object of desire in that room.

Are we humans not like vultures gathering for an accidental feast? What could possibly make God give us a second glance? With His thumb, He could wipe us, like those tiny spiders that ran across my computer screen yesterday on the deck. Bobby's bad influence was not overt, but hung above his head like Schultz's dark cloud over *Pigpen*. The dark cloud was always there. For a while, my own rebellion pulled me into this sad vortex, apart from God's possibilities. Surely I missed a big chance to be a real friend to him, instead of a fun buddy. I believe God still has blessings prepared for Bobby, if he is still on this planet— if he has given up listening to his Nemesis, continually visiting that dark bridge of Narcissus.

When Cain raised the first stone to crush his brother's skull, Noah's Ark was already rising on the flood to come through the first rain and floodgates of heaven. The firestorm of Sodom and Gomorrah had already erupted with a brilliant glow in the far distant sky. The orgy at the base of Mt. Sinai, where every idolater danced around a golden calf, had already being choreographed by the Prince of the Air. The dust had already flown across the desert landscape, whirling into a powerful mirage of another god rising on the Saudi Arabian Peninsula. The Oil Cartel had already asserted control over the world's oil supply, holding many nations hostage to their deep pools of black gold. Entropy escaped its cage, and the Clock started its growl.

> A young male jaguar at the Audubon Zoo in New Orleans slipped out of its enclosure in the dark of night and went on a territorial killing rampage, attacking alpacas and foxes and an emu trapped in their own habitats before veterinarians armed with tranquilizers managed to sedate it . . . The jaguar did not appear to be eating the animals it went after but rather was engaged in a territorial display, said Kyle Burks, the zoo's vice president and managing director.[224]

Entropy was released into the world long ago in the Garden of Eden when the howling jaguar burst its bounds to extend its territory. The Prince of the Air asserted his territorial rights over every corner of the world, breaking the necks of as many as he wanted. Eve, and Adam had abdicated their rights to subdue the earth. The Serpent took control of the spiritual atmosphere. Now, he puts fear into the hearts of the emus, coercing the alpacas and the foxes, extending his bondage and terror to every creature captured in their sins.

---

[224] *Jaguar escapes.* Washington Post.

Eve complained that her inattentive husband had failed to protect her from the mischievous creature with the forked tongue. She demanded reparations, addressing God (without looking directly at His glory). "You knew this fruit would attract my eye?" He understood perfectly her attraction for that particular fruit—He had made it off-limits, telling Adam to take care of it. But He also knew that her life would be rich with beautiful fruit which would not harm her. "This forbidden fruit will kill you!" Since Eve had no personal relationship with the Word of God, her understanding had to come from Adam. "How could He foresee my needs when He failed to tell me anything about the tree?" The lamb watched from the tree line to see what would happen.

20.

BASEMENT BAPTISM.

I clearly remember what God said to me that summer day in the basement shower. The shower water washed my body at the end of a sweaty day, but my sin needed a stronger cleanser. I had no twenty-foot-high flood over the Canadian side of the falls to rinse me. And even the *Ivory soap*, at ninety-nine percent pure, could not wash away my sins. Like Pilate's hands, covered with the blood of Jesus, the water in that silver bowl could not absolve me of my guilt. In that late afternoon shower, the soap could only emulsify the Southern slime, while the treated water from Lake Hartwell rinsed my soiled life down the drain.

My nakedness did not improve my chances with the God whom I still did not know. God required that my soul be bared as well. He required that I come to agreement with Him, offering none of my sophomoric self-justification, or lame ignorance. My sin remained, while my skin got squeaky-clean on that hot day. Somehow this vision of those great waters struck me with the proper dread, and the fear of punishment changed my path at this critical moment. It would be the first of several powerful interventions God had scheduled for me.

My good-guy had certainly come to an ugly culmination as I ignored everyone's counsel during this headstrong period of my young life. This nasty shower in the unfinished basement provided the perfect backdrop for God speaking in a new language to Myopic Me! Directly above my head, the spiders were swinging in their dark webs. The rotting edges of the wooden shower boards became the emblem of my own "whitewashed tomb full of dead men's bones." God was showing me that inside, I was filthy—"full of greed and self-indulgence!" I had become the home to a "brood of vipers"[225] which urged me to jump the rails of peace and self-constraint. This filthy version of myself, beyond the healing of water, had never crossed my mind until this afternoon. This concomitant emotion fell on me like a sudden shroud of fear.

As I cried out to God in that shower, without knowing how to do that, I just hurled my emotions up through the vibrating webs into the dark ceiling. I hoped that Someone beyond myself would answer me. Though God had delivered me from Mt. Guyot's cold grip five years before, I had paid little attention to Him in the years since then. How did I ignore His kindness? How could I disregard

---

[225] Matthew 23:25-33

His encouragement? Why did I not hear His warning about idolatry and fear? I assumed that the encounter was a figment out of my cowardice—and, of course, it was. Gideon was a coward hiding in a winepress when God told him to lead Israel against the million-man Philistine army. Looking backward, my behavior in the intervening years deserved His condemnation, not His kindness.

Having some vague pact with God's grace, I gave little effort to finding out more about my Lord. I made little effort contacting Him. Basically, I had no visible relationship with God at all. I exposed myself to every danger that youthful passions might pursue, and I had no idea that the thrill-ride would soon end in crisis and loss. Not visiting church services during this period of my life, I was living like one who had no need of God's help. I was facing a shameful possibility which could destroy me, taking others down with me. Solomon summed up my situation at the end of Ecclesiastes. My secret thing was overwhelming me.

> That's the whole story. Here now is my final conclusion: Fear God and obey his commands, for this is everyone's duty. God will judge us for everything we do, including every secret thing, whether good or bad. Ecclesiastes 12:13-14

The vortex of carelessness had carried me down into Wonderland. Nonsense had become good sense, and dark Queens had become good rulers. I became a slave to the spinning hands of the Clock. I was living in fear of the Cheshire Cat's appearing. I had no clue that God, the unknown God, could do anything to save me from myself. The Red Sea was blocking my escape, and no Lamb's blood protected my door.[226] I had hidden myself in the wagons of the Israelites, hiding in their clothes. I vaguely hoped that Moses could tell me what to do—after all, he had fled from Egypt with a price on his head. I had not spoken to Jesus since Joseph and Nicodemus placed His body in the Tomb. I didn't want to ask Him how much trouble I was in. The pull-string had broken off of the light fixture high above me, and there was no light in my heart.

In the midst of my authentic cry for help in that basement shower, God spoke to me with irreducible logic, telling me that my fear would pass without the specific consequence which filled me up with terror. His words brought instantaneous comfort, as I crouched down on the wooden drainage boards in awe of Him speaking. The God of All Creation had just spoken to me with succinctness, bringing relief instantly. I hyperventilated there in the dark-become-bright in an unction of awe. With fear overwhelming me, I suddenly understood that it would be okay. An A to Z journey with deductive and induction and logical metamorphosis occurred subliminally in an interval too short to measure with an atomic clock. Overwhelmed with the certitude of God's words to me, I could not

---

[226] Exodus 12:13

wait to share this supernatural encounter with the people near me. I had to tell someone what God had said. But how could I tell anyone, since it was unclear how the other parties would be affected by my good news? I was stunned that God would speak to *Myopic Me!* I was struck by the same wonderment which David expressed three-thousand years ago.

> O Lord, what are human beings that you should notice them,
> mere mortals that you should think about them?
> For they are like a breath of air;
> their days are like a passing shadow. Psalm 144:3-4

The God of heaven and earth, the Creator of all things, had spoken to me in a nasty basement shower in a moment when I was supremely aware of my own sins. My fears went into complete remission as soon as He spoke. I gradually realized that this ostensible good might be construed as loss to anyone I informed. They would see my story as exclusive, rather than inclusive. They would feel jealous or fearful. They would feel condemned, though I could see that God had not condemned me or them. Though God had not used the English language in speaking to me, I realized He spoke clearly to me using some elemental dialect.

"It's okay." I heard this in my soul, body, and mind. He didn't say this out loud, though it was loud enough to rise over the shower's wind and rain. I didn't hear it in the way a preacher would say it. It was personal, internal—a language tuned to my own heart. He put this information in my mind as easily as He had written the Ten Commandments on the stone tablets on Mt. Sinai. His voice spoke words my heart understood. It's useless to try to describe. How can I tell another person about an unearthly language, a script written with heaven's pen? His quiet voice could not be translated into English or Arabic. He used a language that repulsed everyone else while drawing me into the Faith-Time Continuum. As they drew back from my baptismal story, I knew there was nothing to fear.

I told my friend, and she didn't seem happy for me. She looked for the nearest escape from my news, as if I had leprosy. She could not handle this non sequitur message from another realm. For me, it was absolute clarity. The deus ex machina—*theos ek mekhanes*—returned into the clouds.[227] Though the Greeks demonstrated this appearance of their gods in their stage productions by using a crane to lower the god into the dramatic situation, God spoke in an unknown language, fully known to me. He spoke to me with private meanings, in a private message meant only for me, which I tried to share as if I were

---

[227] *Deus ex machina.* Wikipedia,

boasting over this encounter with the Rock Star of Heaven. We had shared a moment—Holy God, with Me.

That sounds sacrilegious, but it has nothing to do with religion. It had everything to do with my direct connection to Him! It sounds like hubris, but Pride had been washed down the drain below those slats in the bottom of the grungy shower. His message arrived like a tornado baby that drops from the clouds in eastern North Carolina on the final straight shot to the ocean. God's message dropped down like a Slinky, and pulled back into the sky before I could get a printout of what He said. Could I outrun this light from God that lit the sky in that black shower? Did I imagine those tornado embryos that sprung back into the black sky that day? Did God not speak into my situation with His mysterious language?

No one could understand how that shower water could have silenced my wicked witch, leaving a fool to spin tall tales of God's love. With an encrypted transmission that only I could decode, I felt the personal nature of it like a sword through my heart. The voice of God is a two-edged sword, I would learn—it cuts to the joints and marrow, revealing the motives of the heart. I wanted to avoid trouble, but I had no intention of changing my ways. But something had to change, or this precious message would be lost.

I heard what I wanted to hear in that shower, but I failed to receive His clear message to "go and sin no more." I had no confusion that God spoke a second important message to me. But I heard Him speak once with relief, and the second time leaving me ignorant of what I should do next—I was fully aware of the stunning connection between heaven and earth, though I couldn't say what this meant. God's intention is always to establish His kingdom within Me, crushing the kingdom of this world with its idolatry. He sees the idols which I don't see. They are obvious and powerful—useless and dumb. I stood at my imaginary dedication of His Temple, just as Solomon had three-thousand years ago. I listened closely, joyfully, to one half of what God's spoke to me about my own idolatry. I heard one-half of that supernatural message which stunned me to my core.

That miraculous language sent me off on a bifurcated mission; yet I only heard the first half of the classic message from God. Since then, I have learned that He often gives a word of hope and encouragement, plus a warning. The auditory filter for Myopic Me! screened out the warning, retaining the words of encouragement. "You will be blameless and untouched by trouble, but you must abandon your destructive and sinful life patterns." This is actually a conditional promise ("untouched by trouble"). I heard the promise of blessing, but I missed His warning positioned as a necessary and sufficient condition for the full blessing: "Abandon your destructive and sinful life patterns" was a clear admonition calling me to confess my utter inability to save myself.

I know now that He was saying, "Turn from every idol that robs you of power and freedom, and worship the God who loves you!" By ignoring God's gating condition, simply put, His warrantee was voided. I would have to surrender everything. His Grace would then empower me to overcome sin. I did not know that the wages of sin is death. I did not know that Jesus would become my Savior and Lord. It would be two or three years before He would become the peace of Myopic Me![228]

In Jesus' three years of ministry, before He was crucified, buried, and raised from the dead after three days, He was condemned for spending time with sinners. He became the scandal in Jerusalem. A tax collector became His disciple. A former prostitute followed Him everywhere, and a sinful Samaritan woman sat with Him at Jacob's well. These relationships proved, in their minds, that He was not sent from God. The religious leaders believed His behavior disqualified Him. His behavior was clearly scandalous. They decided to kill Him, fearing what He would become, affecting their rule-bound religious domain. Jesus said that He came to save sinners, not the righteous.

I was afraid of losing what I could not live without, and I didn't even know it! She had become my false god, and she could not bear that burden. No human being can take on this obligation as the god in another person's life. She could not meet my deep need of forgiveness for the fifth step of my fall from imagined grace—my need for deliverance from sin and death haunted me. Multiple voices were speaking in my ear, and discernment had not yet come to protect me from the lie-twisted-around-the-truth. Only the scandalous Grace of God could stoop down to heal my blindness. The gifts of God would come much later, so that I could learn to defend myself from the wind full of flies and lies that splattered daily on my windshield. God's gifts would become essential in my new life empowered by the Holy Spirit rather than my idolatry.

> *A spiritual gift is given to each of us so we can help each other. To one person the Spirit gives the ability to give wise advice; to another the same Spirit gives a message of special knowledge. The same Spirit gives great faith to another, and to someone else the one Spirit gives the gift of healing. He gives one person the power to perform miracles, and another the ability to prophesy. He gives someone else the ability to discern whether a message is from the Spirit of God or from another spirit. 1 Corinthians 12:7-10*

---

[228] Hebrews 4:16

21.

WITCHES SABBATH.

During these same two or three months at Lockheed, my father had gone in for a simple gall bladder removal—not so simple in that day before laparoscopic surgery. I waited with my sisters and mother in Anderson Hospital until he came out of the recovery room. This procedure was more severe in his day because of the long incision across the stomach muscles under the rib-cage. The doctor arrived a half-hour after starting, and I imagined this was very good news indeed. The surgeon spoke to the three of us in a stern cold voice saying there was nothing he could do. When he found Pop's body already filled with cancer—his lungs, liver, and pancreas were inoperable—the surgeon just stitched him back up. Pop had less than two months to live.

My sister remembers the surgeon's rudeness. Fifty-years later, she still fills-up with anger towards this indifferent messenger. The surgeon was so irritated with having to tell us Pop would soon die. It seemed a great inconvenience for this angry surgeon, who had many patients to lop open before his work day was done. Pop's death struck me in the mouth like brass knuckles—with a sting so deep that it took my breath away. He was dead already by way of this cold medical declaration—spoken like the cruel God whom many know, or think they know. But this was no god who spoke to us about the head of our household, our father, our friend. My hope was instantly gone, and I saw nothing but pain ahead. No one in my family had died, and Pop would depart before the rest of us would see death.

Grandmothers would live beyond his day. My great aunt would outlive him. My mother would survive him, through another thirty-two years in the same house. He was so afraid she would sell the house and squander the money, but she proved a formidable money manager and a frugal grandmother to her expanding family—though she never held anything back from those close to her. I felt the shock of his loss in the Anderson Hospital touching a part of me that was far more vulnerable than my solar plexus. My stomach had retracted and would not return. I could not start up my breathing again, as Death curled around me. It was my death and his death. Death took the stage, and this surgeon had served it up like so much slop on a soldier's plate in a mess hall. Standing firmly in the double-doors, medical people slid roughly past us, and my youth got spun up into the rugged spokes of eternity. Solomon tries to put a positive spin on this hard plate of gruel.

> *For everything there is a season,*
>   *a time for every activity under heaven.*
> *A time to be born and a time to die.*
>   *A time to plant and a time to harvest.*
> *A time to kill and a time to heal.*
>   *A time to tear down and a time to build up.*
> *A time to cry and a time to laugh.*
>   *A time to grieve and a time to dance. Ecclesiastes 3:1-4*

I knew very little about this prescription from God. I knew very little about dying or harvesting. I knew nothing about these activities under heaven. As for our Thanksgiving plans, these events took an unfamiliar turn; and Christmas, the annual joy, passed in the silence of staring straight ahead, passing like strangers in the fog of grief even before he died. His earthly journey ended on the eighth day of January. One moment he was tying tomatoes in the backyard garden. The next moment, the mortician rolled him across our front lawn strewn with acorns from the white oak tree.

I saw him squat down when the vertigo struck hard, and he could no longer find his bearings on Planet Earth. I was terrified that afternoon, in the same manner as Mt. Guyot, where I assumed that I would die at age fourteen. That hot afternoon in the tomato garden, I wondered if Pop had stroked in the humid summer heat. His heart palpitations and blood pressure spiked before the family doctor told him to get a surgeon's counsel. Surgeons surge, but bodies fill up with worms. Pop's surgeon left us with very little air to breathe.

Lying in his bed at home, with a morphine drip in his arm and oxygen clipped to his nose, he quickly lost half his one hundred and eighty pounds of body weight. Pop, whom I scarcely knew as an adult person, had a few more weeks to live. The shock of it, and the suddenness of his decline, brought a scream from deep inside of me. I don't know if the scream came out of my own fear of death, or if it expressed my agony over losing Pop. A mouth inside of me produced a terrible life-changing sound—it would represent a great evil that sought to destroy me, but it would bring me to someone Who is very Good. The wail from an unknown wilderness was independent of my normal emotional functioning. I had not realized that it was there, until I heard it.

I could not corral or manage it. It revealed things inside of me that I knew nothing about. It nearly destroyed me; but God used that sound, and the spirit behind that scream, to save me from the second death. You ask, "What is the second death?" I could not know then that it is the death that comes on Judgment Day. It is the day of death that extracts the air eternally from the lungs of the

186

one who lives apart from God. It is the day when Matt Kowalski slips into the endless black vacuum of eternity, frozen inside his space suit, slipping farther and farther away from home forever.[229]

Immediately after Pop's surgery, my mother rolled her brand-new VW Bug down an embankment as she returned from teaching 11th grade English in Anderson at Hannah High. The little yellow car was so beautiful—her beautiful car was no more than a few months old, and she suffered a compound fracture, with the ulna protruding through her arm. She suffered a fracture of her back as she was tossed multiple times inside the tiny interior of the vehicle. Her life was polished that night by the sharp edges of the cans. They knocked off all of her rough edges—and she had very few rough edges. She was black and blue in the most extreme sense.

Exhausted by anguish over Pop's terrible prognosis, she fell asleep at the wheel. The wrecker driver concluded that the tire got ripped off the rim as she lost control hitting the edge of the raised road surface. My heart was ripped off the rim when I saw her in the hospital bed decorated with those bruises covering her from head to toe. She had climbed thirty feet alone up to the highway surface to flag a passing car down. She only saw the bone sticking out of her arm when she reached the light above. In shock, she had no idea how serious her injuries were. Her tiny, sixty-year-old body, received twenty or thirty blows from the cans of fruit and tomatoes flying from the bags as the car plummeted at fifty-five mph down the steep red clay slope of this new highway. Her back was broken, fractured, and she hardly knew how much pain she was in with the morphine drip they gave her.

She was treated by an ER surgeon before she arrived in a private room on the floor directly below Pop. Family members gathered to visit them, and we spoke very little about her nearly life-ending wreck. Though she had suffered severe injuries, we were crushed by Pop's terminal diagnosis. All we could think about was Pop was dead. He did not know it yet, but we knew it. Pop was as good as dead! My mother's extreme condition hardly warranted a comment between us. We were glad she was alive, with her broken back and her compound fracture of her arm, and her black decorative bruises all over her body; but Pop's prognosis preoccupied our conversation.

In a few more days, I returned home to Clemson to spend the weekend there with Pop, while mom remained in the hospital another few days. I placed the wonderful, terrible, *Symphonie Fantastique* on the turntable I had brought with me from Smyrna. Everything I owned found a resting place in the living room floor. With the volume turned to the maximum forty watts RMS, Berlioz screamed out his own version of my madness. Was he mad? I certainly was. Madness comes in many forms, and I couldn't go anywhere without my home-made stereo and my new albums purchased with my meager Lockheed salary.

---

[229] *Gravity*. Wikipedia.

I took everything with me because I was so proud of it. And I needed this slight grip on control in a world flying off the rails. I could cut it on, place the record on the turntable, and lower the tone arm gently down to the record's first groove. I could invoke Berlioz, though he died one hundred years earlier. I could control the volume of the orchestra, and choose any one of the four movements of the symphony. But I couldn't wash away the growing awareness that my peace had taken wing and flown to an unknown continent.

There I sat in the living room floor. Pop had hired an architect twenty-eight years earlier to design this $8,000 house before stereophonic sound became the norm. In the 1940s, an architect might visualize the piano keys pouring out chords and melodies from the corner of the living room. The stereo sound came from the vibrating piano wires inside the four-foot wide sound chamber of the piano itself. That simple musical potential directed the architect's pen during this WWII season. The tiny price tag possible during that era belied the strong design and beauty of our modest house. This architect could not have foreseen the importance of music and media arising in the late 1960s with the arrival of transistor technologies. No special room could have anticipated my *Heathkit* amplifier, turntable, and *AR* speakers performing Berlioz's scherzo as if the entire orchestra had followed me home.

Sick and dying, Pop lay alone upstairs, only vaguely aware of the sentence of death he just received from his surgeon. The doctors delayed informing him of the gravity of what they found. They gave him a few days for recovery from the surgery before telling him. Of course, that gave them a few days to prepare themselves as well. When I heard the family doctor inform him a week later, Pop already knew that cancer carried a sentence of death. No one recovered from cancer in the 1960s. No cure existed. But the word "cancer" never came out of this doctor's mouth during their brief conversation.

I heard him dropping deadly clues that would help an intelligent man decode the meaning. I listened at the bottom of the stairs as the doctor spoke. I heard Pop bravely ask him, "Is it the 'C-word?'" Even he could not utter that forbidden word, C-A-N-C-E-R. These six letters came straight from the terror of death row. But he seemed calm. The doctor was the prison guard saying, "I'm so sorry to have to inform you, Professor Lane, but you will be executed in two weeks by lethal injection."

We say the word today with hope because of chemo and faith that God is bigger than cancer through fervent prayer. Today, we know people who have been healed by God's intervention—doctors even declaring it a miracle. We know many who have survived the chemotherapy and the cancer. We see miracles, but I had no knowledge of this faith on that afternoon when the sun disappeared in the West. I stood in the living room looking out the front window, and I could see the trees consumed by the sun's small yellow fire. It vanished into the same woodpile where I learned the hard lesson of bicycle riding. Unable to turn the wheel away from the waiting disaster, I struck the woodpile head-on.

I wished that Pop might get up to dust himself off after his humiliating crash—finding himself bruised and embarrassed.

As the final movement of Hector Berlioz's symphony roared with the *March to the Scaffold–Dance of the Witches Sabbath*, the sounds punctuated my own emotional extremes, devouring me. I was wrenched by convulsive tears of grief before he was even gone. The tears came from an unknown place even deeper than death. The loss already seemed deeper than a father dying. It came from somewhere I had never visited before. A brokenness appeared inside of me out of a bottomless pit of despair leaving me full of dread and panic. The intensity of Berlioz's scherzo grew toward the crescendo. His use of the orchestra pushed the limits of the sound production equipment, and he sometimes made use of a thousand musicians to achieve the concussive force he desired. For me, no sound could be loud enough to drown out the scream inside my soul.

Pop's voice gradually rose from upstairs so that I could hear him through the wailing violins and piccolo of my portable orchestra—a thousand musicians were silenced when I finally detected his voice from all the other instruments shrilling. What did he say? I strained to hear the faint sounds. "Are you okay—is everything okay?" he asked my status. Guilt swept through me, as I understood how ironic our contrasting emotions were. I answered him with a lie, saying, "Yes. I'm just playing my stereo." I turned it back up, but not as loud. This spiritual scherzo from several tortured realms flew into my soul on the carrier wave of Berlioz's twisted mind. The irony of Pop asking me, "Are you okay?" Neither one of us was "okay." God had His hand on two sparrows—and the hairs of our heads were becoming more difficult for God to count. Our feathers were being scattered all over the ground below the fragile limbs of our lives.

My music professor taught us to love music in our bleary-eyed 8:00 a.m. Saturday morning classes. He explained that these piccolo-shrills in the fourth movement added unique emotional and spiritual power to *Symphonie Fantastique*. With all the potent orchestration that Berlioz launched in this *Witches Sabbath* finale, he showed us that these tiny instruments could tower over the rest to finish this brilliant piece. The shrill insistence of the piccolo completed the twisted harmonics of the demons' hysteria in this rarely equaled crescendo by the French composer. Beautiful it is. It matched my own barely controlled hysteria. How much longer would I be able to hold it together?

This music professor took his own life when the madness of that piccolo in his head proved too much for him to bear. He was a kind man, and the father of my friend. While I contemplated my own mortality, he was struggling with his own. We passed each other like sentinels in silence. In life, we barely express honest pain to each other, rarely confessing our sins to one another, that we might be healed by the light of God. The Scriptures tell us to confess our sins in order to be healed. Neither of us confessed our true feelings on those mornings, but I still felt a special kinship with him. Maybe we could not articulate what is too terrible to say out loud, and he could never find escape from his own private terrors.

His piccolo never left his frontal lobe, so he found a way to douse the volume of his life. Now, in my family's living room, that same demonic swirling of sound entered the vortex of my personal anguish. Dialing back the volume, I mourned his death while he yet lived. Suffering loss before the day arrived, I mourned without receiving God's comfort and hope. I privately suffered something that I could not share with him. I mourned, not knowing him as I imagined a son should know his father. I had failed to love him, and I would never be able to make him proud of me.

I never vacationed in the Southwest with him, or in Mexico, or shared my future time in Texas, New Mexico, and Arizona with him. He would never see the great 4000-square foot house I built with my own hands, or know my son who needed a grandfather so badly. He never even met my wife, nor did he get the chance to show her the unconditional acceptance that she deserved—a wonderful mother and wife. She could have had a second dad to speak approbation into her life. He never read my grown-up version of *The Old Man and the Sea* which he had encouraged me to write in my own words three consecutive times. The skeleton of the fish haunted me, as I looked into the eyes of death with no defense—death's stinger was pressed into my soul.

He would not read this account of our relationship, to correct my misconceptions and to add his own chapter to my own. I couldn't even invite him to my first apartment to see my new king size foam latex mattress on the homemade plywood frame. He did say before his death that he could hardly believe I would be able to purchase something that expensive. The store manager treated me as if he were my father, helping me set up a four-week payment plan. He told me that this would establish my credit standing, while allowing me to have enough left over for groceries and gasoline.

When the piccolo finally died, so did I. Every tear of loss drained from my eyes. Anger took the place of my tears. The shroud of death hung over the house, floating in the empty living room where music, stairs, doors, and windows of night defined an unspecified loneliness curling around my neck with frightening devotion. With no place to curl up in a ball, and no place to shrink to a dot, I collapsed to nothing like the final note of a song wrung from a dying throat. There was no solace in this night which had no entrance or exit. My uncharted chord of irrationality provided no leverage against the encroaching shadows. Quiet confidence in the face of this ascending grief was swept aside by the brutal clock of death winking at me from every artifact in the familiar room.

The piano he pounded while singing "Littlest Cowboy," was forever silent. "Whoa, what a cowboy! He'll wear his yippee hat that little ole cowboy. Though he'll ride the range all day, he'll never lose his way! He's a rootin' tootin' shootin' little cowboy." This song came out of his love for the Southwest—New Mexico and *Arizona Highways*. His journeys in the Model-T Ford with his friend Henry Rankin were formative events. They stared into the Grand Canyon and the Painted Desert with their South Carolina mouths hanging open in astonishment. They fell in love with the land on those trips, passing through ancient geological time. In this room, full of memories, my emotional and spiritual status was modulating like that stuck needle in the badlands of the favorite record ruined by a deep scratch that cannot be mended. The pain repeated with every heartbeat— every half-second I slumped with the knowledge that this long-play album was unredeemable.

22.

LONG DISTANCE SOUL-TIE.

B y this time, I had a two-year relationship with a young woman attending classes in a distant university. I worked at Lockheed Aircraft in the Atlanta area, and we tried to schedule our dates to occur on her weekends home. As I arrived to pick her up during this time of great stress and shock, she witnessed first-hand my Witches Sabbath instability. After waiting for a couple of minutes for her to appear, I screamed into the darkness while I waited in the car in front of her house. Her father had not heard such a sound since he had walked the *Bataan March* of death in the Philippines during WWII. Thousands had died, but he still remembered this shrill note from fury, fear, and hopelessness.

He returned to Corregidor for the seventy-fifth anniversary of that terrible war-story, to walk the same path where his two college friends had died. They died in the prison encampment at the terminus of their famous walk. They died after saving him with a canned ham and a chicken received in the trade of his Clemson ring taken from his unconscious body. The Japanese guards greatly valued the Clemson ring, above any other possession of these stripped-down prisoners. It is a wonder that the guard didn't simply cut off his finger to take it.

But on this night of screams, I ruptured this brave man's front lawn with that forgotten sound from long ago. It was primeval and frightening. He became the papa bear stepping between his cub and the threat of a deranged man. His daughter could not leave the house with a madman parked on her lawn. Her father could not calculate how the death of my father, his former professor from his college days, could now cause me to make such a terrible sound.

He had watched thousands of boys die beside the highway in the Philippines during that eighty-mile walk into the most perfect replica of hell the war could simulate. He had seen the pitiless treatment they received at the point when their death seemed a relief from terror. He had seen men lose their identity, their dignity, and their sanity in the depths of hatred shared along that long highway to a worse prison cell that awaited a few who survived. He could not abide this terror erupting on his freshly mowed lawn. He knew what it meant. I had lost my mind. He understood that I would be dangerous, like a cornered animal, full of fear, with every survival instinct in a heightened state. He could not release his little one into my volatility.

She walked up to my car with her lethal message of irreconciliation as I rolled down my window on my Corvair Corsa. Her words were terse and unemotional as she spoke her prepared text to me. "I have to focus on my studies now. I can't get distracted with what you are going through. I have exams and projects that are due. We can't see each other anymore." Who knows how these words actually sounded in an authentic, unbiased playback? She could have spoken them through tears, but I just remember the brass knuckles into my solar plexus. It was the second death bell tolling for me. The piccolo flared, and the witches shrieked on their brooms with glee as my world spun out of control. My emotional stability departed in this most difficult season of my life—and I was ill-equipped to process the pain filling my chest with an unfamiliar molten metal.

I didn't blame her, or her father, but her declaration of freedom shattered my frail human thread. My thread of life had apparently attached itself to her orbit, and now it was whirling into the vacuum of space. The dependable camel crumpled when she placed her final feather on my saddlebags—maybe the wing feather from some prehistoric bird that carried rhinos airborne back to their nest. My camel's knees buckled once, then folded with the popping of bones in all directions. That trustworthy beast of burden, which had served me so well, collapsed like a wet cardboard box when she turned back to her distant front door. If I had looked closely, I would have seen her father's face between the curtains—he would have done anything to protect her.

My invincibility lay flattened, with every human confidence when it is stripped away. "No!" I whispered loud enough to fracture the car windows. I found myself captive in a giant room without a single handle of hope. Nothing soft came near me, and I could not remember how I had arrived, and I had nowhere to turn from this sudden denouement at the door to hell. Nothing from man could help me, I was certain; and I could not imagine any god who could now rescue me. I felt filthy and broken down—cast off, and lame in limb, and fractured in my mind.

When I went back to Lockheed, I sank into a practical paralysis, with barely enough money to pay for gas and a few essential groceries. I lived alone in a strange town with the emotional capacity of a homeless man—I got very sick with pneumonia—and I was home alone with no medical help to diagnose or monitor my condition as the scars were forming secretly in my lungs.

Years later, the doctor would find those lesions, thinking them to be the telltale tracks left by cancer. But these unchanging scars turned out to be the scars from my untreated pneumonia in that Smyrna apartment. I could have died there, and it would have been days before anyone would have found me. Having called in sick at my desk at Lockheed, I had no connection to work or to home.

No one could help me. I had no vital connection to anyone on earth. I was on a desert island with my broken coconut, and my only friend a soccer ball named "Wilson." Tom Hanks would understand how far I was from human intervention, having visited every emotional, physical, and spiritual reality of the *Cast Away*.[230] What I did not understand then, and barely know today, is that God was there with me the entire time. He was waiting for me to turn from self-destruction and chaos. He had been with me from my mother's womb the day the D-Day assault was first planned. He wanted, more than anything, for me to know the Prince of Peace, the Mighty God.

> You watched me as I was being formed in utter seclusion,
> as I was woven together in the dark of the womb.
> You saw me before I was born.
> Every day of my life was recorded in your book.
> Every moment was laid out
> before a single day had passed. Psalm 139:15-16

The girl I dated had shed me for more stable surroundings, while my father bravely faced his final days in this world. He surely set the example for me while I tried to control what I could not control. Born 1898, his first daughter had arrived on January 8. I had sat on the side of his bed with my mother as he breathed his final breath at 8:00 in the morning on January 8, 1968. Numbers mean nothing—or something I don't understand—but those Eights stare back from his life coaxing me to understand. I looked up the meaning in the Bible to better define the potential significance of Eight—8, 8, 8, 8, 8. What does this preponderance of eights speak to my soul, my heart, my mind? I live in the New Age of Google Search today, and nothing is too hard for me.

Even in that backward day before computers were never out of our hands, our eyes, or our reach from a sitting position, I knew that Eight was an important number symbolic of a new beginning. Resurrection and Regeneration surfaced during my research. Eight is more than a second chance—it represents a new beginning. Eight equals seven plus one. Since eight comes just after seven (an end to life or an era), eight represents a new era—a new fruitfulness—a new beginning with a different destination. Pop was now linked to the resurrection through Christ. A Christian man, his death from that disease placed him in Christ, receiving the promise of every believer.

> "All mankind is of one author, and is one volume; when one
> man dies, one chapter is not torn out of the book, but trans-
> lated into a better language . . . No man is an island, entire
> of itself . . . any man's death diminishes me, because I am

---

[230] *Cast Away*. Wikipedia.

involved in mankind; and therefore never send to know for whom the bell tolls; it tolls for thee."[231]

John Donne insists through his poetry that every life matters, affecting everyone else—his poem stresses our interrelatedness and interdependency on this tiny blue, green, and rust-colored planet. Did he ride on the Space Station to see the earth with this unique perspective? Did he read Jesus' words to the disciples when He said, "Father, make them One as We are One?"

Today, when the environmentalists release butterflies in the Brazilian rain forest, they measure the wind from their wings pushing the air in tiny puffs over New England. They believe that the condor's nearly extinct flight into the Canyon will alter the fronts over the Rocky Mountains. The reports of the storms in Europe will tip the weather in my Smyrna Georgia apartment as I lay coughing for hours on my fake fur sofa. John Donne was more real to me than many distant relatives in the present age. His words are prophetic, speaking of a day when even Noah would blush. He speaks of an age when God's words are silenced by the mob wanting its own way. Yet, in that day, God so loves the world that He has given His only begotten Son so that anyone who believes in Him will live forever in eternity with God.[232]

But the American Religion cares nothing for butterflies or for Donne's forbidden island, for this American religion is founded upon the fragile flapping wings of Myopic Me! I was still on that island which Donne writes about, and I could not imagine a Creator Who could make good sense of my brokenness and poverty—nor could I know what to make of His desire to have a relationship with Me in the first place. I was alienated from every relationship, and had no way back to that connection with men and wo-men. I had gone past insignificance to this great impotence in the meaningless valley of Myopic Me! I had reached the rutted dirt road leading to my tiny dot on the map of Google world not yet existing. Before Google Maps ever provided a street-view, I had vanished into this empty galaxy, where I had no name or address, fading fast in a faint photograph from Hubble's lost archive of past worlds. I did not exist on any map, or on any road, or on any Atlas where auto, bus, train, plane, or caravan could find me in a fortnight. And no one even knew that I vanished from the human race.

For a long time, I had imagined that the history of the world had featured me as its rising king. I saw my mission as that of the individualist—the poet on a remote island by his own choice. I would be the iconoclast, tearing everything down, sitting atop my favorite palm tree, having no interest in the building up—but only interested in the tearing down. I was the first Deconstructionist, before Foucault saw the paradox of insanity, or the women's studies classrooms

---

[231] Donne, John. *Meditations XVII, 1624,*

[232] John 3:16.

195

deleted every white male human from the historical record. I was the 007 from an ancient culture that had birthed me, and now I wanted to shoot it down with my trusty Walther P99. I imagined that I was something, when I was actually nothing. I wanted to be something, but could not be, as long as I thought I was.

Now, I knew that I was falling to the earth, and there was nothing I could do to stop this divine Gravity. I would be powerless, unless I found my connection to the Vintage grape vine which alone could produce the finest wine. I knew nothing about grapes or grafting of vines. I knew nothing of that root system which every vintner seeks to gain the best wine coming from the proven vine. The world will always spit out the Good Wine, preferring to drink the bad! I had opportunities to receive this teaching in my heart during those years in the Methodist Church, but I never opened up my whole life to hear. How is that possible? How could I reject the Word that could save me from this pain?

They will act religious, but they will reject the power that could make them godly. Stay away from people like that! 2 Timothy 3:5

We can no longer live on our floating island, and Paul told Timothy to stay away from people like me! Staying away from me during this season became the wise thing for many former friends, but I certainly had become an island. How ironic is our carefully planned self-destruction? We shut ourselves off from all help, hating to die alone. Paul himself, did this for a long season of his life. He became the killer of faith. He sided with those who would silence the Genesis Project, seeking to stop the power of the Holy Spirit from saving men across the whole earth. He stood against the power of God with his blind religion as his only armament. "Saul was uttering threats with every breath and was eager to kill the Lord's followers."[233]

Gamaliel, Saul's teacher, tried to give the religious leaders spiritual wisdom when he told them they could not stop the advancement of God's plans, no matter how many 007s they dispatched around the world. If God ordained these events unfolding around Jerusalem, then nothing they did would have any effect at all.

> "So my advice is, leave these men alone. Let them go. If they
> are planning and doing these things merely on their own, it
> will soon be overthrown. But if it is from God, you will not
> be able to overthrow them. You may even find yourselves
> fighting against God!" Acts 5:38-39

What prophetic words by Saul's teacher! He warned Saul, Paul, that God Himself would stand in the road on the way to Damascus to confront him. Then, Paul would be moved from 007 to 777 on that blinding Damascus Road, when he would become connected to the True Grape Vine. Saul encountered 777, the

---

[233] Acts 9:1.

God-number, becoming Paul. Facing Jesus Christ, risen Lord of All, he imme-diately knew who the Lord is. He also understood that 007 is not = to 777.

Saul abandoned the black for the Light. He became the bearer of this Light of the world into the bared teeth of religion across the whole Roman Empire. Saul's commitment to the Pharisaic self-salvation plan had brought him to the inevitable and abrupt encounter with God's unmerited favor on the Damascus Road. Jesus blocked Saul's death march into hell, just as He has blocked my self-destructive progress!

"Saul! Why are you persecuting Me?" Jesus asked him. Paul's answer reveals the full realignment of all of his priorities: "Lord! Who are You?" In a moment, Saul abandoned the unrighteous lord in Jerusalem. Chief Priest Caiaphas gave up Lordship over Saul's life. Paul found Jesus Christ who had always been his Lord. Even when Saul had held the coats for the stoning of Stephen in Jerusalem, Jesus was his Lord. Paul would come to understand that Christ had from the beginning of time been his Lord. Before the world was formed, Jesus had been his Lord. 777 had stopped 007 dead on the Damascus Road.

The meaning of those sets of numbers reveals Satan's solution, which is death. It also reveals God's solution, which is life. Love and Enmity are rep-resented in those numbers. This contradistinction is something that a mathe-matician might understand. Numbers have meaning, even denoting character, authority, and power. For Saul, who preferred the Law to all other written texts, murder had become his life's work! "007" had entered his DNA, and only God's Son could stop him from his murderous rounds. Paul would come to understand that other numbers are important as well—such as the 3rd Heaven, which he visited—which changed his understanding of this life of pain.

I would also come to appreciate these powerful analogies years after my father died. His departure reminded me of many 8s that were connected to his life and death. I learned that the number 8 represents a new beginning. 1898 was his birth year. 1968 was his death year. 8 a.m. was his death hour. January 8 was his death day. I could not avoid the 8s in Pop's story. His first child being born on the day that he died is noteworthy. That he died on January 8, at 8:00 in the morning in 1968, stands out. The "8s" popped in Pop's case.

Looking for meaning in all the 8s, I discovered that Pop's body on Cemetery Hill is directly up the hill from Gate 8 of the 84,000 seat Death Valley Stadium in Clemson. The ironic relationship of Cemetery Hill and Death Valley never even occurred to me before I looked at this. I grabbed the 8s when I discovered this biblical encouragement of new beginnings. God encourages me still when I think of it. The Holy Spirit is the Comforter. But none of this hopeful seren-dipity would come to light until Jesus unlocked the door in my heart in Atlanta at the *Church of Our Savior*. Perspective is best from every mountaintop, and somewhat more challenging from the perspective of the valley below.

My brother and I met at the base of that levee holding Lake Hartwell's waters out of *Death Valley* which was below the waterline. He and I met there to shoot cans with his 25-caliber pistol. I had never known anyone who owned a pistol, though Pop had shotguns for hunting. We just gathered at the gravesite earlier in the morning to watch the casket lowered into the earth on Cemetery Hill. We stood in the warm midday sun on this cold January 8, with the perfect air after many dark days when I could barely breathe. We aimed his pistol toward the carelessly arranged cans which he brought out of a grocery bag. The rising wall of dirt provided a safe backdrop of clay and stone for our impromptu liturgy of the gun. I vaguely wondered if this violated any legal ordinances, or church teachings, but this occasion upstaged every tort of men. Our being there had been ordained by God, and these dikes had appeared on the blueprints as a last-minute concession by the Corps of Engineers and the Holy God.

The vocal assembly had met with these chief engineers at Clemson College to present the necessary arguments to stop this indifferent flood from costing the college millions. They reviewed the devastating impact Lake Hartwell's dammed-up waters would produce on college lands and facilities. The dam along the South Carolina and Georgia borders would send a vast bathtub full of water into the stadium seats. Prime experimental acreage below the campus would also be underwater when the lake filled to full flood. The lake would crawl into the childhood woods behind our house, creating lake-front property when it reached the overflow a hundred miles away in Georgia. Now the Seneca and the Tugaloo were one with the Savannah, their banks long buried beneath billions of tons of water. The tall earthen dikes rose a hundred feet to restrict the encroachment of this rude flood, now taking the insulting thumps from our gun.

Standing at the base of the sloping wall of dirt, we shot holes into the leaping aluminum cans. They jumped one by one when our fingers squeezed the trigger, sharing the pistol back and forth until the bullets were wasted. We reloaded, and fired again and again. Crack. Crack. Thwack. Crack. The pistol seemed to appear from nowhere into our hands. The cans came from a bag with these artifacts from our one-time ordinance with burials. The million tons of earth quietly took these lead bullets into this tsunami of death delayed for years on the other side of this strange morning. Deadly marksmen, fearing nothing, we punctuated the grief and joy with our gentle violence.

How could this miraculous pistol bring us together in this full-blooded ritual? This soundless interlude scribbled a paragraph into our life story, as if some Pulitzer-Prize-winning author had written it for us. The pistol, the cans flying, the dikes holding back the unimaginable waters, and our silence in the communion of brothers writing our mutual ritual of passage as sons of the father. We were no longer Pop's boys; we had become brothers, set free to make a life of our own. We had been set free to mess up our own way, when we knew better than to do the things we did. Pop never held us back, barely rocking our boats at all. He never tried to make us in his own image, and now he was gone. His mark was all over our lives. Someone, or something else, would now have to shape our malleable clay into something useful.

When we emptied the box of 22-shorts, Grayson spun toward his car and vanished into his own Myopic World for private healing. I joked that his life ran according to the script of the modern-day *Tarzan and Jane* movie. Jane is the civilized one, of course, and ill-equipped to live in the jungle with wild animals, Tarzan has to carry the weight of every jungle battle which comes. In his courtrooms, day after day, waiting on the law to rule or ruin lives, his torts and rules of civil dispute had considerable weight. In his jungle world, more comfortable with the animals than with the rules of man, he found every knee bowed to the shredding of decency, with justice coming like a scythe through tall grass. Protecting the evil doer—it could be you or me—became more painful by the day.

When Jane called Tarzan home, swinging vine by vine, he easily translated the shrieks and squawks of the jungle languages into sensible stuff. "Me Tarzan: lawyer; you Jane: Island Princess. You like treehouse? We make babies!" The problem is, no one applies the Law right, but God Himself. And no Princess can live up to all the hype, swinging from vine to vine with his arm around her, tree house to lodge house, branches and tree limbs striking her face again and again.

But on this morning, he and I parted like the smoke of our father passing swiftly through our lives. Transfigured from one world to the next in a moment, we shared our unspoken pain nonverbally through this strange sacrament with the inescapable smell of gun powder. The hardware-store pistol seemed more articulate than either of us, and we shared a crude honesty at the foot of the dike. Our sometimes-amazing-communion had become a strange and imperfect blending of peace and fear of poverty.

The cans flew into that late-morning air—empty—torn by an overwhelming force, ruined and discarded. We had lost our father—whom neither of us really knew or properly loved. I had watched him shrink from 185 to 85 pounds while Grayson completed his studies at the University of Georgia Law School. He spent some of his precious time with Secretary of State Dean Rusk during his time there. While I commuted weekends from Smyrna to Pop's bedside, I wondered if all these riddles would finally be untangled in the earth. For many years after his burial, Pop joined us at supper in the kitchen of my dreams. In these dreams, I still didn't know what to say to him—I wondered if some things, like the relationship of a boy to his Pop, can only be untangled by the Father.

Us siblings had howled, with fear-strangled-laughter, when he drove us out on the narrow earthen dam in that green 1950 Plymouth four-door. We screamed with horror and glee while Mama shrank in her seat beside the door. I sat between them—practicing to be the buffer when emotions peaked a decade later. None of these catastrophes in the making ended badly, though our Pop could scare us so well. We never doubted his skills in these moments of peril. Now, he was gone, vanished across the bumpy front yard on the gurney, down to the graveled driveway and the waiting hearse. The wheels jumped and jittered as they rolled through the large acorns that had fallen from the 120-foot tall white oak tree.

Watching from the upstairs window, an era ended with this anticlimax—this ill-formed denouement. The reversal of fortunes in this tragedy was the C-Word, Cancer. Once it was pronounced into the open air of the upper bedroom, everything ended. Our annual Christmas tree hunt evaporated when the hearse drove away. Family outings to those hay barns in the bottom lands were no more as soon as the acorns flew from the wheels in all directions. The wheels of our futures spun around in pirouettes when the gurney arrived at the open doors of the long vehicle of death. Those memories, better than Disney World could ever offer, ended when Pop's sense of humor was lifted from us on January 8, 1968.

When his Pulitzer Prize-winning former students made their long journeys to visit him one last time, the shock in their eyes was fearful to witness. Mercifully brief, this moment during his dying hours painted a terrible abstract portrait. Quiet horror replaced their memories of familial laughter and intellectual joy. Their beloved teacher and mentor had been tortured by this cancer, and the man who gave them everything he could give, lay gagging on the bed before their naked eyes. Shredded, the man they loved, faced them in his final brave grimace. He saw their discomfort, but his own body turned against him with intractable fangs. His desire to comfort them, and leave them with hope, was devoured by the enemy within.

I stood silently with them, invisible; but important things merged in the silence of this room—Pop, his visitors, and this cancer's imprimatur struck their faces without sentences or paragraphs. Foreshadowing thoughts, silent soliloquies, and vivid synecdoches hung in the air. In that room, they finished their book as colleagues, writing this painful final chapter, too unspeakable for written words. When the heart fills with tears too deep to set free, slack jaws prevail. When we stared together into his death, we saw this monster, drooling creature, completely indifferent to our broken hearts—there was nothing to be said.

Nothing remained of him, but a word or two through nausea and pain— their pain cleaved to the outer surfaces of the terrible room. I stood helpless, as if I didn't exist—not interfering in their final moment together. They departed, after traveling thousands of miles, honoring their mentor with his oxygen and morphine, and his suffocation looming. I stayed to shave his beard that grew as if nothing had changed. I carried him to the toilet less and less frequently as he starved; and somehow in all of this, I had become his brave son—as if bravery could ameliorate the gravity of his final battle—going quietly into that good night. No three-credit hour course, this death march had taken on a life of its own. I had become the soldier with the wounded older buddy. Reluctantly, I watched my comrade in arms die in his war-splattered uniform. I could no longer fix my hearing on the steady sounds of the battle, and the world ended with his dying.

My eyes stretched wide, but I could no longer see—future, past, and present blended into a black void. He ate no solid food, and nothing tasted the way he remembered. His five senses had shut down one by one after that cataract surgery left him oozing and wild in the eyes, with worse blindness following than before. As he lay there moments from death at 7:59 a.m., we placed his thick glasses back on his nose as if he wanted to see the room. He didn't see a thing, for he was already looking into a different room that we couldn't see. That room swelled with new light—his eyes working perfectly there—no cataracts or aqueous humor bulged through his irises as he peered into the bright columns of light. The season for dying had passed, and ended before my eyes.

It was January 8 at 8:00 in the morning. Pop breathed his last irrelevant oxygen as he traveled home to the heaven God had appointed. As the "8s" streamed by me, I still had no foundation, and no rudder, through this storm. I failed to comprehend any of these hopeful messages. My own eyes oozed that morning with spiritual blindness more opaque than Pop's cataracts. My morning revelation would arrive at nine o'clock, eight years later on April 16, 1976. There, in that backyard scene, my eyes would finally receive the gift of the Holy Spirit that could make sense of the Words of God which were still foreign to me.

My spiritual resurrection—that renewal of my mind—would take me through an invisible door into a brave new kingdom to see the Word made flesh, living among us. The most important Nine o'clock in human history would be retold through my own experience, as in 33 AD. Peter interpreted that scene for all the Jews gathered from every country around the world. God's perfect economy was present that day, as it is today and tomorrow.

"These people are not drunk, as some of you are assuming.
Nine o'clock in the morning is much too early for that. No,
what you see was predicted long ago by the prophet Joel:

'In the last days,' God says,
'I will pour out my Spirit upon all people.
Your sons and daughters will prophesy.
Your young men will see visions,
and your old men will dream dreams.'" Acts 2:15-17

Everything happens according to the Goodness of God, and the ultimate manifestation of that Goodness has come to me through Jesus Christ—"Messiah" to the Jews and the Gentiles alike. In the first word of the Bible, the Hebrew language gives us a powerful synopses of the *Alpha and the Omega* journey which lies ahead for us when we believe in Jesus's finished work on the Cross. The first word of the Bible contains powerful allusions to that Cross that will save us, and to the Lamb Who will give His life for us. He will be crowned King of an eternal kingdom which begins in God Himself. In this one Hebrew word, we find the fullness of the Gospel, and we discover that the Lamb of God was slaughtered before the foundations of the earth were laid. God would come to live among us in the form of a man, Who was fully God, and His mission would come directly from heaven.

בְּרֵאשִׁית

When we fully understand the riddle of this Hebrew first Word in the Bible, appearing first in the Torah, we find our Savior and our Lord. The Word of God became a Man, and He cast off His divine privileges to become the Lamb before the slaughter. He became the final Lamb's sacrifice gaining our entry into God's rest. Upon the head of the Son of God, the Crown of Thorns would be rudely placed, so that we might know the character of our Savior and our King, Who is King of all kings. God's Goodness also became flesh, dwelling among us, and this Goodness became the Pioneer of our faith, dying on a Tree, and giving us the authentic hope of heaven[234].

God, therefore, cannot produce Badness, for He is Good from the beginning. Even God's wrath is Good. His seeming indifference is Good, and His rain will fall on the just and unjust alike; but the rains were falling on me and my family that morning—hail from the sky, and lightning flashing in the spiritual realm, and the deck chairs were all piled up against the house in the fierce Wind of God's perfect plan to save us from the sharks.

Peter had experienced the second miracle of a great catch of fish when Jesus told him to throw the net on the other side of the boat. The second miracle came when Jesus, in resurrected body, met the fishermen on the lake. Peter had abandoned the mission of Christ to return to his familiar business as a very successful fisher of fish. When the miraculous catch was counted, there were 153 fish in the nets.[235] These represented the 153 people groups of the known world.

A few days later, Peter stood in front of three-thousand Jews from every known country of the world. He told them that the Prophet Joel had foreseen this pouring of God's Holy Spirit on all flesh. He explained that Jesus was the Christ they had longed to see, but they had insisted on His crucifixion. When they heard Peter's bold sermon, after Peter denied Christ three times a few days before, they were convicted, and they believed in Jesus as Savior and Lord. Three thousand were saved from those 153 known countries of the world. Jesus had been true to His word. He had made Peter a fisher of men. The miracles of the fish had become the miracles for all Jews everywhere. And Peter still could not understand that God came for the Gentiles as well.[236]

When my Gentile mother was shattered by her tumble from the raised highway coming from T. L. Hannah High School, the imminent loss of her beloved husband from all these years preoccupied her attention. She was exhausted mentally. Marriage, the thing forgotten in our modern day, was a

---

[234] Pastor Isaac. *Bereshit.*

[235] John 21:11.

[236] Acts 1:41.

permanent thing in those days. She would have to learn to live without her love for the first time since she was a young woman. She needed her miracle of the fishes. She needed her miracle of hope in this black hour.

She was recovering from the broken back and the compound fracture of her arm. She would take a much-needed break from her grueling schedule while she healed. Her return to the high school teaching could wait a few weeks more. Her students would no longer be allowed to pick her up and carry her around the room like their toy teacher. Jim Rice the Hall of Fame baseball player for the Boston Red Sox had been in her English class that year for his 11th grade studies.

It was a tumultuous time in Southern towns. Southern schools still applied the styptic pencil to the razor's edge of desegregation. Jim Rice tells his closest personal friends about the abuse he lived through in his youth, though my mother never said a bad word to me about any of her students. She loved teaching literature to kids who were often ill-prepared to take on such intellectual challenges.

Jim Rice would go on to be one of the most distinguished sports voices in the Boston baseball scene; and unlike most former athletes, his grammatically accurate speech would have made my mother proud—grammar is most often acquired from the repetition of the parents' voices rather than from the classroom hours with the teacher. We learn at home how to speak "the king's English"—or we learn something else which sounds right to our ear. I have heard so many announcers speak of Jim as heading to the Hall of Fame for sports announcers in Boston. His Hall of Fame status in baseball is unquestioned, but these wordsmiths were acknowledging his considerable contribution to the weekly reporting on baseball in a sports-crazy city. Jim's parents must have taught him well, preparing him for a life well-lived.

She told me about a "large sports hero" who had carried her to her desk. Undoubtedly, it was one of the giant football linemen who transferred her like a flowerpot that day. I didn't know how I felt about that until I remembered my own participation in a similar act of overfamiliarity in one of my classrooms. I remember that several football players in my high school had carried our French teacher to the quad between the classrooms with her still seated at her desk. It seemed a badge of honor in those days to be carried to and fro. It was unnerving for my mother, but she did not complain or disparage these impressive young men in my hearing.

She had a sense of humor about her diminutive stature among the giants around her. Growing pains for the teacher and the student alike were common during this difficult era. I think she came home physically exhausted after teaching all day, and shopping for groceries that night of her terrible wreck on the Anderson Highway. She intended to visit Pop's hospital room that evening; but she was ferried to the hospital by the passerby who picked her up from the shoulder of the road. With no cell phone in this era before Twitter, Snapchat, and Facebook, the Highway Patrol might be an hour away. If she had not climbed the embankment, she might have died from shock and her injuries.

Her mind was fractured by many emotions she never shared with me—this in direct contrast to my spewing over with a flood of feelings. Her new pain, knowing that the love of her life lay dying with lung cancer, brought her to grief she had never felt before. Years later, she printed up several books of her poems from the 1930s through the 1990s, and one poem strikes me as central to her emotional state the night she flew into that darkness in her little yellow VW Bug. Having no reasonable hope of a safe landing, her mind had traveled back in time to remember the love of her youth. The poem expresses beautifully her relationship with Pop during all those years of marriage and raising a family, teaching at Clemson University, and being a wife and friend.

I Unworthy Am to Be

There is no certain reason why
I love him that you might descry.
No patent beauty evident,
Or obvious enchantment
To lure my heart that it should be
Surrendered to this constancy—
This sweet delight from day to day;
And if you ask I cannot say
In what his subtle charm consists
That after long my love persists.
I only know that there is grace
In every outline of his face;
That there is beauty in the mind
Of him who holds my heart confined;
That there is loveliness in fact
Beneath his every gentle act—
And I unworthy am to be
Beloved of such a one as he. Bessie Mell Lane, 1936

Wow, to have such a poem written about me by my wife would be amazing. My mother loved my father, ignoring his spots and blemishes. I shudder to think what my wife might divulge about the flawed and broken man she has lived with for nearly fifty years. She has always supported me, though she might have bolted over many things.

During this painful interregnum, my reality was suspended between space-time and faith-time in Smyrna Georgia. It was a perilous moment in the time-line. Poverty and shame drew me into an air so thick I could not breathe it any longer. I suffocated on my every breath—wrecked by every wild thought careening. I had fallen headlong, and I lay in the darkest pit of Myopic Me! Pop, the man, was gone. Pop, the father, was gone. My girlfriend was gone. I found no landing place alone. In my empty living room in Smyrna, I found no comfort or peace in the familiar surroundings.

Weighted down by my own sins, unconfessed and barely understood, the years "going to church" could not help me decode my spiritual crisis. I had no relationship with God's Son. I had no relationship born of faith and believing, as much as I had wished to have one. I did not know how to believe in Him. I could not even see the need I had of being filled with God's Spirit to fight this battle in my interior. I had no one to talk to about my troubles. Prayer was unknown to me. There was no hero in my life. I knew that soul-sickness placed me so far from peace that no doctor could help me. I went to the family doctor. It made things worse.

Like Patricia in *Joe Versus the Volcano*, my soul's progeny brought more trouble for myself and for others. My spirit did not know how to consume true food. I yearned for home, not even knowing the direction home. Home could no longer be found by traveling along that icy Atlanta highway. I had driven eleven hours, going 140 miles, only to slide in a ditch twelve miles from Clemson a few weeks earlier. Better that I had not made it there—for what happened after arriving. I had passed hundreds of eighteen-wheelers and autos that slid helplessly off into a hundred-mile ditch—trucks fell on their sides against the vertical red clay and gravel embankments along much of the road. The worst ice storm in a generation finally shut down I-85. Those experiences did not come close to what I experienced hours later in Clemson. I should have stayed in Smyrna to read what Jesus had spoken to the ancient Greek City of Smyrna, currently on the western coast of Turkey.

> "Write this letter to the angel of the church in Smyrna. This is the message from the one who is the First and the Last, who was dead but is now alive: 'I know about your suffering and your poverty—but you are rich!'" Revelation 3:8-9

In modern Smyrna, I was convinced of my poverty. I felt poor, living on my own for the first time in a strange town. In ancient Smyrna, they faced imminent death with their physical poverty. So, I was facing death as well. But my death throes were self-induced. My battle with death came because of my refusal to hear God and accept His strong foundation so that I could face the storm that lay ahead of me. When He said, "Go and sin no more," I didn't listen. Now I was in deep shock. Now, I was suffering inextricable anguish.

I felt certain that no one could untwist the python from my throat. Like Dorothy, I had no idea where this vortex would deposit me. A mute phone hung on my apartment's blank wall. It had never rung, and I never lifted it to make a call. In this time before cell phones, the phone book of greater Atlanta contained a million names. I had never opened that giant white and yellow tome to make a call. It lay there unmolested on the Formica counter. Though my whole family had not died, I felt completely alone. My mind ran amuck with no place to land. A deadly panic jumped my soul, and I could not risk another wild thought.

I had no money, so I couldn't drink to dull this unbearable pain. I had no drugs, though drugs couldn't help me at this point—I fully understand how someone could end up using drugs to kill the pain. The room was spinning, empty, and baron. The Chinese red table with the screw-on legs no longer glowed in front of the homemade black fake-fur sofa I made. The blank walls mocking me in my homemade room seemed useless and obscene.

The trash remained in a tall pile at the end of the single Formica counter. It had migrated out into the room by now, and the spaghetti sauce had long-since dried on the ceiling—dispersed there by the steaming pressure-cooker months earlier. None of these details attracted my attention on this night. My $4.00 per month electric bill did not improve my outlook. Nothing mattered to me, while the clock hands moved silently toward the midnight of my soul.

The saliva of death already digested my father's body in the ground. The memory of her excited smile leaping into my arms with her legs locked around my waist seemed little more than a nightmare as the second hand made its final circuit around the dial. I switched for the first time to inevitable suicide. This final act from *King Lear* found me walking into the fierce storm with no defense for the shrapnel flying through my mind. This final act brought pain too great to bear.

A thousand fractured synapses dragged down a billion photons coalescing into a fleeting image of God—as if God's presence could help my situation! I had no idea that Revelation depicts a time when men will be so spiritually empty that they will want to commit suicide to escape God's searching eyes. He was searching for me while the Locusts arrived with the Fifth Trumpet's blast on the final day. A great spiritual battle had arisen in the earth, and my soul felt this battle raging in my sparse room.

> Then locusts came from the smoke and descended on the earth, and they were given power to sting like scorpions. They were told not to harm the grass or plants or trees, but only the people who did not have the seal of God on their foreheads. They were told not to kill them but to torture them for five months with pain like the pain of a scorpion sting. In those days people will seek death but will not find it. They will long to die, but death will flee from them. Revelation 9:3-6

23.

A TRAIN THROUGH
SOLID ROCK.

When no man could help me, God intervened. Ready to kill myself as the only relief from unbearable pain, I made one final choice. When I could not face another thought, each one coming like a demon loosed in my mind, I picked up the phone. By some miracle, Phillip's name appeared through the chaos of my wild thoughts. I hardly knew Philip, my oldest sister's husband, and I didn't like Philip. His direct ways made me very uncomfortable. I avoided him, but never seemed to escape his invasive personality. He seemed intent on penetrating my defenses, seeing my defenseless position in this world all too clearly. He had prayed for me once, when I was feeling sick while visiting my sister and him. Being prayed for felt very peculiar, and I did not enjoy that needy, religious feeling.

When this explicit name arrived in my mind, I suppose that I picked up that phone from the wall hook to make the call—how did I find his number? I don't remember calling information or even holding the phone in my hand—or to my ear? I don't remember ever calling anyone on that phone. A sound from a tin can on the other end must have come when we stretched the string hard across 500 miles.

It might have been 500 light years for all I know; and by extrapolation from this history, he must have climbed aboard a train in Lexington to travel through the long night and a hundred silent stations to find me at the Atlanta train station. He had to travel far from the path the crow would fly because the mountains in between blocked every train I have ever heard of. Maybe that flying train from *Back to the Future* could have done this, but none other. This was past time, but future time still has no way to travel the crow's flight from Lexington by rail.

There is no way by train—I don't know how he made it overnight. Even today, the trip takes twelve hours, and I called him near midnight. He watched street lights from night to morning as the organized tonnage navigated, clackity-clacking along, on more than a hundred-thousand forty foot steel rails. I found him waiting on the sidewalk in the morning at Peachtree station. I picked him up where Sherman's fires were still smoldering. But I do not remember how I survived from that midnight until I prayed, asking Jesus to forgive my idolatry the next evening. I vividly remember kneeling before a stranger in an unfamiliar church on North Highland Avenue. In a few moments, the heavens would come down to touch *Untouchable,* Myopic Me! The unfamiliar quickly became the unforgettable for a new creature in Christ.

Philip's voice had somehow calmed me to survive that night. Knowing he would soon arrive kept me calm until the next day when he and I talked about God's love. Philip explained that God revealed His love through His Son Jesus. We walked somewhere in a field or park, though I can't recall where we were. I could see the Door waiting for me, bored into the steep side of eternity. Through that Door, God's forgiveness awaited me. That very evening, as Philip rocked along those same rails returning to Kentucky, I drove my Corvair Corsa quietly down the interstate highway into Atlanta, pulling to a stop at 1068 North Highland Avenue.

The Anglo-Roman, *Church of Our Savior*, looked similar to my mother's favorite church in Clemson—an Episcopal Church. Father Petway waited to intercept me before the start of evening services. Phillip had spoken to him at a conference a month earlier. The only person Philip knew in Atlanta, Father Petway, told me to get on my knees and ask Jesus to forgive my sin of idolatry. I prayed, asking Jesus to forgive me, and to take over my life—I surrendered to Him. Jesus heard my prayer, and I knew with certainty that I had passed through the only Door which could take me from suicide to Peace. I did not fully understand "idolatry," or "Savior," or "Lord," but I knew now that those evening services were going to help me get to know Him better.

God knows what took place in the heavenly realm on that night—He pierced the membrane between space-time and faith-time. God carried me in His arms from idolatry into His monumental peace. I gained a new identity as a child of God. The Holy Spirit guided me through the valley of the shadow of death, pointing out the dangers coming with every inordinate love. For the first time, Myopic Me! understood the core principle of Perfect Love that is highly motivated to protect all those created in His own image.

God did not send His Son to condemn me, but to save me. I could not stop crying as we sang the plainsongs containing His name in Latin, with every reference to the Lamb of God piercing me. Since He was pierced for me, loosing deep gratitude in my heart, I started Day One of my life. The old had passed away, and the new had come. I did not know this in any intellectual transaction, but my heart understood this.

Through unmerited favor from God, I had been saved. God's sovereign choreography brought me to this dance of life which I had been thirsting for, but didn't know it. By sending my brother-in-law from Kentucky, I was connected to the only man Philip knew in a city of a million people. This serendipity of God opened me to a long-distance connection to the God of heaven and earth, bringing Him as close to me as my own breath. God had already performed the heavy lifting two-thousand years earlier when He laid His arms down on a Cross. His suffocation made it possible for me to breathe. He pulled me out of the toxic entropy of sin. Though I still imagined that I was a good guy, the Holy Spirit provided the answers to many of my questions now. He gave me all I could handle at that time. I knew nothing! But He was now my Teacher. He declared succinctly: "Jesus is the answer."

While vast numbers of people are trying to push every thought from their minds, Christ is teaching me to think continually on His grace and the beauty of His holiness. I didn't say that I do this very well, but I have become more intentional about it. It is the Holy Spirit Who comes through, reminding me continually of Jesus' commands and promises. He, the Holy Spirit, models for me the continual praise of His glory. God had moved me from poverty in Smyrna to the riches of every little thing He was doing in my life. It was happening now, nearly every hour of every day. His great concern for Me at every stage of this journey caused me to begin to learn how to love others at every difficult stage of theirs. I still had the problem of falling in love too quickly, or remembering the lost love too painfully. But He never stops teaching me to keep my thoughts trained on what is worthy of praise and what is lovely. It is Christ in me Who reminds me that He is all of these, and He alone is truly worthy of my worship.

The long-running and often unworthy show, *Saturday Night Live*, had a recurrent skit in which Jon Lovitz repeated the phrase, "Get to knowwww me!" I don't really recommend stemming on Jon's vapid character portrayal, but Jesus Christ is certainly worthy of our attentiveness to our final breath. Getting to know Him is everything. Though He didn't say, "Get to know Me," He did say, "Follow Me!" There is an important difference. Following Him causes us to discover the Way, looking directly into His Truth, and finding His new Life. It caused me to watch what He said, and to try to emulate what He was doing. It brought me eventually to hear Paul's admonition from the jail cell at Philippi. Paul was speaking directly to every Christ-follower, telling every believer, to keep their eyes on Jesus—Who alone is Worthy of our Praise. With my attention focused on Him, and my feet following Him, Paul said I should keep my thoughts fixed on His Glory and Beauty.

> "And now, dear brothers and sisters, one final thing. Fix your thoughts on what is true, and honorable, and right, and pure, and lovely, and admirable. Think about things that are excellent and worthy of praise." Philippians 4:8

For weeks after I prayed for Christ to forgive me and live through me, I started seeing God's miraculous hand in everything that happened. In a sense, my fourteen year old prayer on Mt. Guyot was recapitulated, but with the confession before men. The Coward was silenced, at least for a moment, and I was willing to do whatever God told me to do. I now had ruby slippers empowering me to go Home—not to Kansas or Clemson—but to the Home hidden in God with Christ—God's glorious Son. The home my heart yearned for was embedded in this new relationship—in ways I could not yet know. By faith, I would take the next step, and the next, sometimes as the fool, and sometimes as the one moving in the visible counsel of God.

I knew all of this instinctively, as my life had received His message twice before I arrived at my parking space on Highland Avenue. God intervened in the Smokeys, but that baptism in the driving rain at the top of the world could not wash away the sin from my life. He came close to Myopic Me! in the shower in the basement in Clemson, but that could not turn me from sin. I did not know Jesus Christ; nor did I understand the Good News of the kingdom made possible through His sacrifice on the Cross.

Jesus now came to me as *Prince of Peace*, when I could not bear to think another thought. Suicide was the only way I could escape the pain. After His inexplicable peace, I would come to know Him as *Wonderful Counselor*. That hymn from the Christmas carol came back to me with those three manifestations of Jesus in my life. When I was baptized in the Holy Spirit eight years later, I came to know Jesus Christ as *Mighty God*. He became my constant *Advocate* with the Father, leading me into all truth, ending the reign of fear and cowardice in my life.

> My dear children, I am writing this to you so that you will not sin. But if anyone does sin, we have an advocate who pleads our case before the Father. He is Jesus Christ, the one who is truly righteous. He himself is the sacrifice that atones for our sins—and not only our sins but the sins of all the world. 1 John 2:1-2

These names changed me from the inside out, arriving from the Gospel of Luke and from the Letter of John speaking to the Church about the divine nature of Jesus Christ, who existed from the beginning, being the very *Word of Life*. "God is light, and there is no darkness in him at all."[237] These names and descriptors would draw me deeper into the stunning reality of a personal relationship with the Holy God. Heaven and earth would be joined in me through this supernatural benevolence of a God who demonstrates His desire for a relationship with each one of us. Jesus' final prayer in the upper room on the night He was arrested, whipped, and crucified, still speaks today of this eternal relationship between God and those who believe in His Son. Jesus spoke into future time, our time, praying for you and me as we come to believe in Him.

---

[237] 1 John 1:1-7.

> "I am praying not only for these disciples but also for all who
> will ever believe in me through their message. I pray that they
> will all be one, just as you and I are one—as you are in me,
> Father, and I am in you. And may they be in us so that the
> world will believe you sent me." John 17:2-3

The day that I asked God to forgive my idolatry—asking Him to take over my life—my confidence leaped. Though I did not fully know how to get Home, I now understood there would be no need for maps or futuristic GPS tracking to take me into the future from the tiny chapel in Atlanta. God gave me the holy tracings of His purpose to lead me on. He said to follow Him wherever He goes. When I complained that I did not know where He was going, He pointed to His Son: "Follow me."

I could see that something akin to the Faith-Time Continuum had broken through the very roof of my life—and I had been lowered like the crippled man on a litter through that opening. I had been lowered to the feet of Jesus for healing and instruction. God wrote new flight plans for me, as He led me out of the wilderness of my own sinful life. He repaired my eyes, and He strengthened my legs so that I could keep up. He reset my compass to a new destination with an inheritance anchored by His eternity.

That old Myopic Me! had officially left the building, though I insisted on dragging that dead body around in a body bag behind me for a while. I didn't know how to let go of that ugly broken me who had been with me for twenty-three-plus years. Chasing after the wind came to an end when I received God's Son—but I sometimes reverted to old patterns when things didn't go my way. When I read Jesus' Words, years later, it frightened me; for I did not want to be known as the lawbreaker whom Jesus had "never known."

> But I will reply, 'I never knew you. Get away from me, you
> who break God's laws.' Matthew 7:23

The *Good News* is potentially wrecked if Jesus' Words come home to roost. These Words were aimed primarily at the Pharisees who pretended to be in right standing with God, though their hearts were far from God. Their entitlement included self-righteousness and legalism devoid of any pretense of mercy or grace. Jesus told them that their father was the Devil, not God. He painted a terrifying picture for them, or for anyone, who does religious works to get ahead or to impress men, without fearing God.

211

> "Not everyone who calls out to me, 'Lord! Lord!' will enter the
> Kingdom of Heaven. Only those who actually do the will of
> my Father in heaven will enter. On judgment day many will
> say to me, 'Lord! Lord! We prophesied in your name and cast
> out demons in your name and performed many miracles in
> your name.'" Matthew 7:21-22

His Wind, I was learning, is better than vanity or narcissism, or lawlessness;
but His full healing unfolds over time. Amazing things, with practical benefits,
seemed to pop up everywhere for me after I had declared my idolatry, agreeing
with what God already knew of me. Events invisible to the naked eye arrived
on a spiritual plane now, for my mind was opened to see them for the first
time. It was naturally supernatural. I had entered into this paradoxical reality in
which flesh and Spirit were somehow dancing together with a beautifully choreographed balance.

> So I say, let the Holy Spirit guide your lives. Then you won't
> be doing what your sinful nature craves. The sinful nature
> wants to do evil, which is just the opposite of what the Spirit
> wants. And the Spirit gives us desires that are the opposite of
> what the sinful nature desires. Galatians 5:16-17

I sat in my apartment with the phone pressed to my ear calling unknown
dormitory phones in the halls at Emory University in Atlanta where my uncle
had received a degree decades before. I shared my primitive story with whomever would answer, telling them that God had given me peace which I couldn't
describe. Suicide had been lifted from my heart, and I could not wait for all the
day promised now. I was compelled to tell others what had happened. This Good
News seemed irrepressible.

The Spirit of God inside of me seemed to take over, putting me in touch with
the smartest young people living in this large city population. I told them the miracle that had visited me at the brink of death. I told them it was "so simple, and
not at all intellectual, as I had imagined it would be." I knew nothing else to tell
them, except this story of miraculous peace replacing the utter panic and terror
that nearly destroyed me. This was my early testimony of Christ in my life. This
story would change, and it would grow stronger, more articulate—none more
articulate than the blind man who told the Pharisees in Jesus day: "I don't know
whether he is a sinner . . . But I know this: I was blind, and now I can see!"[238]

---

[238] John 9:25

Clearly, I had nothing theological to share with them. There were no spiritual laws which I had memorized to share with strangers and friends. I couldn't tell them that Mary appeared in a vision in the wall of my apartment, or that I felt wind blowing through the closed window of my room as the Holy Spirit filled me with His power. For the first time, I used the phone for something other than dull errands. I had been blind, but Jesus created clay with His Own spit to press into my eyes. Seeing for the first time in my life, I could only tell them, "I can see. I was blind before, but now I can see." The blind man whom Jesus healed fit my story perfectly. To anyone who would listen, I said, "I don't know who He is; but I know I was blind from birth, and now I see things that were not there before." I was a dead-man-walking, but Jesus rescued me from the gallows of death. I heard the terrible sounds as that trap door rattling above me in the air, and I could see all around me when the rope jerked their necks hard with those thirteen terrible knots. I was scheduled next, for the trap door's click.

My rusting Tin Man had just been oiled by the Holy Spirit, and a new heart pumped blood through my body with a proper sinus rhythm. The Tin Man had gotten up from the golden gutter of Oz, to walk without a squeak into the Emerald City where he would be led by a child to the altar of his full identity. I had the Tin Man's sense of paralysis and wonder, not fully understanding this promise of a new life. He made me a new person, but I had no clue how completely my life would soon change. With no merit of my own to recommend me, Christ made all things new. I buckled my seatbelt for a wild ride, confident in this powerful new peace in my heart.

> "So then, if anyone is in Christ, that person is part of the new
> creation. The old things have gone away, and look, new things
> have arrived." 2 Corinthians 5:17

It is amazing, as I look back today, that I did not attempt to convince these academic geniuses at Emory of anything. I only wanted to share what had happened to me as best I could. I can see those phone booths in the long halls of the Emory dorms to this day. Of course, I have never been on those halls in the flesh, but I am convinced that I was transported there on that evening of joy. I shared what I couldn't contain or keep private any longer. They ran down the hall from their casual conversation with a friend when they heard the phone ring. These calls could mean their parents had news from home, or the boyfriend wanted to talk about the time they spent in the library reading Wordsworth with soft whispers. The dramatic sound of the ring could bring life or death, joy or sadness, excitement or awkwardness. These rings from Smyrna, by way of Jerusalem, brought news of great joy: For this day in Bethlehem, is born a great king, and He is Christ the Lord—Prince of Peace, Wonderful Counselor, Mighty God!

> That night there were shepherds staying in the fields nearby,
> guarding their flocks of sheep. Suddenly, an angel of the Lord
> appeared among them, and the radiance of the Lord's glory
> surrounded them. They were terrified, but the angel reassured
> them. "Don't be afraid!" he said. "I bring you good news
> that will bring great joy to all people. The Savior—yes, the
> Messiah, the Lord—has been born today in Bethlehem, the
> city of David!" Luke 1:8-11

My call came from the Faith-Time Continuum which I had encountered through the gift of God's grace shown to me. I had to tell someone what Jesus had done, born in a manger, living in seclusion to avoid Herod who wanted to kill Him, working as a laborer and carpenter before arriving from Nazareth in the walled city of Jerusalem. He confronted the hypocrites of the day, and He brought hope to those who were captive and downcast, healing every one. Those on the other end of the copper phone lines listened to me with kindness and attentiveness as I shared my little story— I told them how I had been raised from death to life, literally and spiritually. I had many amazing conversations with strangers who may remember to this day, the day when God called them on the hall phone to tell them the glory of His beloved Son.

They were so kind to me, likely concerned that I might yet take my own life. But I had become like the woman at the well, who had lived in the intentional solitude of her shame until she received the living water from Jesus. He sat down beside this broken Samaritan woman, and she knew the audacious nature of His act of kindness. Though He was clearly a prophet, or the Messiah, He spoke to her about Living Water that would keep her from ever thirsting again. Her long-time false security, sharing her bed with one drifter after another, would now come to an end. She had this living water from the Promised One, and He would woo her all the way to heaven. She had no reason to hide any longer, for the God of gods had drunk from her cup from Jacob's Well. He had sat right there, beside her, and she could tell Him anything. There was no condemnation in this Christ Who restored her lost dignity during the brief time of their conversation.

Now, I spoke to strangers out of irrepressible joy. No longer ashamed or driven by self-interest, I could not stop talking about God's peace, telling everyone that Jesus had plucked me from Niagara Falls with His Shepherd's crook. Peace is the most profound gift which came from that simple conversation on my knees that evening: "Forgive me, Jesus. Save me, Lord." From agony to peace with a simple prayer—but the words should never be construed as a magic trick. Knowing Christ is not an excuse to practice superstitious rituals born in hell. He came to remove superstition and occult bondage from our lives. It would not matter if the words had been different words when I prayed. The peace that came as a gift, arrived from God's throne room. I came to Him through the faith of a child, surrendering to Him as Savior and Lord—knowing

214

that no man could help me. Peace did not come through the shrewdness of an insight or through great intelligence opening some intellectual world to me. It came through a relationship with the One Who gave His life on a terrible Cross before being raised from the dead.

God does not reveal His love to those who are still fighting against Him, full of pride, still boasting in their own accomplishments. When He confronted Saul on the Road to Damascus, He asked him, "Saul, why are you persecuting Me?" Saul, Paul, answer simply: "Who are you Lord!" When Christ confronted me in Smyrna, He asked me, "Why are you worshiping other gods before Me?" He took me from the bottomless pit to a place of deep peace. By unmerited favor, he picked me up before it was too late. I did not deserve His help, and no amount of money could buy the peace He gave me as a free gift. Nothing I do gains me this peace. It doesn't come through my own will or expertise. It is miraculous and transformational.

My brother-in-law spent his meager salary as a new priest to travel by rail to my rescue. The Priest at the church charged me nothing for his trouble. The free gift of God is available because of Jesus' compassion. His servants give their lives for those who are lost to this very day. More Christians have died for their faith in the first seventeen years of the twenty-first century than in all the years since Christ rose from the dead. God's servants today don't hesitate to push back the darkness to encourage my steps of faith. But only Christ, I have learned, can help me complete this long race. Most recently, I have referred to it as a fifteen-rounder rather than a race.

After my new birth by God's Spirit in Atlanta, I wanted no part of my former life, casting it off like a flaming garment. When I surrendered to Christ Jesus, God started to bring me to life in ways that meant everything to Me. Unique things started happening that touched, moved, and motivated me. These were things others might not have noticed or cared about, yet they brought great encouragement and excitement into my life. God knew me in these personal ways that spoke of His Omniscience immediately.

I don't know that I even knew the word "Omniscient," but I learned the personal benefits of His great gift of knowing—Past, Present, Future, and even beyond time. He did not give me the things that would bring someone else to life—He opened me to a personal relationship with the Omniscient God Whom I had not known before. That rare covenant in the cold rain on Guyot, now came my way, and constantly impacted my life. More and more, we saw eye-to-eye, as Jesus' Lordship enveloped me.

This wonderful sloughing off of Myopic Me! brought a more personal and vivid connection to the *Faith-Time Continuum* which speaks to me to the present day. I started hearing His Voice. Who is speaking? There are three voices trying to get my attention. This auditory stream runs nonstop in the mind. It is either God the Father, the Holy Spirit, or Christ Himself. They speak in contradistinction from the many dialects of the present Culture. These counterfeit voices come through the whispering of demons which appropriate any of the fleshly appetites,

215

the pride of life, or the inordinate love of the present world. The Culture seeks to seduce with the latest rationalizations of every human appetite. The Culture is the Excuse Machine for everyone who has rejected God's good counsel.

> "You're worth it! Grab all the gusto while you still can. Join into the writhing night scene. Marijuana is not addictive, and it never leads you to a more addictive drug. Sex is your inalienable right, male on male or otherwise. Sink your teeth into one of our juicy steaks and add one of our delicious lobster tails. When you use our credit card, you get things free."

Meanwhile, the average credit card debt in America is measured in the thousands. Satan entices us through various temptations, always quoting God, but with a twisting of the meaning of the Words. God's Omniscience orchestrates every aspect of my life today, continuing to lead me through every self-destructive urge. Paul describes the flesh of man as "this body of death."[239] I soon learned after being born of God's Spirit, that there is a Person speaking through the Faith-Time interface. His ubiquitous voice is speaking to every believer. The bible calls Him the Holy Spirit, and He lives inside of every believer. The Holy Spirit is everywhere at once, but He also speaks to me revealing the glory of Jesus Christ, and reminding me of Jesus' Words. The Holy Spirit is known as the Comforter, and the One who leads the believer into all Truth—Jesus Christ.

God's graciousness is revealed to me through these three distinct Persons, the Triune God: God the Holy Spirit connects me to the glory and the Words of God the Son—Jesus Christ reveals the Father to me as "Our Father Who is in heaven." Hallowed is His name! As the Lord's Prayer ("teach us to pray") speaks to my heart about the power of Our Father, the Holy Spirit maintains my connection daily to God's Comfort, Counsel, Provision, and Advocacy. I come boldly to the throne of Grace, while the Holy Spirit is speaking to the world, bringing conviction of Sin, Righteousness, and Judgment.[240]

> Our Father in heaven,
>   may your name be kept holy.
> May your Kingdom come soon.
> May your will be done on earth,
>   as it is in heaven.
> Give us today the food we need,

---

[239] Romans 7:24 (NKJV).

[240] John 16:8

and forgive us our sins,
 as we have forgiven those who sin against us.
And don't let us yield to temptation,
 but rescue us from the evil one.

Jesus finished His brief teaching on prayer, saying, "If you forgive those who sin against you, your heavenly Father will forgive you. But if you refuse to forgive others, your Father will not forgive your sins."[241]

Wow! The only issue He repeated is the warning about forgiving others. It is only possible when we accept His forgiveness from the Cross. Out of Grace, given to us without merit, we can see clearly the brokenness of the one who sins against us. We are just like them. They are just like us. We all need God's Grace through His forgiveness of our sins; but equally, and in like manner, we are empowered through our forgiveness of others. Holding back our forgiveness thwarts this power to be the grace of God, with powerful prayers being heard before His throne daily.

The Body of Christ, the Church, receives the gifts of the Holy Spirit as powerful manifestations of God's presence and interactive love. God's Unity, Power, and Authority are given in the Body for the accomplishment of His will, advancing His kingdom in the world. God the Holy Spirit is the ubiquitous Presence of God in the room, but also inside of each believer. The Holy Spirit speaks God's warnings, and His love, into a narcissistic world. This triune God is experiential from day 1, but intellectually He is unpacked in my life as the Holy Spirit teaches me the Word of God revealed in Scripture. He teaches me the Omniscience of God when I go, and when I stay put, when I run from Him and when I hide. Such knowledge is too much for me to comprehend: "What are mere mortals that you should think about them, human beings that you should care for them?"[242]

Omniscience is complex and simple: Knowledge, Awareness, Sagacity, Wisdom, and Insight encompass the Dictionary's vain attempt to sum God up. Omniscience is more profound than *Google* can possibly explain, though *Google* seems to answer every one of my questions by connecting quickly to the Words of Christ through its intricate search engine's expertise: Sometimes today, I am foolish enough to think that Google stands for: God Ordains & Orchestrates Goodness & Love Everywhere. The Omniscient God has ways and means which we cannot imagine, and His thoughts are beyond ours, even on those clear days when we can see forever.

In point of fact, God's knowledge extends beyond the edges of the universe and beyond time, into a realm we cannot wrap our primitive logic around.

---

[241] Matthew 6:9-14

[242] Psalm 8:4.

Our rational mechanisms falter at the discovery of His Great Design and glorious Righteousness. Just as Google seems to anticipate my myriad inaccurate phrasings while linking me to incredible and detailed knowledge, God's Omniscience arrives before me, knowing everything, and seeing into every context through His lens of compassion and magnanimous reconciliation. Our God reveals Himself through the Cross, not through Google. For some, the idea of the Google god is a helpful metaphor; but Google can never challenge God in knowledge or wisdom or understanding. God is the Alpha and Omega version of Google, the One Who existed before any question had ever been asked.

His Omniscience comes like that friend who always gives you the most profoundly insightful gift on our special day. "Ohhhh!" we gasp, "That is so special. You heard my heart's desire from one mention of it. How did you find it?" When David sang his song to God in Psalm 139, he said, "Search me, Lord; and see if there is any evil way within me. I know that you already know everything about me. Even if I go across the sea, you are there. You even knew me when I was in my mother's womb. Such knowledge is too wonderful for me!" We search Google in vain, but God searches us, so that His Son can be perfected in us! God's omniscience is like that, but with a much bigger budget for gifting than Google can dream. God has no spending limits and no stingy accountant to countermand His plans. No one can look over His shoulder to say that He is wasting a year's wages.[243]

God can choreograph the nations and their armies, bringing His generosity directly into your life, while the boundaries of the Middle East and Europe and Africa are being transformed. "That is too great an expense for a man's soul," we complain, loving money more than we Love. But God's perfect budget has already accounted for His Son's blood shed for our sins. He has withheld nothing in the funding of our rescue. Now, and then, He is not restrained by the Federal Deficit, or the capacity of the Printing office to mill ten thousand dollar notes with Salmon P. Chase's portrait. Some Presidents believe that Chase is surely god, and God is surely dead. But others believe that ignorance of Him is a medicine to be swallowed at your own risk. His portrait comes into view when I look at Him without making excuses.[244]

His face comes into view like the slowly developing print in the Kodak Dektol. I would discover that mystery in the photographic darkroom at Lockheed Aircraft on that curious and completely unexpected evening when my idol appeared in those magic waters. God loves us so much, He even speaks to us through our idols, through the poisonous chemistry of our lives, always calling us into His untranslatable freedom. He will use a donkey to change

---

[243] John 12:5

[244] Luke 14:18

our direction.[245] His gradual appearing comes to fullness, revealing the already existing God through the perfect chemistry and exposure of His Son—bringing Light into our dark room from far more than 2000 years ago.

He rarely gives one of His good gifts to me that it is not also intended to bless someone else. Though he encourages me, filling my heart with appreciation for what He has done, He most often gives that which I will give away immediately. The gift and the person with the need are given together by the Spirit's urging. This sounds self-righteous, or self-aggrandizing, but it is not. It is a gift from God's goodness which is in me more often than I really appreciate or celebrate enough. His goodness somehow passes through my flawed reflection to reveal His mercy and grace. I deserve nothing from Him, but His love for you is so great that He will even use the likes of Me to show His love to you. This is truly scandalous! How could He? How could he use the worst sinner to reveal His Son's glory? I still don't understand this.

---

[245] Numbers 22:21-39.

24.

GOD'S WANT ADS.

aving played football for two years in college, an ad in the Lockheed Employee News caught my eye. The submitter of the ad was fishing for a quarterback for one of the Lockheed flag football teams. As far as I know today, flag football was not the giant gay setup (*Friends, Lesbians, and Gays*) it has become today in the Boston vicinity.[246] Back then, "No one was gay." Flag football was merely an alternative for exercise and competition without the extreme danger of injury that comes when the pads are put on.

Before Christ, I had not been aware of these Lockheed want ads placed by a few hundred of the 27,000 employees at Lockheed. These tiny want ads populated this weekly paper, and I learned that Lockheed had attracted many very talented ex-ballplayers into this no-contact league. It sounds silly that this would mean so much to so many, but every frustrated high school and college player wants to continue playing the game they love.

I signed up, and found my new team very happy to have a former college quarterback on their side of the ball. In this amazing post-Salvation season between the goal posts, I discovered a new healthy life, with deep gratitude in my heart, and my trivial pursuit on the gridiron brought much enjoyment my way. It helped me rise from the grave of my despondency. In our first game on the field of play, things went very well indeed. After seven offensive plays were completed, we led our opponent by a score of 28-0. Seven plays led to four touchdowns with extra points added by four more passes.

It was my miracle catch of fish which Peter and several other fishing disciples had experienced when they met the Lord of Life on Lake Galilee. Our football opponent was stunned, and afterward they asked for an explanation. My teammates seemed happy enough. I had just joyfully thrown consecutive passes to one of the best pass receivers and route runners I had ever seen, including the All American at The Citadel and the New Jersey boys I loved at Clemson University. Today in New England, that five-foot, nine-inch Julian Edelman of the New England Patriots reminds me of this talented, and instinctive route runner from that Lockheed team. Julian is truly one of the great receivers ever, and that guy at Lockheed could run a pass pattern in much the same way.

---

[246] Flag Flag Football.

If this whole vain discussion seems like *Shallow Hal*[247] to you, just realize that God gives us things that we love—salt sprinkled over the food of our lives. These experiences revived my confidence, as God showed me a whole new world in Marietta, and then in North Carolina a few months later. From death to life, I traveled in ways indescribable *Before Christ*. I would soon learn that these blessings from the Garden can be folded together with the seductive tricks of the Serpent. God has since shown me that, "Everything is permissible, but everything is not edifying."[248] Everything is permitted in God's miraculous liberty, but some things will not please him; nor will they reflect His love. He calls me, not to legalism, but to freedom through perfect love which casts out all fear.

God has since shown me that there are binary destinations for our idolatry and religious bondage to pursue: *Legalism* and *Relativism*. On one end is the futility of the law. On the other end are the self-destructive aims of licentiousness. Each is wrongly interpreted as God's best salvation. Neither place is born of God's salvation through the Cross. Freedom is not to be found in religious bondage, any more than it can be found in unrestrained lifestyles. Christ is the umpire, and he calls the balls and the strikes. He is the Way, the Truth, and the Life.

I am still grasping the full ramifications of this great freedom today. I know that He is the death-lifter. He is the One Who calls us to be born-again of the Spirit—He said not to go anywhere without Him—the Holy Spirit. These two truths, tied to His promises, can carry the believer through every storm. I understood that I could not go back into my mother's womb, but I had been born again and filled with His Spirit. His constant message to me, then and now, is to leave every idol at the foot of Jesus' cross where it belongs. I had stared into the double-barrels of death's buckshot just days before, but I knew my Savior now. When I was on Mt. Guyot, I did not know Him. On Satulah Mountain, I did not listen to His voice or hear Him warning me. In the shower in Clemson, I had no idea that Jesus had died for my sins, washing me with His Own blood.

Like the Israelites who had seen the Red Sea open to a depth of more than a hundred feet, I had seen God's deliverance, moving me from death to life. Though the Israelites could imagine their blood squirting when they saw the Egyptian spears and chariots in the distance, they soon forgot the Great I AM. Though He gave them safe passage over dry ground through the sea, drowning the Egyptian army, they melted their jewelry to make a Golden Calf. They soon worshiped again what they could see with their own eyes—like Thomas later in the Upper Room, they lacked the revelation of God in their hearts.

God, they could not see; but this golden calf, they could control entirely, bowing down to what they made with their own hands and craftsmanship. Diving into the orgy, they imagined that God could not see them from the mountaintop.

---

[247] *Shallow Hal*. Wikipedia.

[248] 1 Corinthians 10:23.

Their orgy is deeply printed in our hearts, as well. This metaphorical orgy is always lurking there. Our orgy is the name of our god that hides in our hearts. It is the Orgy that we minimize as a minor issue. But God is greater than our Orgy—and our self-deception! Jesus' blood is better than our Sexual Ecstasy or our Opiate Door. Success in life will never be enough to satisfy, and chasing the brass ring can never save us.

Nothing God gave me in my new freedom could truly become an idol because of His monumental grace in the midst of every circumstance. His divine appointment always awaited me, whether I saw it or not. No god could preempt my Lord. He showed me the keys to death and hell He clutched in His hand. The temporary pleasure of playing football in my hours away from work merely increased my gratitude for what He had done for me. I was truly enjoying the amazing skills of my teammates. This activity gave me an amazing boost in this brief season, and I made new friends with several of these teammates and co-workers during this time. It was a season, like salt on dull food devoured in a moment. The food was memorable, and these providences brought me back to life from death's door.

One morning, as I hiked from the B-25 building toward the half-mile long B-1 building at Lockheed Aircraft, the super-secret *SR-71 Blackbird* spy plane passed over my head to land in the adjacent Dobbins Air Force Base—only a handful of people even knew of its existence. The fortuitous timing of my routine trip to the manufacturing line from my desk in B-25 gained me this serendipity of God. I don't know why it made an emergency landing, but my reading has revealed that 14 were lost due to various accidents, none by enemy missiles. One was lost three days after Pop's death. The titanium skin of the jet reached temperatures of 550 degrees Fahrenheit.[249] The passage of the air-breathing supersonic airplane took no more than fifteen-seconds, as I was walking in the wet morning air.

It passed directly over me a hundred feet above my head. I could have thrown a rock as far. I could read the numbers on the belly of this *Blackbird* in flight. I looked around to compare notes with another soul walking the landscape of my moon, but there was no one! I saw not one soul on the sidewalks or roads as far as I could see. I was the only one walking so close to the nearby runway on that Georgia morning. I stood, looking straight up at its lowest trajectory before it touched down on the nearby runway! The *Blackbird*'s first mission in 1964 had verified the supersonic aircraft's capabilities, reaching speeds above Mach 3—nearly 2500 mph. Five decades later, the *SR-71* still holds the air-breathing speed record.[250]

This incredible, complex culmination of the engineering efforts by the *Lockheed Skunkworks* had just landed a few hundred yards away from me, and

---

[249] *A-12 Oxcart*. Gizmodo.

[250] *Lockheed SR-71*. Wikipedia.

it looked like *Batman* morphed with a giant black stingray and *Ironman* in one super-natural flying machine. From the front, it reminds me of the alien aircraft flown by Will Smith in "Independence Day." The two jet engines are the same diameter as the fuselage, each one taking up most of the surface area of its wing. To this day, the *SR-71* is very advanced, with its optimal form-to-function design and its stealth technology—considered the "femme-fatale" of all jet air-craft.[251] Dobbins Air Force Base closed down immediately upon its touchdown that morning. It had passed above me flared wide for landing. No fuel dripped on my head, as I learned later that the swing-wing function was not a perfect fit at very low air speeds. The leak disappeared at altitude and at top speed as the surfaces heated up and pressures increased.

Every human idol has its deep flaw, and the *Blackbird* was no exception. I doubt that very many people have ever seen this plane fly. Its takeoffs and landings were always well guarded, and they were always completely private. Why this jet had to make the emergency landing on that particular morning remains a mystery to me, but I know that it was God's little serendipity for a tech-crazy young man. I knew God's Son, and Jesus made a way for me into the throne of grace.

I found myself in a wonderland of advanced technology between Lockheed Aircraft and Dobbins Air Force Base, and God said to me, "Take a walk, John. Look up." When I looked up, I saw Him flying over me—that's right! I could see His love for me in that sweet serendipity. This funny S-word, serendipity, always significant, had become a very personal God-word for me after I prayed on my knees on Highland Avenue—changing my whole life and understanding of past, present, and future.

God's love is spherical, and His coming brings all clarity to complex things. Jesus' death and resurrection had become a mushrooming reality, just barely understood by me, but opening me up to a profound awareness of what a great price had been paid for my peace and joy. God was speaking to me personally now about the miracle of my Salvation, and through myriad gifts coming to me with His fingerprints all over them. The miracle life had become my reality, though I still barely understood what a miracle is. Eric Metaxas, best-selling author of *Bonhoeffer: Pastor, Martyr, Prophet, Spy,*[252] addresses this miracle interaction we begin to have with God.

> The following stories [about miracles] illustrate that these kinds of experiences are not only for nuns or monks or priests or "certain people." They illustrate that the God of the universe wants to communicate with every single one of us and

---

[251] *Sexiest Military Aircraft*. We Are the Mighty.

[252] Metaxas. *Bonhoeffer*.

that there is not only one way in which he does that. Because he created each of us differently, he will communicate with us individually. Though he is the same God for every one of us, in his tenderness and desire to reach us he is able to speak to us in ways that are very specific to us. [253]

Wow, Eric! Holy Spirit! You speak to us in the same language, with different dialects, and some people explain it more succinctly than others. Since 1964, four years before the Holy Spirit started translating reality for me, more than 4000 missiles were fired at the *SR-71 Blackbird* as it flew along at 80,000 feet. But none found their target! I imagine that the high-resolution cameras on board could photograph the lettering on your favorite "T-shirt" from sixteen miles up in the sky. Nothing like it ever arrived in the thin air of the ionosphere before it ruled this realm.

The *SR-71*'s mission to expose the plans of belligerent nations before they could be unleashed continued in the sky for years after. It carried no weapon other than that camera's eye in the sky—like David's Omniscient God looking down into our plans, the spy-plane discovered evildoers everywhere. God's little gift came wrapped in a bow for me when I was transfigured as His little one. I didn't deserve anything from God, but He regarded me in a different way because of my new Friend and Advocate—Jesus Christ. My new Attorney took my part now, handling all of my cases, paying my debts, and assuring that God the Father accepted me.

Shortly after that supersonic highlight reel over my shoulder, I also found my way into the *Lockheed Photography Club*—this adventure, like all the others, came with an instructive dose of spiritual warfare and eventual insight—I didn't know then that this battle was not between flesh and blood, but unfolded in me and outside of me through powers and principalities, dark kingdoms, and demonic forces in the heavenly realm.[254] I had no idea that dark kingdoms existed, and I certainly did not connect this to the darkroom I discovered in the *Lockheed Photographic Club*—ironic language, Darkroom, at its finest—nor did I know anything about spiritual battles seeking to control my thinking as I entered this new venue in my life. My total photographic experience previously had seen the completed roll of film depart from the Post Office on the way to the nearest Kodak Processing Center. In those days, film reappeared two weeks later as negatives in a box with a corresponding set of black and white prints.

I didn't know what a darkroom looked like, and I had no idea how the film turned into printed photographs in an album. In this day before digital photography made the chemicals and yellow lights irrelevant. There, in that

---

[253] Metaxas. *Miracles*.

[254] Ephesians 6:10-18

strange glow, I learned how to process negatives and make prints as large as 24 x 36 inches in size. The process seemed miraculous every time, with the image appearing in the chemicals, growing stronger and brighter with the passing seconds—entropy, time, and this imitation of the created thing appearing. It seemed magical and addictive.

That exposed image from the projector appeared as the positive image even though you projected the negative image in the dark room. The light negative areas produced the darker image content; the dark negative projections produced the lighter image content in the finished product. Why? Because less light from the projector strikes the photosensitive silver halide crystals suspended in gelatin on the printing paper surface. Also, the more silver halides in the paper brand, the more sensitive to light the paper is. There are many details, but the process begins with the exposure of the paper in the darkroom with a yellow or red light allowing you to see.

Throwing the paper in the Kodak developer brings the image to life, darkening the emulsion fairly quickly. The stop bath halts the darkening by neutralizing the developer with an acid. The Fixer hardens the image to the effects of light exposure outside the darkroom. The hypo clearing agent removes residues of the chemistry so that the picture will have no stains. It is entirely logical, predictable, and beautiful. I loved this process immediately. It is the combination of Science, Art, and Love. This intoxicating experience could hold my attention for hours as if no time had passed.

The former girlfriend now appeared from those vague negative projections into black and white realism in the darkroom. She smiled at me from that finished print. And I was hooked again on those very real feelings engendered in moments and memories. Printing my photos in the evenings, I grew in skill and knowledge. I dove into this mixing bowl of light, acids and silver salts. The high-quality projectors in this dark room facility made the work easy and accurate. Her face appeared, again and again, and this dangerous business came far too easily with my new freedom. The wonder and the power of this process came with God's simple warning: "Beware of idols. But know this: The darkness cannot extinguish the Light."[255]

Taking an extreme metaphor to help explain, the gun is not the murderer. But the man who uses it to kill might be a murderer. The implement, even the person, is not evil in itself, herself; but the one who uses the implement for evil purposes is. One night in the darkroom, a guru of the world of red and yellow lighting was present with a large number of his photos lying face-down in the wash water. He asked me to run them through the dryer later. I was pleased to take his photos out when mine were finished washing.

So, when I turned one over about a half hour later, I was shocked by what I saw. He had photographed a man and his wife in private intimacy. I turned it back over, took mine, and never came back to the darkroom again. Satan ruined

[255] John 1:5.

my enjoyment of the darkroom. Or did he? I believe that God used this event to warn me before it was too late for me. God would deal with him later—even dealing with him through this rebuff of his dancing with the devil. But God stopped me in my tracks. In effect, he kicked me out of the darkroom reverie. He is always looking out for His Own, and sometimes we don't realize that He is protecting us from worse troubles.

During the day, I climbed all over the C-5A cargo planes during their assembly journey inside the half-mile long B-1 building. Their sixty-five foot T-tails came together in pieces assembled inches below the horizontal beams of the ceiling. This gigantic, endless building contained the most amazing aeronautic wonders in all stages of the assembly journey. The riveters fired their tools that sounded like machine-guns, and ear plugs kept the hearing loss to a minimum as I walked amongst those behemoths.

At night I went to the evening services at the Church of Our Savior in Atlanta. I loved every second of those times worshiping my Lord and my God, Jesus Christ—Christus, in the ancient Greek. I had no prejudice now, for Christ had changed my heart. Though I had little connection to the other believers, except to smile, I loved every minute worshiping God in this intimate and holy way. We were set away from the world, in a world of our own, exalting Christ with our tears—and I can only assume that I was not the only one who overflowed with deep emotions every time I heard His name.

Each day I watched the C-130 Hercules being built forty-five years ago. This process continues to the present day! They are still being retrofitted with new engines, weapons, avionics, and capabilities to meet the needs of a new day: "In the final days, there will be wars and rumors of wars."[256] These tiny airplanes [132-foot wingspan] were on the far side of the long line of monster aircraft in the assembly line along the far wall of B-1. The C-5A [223-foot wingspan] dwarfed the smaller cargo planes. The largest aircraft in the world at that time, it would carry cargo around the world for military and various rescue missions, but the C-130 Hercules would outlive them all.

I clicked my camera again and again as President Johnson and Ladybird Johnson christened the first production C-5A with champagne. Ladybird broke the bottle over the sturdy nose of the first aircraft that had finished the production and testing processes—it was ready to fly in 1969. After the appearance of wing cracks in the 1970s, the wings were redesigned in the 1980s. The original Lockheed wing design used the outer wing surface as load-bearing. The new design added structure internally to bear the load of up to 120,000 pounds for long flights over water and land. The new Super 5M Galaxy is being made today with increased load capacity and with no need to refuel from the U. S. to any operating theater around the world. [257]

---

[256] Matthew 24:36

[257] *Lockheed C-5*. Wikipedia.

A C-130 had already landed on the USS Forrestal aircraft carrier in 1963 without a hook to slow it down. No one thought this was possible, but the emergency landing at sea revealed the potential. Many landings have been completed since then on aircraft carriers, though it has a 130-foot wingspan and is one hundred feet long. It is the only military aircraft still in production after fifty years. My time at Lockheed coincided with the buildup of Vietnam hostilities. Fifty-Five C-130 Hercules aircraft went down or had accidents on the ground during the Vietnam war, with thirty-four lost in direct combat encounters.[258]

Immersed in these technological beasts every day, I marveled at the prowess of mankind spread out before me in this great manufacturing arena. Every evening I drove the forty mile roundtrip for services in Atlanta which revealed the handiwork of God. I loved everything about my routine. My life was full in ways I had never dreamed. I drove to the little church for fellowship with other young people who had found God in the sacramental protocols of this "high church" setting. It went way beyond my mother's favorite Episcopal church. It meant everything to me, but more than those rituals, Christ meant everything to me now. The form of the service only brought me to a place where He could be exalted and worshiped. I wanted to be with Him. When I left that safe place, I had to go through the eye of the needle again to find another safe place in the body of Christ—His Church.

On one of those nights at the evening service, a young man presented me, with great dignity and display, the newly published book, *The Day Christ Died.*[259] It was a gift of love. This exchange was one of those God-moments which Christians talk about, and no one knows what they mean. This young man played his part in puncturing my space-time. His voice spoke to me through the faith-time manifold where our gravity merged for just a moment. Time bulged as we stood face to face, with his hand moving toward me. He was holding a book, offering its contents to me. He knew that it contained the code to unlock another room into that knowledge of God's love which I so desperately required.

We briefly spoke, and I thanked him for noticing me—for seeing I was now alive and no longer dead. The divine foot had pushed through my door, and God knew me in this vague intersection of the Faith-Time Continuum. I had survived the visitation with death, and survived by Grace. Since this had been a very lonely time, this special encounter with a like-minded human being was special. It was fleeting as a shooting star, but bright as the face of God. The Holy Spirit's overwhelming presence had filled me during the hour-long service, and He moved again in this extended fifteen minutes of fellowship with other God-seekers after the service.

Unfortunately, this lone encounter with another believer would be the last one before I took a job with *Western Electric Corporation* in North Carolina. I

---

[258] *Lockheed C-130.* Wikipedia.

[259] Bishop. *The Day Christ Died.*

would be working on the *Antiballistic Missile (ABM)* system on the eighteenth floor of the Nissen Building on Fourth Street in Winston Salem.[260] The young man's gift in Atlanta, 320 miles away, touched me in a powerful way. Though he never knew the great impact his book had on me, the gift opened to me the very real potential for family in the body of Christ—in the Church—through the very real suffering, death, burial, and resurrection of Jesus Christ. It is strange to remember how vague was this bond at the time, but the nature of salvation is so incredibly personal—and powerful.

Moving from personal to corporate would take me another eight years to understand with any intimacy at all. Knowing is intimate, visceral, sometimes painful, and always essential. I would learn something of this pain which Jesus endured, though my pain would be mostly self-induced. Much of my pain would come from the self-inflicted wounds of the past life, before Christ. The book had revealed powerfully to me the price Jesus willingly paid for the family bond which I so blithely postponed from that meeting in my equivalent of the "upper room." It is God's most emphatic intention, to make us one with Himself and one another. Jesus' prayer in that first "upper room," on the night when Egypt's lamb became Jerusalem's Lamb of God, was a prayer for Oneness. When that book was pushed through the membrane between heaven and earth, my understanding of Christ's sacrifice changed forever. When I remembered Him thereafter, I could not escape the memory of His suffering and death on a Cross.

I did not even know the young man's name—but he is my strong spiritual brother in Christ. "Thank you, brother! If you are reading this, you are more than seventy years old. I pray for God's great freedom in your life—His great adventure and purpose in everything you do. The night you gave me the book, I started to understand that I could, and had to, live a new way as a member of His Body. I understood that I was becoming an authentic member of His Church in the earth. I had been adopted into a new Family, and I owed everything to Him."

> He gave up his life for her [the Church] to make her holy and clean, washed by the cleansing of God's word. He did this to present her to himself as a glorious church without a spot or wrinkle or any other blemish. Instead, she will be holy and without fault. Ephesians 5:25b-27

This feminine thing, the "her," is anathema for men who are urgently masculine in this world. Male or female, we all were being made holy, washed by the cleansing of the Word. We were instantaneously clean, and progressively we were being made holy—set apart for His purposes. Men struggle to bridge the mental and cultural gulf when they become the Bride of Christ. But men

---

[260] *Lockheed C-5 Galaxy*. Wikipedia.

fully realize that they have spots and wrinkles and blemishes that need healing. Actually, men can only bridge this chasm when they adore Christ as Deliverer, Friend, Savior, Lord, and King.

But the intimate relationship with Christ is understood best in the marriage covenant with God—We know that His "body was broken, and His blood was shed," making possible a *New Covenant*—not a covenant of Law, but of Grace. This covenant reaches through the social haze between us, full of promises, love, as well as commands. We share Christ in this intimate Communion of love. Even God's commands are commands to love Him, and to love each other—as we love ourselves! Forgiveness is the medium for this love to exist and persist.

I never shared an overt spiritual conversation with this young man in Atlanta beyond our common faith in salvation through Christ. The exchange of the book that night is a metaphor of Christ's suffering bearing fruit into eternity. Two thousand years after His sacrifice, a medical doctor's eyes were opened to see the profound act of love that could save a sinner like him, and me. Men don't easily partake of this kind of soul intimacy. Men need to become as little children to approach His offer of peace and purpose. The intimacy has nothing to do with homosexuality, as some imagine. Though there is a sexual component to our relationship that is revealed in the Song of Solomon, that Song of Songs addresses our intense intimacy with Christ's death, burial, and resurrection. The Church reciprocates that love.

I took the book from him, saying, "Thank you for your kindness." Then I headed out on I-20 to I-75, and drove a car full of God's peace back to my apartment in Smyrna thirty minutes away. I started reading the book that same night. The author, Jim Bishop, describes the crucifixion from the perspective of Christ's physical suffering. As a medical doctor, he reconstructed the Gospel story from the vantage point of the Medical Examiner doing an autopsy. Not just any autopsy was performed; this autopsy reveals the extreme suffering which comes through the Cross. It reveals the terrible suffocation which finally kills those who survive all the other shocks to the body and to the heart.

I witnessed the cruelty of the crucifixion with none of the sanitized abstractions learned in my childhood Sunday school classes. The intentional cruelty of the cross—the most painful way to kill a man—came directly from the Roman ruler's desire to publish fear into a wide-flung populace. The fear of punishment they created was in stark contrast to God's perfect love which casts out all fear. One kingdom threatened hell on earth for breaking Caesar's law, while the other promised eternal life with God, saved by grace, and not by God's demanding Laws. Our freedom comes through Christ's suffering, and the spiritual war rages still. The ultimate battle is won, but God is transforming our minds through His kindness, and the mind and heart and soul have become His fields of victory. God is breaking every contract with darkness we signed in ignorance: "Father, forgive them, for they know not what they do."[261]

---

[261] Luke 23:34

The Empire of Rome united many nations around Roman Law and under the fear of punishment, instituting the horror of the crucifixion for nearly any crime that might be committed. This cruel choreography of death, put every perpetrator on public display—naked display—in agony and a final shame. Jesus' clothes were raffled off, and He was mocked with a crown of thorns. The crucified criminal most often died of suffocation when they had no more strength to support their weight against the spikes driven through their hands (wrist tendons) and feet. Their last breath followed the pitiful thrusting of their thigh muscles, hoisting their body a few inches, unable to gain another breath. Some died of shock when the primary nerve system in the wrists delivered severe shock directly to the heart.[262]

The strong ones who continued to lift themselves up for air would die when their lower leg bones were broken by the Centurions. They quickly suffocated and died. I discovered in this narrative account of Christ's crucifixion the powerful truth that God is the giver of every good gift; and He held nothing back in order that I could be rescued from punishment and death—from the death which never ends in hell. I came to deeply understand that the Lord of my life had suffered greatly to save me. But I must tell you that idolatry is not easily removed from the mind's convincing games, and I soon entered into a season of spiritual warfare so formidable that I barely survived it.

Looking back, I see that spiritual warfare happens in the mind before it invades the concrete rituals in the appetites—it occurs first in the heavenly realm before arriving in the thoughts, shifting the will of man. It is a battle for control and lordship. It is a battle of confidence, where confidence is akin to confiding. It is a battle between light and dark. The Prince of the Air spins up his perfect stronghold, planting it in our mental process. Even a believer can suffer from this kind of stronghold, not knowing how to find victory in the minefield. For the most part, it is ignorance that takes us captive, for we already have this victory through faith in His name.

Paul said we should take every thought captive to Christ. We can take a thought captive to various philosophies, to a counselor, to an advisor or family member. But it is only truly effective when we take the thought captive to Jesus Christ's words, promises, and commands. When a thought, full of threats and forebodings, is placed inside of Christ, it is disarmed of all its power by the great light of His glory. His name makes the demons tremble. His great name is above every name, in heaven and in the earth. He is the One Who can handle the temptations which come—He endured those same temptations without sinning.

He is therefore the One Who can "lead us not into temptation." This battle rages in the paradoxical landscape of Christ's perfect victory. It is a paradox because we are free while we struggle to function in this new freedom. It is an enigma in a riddle, inside of a puzzle, which God permits for our ultimate good.

---

[262] Bishop. *The Day Christ Died.*

Soon, the problem area becomes the area of discipline and faithfulness. The pattern of this world which held me—the idolatry captivating me—fades away.

My honeymoon with Christ came to an end in a matter of months. Now, God started to show me my depravity and the persistence of my sin-nature which had made me a slave (though I had no idea to what degree and kind). He also showed me what Christ accomplished in the flesh, while He was fully God, walking among us without sinning—the Pioneer of our Faith. I realized eventually that Jesus received the baptism of John in the Jordan River as the pivotal action before He took on these temptations which I experienced in Atlanta and points north. At that time, I knew nothing about Jesus' victory in the wilderness. I had not heard or read that He rose from the baptismal waters in the Jordan River to enter into a battle to settle the issue of the appetites, the love of the world, and the devil's deadly soul-traps.

I did not understand that Jesus intentionally traveled to that lonely place to be tempted by Satan! The love of the world, an institutional disease of flesh and eye, had to be subdued in His flesh. His appetites had to be brought into submission to the Father's will, so that God's words were greater than the taste of bread, drenched with butter and extra virgin olive oil. Satan had to be told that only God should be praised and worshiped, and that his glory was dwarfed by the great light of God, the Creator of all things. Jesus carried a weapon which the devil also knew about—the Words of God. Every time Satan pitched his filthy deal with Jesus, the Lamb of God answered with the Words of God. Though Satan quoted the Scriptures, he always demoted God, promoting himself. Like the false church that promotes itself above Christ, Satan claimed glory that can only be accorded to God Himself.

At the end of forty days of Jesus fasting and praying, Satan realized that Jesus could not be tempted by his best tricks. Jesus carried in Himself the Words of God which crushed every argument, every appetite, and every temptation that Satan could bring against Him. Jesus twice quoted God's word from Deuteronomy 6—God's word to Moses in the wilderness. From Psalm 91 Jesus quoted from God's promise to protecting Messiah's heal from bruising. Quoting these two chapters from the Torah, Jesus cast Satan out of His ministry which would come through the Cross. "If you faced the Cross," I asked myself, "would you be tempted by Satan's offer to avoid that suffering?"

Then, Jesus demonstrated the power we have through His name: "Satan, get out of here!"[263] Satan knew that he had to obey Jesus' command—on the basis of the scriptures quoted. Standing according to the Father's words, Jesus had all the authority of the Father over matters impacting the heavens and the earth. Satan left immediately, until he found another opportunity to trip Jesus up, keeping Him from performing God's good and perfect will. I have learned that the same challenge faces me. Satan leaves, but he looks for another moment of vulnerability to tempt me, keeping me from God's will. When I resist, God

---

[263] Matthew 4:1-10

always comforts me. In Jesus' case, the Angels came to take care of His needs in His greatly weakened state.[264]

God wanted to begin to write His Words on my heart with indelible ink— with the blood of Jesus. I would struggle eight years—seventy-three-times as long as Jesus, before I learned the Words that could protect me from the lies of the enemy. I would struggle against many powerful forces, not having any understanding of the scriptural truths that served Jesus so well in the wilderness of His testing. Jesus modeled for me the attentiveness to every Word from the Father's mouth. God's Word would eventually become a place of safety for me. It is a rite of passage for every believer, moving each one of us from the kingdom of this world into the fullness of the kingdom of God.

---

[264] Luke 4:1-13

25.

FANTASIES OR SPIRITUAL STRONGHOLDS?

When I had fantasies so real they triggered glandular responses, I had no answer—no Words to thwart Satan's plans. I just said, "Give me more of the same. I have to stop thinking this way! Give me more; I have to stop!" But this fatal flaw came with shame and confusion about what had happened to me. I didn't understand how this idolatry could still cling to my mental routines. I didn't understand that Christ had decisively broken sin's power over my life, giving me the power to say, "No!" I questioned whether I could be a Christian while entertaining these more-real-than-life sexual fantasies.

I had a photo album with me when I moved to Winston Salem, and this album had become a great distraction. Of course, I did not initially see this as a negative. Please hear me say that these photos were just photographic images of my former girlfriend. She had not posed for the purposes of seduction, but my inordinate affection for her produced a distraction which became an idol in my daily routine. Confessing my sins here should never shift any blame to anyone else. Jesus entered into a personal relationship with me, and He told me and John the Apostle, "Beware of idols."[265] After the resurrection, Jesus asked Peter, "What is that to you?"

He was speaking about Peter's eventual death, crucified upside down on a cross at Mamertine Prison. Peter would share the Good News of the forgiveness of sins and reconciliation with God the Father through Jesus' Cross.[266] He would speak to his crucifiers for hours before he died, explaining to them the Gospel of the Kingdom. But on this occasion, before the Holy Spirit had come to fill Peter with boldness, he wanted to know how come John was not going to die on a cross as he would. Why did John get to live a full life?[267]

---

[265] 1 John 5:21 NIV.

[266] *Mamertine Prison*. Wikipedia.

[267] John 21:22

Jesus told Peter, and you and me, to be accountable for what we have heard Christ say to us. We should blame no one for the outcomes of doing what He tells us to do. Each of us is different, though we are tied together in the perfect unity of the Holy Spirit. Jesus eventually gave me this explicit instruction: "First get rid of the log in your own eye; then you will see well enough to deal with the speck in your friend's eye."[268] This dealt with my version of Peter's dilemma. Each of us has a personal relationship with the Word of God. Each of us is accountable for what we hear. Stop your ears if you must, but He will cause you to hear His voice with the best noise cancelling head phones strapped to your ears.

My photo album contained nothing but candid and posed photos taken with a little *Kodak Brownie* camera of that day—grainy, black & white snapshots. This was my issue to hear Jesus' voice. How would I deal with this fly buzzing inside my head? How would I deal with this ongoing symptom of my idolatry? The flash bulb had done its supernatural work in hues of gray, and nothing could change the effect those images produced in my soul. They had become a place of comfort and pleasure for me.

The videos and the sculptures of this world can become the ritual altars for our inordinate worship. These can so easily become the obsessive compulsive disorder of our rote behavior. That movie scene can take us captive in a distorted and vain chasing of illusions. We were made for worship, and we will find something or somebody to worship as our default god. But God is a jealous God when it comes to ultimate relationships. My attraction to that altar spoke of a deeper calling by God to seek Him for my greatest intimacy and pleasure!

I had to ask God's Spirit to shake me loose from all those cravings of the flesh, those distorted, wounded ways of relating to the world around me. In my weakness, I discovered that Christ is always strong. In my weakness, God was working out His holiness in me. My wounds, I would learn, are intended to be exchanged for His glory. The thief on the Cross stole Paradise from the jaws of death at the last minute while he waited to die beside Jesus. Mary Magdalene poured out on Jesus' feet the perfume left over from her life as a prostitute. She exchanged the nard of her wounded lifestyle for the glory Christ's would receive a week later when He rose from the grave. Christ's wounds were exchanged for the Victory that eventually saved me. His battlefield on the *Hill of Skulls* would defeat the power of my old sin nature.

I would learn to embrace these battles. There, the flesh is crucified, and the resurrection becomes the supernatural reality. In that spiritual place, Jesus has already broken the power of sin and death, empowering me through the Holy Spirit to lay down my sin-life at the foot of His Cross. Greater is the God of my salvation than this forked-tongued Prince of the Air with his library of lies. At the Cross, Satan was shattered by God's inexorable, good, and perfect will. On the third day, the dark crypt opened, and the demons fled from the power of

---

[268] Matthew 7:5

Jesus' name. They could not survive His presence, glorified as He was in the resurrected body, for they had already cried out for His mercy before He took the keys to death and hell. Jesus walked back into our Myopic World to give us our final instructions:

> "I have been given all authority in heaven and on earth. Therefore, go and make disciples of all the nations, bap-tizing them in the name of the Father and the Son and the Holy Spirit. Teach these new disciples to obey all the commands I have given you. And be sure of this: I am with you always, even to the end of the age." Matthew 28:18-20 "But you will receive power when the Holy Spirit comes upon you. And you will be my witnesses, telling people about me everywhere—in Jerusalem, throughout Judea, in Samaria, and to the ends of the earth." Acts 1:8

When Jesus spoke, He stood in the center of the Middle East near Jerusalem. He had conquered death, and was minutes from ascending into heaven. He spoke of distant lands and unknown peoples. He spoke of us, in America, seven time zones away. The Pilgrims brought His words into the new world nearly six-teen-hundred years later. In Jesus' day, this ocean journey was inconceivable. Today, the journey to freedom is unaffected by time zones, weather, or commu-nication challenges. We don't need a good *FaceTime* connection to reach God's Throne. Christ has made a way, piercing time and distance. The God of the impossible takes on our brokenness, for sin is no obstacle for our Mighty God.

This grace reassured me during this brief season—encouraging me in some deep, deep, unshakeable place—the lying voices whispered, "You are doomed," but I couldn't be shaken from my certainty that God had sealed me. Those potent fantasies stirred hormonal responses so authentic they cannot be replicated on this page, and it would not be edifying to do so. But these vain imaginations were fabricated by demons seeking to introduce me to a *Brave New World*.[269] They tried to revive the sloughed off narcissistic propensities of Myopic Me! In this dark night of the soul, doubt creeped into my thoughts like a serpent. They dragged their shame, a sack of fear, and a dose of terror, but Christ shattered their split-tongued accusations.

I would learn that the Father of Lies always carries a bag of flaming shame, splattering it on anyone who stands still long enough. But God brings redemp-tion and a garment of praise. When the enemy comes with his invisible terrorists, God disarms their AK-47s and their air to ground missiles with His great love.

---

[269] Huxley. *Brave New World.*

> And the Holy Spirit helps us in our weakness. For example,
> we don't know what God wants us to pray for. But the Holy
> Spirit prays for us with groanings that cannot be expressed
> in words. And the Father who knows all hearts knows what
> the Spirit is saying, for the Spirit pleads for us believers in
> harmony with God's own will. And we know that God
> causes everything to work together for the good of those who
> love God and are called according to his purpose for them.
> Romans 8:26-28

My brief season of condemnation is typical of Satan's tactics, for he never desists from his attempts to shake our faith, stealing our soul for delivery to hell. The enemy wants to pull the shawl of hopelessness over every head. His goal then, and now, is to steal, kill, and destroy. God says that I should put on the full armor—every piece of armor which comes through what Christ has done. This is not the armor of striving, for there is nothing I can contribute beside believing—even the believing is a gift from God. God tells me to put on the helmet of salvation. He tells me to put on the righteousness Christ won for me through His sinless life and His perfect alignment with the Father's good and perfect will. Through Christ, I should remind myself that the Truth is not a philosophical construct, but is a Person. The Belt of Truth is Christ's Character, His Mind, His compassion, His nature, and His Words. When I reference the Truth, I reference His Words in the Bible. Everything is tested with His Words. The only complete Truth is Christ. Anything else is a shadow or a lie.

Why should I need this armor since I have been set free? It makes no sense. Why should I need the Gospel of peace on my feet, or the shield of faith on my arm? What could provoke me to draw the Sword of the Spirit, the two-edged Sword which is the Word of God? Since I am saved eternally by the blood of the Lamb, what more is there to do? Why do I need armor when I have on the Kevlar of God already covering my soul?

> God exists everywhere and everywhen. He is eternal and
> omnipresent. And not only is he present everywhere, he is
> everywhere pursuing us. He is the hunter, the king, the hus-
> band, approaching us at an infinite speed. Central to C. S.
> Lewis's vision of the Christian life is the basic fact that we
> are always in God's presence and pursuit.[270]

---

[270] *John Piper Preaching.* U-Tube.

While Paul was held in that little room in Mamertine Prison he saw something profound in the armor of that centurion in that dark cell.[271] Paul found God's parable as his own mind was whirling with dark thoughts of death and fear of the sword that would remove his head very soon. Paul learned to hold up that Shield of Faith to stop the fiery darts that burned into his mind. He learned to take those foreboding thoughts captive—each one disarmed by the promises of Christ. Paul had personal promises from Christ that he would be translated into heaven when that sword of Nero took his life.

This confidence empowered Him to speak into the centurion's life and indirectly into his family. Though Paul often drew the Sword of the Spirit from its sheath, he approached every authority wearing the shoes touched with the Gospel of peace. He understood that fear did not disqualify him, for he had put on the righteousness of Christ, and not his own righteousness. He put on the love of God which he had written about in the Letter to the church in Corinth. Paul was able to bear all things, believe all things, hope all things, and endure all things.[272]

Paul and I need the armor because of that roaring lion, that toothless beast who tells me I will never change, coming at me in the heavenly realm, and in the earthly realm when he finds my flesh is vulnerable. World War III was declared when I believed in God's Son. The peace Christ gave me that day placed me in the supernatural eye of the World War that rages all around me to the present day. When I move in Christ, the eye of the war moves with me. The Hurricane storm of war follows me, but the eye-wall holds if I yield myself to the Holy Spirit. He brings comfort and help when I cannot make it on my own strength.

That feeling many of us had on September 11, 2001, was a picture of this battle in the heavenly realm that looks for a chance to devour us. Many people were shaken that day, and some have not recovered from that hovering fear. The PTSD from those events haunts their dreams. But God is sheltering many under the shadow of His wings. The Revelation of Jesus Christ brings a picture of this battle, this world war. The war of Armageddon grows closer, and the Seven Seals become more real. The Spector of the mark of the Beast seems more possible daily in this era of identity theft and hacking of vast data bases to steal our profiles and money. But the eye-wall holds in this present and future storm unfolding. The eye-wall is Christ Himself, and His Cornerstone keeps our building from collapsing in the buffeting which comes.

The Scriptures say, "Resist the devil, and he will flee," but I knew nothing of this instruction in the beginning. Jesus' half-brother, James, encouraged every new believer with words explaining how faith works during the storm. He said,

---

[271] *Mamertine Prison.* Wikipedia.

[272] 1 Corinthians 13:7

"When troubles of any kind come your way, consider it an opportunity for great joy. For you know that when your faith is tested, your endurance has a chance to grow. So let it grow, for when your endurance is fully developed, you will be perfect and complete, needing nothing."[273]

Paul warned the church in Corinth to address the sexual sin that is still shocking in our jaded age. A young man had married his step mother, and the church had been supportive of this union though it is forbidden in Leviticus. He told them to "cleanse [themselves] from everything that can defile [their bodies] or [their] spirit[s], [working] toward complete holiness because [of their] fear [of] God.[274]

It took me years to learn these warnings. God wanted to teach me more than cold military obedience. He wanted my heart to understand how much He has loved us in the midst of His stern commandments. Otherwise, we cannot be changed into the likeness of His Son. When He urged me through the Holy Spirit to deal with these innocent photos, He wanted me to fully understand that an inanimate album could become my false god, undermining my relationship with Him. I gravitated toward this private affection which could divert me from God's brand-new plans for my life. Is the bird to be blamed for the worshipers who gather in the golden rooms in Thailand to worship before their images? Is the snake to be blamed, or is the sun complicit for the sacrifices made before its likeness? God did not blame the album, but He confronted the inordinate affection in my heart.

No one is to blame, except for the idolater himself. When he eschews the voice of God, preferring the messenger of antichrist, he chooses to commit adultery against God. Did I overreact in those first days? Somewhat, but I had to learn how to fight for the will of God as the best possible outcome in every case—just as the Thief on the Cross learned, under fire, how to fight for Christ. "Don't you fear God [he said to the murderer on the other cross beside Jesus] even when you have been sentenced to die? We deserve to die for our crimes, but this man hasn't done anything wrong."[275]

Accusing the brethren is Satan's most common method of bullying the one who is vulnerable, but he can't steal what belongs to Christ! Greater is the One who is in us, than the one who is in the world—the evil *rulers of this world*.[276]

---

[273] James 1:2-4

[274] 2 Corinthians 7:1

[275] Luke 23:40-41

[276] Ephesians 6:12

Since God is the lover of our souls, the devourer, the sin-tickler, is unable to take our peace, or to break up our relationships, or to wreck our lives. Christ is our Advocate, and He blocks the Accuser's U-Tube videos from playing on our smart phones. He is trustworthy, even when we are unfaithful. His promise holds true, even when our promises crumble. This bullying by Satan overflows beyond my little story in Smyrna Georgia. His bullying is famous in Hollywood, and those who agreed to worship him are finding out that his promise of power, sex, and money does not nullify the Law.

Even in our broken world, God's law continues to be a mirror of our failure to love our neighbor. No one is good! Please don't misunderstand this, for you and I are not good either. The Pope is not good. The policeman is not good. The President is not good. Why do we expect him to be good, when we aren't? The King is not good. Why are we shocked when his actions violate our strict moral code—which we ourselves fail to follow? Not even those housewives of Orange County are good. Sometimes people think they don't have to be accountable, and they get caught in gross sin according to our shifting code and standards in the society. But God misses nothing that we do. He already knows us better than we know ourselves. He knows that our hearts are continually wicked and perverse. If you truly see goodness, and you are not the best judge of it, you are seeing God's goodness being worked out in the world. While the Holy Spirit is present in the world, goodness will be seen in myriad ways. When He is removed, nothing but evil will remain, and even Noah's day will seem like the "good old days."

In the entertainment industry, the performer becomes the target of stalkers and paparazzi. The performer, the actress, or the movie itself becomes a shrine for illegal pleasure. The forbidden fruit is picked again and again, as if there will be no consequence. The movie star becomes the private love interest of the fan or the director. Is the actress guilty of crossing some line? Maybe, but this is not always the case. Within the movie, there may be scenes depicting exploitation. Potential complicity can occur when an actor portrays deeds done in darkness. Has the actor sought to be worshiped as a god—or to seduce the viewer? Has the actress intended to seduce the audience with her romp? Certainly, some have sought to be worshiped by their fans?

If so, they are complicit in any ramifications from their actions—are they not? Clearly, most performers don't think it through fully. They don't understand the distortions that occur when they sing their little song causing many to lift their cell phones in worship. Fans often hold their hands up in worship of their idol, not realizing how their ecstatic adoration offends the God whom they ignore. God's displeasure does not change the love of God toward His creation. He did not send His Son into the world to condemn the world, but to save the world through Him.[277]

God's solution for my own idolatry became clear to me one night like the fire of Elijah coming into my mind. Jesus and Elijah moved me to place the

---

[277] John 3:17.

photos from that album on the hibachi flames, burning each one entirely. The Greeks have their catharsis. Medicine has its therapeutic qualities. But Christ gives the forgiveness of sins and the promise of eternal life with God. A contrite heart is better than any medicine because it removes the object of false worship. Burning the photos was efficacious because contrition accompanied this act. With the living presence of Christ in my heart as I went to that hibachi, the soul-tie was broken which had held me to a dark spiritual bondage in the heavenly realm. Keeping the photos would keep me from truly turning from my sins. We cannot do this in our own strength. Don't even try. Only God can make this happen.

I had to feed each one of those precious photos into the fire, watching each one as it was consumed. Each one had tentacles of power into my private reverie. Each one was now burning before my EYES. My appetite was burned in the fire. My adultery before God was burned in the fire of His authentic love. My inordinate love was consumed in those flaming photos. In case the female readers still don't understand this "burning," imagining that the fire is burning you up, this is not the case. Ask your favorite man to explain the need. Men know how images become altars. If I still had those photos today, I might be tempted to go back to that little shrine! It was my aberrant response to her photographs that created the shame-game. God did not create this game—Adam and Eve first found the delicious territory of good and evil. They stumbled into this lie, wanting to be like God.

Adam and Eve learned to blame God in the very moment of their shame. God does not blame, but He will judge us all on the final day. His judgment will be perfect, with no ulterior motives. And the consequences of His judgment will only find remediation through the shed blood of His Son Jesus. My idolatry pierced my soul through the orifice of my eye, inflaming my mind, heart, and soul—"Love the Lord with all your heart, soul, mind, and strength." The young woman did nothing to deserve God's judgment or Adam's self-righteous finger-pointing. I had simply chosen to build my altar around these images of her. This creepy worship service is not a new thing, for it has been there since the beginning of the world of man.

For a vast number of men, this spiritual cleansing exercise will make perfect sense. Those photos became the problem, and I had to do something about that bifurcation of my soul's affection. I could have left them on the living room coffee table, but I couldn't be left alone with them. There was nothing sexual about these black and white photos. The album was very much like the album full of your baby pictures. But this album had become a shrine, chaff in my life, and it had to be burned and renounced as an object of distraction, pleasure, and idolatry.

I wasn't burning the person up, but I might have been freeing that person in some way. I might have been freeing her from some relational bondage that had come into our relationship—what some call soul-ties. I have come to understand that Soul-ties, my own definition, is a spiritual, and body-contract, signed wittingly or unawares in the heavenly realm, as well as in the earthly realm. This soul-tie drains us of strength, focus, and hope. It appears to be an affectionate contract with a person, but actually is a contract with the Evil One who seeks to destroy, steal, and kill. The only safe place in the universe for love and war is spelled out in the simple words spoken to Moses by God Himself after God freed the Israelites from slavery in Egypt.

> And you must love the Lord your God with all your heart, all your soul, and all your strength. Deuteronomy 6:5

"All your soul" is a crucial phrase in Jesus' two Love Commandments. This soul bond with God brings perfection, wholeness, and is never bifurcated by idolatry. This is the 100% love of God—with the healthy soul all-in for God. No part of the soul is reserved for any other gods. The love of any other god is a spiritual sin-tie, a bifurcation of the soul's entire commitment to God's will and purposes. Where is your soul?

I had to admit that my soul was bifurcated by this powerful divide. I can't say that I fully understand this conception of the soul to this day—what is it? Scores of verses connect heart and soul together, as if they are inextricably blurred. But there is a different meaning of soul which appends to eternity and cries out for protection in the earth. "Dear friends, I warn you as 'temporary residents and foreigners' to keep away from worldly desires that wage war against your very souls."[278]

My soul is particularly vulnerable in love relationships. Since God restricts the sexual union to the covenant of marriage, violating this prohibition creates trouble in heaven and in the earth—a foreign concept in a world which disavows the covenant of marriage as having any heavenly import. Truthfully, it doesn't matter if a Justice of the Peace or an Elvis Impersonator performs the wedding— the soul knows that marriage is consummated. There is also a powerful contract formed in the flesh, and this contract comes with dark spiritual intonations forming a web of bondage outside of the will of God. We bind ourselves to the dangerous undertow of demons who plan nothing good for our lives. That is a problem. Fixing the problem is possible in Christ alone.

These contracts have power to bind, taking you prisoner. Terms are set in the heavenly realm which you never actually agreed to. The covenant of marriage is much more than a legal bond. It is a bond of love that is formed in the character of Christ's love for the Church—giving His life for Her. The first mention of marriage is in Genesis, within the first five-hundred words of a multi-million-word Bible. Marriage is a covenant made in God's presence, formed in His demonstrated relationship with Jesus Christ and the Holy Spirit. This covenant

---

[278] 1 Peter 2:11.

is reinforced in the New Covenant writings by the Apostles. Jesus Himself, in many discussions of marriage and divorce, makes it plain that our failure in marriage is due to our selfish hearts.

Old Testament prophets speak of the sexual union being restricted to marriage. Malachi was the final prophet to speak to Israel, until Jesus became the Lamb sacrificed for the sins of the whole world. Malachi makes it clear that God hates divorce. He says that a man divorcing his wife performs violence against her, as if he were dragging her through public streets by her hair. Jesus said that we injure each other continually because our hearts are wicked.

For marriage to be fruitful, with children being nourished spiritually and physically, Myopic Me! will have to surrender to God's perfect love. "Self-consumed and short-sighted," partially describes the character of Myopic Me! But Jesus sees us in our brokenness with His X-Ray vision. He longs to be our Shepherd, to keep us from the rushing waters, from the toxic clover of our lives. He longs to be the Counselor of our Marriage Vows and our Covenant of love. He longs to show us through His own actions, that love conquers our most convincing feelings. "Once you were like sheep who wandered away. But now you have turned to your Shepherd, the Guardian of your souls."[279]

The Shepherd, Jesus, was guarding my soul on the day when I burned the photo album. The Shepherd told me to burn this doorway into my idolatry. He understood there was a spiritual tie that was keeping me from loving God with my entire heart. He understood that my soul was tied up in the heavenly realm because of my sin. If you don't believe in this spiritual reality, then you might think back to that relationship that tied you up with the same rope we used on our childhood "General Albert." His neighborhood army, replete with wooden tanks and cement grenades with cherry bombs inside of them, battled our neighborhood. We tied the General to the oak tree in the back yard until the mail man arrived to cut him down. Soul-ties are powerful bonds, keeping us tied to our past. It gets lonely out there in the dark back yard, struggling against the bark of that old white oak tree. The Mail Man, bringing the Good News, is the only one who can set us free from that terrible tree.

Keep in mind that when we draw near to God, He draws near to us. He doesn't leave us chaffing and struggling, but comes to free us. But another one, with darker motives, draws near as well. The accuser jumps into our path with his enticements. He offers us a cruise in the harbor with prime rib and fresh fruits. He offers us a front row position when Wild Cherry drops all pretenses before our eyes. As our faith grows, we are tested according to the parameters of our new commitment to follow Him. How we handle these new temptations, determines what happens next. The former contracts in the heavenly realm are not dissolved without the assertion of our trust of the One Who is the Pioneer of our faith. The enemy of our souls will do everything possible to retain us as his

---

[279] 1 Peter 2:25.

client. The desires tumbling around in our souls become a matter with eternal consequences.

> So get rid of all the filth and evil in your lives, and humbly accept the word God has planted in your hearts, for it has the power to save your souls. 1 Peter 1:9

God had planted this word in my heart—the Shepherd had spoken to me to get rid of the evil rituals. I was propelled to burn this linkage to bondage in a symbolic sacrifice, breaking free according to my commitment to follow Jesus Christ. Immediately after this spiritual breakthrough, the tempter fired another salvo across my bow from a whole new direction! I was being tutored in this phenomenon of the spiritual realm. Binary is the war. The battle between Good and Evil is a law, though the battle is already won.

In that darkroom at Lockheed, the stranger (devil or angel) had left sexually explicit photos in the wash tank just days before. Unaware of this potential influence, I was swept into raging fantasies that were so real that real no longer seemed as real. He had photographed a man and his wife in very private sexual positions. I did not discover this until my own photos were dropped in the wash water, and I flipped a couple of his randomly. I was shocked that he did this, asking me to dry them. I don't even remember what I saw, returning them face down immediately. Quickly, I washed mine and left everything as it was. I never came back to that dark room, and his photos are floating still in that ancient bath tub full of shame.

A year later I found myself living in a two-story apartment building where I burned the photos which had become more than an album for me. These photos were the ones I had pushed through the darkroom that night when I resisted looking at the explicit photos left in the bath water. The spiritual realm had become partially visible that night, though I did not see the full ramifications of these events on that occasion. I committed the mistake of the Pharisee, justifying myself as good in contrast to this evil man. From that man's idolatry, I had found victory over my own idolatry formed in that common bath water—as if the demons had migrated from his emulsions into mine. The transference went all the way back to the original bath water in the Garden of Eve's original temptation. My photos were in direct disobedience to God's miraculous deliverance. He had freed me from the idol that had tied me to the spirit of death—now I was making a new idol in the image of the old one!

On this subsequent night in a different city, I was walking on the dark side of my two-story apartment building in Winston Salem. I was walking into shame and Pharisaism again. I carried my basket of dirty clothes to the shared laundry machines at the far corner of the building. I was doing more washing, but this time it was not dirty photos left in the bath water. I was washing my dirty clothes that suddenly became connected to a brand new deed performed in darkness. Clothes can be washed again and again with soap and water, but my mind would soon need a different kind of soap. A different version of the wash water would be needed to cleanse me.

As I walked the last twenty-feet, passing by the final apartment, I looked through the bright window on my left to see the young woman inside. Her curtains were wide, and her screen was like one of those large flat screens that had not yet been invented. She was involved in some sexual ritual on her knees, and she was naked. I had dated her once, but I hadn't seen her for a while. As I stopped in the hot-flood of visual stimulation, she moved slowly on her carpeted floor. The fully illuminated room became my X-rated scene from some late-1960s movie. Since she had no way to anticipate my arrival at her window, I was convinced that this was another spiritual trap set just for me. All I had to do was step on that convincing concrete walkway at her window's ledge, and I would fall into another dark prison. Mid-fall through that thin concrete veneer, I could already see that nothing good would come of this incident. I had to flee, or I would surely die.

I had just a day or two earlier burned the photos from that album, when this window filled my eyes and my endocrine with a new synaptic stronghold. Despite my effusive reaction to what I witnessed, I felt compassion for her loneliness and obsession. I was stunned, watching a car-wreck, unable to look away. She was revealing a deep need for affection and connection that I knew I could not supply—for whom, or for what purpose, had she become this X-rated shop window display? She was demeaning her body and soiling her soul, and I was certain I had become her accidental predator and her sober priest—such a terrible metaphor in light of what has transpired in the priesthood in Boston and in the churches around the world.

> "God forgive us, for we have all fallen short of Your glory. Hear our prayers from brokenness, and transform each one who has exploited proximity for sexual advantage. Remove the millstone from every neck,[280] and let Your redemption come to the cities and to the men and women who are drawing near to You. Heal the hearts of those who are wounded, those who have been violated, that they might know Your forgiveness and Your gift of peace which passes understanding."

There was something deeply wrong through that open window which broke my heart while flooding me with intense attraction and revulsion. I knew that I could not solve her soul's fractures, but I could pray for my own—I could

---

[280] Mark 9:42.

pray for her and I could pray for myself! I had just burned the images from the album on a hibachi fire! Now, with the embers still warm, these uninvited images arrived inside my brain—coincidence? Not possible! Regardless, I had a new batch of synaptic messengers whose mouths were providing me with puerile post-it notes for my wall. Before these images might become a new photo album for my Chinese red coffee table, I had to pray that God would silence their invitations to sin.

Even on that night—very early in my spiritual education journey—I had become deeply moved in ways that could only arrive from Jesus' pure motives pouncing on my illegitimate instincts. This new secret room could not be allowed to send down roots in me again. God wanted my sexual adventures to be developed inside of marriage, or else they should remain unfulfilled. Endocrine is a wonderful blessing within marriage, but was a toxic dessert cart trolling my table in the realm outside of marriage. It was a trip-wire pulled across the entrance into several dark rooms. While endocrine connects mates, body to body, heart to heart, and soul to soul, Jesus had me praying, "God heal her wounds!" I prayed that He would touch her with true love. God kept me from that temptation and delivered me from that potential for evil. Even today, I pray, "Lord, it is not too late to wash away her shame and her guilt. Show her Your perfect freedom! And it is surely not too late for me to learn to love in the present day!"

Her identity had been fractured by some wounding in her past life. She craved a sexual bond with another human being, with me, through the only means she had available—the only means possible. I know that she felt ashamed, and exhilarated, but I felt her pain as well. I too often have considered illegitimate means acceptable for the gaining of something which I cannot have. Illegitimate gain is toxic, poisoning the well water. There is nothing more repulsive than prostitution. It is such a pure corruption. Though I would learn that everything in Christ is permissible, everything is not going to be edifying. Everything is not going to please God. Neither exploitation, nor prostitution, brings honor to man or to God. What motivates each one of us to become the prostitute will vary from case to case. It may be pleasure or fame. It may be money or the adrenalized libido which produces the prostitute. Prostitution always devalues self, life, honor, and health. It devalues family, relationship with God, and even common sense. The devalued soul will accept this dark shadow, and the body of the narcissist will be released in the pursuit of every unhealthy pleasure.

Did she decide that she could never forgive herself for some youthful crime she had committed? Did she no longer resist shame? Did her soul become divided that day when she was seduced by someone in her past? Had she learned this extreme tactic when someone used it on her? Did she ache for love so much that she could not resist this counterfeit rendezvous? I understand. Did I not yield my soul to her that night when her large glass window glowed with forbidden possibilities? On the other hand, did I not stop on a dime when the light struck my eyes—did I not celebrate the arrival of evil in that secret moment? I had to immediately give this to God.

Otherwise, whose lackey would I become? Was my uniform to be woven again from sin, my robe dyed in a new slavery? Would I submit again to those unseemly spirits, yielding to her worst gods? Only God's grace can ever make sense of the sin-nature that comes with the territory of the flesh of man. It would be easy to blame her, condemn her, judge her, but with my finger pointing, I would have three fingers pointing back at me: Father, Son, and Holy Spirit. Fortunately, I was slowly learning that, "There is no condemnation for those in Christ" [I have to tell you that I did not know these promises of God at that time through memorization, but I knew them instinctively, as the Spirit of God took my part, encouraging me].[281]

The scandal of grace is best revealed when the prostitute is thrown at His feet. The scandal includes the dust of man, the stone of judgment, and the mercy shown by God. The Law requires our death, but Jesus stands between us and the Stone Thrower—His Father in heaven. He becomes our Advocate and defense. I pray for God's redemption to come to everyone I have injured in this life, coming even to those I have wounded through my fits of futility. "Resist the devil, and he will flee. Draw near to God, and He will draw near to you."

> Now may the God of peace make you holy in every way, and may your **whole** spirit and soul and body be kept blameless until our Lord Jesus Christ comes again. 1 Thessalonians 5:23

God wants me to war against any counterfeit choreography that causes me to dance in ways unbecoming of a child of God. James, brother of Jesus, wrote about the fiery trial that comes with an authentic purpose. As I draw near to God, there is a concomitant fiery trial which seems to follow immediately upon every action taken in faith and trust of Him! I call this fiery trial a necessary part of the choreography of this dance with God the Holy Spirit and with the Body of Christ. God is bringing unity out of disunity. He is making clean what is filthy. When I embrace the trial, not running away from it, the dance steps become powerful through reconciliation, ending lust, shame, and fear. Faith and endurance come out of the mini-wars I have waged in the flesh. There are witches in the world, but much of my trouble has originated within myself.

> This is what the Sovereign Lord says: What sorrow awaits you women who are ensnaring the souls of my people, young and old alike. You tie magic charms on their wrists and furnish them with magic veils. Do you think you can trap others without bringing destruction on yourselves? Ezekiel 13:18

---

[281] Romans 8:1.

God is calling me to put immorality behind me. God pulls the man-pleaser and the God-pleaser through the same eye of the needle of salvation—through His Amazing Grace. How sweet the sound of this Grace that saved a wretch like me. Like the rich man, whom I imagine will have to leave all of his idols on the input side of the needle's eye, I readily see every one of my own self-medicating patterns coming out in the powerful suds of Christ's new work of creation in me.

> The man answered, "'You must love the Lord your God with all your heart, all your soul, all your strength, and all your mind.' And, 'Love your neighbor as yourself.'" Luke 10:27

Jesus knew that the rich ruler loved the law far more than he loved the Law-Giver. The man's soul was divided, and God had no part with Him. He was an idolater, and his idol was one of the most familiar of all idols—he lived under a self-imposed set of rules which he could not keep. He had no idea that his soul rejected God entirely, believing that his own performance was the measure of his salvation. But God is the lover of our souls, and the love of the world is a powerful magnet that pulls the soul of man away from God's influence. The world was made for man to enjoy, but God imposes one rule upon our happiness: Love the Lord with all your heart, soul, mind, and strength—worshiping no other gods before Him.

> And what do you benefit if you gain the whole world but lose your own soul? Is anything worth more than your soul? Matthew 16:26

On the Mount of Transfiguration Jesus demonstrated that Father God, Who is Spirit, is strong enough to confront any idol and destroy any empire through His eternal plan of salvation. He sent His Son, and Rome fell before the power of His victory, giving His own life on the Hill of Golgotha. The members of Nero's household were worshiping Jesus Christ as their Savior by the time Paul was executed in Rome. Standing there with Moses and Elijah, God told the disciples to listen to Jesus, and Him alone.

He didn't even say to listen to Moses or Elijah—for both of them pointed to a future time when they would know Him in glory after His victory was won. For Jesus has all authority, and He can disarm the emperor or the despot with a word. There is no Caesar who can survive His wrath. And no one can avoid His final judgment. King Herod picked the wrong battle when he tried to kill God's Son, never looking to find Him in a manger for animals in Bethlehem. Therefore, God permitted Satan to devour the narcissistic king. When he made himself to be god, the maggots came into his flesh, devouring his most private parts at the very point of his dying.[282]

Moses led Israel from idolatry and slavery. Elijah rebuked Ahab and Jezebel, slaughtering the Baal prophets. Each of them pointed to the coming of Christ the King of kings, the better deliverer and shepherd, and the better destroyer of the false prophets and the false kings. Jesus' work is finished, His authority is absolute, and He is speaking to His Church. He intends to lead us from the fraudulent philosophies of men! This verse in Hebrews is not terrifying when we understand that Christ's blood, not our weak efforts, has washed away our sins. My goodness is not what saved me. God's mercy saved me, and Jesus Christ is the necessary propitiation for my sins.

> Dear friends, if we deliberately continue sinning after we have received knowledge of the truth, there is no longer any sacrifice that will cover these sins. Hebrews 10:29

Only Christ can forgive sins. His blood is the final blood. His sacrifice is the final solution for our reconciliation. There is no backup plan if we reject Jesus. True heart repentance and godly sorrow are the only remedies for our rebellion. This heart condition is born from the Love of God, not from the narcissistic selfishness of humankind. One day, when Jesus was speaking to His disciples in Jerusalem, He could see that the Pharisees had forgotten the Law of love. They said some of the right things, but they could not apply these things in their own lives. They spoke of religion and law, but they had forgotten justice and mercy.

> "I tell you, many prophets and kings longed to see what you see, but they didn't see it. And they longed to hear what you hear, but they didn't hear it." Luke 10:24

Spiritual deafness is the barrier to hearing this Good News. The longing to hear can connect anyone to the Faith-Time Continuum. When the Scriptures refer to "a great cloud of witnesses," the writer of Hebrews is speaking of all those who have gone before us in the faith. Did King Solomon see or hear God's secret information revealed in Christ? Is he mentioned in Hebrews 11, the Hall of Fame for the faithful? Abraham, Rahab the prostitute, Sarah, Jacob, Sampson, and Joseph are all mentioned. Solomon's father, David, is mentioned. But Solomon is not listed in Hebrews 11. He is not listed among the heroes of the faith. The great King missed the cut. Though he did not live during the time of

---

[282] Acts 12:22-24

Jesus Christ, neither is he mentioned in the context of the faith that reveals belief in God's deliverance. Was he so myopic that he could not see beyond his own personal needs, his own potent self-interest? That journey is provided through the Word of God in 1 Kings and 2 Kings and in the Chronicles [of the Kings]. But our best answer to that question is found in Ecclesiastes 12, the final verses.

We find the old, idolatrous, broken king, bowing down to the Holy God. He had tried everything—EVERYTHING. He had pioneered eating and drinking, whoring and thinking. He had authored many books, wined and dined fawning kings and queens, surrounded himself with solid gold everything. He had become the ultimate king of the world, the answer to the question, "What happens when someone says, 'Yes,' to Satan's third temptation of Christ?"[283] Solomon had gained the whole world, with fame, and every possession his heart could imagine. The most beautiful women were around him from morning to night at his beck and call. To this day, he is known as the wise king, and the modern dictionary defines "wise" as "having or showing experience, knowledge, and good judgment." What?

Yet, life on Solomon's own terms became a "meaningless chasing after the wind." He did not show "good judgment." At the end of his Ecclesiastes, the final conclusion revisits the script of God's best wisdom. It reveals a king laying down his kingly prerogatives before the throne of the One Whose name is above every name—the Word of God raised in glory forever. Solomon finally bowed, after all, to the King of kings, Who is Lord of All: "Fear God and obey his commands, for this is everyone's duty. God will judge us for everything we do, including every secret thing, whether good or bad."[284] Solomon, with wisdom like no other king but Jesus, could not foresee the Good News that Jesus would reveal in a thousand years. Yet Isaiah 53, 61, and Psalm 22 all point directly to God's incomprehensible Salvation for every Myopic Me!

> The Spirit of the Sovereign Lord is on me,
>> because the Lord has anointed me
>> to proclaim good news to the poor.
> He has sent me to bind up the brokenhearted,
>> to proclaim freedom for the captives
>> and release from darkness for the prisoners,
> . . . to bestow on them a crown of beauty
>> instead of ashes,
> . . . and a garment of praise
>> instead of a spirit of despair.

---

[283] Matthew 4:8-11

[284] Ecclesiastes 12:13-14.

They will be called oaks of righteousness,
a planting of the Lord . . .
And you will be called priests of the Lord,
. . . and instead of disgrace
you will rejoice in your inheritance . . .
and everlasting joy will be yours. Selected from
Isaiah 61:1-8

26.

VIET NAM BOUND.

O ur preference for war to reconcile our many nationalistic interests resurfaced in Korea and Viet Nam. I lived through the general rebellion in the US when a whole generation resisted the muddled battle cry coming out of a jungle outpost in Southeast Asia. Soldiers historically rely upon harsh discipline to bring together a band of brothers out of the disunity of many voices speaking. Military discipline is famous, and infamous, in applying these methods. I had bolted after a year at The Citadel, where hazing had taken discipline into the deep woods of the cult. In my Basic Training Dorm in the Air Force where I was designated the Dorm Chief, I would use very little of that culture or those stock techniques.

The boys from South Philly would likely have executed me during the night if I had bullied them with blind discipline; yet we went on to win the "Outstanding Dorm" award. I told them, "We're in this together." We have to do what the Air Force requires in terms of polished shoes, marching together in step with each other, bouncing quarters off of our olive beds, with socks folded in little rows. The blanket on the bunkbeds was there in case the temperature in San Antonio Texas ever dropped below ninety degrees during the night. It never did while I was there.

I told these kids that we could just do it, or we could get busted together. I said, "It's easier to do what they ask, rather than spend all our time with disciplinary actions. The threat of discipline should be sufficient." I told them how many tours I had walked at The Citadel. One Tour is an hour in full dress with an M-1 rifle marching back and forth on the quadrangle of our R-Company barracks. It was supposed to be humiliating, but it was mostly a time to think. I had 20-hours to think before my punishment ended.

Somehow these stories and vague instructions worked with these guys from the Philly gangs. Just kids, they didn't kill me, though they did come to my crow's nest one night with mixed motives. In truth, God was with me at Lackland Air Force Base during that season after college graduation and a year and a half working at Lockheed and at Western Electric—Post-Atlanta, *After Christ*—grace covered everything I did, no matter how dangerous or stupid. I don't think God intended for me to be a soldier, for I couldn't kill the rabbit in the woods, and skinning the squirrel had nearly finished me. Pulling the hook from the fish's throat had seemed too much to bear on those fishing trips with Pop.

251

I believed that God was with me in those days "Before Christ," BC. Through of all those years, I tried hard to believe in Him, but I could not see Him. Neither did I surrender to Him through faith in His death and resurrection. I knew Him like I knew a sports hero whom I had never met. Now, I was saved by Grace, and He had become the Person of persons in my life—He had become my Super-Hero. In Basic Training, He gave me favor with these forty-eight teenagers who were heading for war in Vietnam. Those kids followed my lead because God blessed them with understanding and courage to yield to the immovable mandates of military life. All of us knew that we were heading for Viet Nam after training. For me, the next stop was *Officers Training School*, then *Pilot Training* seemed inevitable.

Whereas WWII arrived at Pearl Harbor as a crystal-clear trumpet note calling the world into essential liberty, Viet Nam left the critical questions unanswered. The motivations for another police action (restraining communism in Southeast Asia) remained shrouded in secrecy. When I spoke-up in my *Officers Training School (OTS)* classroom, my question was already in the minds of many commissioned officers in the military.

> "What would we say if the Soviet Union came to Cuba and said that they were placing their military might ninety miles off of our coast? We would be up in arms—nuclear arms. We would resist them at all cost. We did resist them to the point of mutual nuclear annihilation. Well, North Viet Nam is not much more than ninety miles to the north of Saigon in South Vietnam. How is this Vietnam Conflict any different on the other side of the world, in a country we had known nothing about until a couple of years ago?"

The answers to my question would become highly complex and poorly understood at the highest levels of government. Uncle Grayson's close childhood friend, General William Westmoreland, attempted to orchestrate the war from his desk in Washington DC, according to his many critics. He was certain that, "Politicians start wars—not Generals." But many blamed him for losing the fight once it started. A new biography gives ten reasons that he should be held responsible for losing the war. [285]

Lewis Sorley writes that Westmoreland was fighting a conventional war on grand battlefields. The North was willing to take great casualties in these battles while the Viet Cong increased their stranglehold on the people of South Vietnam in the huts and villages. The enemy gained tight control of the South while Westmoreland counted the ratios of the dead in the North. A ten to one

---

[285] Sorley. *Westmoreland.*

ratio seemed to point to eventual victory—but this was not to be. Westmoreland was the commander of the American and South Vietnamese forces from 1964 to 1968, a critical build-up period in the war. While Sorley insists Westmoreland tried to cement his place in history, the war got away from him, and he didn't seem to notice. He greatly contributed to the first loss in American history when, seven years later, the top people were lifted from the top of Saigon buildings by helicopter to escape the arriving North Vietnamese army. Was Westmoreland the one who lost America's first war?[286]

Myopic Me! always loses the war waged for vanity. It is a chasing after the wind. When Westmoreland, and America, opened their hands, there was nothing there but the wind. Fifty-eight thousand American dead, drug addictions to last generations, loss of confidence in authority, rebellion in the streets, and the crown of war was wilted in Westmoreland's hands. With hundreds of thousands of Vietnamese dead, the glory could find no fitting head. The glory never sits well on a man, or a nation; but on God's brow, glory is fitting and beautiful. His Words cut between joint and marrow, revealing the very motives of the human heart. No one but God can sort out the meaning of these years in the jungles of South East Asia. Today, when I see my Cambodian friend at the altar for prayer, I am thrilled that God has made a family out of the warring parties of the earth. He is binding everything together, reconciling everything to Himself, joined in our bonds of love for the One who is worthy of all praise.

More likely, no one could have led the American and South Vietnamese forces to victory. Doomed from the beginning, misconstrued in every way by the politicians and generals alike, the strategies never included the political will to win. When the Pentagon Papers were released in 1971, the fabrication of lies into a web of false hope were exposed for the first time through the newspapers. Though Daniel Ellsberg was never prosecuted for stealing the top secret papers enumerating the lies spoken to the American people for years, the revelations finally led to the end of the war—and indirectly to *Watergate* and the end of the Nixon presidency through impeachment.[287] It wasn't Nixon's fault that we lost the war. It wasn't Johnson's fault that we dove in too deep at the Gulf of Tonkin. It wasn't Westmoreland's fault that we lost the war. The very name, "Conflict," bespoke the deeply planted problem. War had changed with President Truman's stonewall of General MacArthur in Korea a few years before. There was no more will to fight in strange foreign lands defending principals which have been poorly explained. Without vision the people perish. Without vision, the war is lost.

I was thankful that I missed this war. I would have loved flying jets, but not so much dropping napalm to burn the flesh off of the enemy and the friend alike. Truman's determination not to widen the war in Korea spilled over into Vietnam, and the jets were not allowed to even follow the enemy jets into the North. The

---

[286] Ibid.

[287] *Pentagon Papers*. Wikipedia.

entire army was hamstrung from the start. Endless Conflict, still extant in the Korean Peninsula to the present day, drove a stake into the heart of the American forces, leaving them to die, but never win.

Nuclear Annihilation has come full circle, and any false step can mean the end of the world as we know it. The MIRVs in Russia and America represent the end of all life if they are ever launched by mistake or through cunning motives. It all started the day that Einstein's definitions of insanity were published across the world of politics and warfare. "Repeating the same thing, expecting a different outcome," plus $E = mc2$ spells disaster for Generals and the World today. It spells disaster for Nations and Rulers today. In Vietnam, the repetitive, and futile patrols exposed men to certain death daily: Einstein's Insanity Prime. With no military benefit, these bloody strolls turned into body counts on the evening news—one hundred of them died, while only ten of ours died, and the Generals were happy. This seemed to be very good mathematics; this provided the new evening optics for the national television news.

The jets continued to turn back at the DNZ, near the 17th parallel,[288] allowing the enemy a sanctuary in the North. The fear of China's entry into the war hung over every rule of engagement. But this was no board game to be fought between Boardwalk and Atlantic Avenue. 58,000 Americans died, and hundreds of thousands of Vietnamese died. The war was finally won by the communistic Vietnamese freedom fighters. [289] Another seven-year war for the Americans turned the streets of America inside out. Nevertheless, more capitalism than communism is visible in the streets of Saigon today. My long-time friend says that he loves these Vietnamese people who have lived through more bloodshed than most nations have endured.

The Viet Cong, wearing black-pajamas, fired their far superior AK-47s, when Johnny came marching by, and the jungle cover hid a multitude of sins in the war that added opium as a staple in the American soldier's diet. Though Westmoreland's army killed ten-times as many of the enemy, the decade-old conflict never moved the locus of the war to victory. Nixon's carpet bombing of a country which had no carpet was another ironic twist that failed to produce positive results.

The Viet Cong hid in underground tunnels, and some died where they hid; but the survivors came out to fight again and again. Nothing could stop them from defending their country against the interlopers from foreign lands. The complexity of this war revealed a new battlefield where boundaries were blurred and enemies looked exactly like allies. Much of the time, the North Vietnamese army could not be distinguished from the villagers, since they lived side by side and often dressed alike.

---

[288] *DMZ*. United States History.

[289] Sorley. *Westmoreland*.

The Viet Cong infiltrated every village in the South, bringing this conundrum into a bitter focus. The fresh new gods landed on our planet, and each one had an eye set on destruction. Satan's disguise might have been his best deception yet. When he couldn't outgun us or out-bomb us, he hid himself in black pajamas until we walked right into his AK-47's range. When we finally quit the jungles, he bound us up in a reconstituted religion. Instant Gratification became a single formidable reaction to great suffering and sacrifice for decades. Opium and materialism opened two doors through the bombed-out walls of the American consciousness.

Today, *Apple* offers a purchasing transaction system which only requires facial recognition to trigger the completed transaction with the bank account, debiting the person's account. This is the next version of our commercial doorway which will simply end as Revelation describes. The facial recognition system is not the final step in this evolution to what has already been foretold in the final book of the Bible. Failure to submit to this economic plan will become a capital crime. This doorway is opened when Instant Gratification is demanded by the people of the world. When those same people demand to have the end of war, this will happen. When we insist on having a global emperor who promises peace, who collects every weapon and every nuclear bomb for himself, then this will happen. Upon the penalty of death, POD, the emperor will take control of all commerce through the *mark of the beast.*

> He required everyone—small and great, rich and poor, free and slave—to be given a mark on the right hand or on the forehead. And no one could buy or sell anything without that mark, which was either the name of the beast or the number representing his name. Wisdom is needed here. Let the one with understanding solve the meaning of the number of the beast, for it is the number of a man. His number is 666.
> Revelation 13:16-18

When Solomon got lost in gold and women and foreign gods, he was receiving 666 talents of gold each year. The number of the beast is the number of the most seductive idolatry, which will even pull the Jedidiah's of God into gross disobedience. This ultimate war is the war which Solomon, famous for bringing peace, wrought in Israel. He is the king for whom peace was worth any price. This false peace brought him to declare that life is meaningless, empty, and a chasing after the wind. He found himself in a war in the heavenly realm which was more deadly than the visible war he avoided through many alliances with evil kingdoms. For worldly peace, he gave up his soul, and the souls of his people. This invisible battlefield even seduces those who start in the Spirit, causing them to end in the flesh.

> Now the Holy Spirit tells us clearly that in the last times some will turn away from the true faith; they will follow deceptive spirits and teachings that come from demons. 1 Timothy 4:1

It will not go well for the ones who lead the elect astray.

> And the beast was captured, and with him the false prophet who did mighty miracles on behalf of the beast — miracles that deceived all who had accepted the mark of the beast and who worshiped his statue. Both the beast and his false prophet were thrown alive into the fiery lake of burning sulfur.

War is Hell.

27.

LIZA WITH A Z.

I met Dorothy's daughter in the Huntsville Airport in the early 1970s. She had already become a star in her own right—and she had made movies about youthful struggles trying to answer the eternal question, "Who am I?" Her movies encouraged any number of misfits and losers in their quests to find their own golden walk through a world that devours its young. Liza Minnelli was already an actor of some renown when I spoke to her in that unlikely outpost in Alabama. It was the same town from which the General had come to R-Company to find out what happened to his son. But Liza's great fame came partially from the fact that Dorothy was her mother! Imagine that twisted reality. Her father's name helped her avoid the charge of nepotism in the shark tank of Hollywood, but everybody knew that she was born on that Yellow Brick Road leading to the Emerald Utopia.[290]

I was visiting the US Army Engineering and Support Center for validation of our Testing and Trouble Analysis Procedures written in North Carolina. These procedures would assure rapid and accurate repair of the circuit boards used in the phased-array radars poking through nine feet of reinforced concrete planned for several northern US sites, including one near Grand Forks North Dakota. The *Antiballistic Missile System (*known also as *Safeguard* or *Sentinel*) was designed to stop incoming intercontinental ballistic missiles in outer space with a nuclear blast from the Spartan missile, or as a last resort, with the short-range Sprint missile. The missiles were loaded in underground bunkers to protect America's nuclear deterrent from the continual threat of nuclear attack over the North Pole by the Chinese or the Soviet Union. The program was scaled back in favor of a *Nuclear Proliferation Treaty in 1972.*[291]

But these radars would not be able to protect Liza's mother from the trouble that was coming from the wretched witches of Oz. The northern radar sites were so near kin to the Scarecrow Dorothy met along the road in Oz, that he might have doffed his hat in that northern direction had he known. Liza could not shield her mother from the flying monkeys that would follow her home to Evanview

---

[290] Karp. *Utopian Tension.*

[291] *Sentinel program.* Wikipedia.

Drive in the Hollywood Hills. I spent a few moments chatting with her and her anonymous travel companion, before heading home to North Carolina.

On a business trip a few years later, I discovered that Liza was singing in a one-woman show in Washington D. C. I called the ticket office from my hotel room an hour before the evening performance. "No chance I can get a ticket; but at least I can try," I thought, as I dialed the number. "We had a cancellation just now," and I said, "Great," without even knowing where the seat would be in the giant theater—not knowing what the ticket would cost.

I could not believe my good fortune getting to see Liza at the last minute. I put on my suit and tie and headed for the *Kennedy Center* in my rental car. When I was led to my seat, I was front row-center, directly in front of her microphone. I was six feet from Dorothy's daughter! The ticket cost me $20.00—a lot in the late 1970s—but I was thrilled. I was thinking of my wife as much as anything as I headed for the rental car and out the door. She loved Liza and would be amazed at my good fortune. We had seen her movie, *Tell Me That You Love Me, Junie Moon*, and we loved it. She was making the movie in Boston, playing a recovering acid-head girl, when the news came from London about her mother's death. Try growing up with that kind of life and tragedy swirling around you.[292]

Her top movies were *The Sterile Cuckoo; Cabaret; Arthur; New York, New York*; and *Stepping Out*. Liza arrived to grand applause from the 2400 attending her performance. She looked right at me when she grabbed her microphone on the slightly raised stage! Did she recognize me sitting there, eyes wide? How could she remember a guy on a business trip at the Huntsville Airport a couple of years before? She certainly looked me over, peering down from her focal point above me, as she belted out several New York show tunes. [293]

Her performance was amazing. *Liza with a Z* entertained the large crowd with her energy, and I couldn't believe my good fortune seeing her from my perfect perch. My wife and I loved her ingénue movies, and now I was a fan of her amazing presence in the great hall. Someone had canceled their ticket in my cat-bird seat just five minutes before I called. I would have stayed in my room nibbling on cold pizza rinds had I not seen her name on the flyer in the room. I thought of the girl I had met, wearing no makeup, hoping to slip past every eye in her traveler's drab, wearing an out-of-the-bag sweatshirt and sweat pants for good measure. Now, I watched her, dressed to-the-nines, with every inhibition cast aside. These two Lizas were completely different people! Her mother had taken prophetic Oz by storm when she was sixteen-years old, and now her daughter was giving me this private ride on the stage of the *Kennedy Center,* on this night of serendipity.

Surely, the Wizard of Oz had led me there. Surely, God will give her help finding her way home. I prayed for her ruby slippers as I watched her burn

---

[292] *Minelli*. Arizona Republic of Phoenix.

[293] *Minnelli*. Wikipedia.

through all those tunes—can you imagine standing alone on that great stage, out of a bag, wearing a sweatshirt in Huntsville, to have enough confidence to stare down that great crowd of folks who came to be entertained? By herself, she carried the show, and I prayed that she will not end her days in her own version of Auschwitz. Dorothy's final days by the Pacific Sea left her looking like one of those women the allies found in the infamous death camps in Europe. The promise of Oz faded when Dorothy grew up and found out that witches also live in houses, and Wizards struggle to make a go of it in the Emerald City. The flying monkeys circled her house until she finally fell down from exhaustion in the back yard. Her legs were as thin as toothpicks. And I don't know if she found her ruby slippers.

As Liza made eye contact with me again, her makeup still perfect, her voice powerful, I witnessed the pluck and confidence that Dorothy had displayed in Oz. Dorothy skipped along the golden boulevard with her entourage on the way to see the Wizard—Toto could be seen, if you look closely as they pass by. She was on her way to Hollywood where she would discover the pot of gold at the end of her journey. Liza's mother had emulated Dorothy so beautifully thirty years before; but now, the gold was running out, and no one wanted to hire her. She had touched everyone with her pluck and perseverance, belying her real-life suicidal outcome in 1969 at the age of forty-seven (barbiturates overdose).[294]

Near the end, with legs shrunk to nothing but bone, her financial struggles brought her to the edge of ruin. "Whither hath fled that visionary gleam" of gold in the city of Oz? How could this reversal of fortune occur in the land of the gold reserve that guaranteed financial stability in the Golden Hills by the Placid Sea? How did Liza's mother fall down beside the road in the Pursuit of her own Happiness? God does not guarantee happiness, but He guarantees joy. I hope she experienced His joy.

With her childhood behind her, her public career seemed to vanish, just as Oz vanished with the clicking of Dorothy's heels. The vicissitudes of vanity and fame left her in need of rescue. She rescued others who had fallen down, but she could not save herself! It seems a national crime that this could happen to "Dorothy," the heroine of our youth. Losing her seems more like losing a family member. Liza's mom looked in her hand to see what she had won for all her fame, and there was nothing but wind.

She never found the *Faith-Time Continuum*, as far as I know. I hope I am ignorant of her relationship with the Voice and Name which saves the one who listens and does what He says. When she has her review before the Better Wizard of Oz and Wonderland and Nazareth, the One who is King of kings and the Lord of lords, I hope she is in His arms of love. Her golden highway through the hills of Hollywood dumped her unceremoniously into Alice's *Wonderland*, where the dark Queen spit her out beside the road. Like the once successful factory worker

---

[294] *Judy Garland*. Wikipedia.

from New England, she was cast off and forgotten, rusting and powerless on her back. Liza had to watch Dorothy fall down, and she could do nothing to save her.

Sweating behind his theater screen, Solomon turned out to be the imposter from L. Frank Baum's story of broken dreams and shattered hope. All of Solomon's power, wealth and upbringing, could not save him. Isn't that the most frightening thing of all? He was called "Jedidiah" by God, yet he could not save himself from destruction. He is my doppelgänger, for he has gone the windy way of vanity to find a short cut through life—a life drenched in pleasures of every known variety he pursued and won. When Jesus refused the temptation to turn the stone into hot steaming bread, Solomon ate his fill, with real butter and extra virgin olive oil. But God remained faithful to the promise He made to David.

> Out of the stump of David's family will grow a shoot—
> yes, a new Branch bearing fruit from the old root.
> And the Spirit of the Lord will rest on him—
> the Spirit of wisdom and understanding,
> the Spirit of counsel and might,
> the Spirit of knowledge and the fear of the Lord.
> He will delight in obeying the Lord.
> He will not judge by appearance
> nor make a decision based on hearsay.
> He will give justice to the poor
> and make fair decisions for the exploited.
> The earth will shake at the force of his word,
> and one breath from his mouth will destroy the wicked [on
> the final day]. Isaiah 11:1-4

This promised Messiah, this Jesus, would advance His kingdom around the earth, exceeding the territories of Alexander the Great or Stalin, Julius Caesar or Hitler, John Kennedy or Barrack Obama in modern times. Jesus Christ's political Plank would come directly from God's words, and not from motives to exploit the people. His rule would be unprecedented, since He would become as the Servant of All. He would temporarily lay down His divine privileges to rescue every man who believes in Him. No king or president has ever intentionally given his life, His sinless life, to save his citizens. But Jesus did this. He spread His arms upon the Cross, permitting sinful men, whom He loved, to drive the spikes into His hands and feet.

President Grover Cleveland's reign as a lesser king in Oz in 1889, is the likely model for L. Frank Baum's Wizard in Oz.[295] The history of earthly kings and presidents is replete with a continual string of failed marriages with the

---

[295] Shirvani. *The Wizard of Oz as a Monetary Allegory.*

people they govern—the first example is Saul in Israel's history. He failed to do what God told him to do, caring only for his constituents material welfare—ignoring their spiritual welfare. Strange, this very idea is in direct contradistinction with our political system which promises a "chicken in every pot!"

President Grover Cleveland arrived in Oz as another purveyor of broken dreams, promising everything according to the stock political mandates for reelection.[296] Hope springs eternal in the human heart, but the ruler always disappoints.[297] Self-interest, not self-sacrifice, is the governing DNA for all these relationships. The people want something to benefit themselves, while the ruler wants power, fame, and money—Solomon's big-three. God's instructions are only rarely understood and scarcely followed by political leaders. The Promised One alone has addressed the real needs of the nations of the earth—He gave His own blood for the forgiveness of our sins. He gives every man peace, purpose, meaning, and dignity.

Clarence Thomas, the Supreme Court Justice, arrived in Washington DC from the most overwhelming poverty I have ever read about. No Dicken's character even comes close. His childhood years in Savannah Georgia should have prevented him from being anything more than a junk dealer or a janitor. His track to Congressional approval as a Justice of the Supreme Court reads like Jesus' Own trail of tears in Jerusalem. When my brother spoke to him in the Queen's Theater in London, Justice Thomas grimaced at the approach of a white man who might harbor malicious motives. When Grayson spoke to him about their close mutual friend, their chance encounter produced a happy serendipity instead of an ugly scene. When the *New York Times Best Selling* author tells his story from Savannah to DC, he aims his bright lights on every ugly underpinning of our political system. In so doing, Justice Thomas, not the "janitor," exposes the cruel political stratagems which he endured in the years before he became a Supreme Court Justice.[298]

President Cleveland served three terms, failing to change any part of the world for the good during his twelve years in office. His long Presidential reign oscillated back and forth from a paternity suit to a Railroad bankruptcy, followed by a Stock market crash and several bank failures, until finally he lost his cushy job behind the curtains in the Emerald City. His marriage to a twenty-one-year-old woman during his time in office (twenty-seven years his junior), was the only fruitful outcome of his presidency, yielding five children during an otherwise unproductive reign. In his first term in office, he vetoed 414 bills—a record for hindering the advancement of the people's will. He stifled the government, and nearly silence the work of the Legislative Branch of government.

---

[296] Ibid.

[297] *Grover Cleveland*. Wikipedia.

[298] Thomas. *My Grandfather's Son.*

The unemployment rate peaked at nearly 20% while Cleveland masqueraded behind the curtain in his *White House* in Oz. [299]

The Wizard's impotence in Washington rivals the Wicked Witch, among all the characters in Oz who have lost their way. As the foremost imposter in Oz, the Wizard's ineptitude barely hides his fear of failure with the imposter's clay feet. He couldn't live up to his own hype or to the fantastic expectations in Oz. L. Frank Baum made no bones about his failings, as he pulled back the curtains on every false god in the Emerald City and beyond. He exposes the paradox of great power for children to see—revealing that the most powerful Wizard on earth is nothing more than a pretender cloaked in smoke and mirrors—the trappings and artifice of his authority wilt when the puppy arrives on queue with Dorothy. Please notice that Dorothy did nothing to expose the Wizard. Toto, the pup, exposed him! Children can understand these simple portraits of weakness and failure—and Serendipity, the dog. The most fearsome bluster may bring kids the greatest sense of relief, causing them to erupt with nervous laughter.

When we focus on each one of Baum's characters, including California Dorothy and her Liza with a Z, we come to see ourselves. We come to realize that we too need redemption, and we need God to change us from the inside out. We cannot change by following the Law—we know the Law, and we know that we cannot keep it. We can only be changed through God's unmerited favor. His Spirit alone will change us. We can readily see, even children can see, that neither the Wizard nor Dorothy herself is good in her own strength. Not even Liza with a Z, with her monumental talent and charisma is good. We all fall short of God's impossible standard—none of us come close to obeying God's mandate to love Him, our neighbor, and ourselves. None of us is innocent, for we have all sat in the famous seat of the scornful.[300] We all need God's intervention to lead us from the sin-life, the brokenness, the heartache and pain.

While the Millennials flirt with the faint trails of Myopic Me!, the euphoria of heroin is seducing an entire generation. Liza understands this malaise better than most citizens in the Land of Oz. Growing up during Liza's era, I never witnessed such a dire choice as heroin. But she was growing up in the dark shadows of Oz. When someone tells me today that he is a heroin addict, I am incredulous. "How could this happen?" Naive, I know, but how could anyone step off this cliff?

Driving by the police-tape on the side of the road where a crowd had gathered, I learned later that the thirty-one year old woman had died in the field across the road from her perfect Home in the million-dollar houses of *Westwood Estates* near my own neighborhood. This neighborhood is the place you go when you feel like a king or a queen. It is the house that will become the perfect home with perfect neighbors and happiness in every room. It is the neighborhood for

---

[299] *Grover Cleveland.* History.

[300] Proverbs 21:24. Psalm 1:1 KJV

wealthy *Patriots* football stars and corporate magnates who strike it rich. It is the neighborhood where the Wicked Witches are not allowed to fly on their brooms over any of the houses—the hopeful name of the entrance road into Westwood Estates is "Homeward Lane." The hopeful name of my story is the same.

I don't know why she died in a field of loneliness and hopelessness; but my mind immediately leaps to the flowering fields of Fentanyl. Heroin and Fentanyl have become the tag-team-from-hell which seems to visit every family. This "Blue Caterpillar" in Wonderland is the greatest imposter of all. This breath-stealer demonstrates Satan's cruelest tactics, beginning with the innocent toke, munching the hilarious mushroom, and bursting through the roof of the house to make us laugh out loud. He comes to steal our breath, destroy our peace, and kill us when we perform his little experiments in private. We call it self-destruction, but it looks more like suffocation. We want to feel better, feel closer, enjoy life more, but the Breath-Stealer ruins all of those dreams! Christ is the breath-re-deemer, breathing life back into the captive soul of man, even though we may have signed a deal with the devil.

This universal theme comes through with amazing subtlety in *Oz* as Dorothy, the child, Liza's mom, leads her tribe toward home. The humility of this full-grown child opens doors which only innocence can walk through. Her broken down bunch follows the child's lead, entering a kingdom where hope springs eternal. Unless you enter as a little child, this kingdom will bar your entry. If you are neither hot nor cold, this kingdom will spit you out. Those who have been greatly disappointed by life's harshness learn the lesson of trust from the girl from Kansas. She loves family and home in a multicultural world that no longer functions in perfect love.

She sees evil for what it is, no longer confused by its seductive tones of gray. As a child, she enters through the only door that is open to her. Her trust of authority brings her to the moment of truth when she believes. The slippers are inanimate, but she understands in the manner of a child that the supernat-ural power is released through unmerited favor which is available to even the impotent man. When I discovered this same kind of childlike trust in Atlanta, the Cause and Effect of spiritual mathematics gained me a pair of Ruby Slippers (not gender restrictive) that carried me through the eye of the needle.

Like Dorothy, I understood 10% of what God was doing in Atlanta. I could say honestly, that, "When I clicked my two heals together, He wrote His Truth in my heart, gave me His own breath, and showed me the Way Home!" His finger prints are on every part of my life today, and the influence of that Cowardly Lion from Mt. Guyot has been thwarted. Like Dorothy, I recognized Uncle Henry without knowing his name—and the yearning for home has impacted every person I have encountered along the way. My slippers are as real as the ones still visited in the Smithsonian Museum to the present day.

The Wonderful Wizard of Oz was published more than three decades before the movie arrived during the 1930s Depression era. Fear already gripped the world like the Plague—but this movie technology articulated a multi-colorful story of redemption in the critical moment. Online today, the first-edition hardback of this book can be purchased for $100,000. The picture book edition from 1900 is available for $66,644.10. The plucky little girl from Kansas ignored every sophisticated critical review and the black face of evil, to sort through the good, the bad, and the ugly spirits thriving in Oz. All of these were enunciated with historicity and with technological timing in the first major color movie in 1932.[301]

While the winds gathered with unrelenting strength during the Dust Bowl years, the imaginary tornado through Kansas took Dorothy into the bounded horror and joy of the Emerald City in Oz. Dorothy showed children and adults how to survive overwhelming doubt during these difficult times. Ironically, the farmers contributed to the conditions which precipitated the Dust Bowl during the Dirty Thirties. They deep-plowed the topsoil in mid-western states, removing the billions of roots of the protective grasslands that held the soil in place. With the sturdy grasses gone, the topsoil turned to powder in the fierce winds that continued until 1940. Advanced technologies brought great benefits, but these boons for the bread-basket had unintended consequence.[302]

Baum sucks us out of our naive neighborhoods, but he puts familiar words into our mouths: "I want to go home!" Prophetically, Baum addresses the false-security of every earthly home and every national currency. Though our Dollar bill states emphatically, "In God we trust," we really find security in our money. Money is our deliverer, and in Baum's day, this Mammon god was being threatened severely with confidence wavering globally.[303] Before Remarque's war arrived, the Germans took down their financial shield, discontinuing the gold reserve. Soon after the war, the defeated nation of Germany spiraled down into hyperinflation. The level of desperation can hardly be exaggerated, as we look back to see them loading Deutsch Marks in a wheelbarrow to buy their next loaf of bread.[304]

Two thousand years earlier, money was also the issue. It has always been the issue with men. Jesus said that it is impossible to love God and Mammon (money), simultaneously. When Peter and John arrived at Solomon's Portico with no silver and no gold in their pockets, and no money in their *Bank of America* debit accounts, the crippled man was disappointed. Pulling his hand back from their poverty, he waited to hear what they would say next. He discovered that they had something much better than money. They had gold and silver of a far purer kind. The name of Jesus is worth more than much fine gold. Peter put it

---

[301] *The Wonderful World of Oz*. Wikipedia.

[302] *Black Sunday*. NOAA.

[303] Shirvani. *The Wizard of Oz as a Monetary Allegory*.

[304] *Hyperinflation*. Wikipedia.

this way: "For you know that God paid a ransom to save you from the empty life you inherited from your ancestors. And it was not paid with mere gold or silver, which lose their value."[305] It was paid with the blood of God's Son.

Their gold did not come from the six-hundred and sixty-six talents which Solomon collected annually from the gold mines and gifts from kings and queens. Peter and John's gold came from the unlikely account in the name of Jesus Christ—seven-hundred and seventy-seven was the number of His pure Gold, gold so pure that a man can see through it. This Gold breaks the jaws of death. His name raises the dead to life. This Gold silences demons, sending them away begging for mercy. Peter and John carried this infinite, transparent Gold, exceeding Solomon's wildest fantasies, even though the great king had hundreds of gold chariots, gold buildings, and gold plates and cutlery. The Queen of Sheba was move to give him gold when she saw the goodness of God in Israel.

> "Praise the Lord your God, who delights in you and has placed you on the throne of Israel. Because of the Lord's eternal love for Israel, he has made you king so you can rule with justice and righteousness." Then she gave the king a gift of 9,000 pounds of gold, great quantities of spices, and precious jewels. Never again were so many spices brought in as those the queen of Sheba gave to King Solomon. 1 Kings 4:9-10

But Solomon did not receive the Gold which Peter and John received from Jesus. He gave them the very inheritance of God, with all the cattle on a thousand hills and all the power in Jesus' name. They received the riches which kings and princes desired but never received. Jesus' core disciples carried in their souls the supernatural Gold of Jesus' name. At Solomon's Gate, the glory of God was revealed. At the doorway of Solomon's Portico, the Doorway into God's throne room was unmasked for every witness to understand. The great wealth of God was unveiled in Jerusalem when these two fishermen lifted a crippled man from his lifelong condition. Solomon's greatness was trumped by the glory in Jesus' name.

> Peter and John looked at him intently, and Peter said, "Look at us!" The lame man looked at them eagerly, expecting some money. But Peter said, "I don't have any silver or gold for you. But I'll give you what I have. In the name of Jesus Christ the Nazarene, get up and walk!" Acts 3:2-6

---

[305] 1 Peter 1:18.

On this good day in Jerusalem, the name which the religious authorities had forbidden, went walking and leaping into newness of life. The crippled man was transformed when God's Gold was invested into his life. The healed man would now be able to earn his daily bread, also through God's provision. He was redeemed at Solomon's Portico. Putting down his tin cup, He became praise unto Christ's name! "What a beautiful name it is!" he likely shouted to anyone who would listen. "What a wonderful name it is," he insisted. "What a beautiful name it is: Jesus Christ my Lord!" He could say, like no other man in Jerusalem, "I was crippled from birth, but now I can run and leap, praising Jesus' holy name!" If the man could sing, he would have sung the lyrics to the contemporary song, "What a Beautiful Name." He would have stood beside the *Beautiful Gate* to herald that, "He has no rival, He has no equal. His is the name above all names! What a wonderful name it is. What a beautiful name it is! The name of Jesus Christ my King!"[306]

Whatever God had intended for him, his new mobility would greatly advance. He became the walking, talking testimony to the name above all names—the name which healed the blind man and the ten lepers, raising the dead daughter of Jairus to newness of life. This name which raised Lazarus from the dead, had become the Way, the Truth, and the Life for him. Now, he could see the Gold of God through the eye of the Needle he had passed through on that miraculous day when the two disciples gave him no money for his tin cup. Few men, then or now, could decode the power and beauty of the name of Jesus, like this lame man. Was Jesus' name some kind of magic? He had no clue about such things. He had been set free! In that name, he had received a new life that was unimaginable a few moments before. He would be able to say with Mary Magdalene that the name of Jesus had changed his entire life direction, his lifestyle, his way of thinking, and his plans for the future. Jesus had become his Hero, and there was no Hero like Him.

Dorothy was Liza's heroine when she was young. Liza suffered greatly through the final years of Dorothy's life, She endured the reversal of her mother's fortunes in their Hollywood Hills home. She watched her Dorothy waste away, while the young people in her own world became junkies, disillusioned with life, unable to bear the pain or boredom of living. Her friends were falling down all around her on the Yellow Brick Road. While Liza was in New York City filming her story of a young acid-head trying to get clean, she found out that her mother had died of an overdose in Alice's London. In the same city where Alice tumbled down to face the blue smoke of the gatekeeper in the London Underground, Dorothy had succumbed to a toxic dose of barbiturates that helped her sleep.

Meanwhile, and long ago, Mary Magdalene had stood in front of Jesus' crumpled form on Golgotha. She watched as He was nailed to the cross, one spike at a time. Seeing her Hero suffering in this way had taken her breath away.

---

[306] Fielding/Ligertwood. *What a Beautiful Name*.

She gasped when the soldiers jammed the crown of thorns on His head, mocking Him as the King of the Jews. When they lifted Him up so that all men would be able to see Him, she could not believe that anything good would ever come into her world again. Everything turned black on the Hill of Death, and the earth was split open tearing the Curtain of the Temple from top to bottom. She knew that the world hated Jesus, but she could not see the big picture. Though she poured out a year's income on Jesus' feet a week before, anointing Him for His burial, she could not see that His death would open the way for her to come boldly to the throne of God.

In New York, Liza must have wept, when she hung up the phone. Her knees must have buckled from the shock of her young mother's death. She must have felt like giving up when the brokenness of her story overflowed into the whole world. She must have lost all hope. Could she not sit down with Mary Magdalene to talk about what she had felt when Dorothy died so tragically? "She didn't deserve this," Liza would have whispered, hoping Hollywood could hear. Hoping America might hear her, she surely hurled an admixture of anger and despair into her private quarters. Mary could have told her she understood. "The Lord didn't deserve to suffer and die for evil men!" Yet He did suffer and die because of His love for Liza, Dorothy, and every Mary in future-time. Jesus made this clear when He sweated blood on His knees in the Garden: "Father, not My will, but Yours be done!"[307] Then Mary would have recounted what happened next, speaking to her new girlfriend, Liza:

> Early on Sunday morning, while it was still dark, [I went] to the tomb and found that the stone had been rolled away from the entrance . . . [I] turned to leave and saw someone standing there. It was Jesus, but [I] didn't recognize him. "Dear woman, why are you crying?" Jesus asked [me]. "Who are you looking for?" [I] thought he was the gardener, [Mary laughed, relating the events to her new friend Liza]. "Sir," [I] asked, "if you have taken him away, tell me where you have put him, and I will go and get him."

> "Mary!" Jesus said.

> [I nearly fell from fright! I] turned to him and cried out, "Rabboni!" (which is Hebrew for "Teacher"). "Don't cling to me," Jesus said [to me], "for I haven't yet ascended to the Father. But go find my brothers and tell them, 'I am ascending

---

[307] Matthew 26:39.

to my Father and your Father, to my God and your God.'" [I ran and] found the disciples and told them, "I have seen the Lord!" Then [I] gave them his message. John 20:1, 14-18

28.

CRUSHED BY THE CROSS.

A little-known story involves a famous man whose name you may have heard in your biology class. This iconic figure among men has had profound impact on the culture, on religion, and on the identity of us human beings. He partially or completely recanted his own theories in his first book, or else during his lifetime, yet thousands carry the torch for his provocative ideas to the present day. The essence of these theories is a godless religion which unlinks the origin of man from God the Creator. Man in God's image becomes man in the image of the apes. Man is the result of random accidents (*natural selection*) in the chemical and evolutionary domain. Our famous man regretted that he had no good explanation for the *Cambrian explosion* of animal categories which seemed to undermine his entire thesis of natural selection.[308]

His personal chronology, bulleted below, reads like every Greek drama, except that few of us are even aware of the reversal of his fortunes midway through his journey.[309] If you look closely at this brief portrait of a young man, you will see that the Cross crushed him gradually, as it will crush everyone who discounts its transformative symbology and redeeming reality. Though the Cross itself has no intrinsic power to redeem, being the most hideous symbol of death, the symbol of the Cross pierces the tough soul of man. Behind this symbol we discover a treasure trove of redemption, love, suffering, and death. We find resurrection, forgiveness, reconciliation, and deliverance from nearly two thousand years ago.

When the famous scientist rejected this treasure, throwing it down beside the *Yellow Brick Road*, he had no clue that the Hound of Heaven would pursue him to his final breath. His story is like our story, with all the trials and tribulations which come with this life. The shadow of the Cross is unavoidable when we visit his history.

- He was schooled as a Christian minister

---

[308] *On the Origin of Species*. Wikipedia.

[309] D'Souza, *The Evolution of Darwin*.

- He became agnostic, believing in material explanations for the universe and this life.
- Corrupt pleasures consumed him, and he found no relief from them.
- He killed birds with a hammer, revealing his deeply fractured personhood.
- He veered off into many twisted and self-destructive behaviors, unable to love himself.
- He believed in eugenics for the manipulation of racial purity.
- He slid down into deep depression, dizziness, and other physiological symptoms and infirmities.
- He was completely incapacitated by the age of twenty-eight, not understanding the causes.
- He lived forty-three years in this twisted condition.
- He was known then, and is known today, as "Charles Darwin," the father of modern biology.

Children are required to study his godless religion, "Evolution." Children's brains are indoctrinated in Darwin's accidental or intentional promulgation of faith. Like many scientists who do not believe in God, he intended to separate the science of biology from God entirely. His mind jumped the rails when he turned against God, becoming agnostic. When Jesus finds us off the rails of Reality, He offers to restore our right minds to the Last Known Good. The Last Known Good takes us all the way back to the Garden in Eden, in that time before Eve ruptured the forbidden fruit—and Adam blamed God for pulling Eve out of his side.

The Narcissist will resist this dangerous brainwashing of the *Last Known Good*. He will believe in, trust in, and rely upon Evolution, born of Human Ingenuity. He will buy the failed gospel of Darwin who died admitting he had made a mistake. The Cambrian explosion of animals, without any forebears, has never been explained by scientists to this day. Darwin admitted that he could offer no explanation for this sudden eruption of lifeforms in vast array. "And God said, 'Let the land produce living creatures according to their kinds: the livestock, the creatures that move along the ground, and the wild animals, each according to its kind.'"[310]

When he abandoned God's call on his life as a minister, he turned to humanistic explanations for creation, denigrating the purpose and meaning for every man's life. Evolution was the deformed progeny of his loss of faith. He abandoned God's wisdom, as Solomon had done for decades when he lost his right mind chasing the wind. Darwin abandoned God's love for him, turning to fragile theories leading many astray. Darwin clung to his idolatry with a death grip. He had become frightened when Jesus knocked at his private door—that door hiding his own bitterness, cruelty, and fear of failure. He left us swinging in the wind

---

[310] Genesis 1:24.

of his cold philosophies of evolution and materialism. The Cross leads to the deepest friendship, acceptance, forgiveness, and hope, while Christ transforms our hiding. The Cross addresses every aspect of Darwin's brokenness, and ours. Charles had many dark veins running through his public and private persona. God's Light could have healed him, but he translated himself as a god among men instead. The Cross fell on his life, and will fall on ours, bringing redemption or total alienation from God and neighbor. [311]

When I wrote a terrible short story for Fred Chappell's fiction class in graduate school, I was told by my astute peers in that writing workshop to stick with poetry. I can still remember the sounds from my imaginary nighttime train ride. Like a rubber glove snapping off of a sweaty hand when the doctor completes the open heart surgery, I heard my fellow passengers on that train being turned wrong-side outward in their seats. Rather than pathos, I filled that train full of bathos. Seated in that otherworldly train into the darkest night, I heard their organs flop, pop, and snap, as the inside of each person became the horrifying outside.

Are you glad that God saw fit to put our organs inside of us instead of outside? Would Eros have the same pull on our lives if we were organ trees instead of these beautifully shaped figures we maintain today? That long night's train ride was punctuated again and again by these terrible sounds as face and chest, abdomen and feet, fingernails and knee caps, became organs dangling in the air, with brains and intestines scattering down the aisles. Every stranger on that all-night ride into hell fell under the spell of some alien power. The smell was unbearable, and the sight was too much to describe on this page.

After the class heard my story, I was informed gently by each one of them that I should not write any more fiction. One said that I had provided the transparent overlay, but there were no maps beneath to give the story its substance or meaning. I had left those elements out because I hadn't understood my own metaphor. I couldn't give them maps when I had no idea where the train was going. Wrong-side-outwards meant nothing to me as I shuddered at the feedback from my peers that night in Fred Chappell's class. Since I barely understood God's ways, still misconstruing His mysteries, God was showing me that one more shallow story could add nothing good to the world.

When God finds us in our sin, the heavens are continually declaring His glory. As Paul observed in his letter to the Romans, we are focusing on the created things rather than the Creator.[312] He therefore finds us twisted loosely around the self-evident revelation of Himself. But He finds us, predictably, swallowing the lie, hook, line, and sinker. We are fed this dangerous diet from birth, one way or another. Our understanding and status is interwoven with the generational curses from our forebears. We are living the inverted dream, still denying the

---

[311] Bergman. *Darwin's Passion for Hunting and Killing.*

[312] Romans 1:23.

very purpose for our lives. We imagine that life is about gusto and happiness, but our understanding is turned wrong-side-out. He has to change our understanding and acceptance of the True Reality—which is Jesus Christ. Focus on the things above, and not the things below.[313]

The old ways have been developed honestly through indoctrinations, social and political encodings, all coming from our environment. Our parents taught us a few lies and half-truths, and even our religions twisted the meaning of the Cross. We went to college, and our professors crossed their legs and told us their version of the way things really are. We bought it. We believed what Norman Mailer wrote about the faith in a drop of urine on a ceramic toilet bowl. We didn't just read it, but we got excited about it. We believed the stories about spontaneous combustion and aliens from outer space reported in the *National Enquirer*. We believed everything they told us, like fools, and we didn't even know who we were. We were blank slates, smudged hopelessly, waiting for the New Chalk to write His name. We took many counselors, but we rejected the One Who is faithful and true. We were wrong-side-outwards, and only God could make us into new creatures on our brief commute.

God sees our inverted mess, but He wants us to know that He transforms us through the perfection of His Son when we believe. He loves us in the same way that He loves His Son. We desperately need His rewriting of our miswritten story, but we can't do it without going through the Cross. We can't understand our wrong-side-outward brokenness, but He explains that the Cross renders our mess null and void. Sin has turned us wrong-side-outwards, but God's antidote comes through a bloody Cross. There is no ugly story too far gone for this redemption. The blood of God covers a multitude of broken lifestyles and rebellious fantasies. "Antidote" comes as an apt rhetoric of what God has done, since sin has poisoned and disfigured us all. Sin separates us from His fellowship, love, and provision. The Antidote restores us to the Last Known Good.

When we are born again, we are turned right-side-outward by the Spirit of God. Our organs are tucked back in, and our intestinal horrors are folded into His righteousness. Our surrender to His Son collects us from every strange train ride that brought us to Him. Our insanity and shame caused us to misinterpret every message of hope, while the horrors of life exploded like popcorn around us. We were swimming in blessings, blaming God for every disappointment resulting from our flawed character. Every rebellious choice we made caused us to shake our finger in His face: "Why is the world full of such evil!" we shouted, with our pants down around our ankles, and the heroin needle still in our arm.

Our own story popped and snapped, as we traveled on into the night, refusing to receive His deliverance. With our inner motives completely visible to strangers and friends, we could hear Him whispering, "I love you. Let me take your heavy burden of sin!" Nothing about this riddle of love made any sense to us, for we were cursed by our false gods who held us like a cat holding a mouse

---

[313] Colossians 1:15-20.

in its paws. His Words come to heal us like the scalpel of a great surgeon, cutting us open to heal our deepest maladies.

> For the word of God is alive and powerful. It is sharper than the sharpest two-edged sword, cutting between soul and spirit, between joint and marrow. It exposes our innermost thoughts and desires. Nothing in all creation is hidden from God. Everything is naked and exposed before his eyes, and he is the one to whom we are accountable. Hebrews 4:12-13

The Holy Spirit hovers over our unformed waters,[314] over our wrong-side-outward theology, protecting us, convicting us of sin, righteousness, and judgment. He comes to us as Comforter, Advocate, and Counselor—the One Who leads us into all Truth.[315] There is no living and active Truth without Him, and there is no understanding of that Truth without Him. He is the translator, who illuminates the Word in our hearts. We are no longer orphans, abandoned, unloved, forgotten, hopeless, and alone. He will never leave us or forsake us.[316]

When I entered the Center-City Philadelphia theater in 1964 to watch *A Hard Day's Night,* I was a little late arriving. The theater was completely packed with young girls who never stopped screaming for the entire one-and-a-half-hour film. It was impossible to hear the dialogue or the songs inside that jet-engine-noise. It was hysterical worship offered by girls who were convinced they had finally found their knight in shining armor, their savior.

The *Beatles* became famous for their twelve-string sounds and their studio modifications that were revolutionary. They were shaggy and handsome, boundary-bashing, brash, drug-promoting song writers and singers who had taken the whole world by the eye-balls. These girls were in that dark theater to worship their new god. Turns out their new savior was decidedly anti-Christ at that exact same moment. Their press officer described their philosophy of life in an interview for *The Saturday Evening Post* in August of 1964.

Derek Taylor stated that the *Beatles* were "completely anti-Christ. I mean, I am anti-Christ as well, but they're so anti-Christ they shock me which isn't an easy thing."[317] John Lennon cut through every pretense to the contrary when he boasted two years later: "Christianity will go. It will vanish and shrink....We're

---

[314] Genesis 1:2.

[315] John 16:13.

[316] John 14:18

[317] *Religious Views of the Beatles*. Wikipedia.

more popular than Jesus now." [318] That turned out to be their swan song year: "Christianity will vanish," John Lennon declared; but Jesus said that, "All the powers of hell will not conquer [the Church]." [319] Before that year was finished, the *Beatles* had gone their separate anti-Christian way.

In 1966, the *Beatles* played their last time together until their uncomfortable reunion in 1970. [320] The arrogance of Lucifer had crept into the thinking of the one who "thought himself better than he really was." [321] It is a malady common to Myopic Me!, but God never stops speaking the Good News of the Cross through the *Faith-Time Continuum* to the most fervent naysayer. He desires that none shall be lost—even those who were mocking Jesus on the Cross heard this same offer of forgiveness: "Father, forgive them for they know not what they do."

When the evil of Pride came to roost in their camp, a single motivation was launched: Death. Satan comes to steal, kill, and to destroy. He accomplished all three with the *Beatles*. A few years later, the world was shocked when John Lennon was murdered at age forty. Cancer took George at age fifty-eight. Meanwhile, Lennon's Yoko Ono gained the whole world, being worth more than 600 million dollars today. The peace activist likely doesn't believe that true peace comes through the Cross of Jesus; nevertheless, Jesus died for Yoko, for John, and for George. He still wants to give them His peace.

The terrible cost of sin is a fundamental aspect of the complex symbology of the Cross. The Cross is a reminder of the miraculous and intentional salvation flowing out of God's love for the world—planned before the world was even formed! [322] Father God did not send His Son to condemn the world, but to save the world through Him. [323] The Cross highlights the failure of every human institution to effect Justice with Mercy in the world of men. Jesus Christ had come to save all men, yet He was chosen for crucifixion as a common criminal after a mock trial with false witnesses assembled under the cover of darkness.

Political motives were central in the crucifixion of God's only Son. He was chosen to be the Scapegoat for Israel, the One sacrificed for the many. [324] Like Solomon's evil alliance with Egypt, which brought decades of peace with idolatry, this alliance between the Chief Priest and the Roman authorities slaughtered

---

[318] *A Hard Day's Night (film)*. Wikipedia.

[319] Matthew 16:18.

[320] *A Hard Day's Night (film)*. Wikipedia.

[321] Romans 12:3b.

[322] Revelation 13:8.

[323] John 3:16-17.

[324] John 18:14.

the Truth[325] and opened the floodgates for spiritual adultery. Mercy was affirmed when Jesus forgave the sinner crucified beside Him, and then promised him the first place in *Paradise* that very day.[326]

The Cross became infamous in Italy recently when a terrible tragedy occurred at a religious site on a mountain top. A young man had traveled to Cevo Italy to celebrate the installation of Pope John Paul's crucifix on that mountain. While the young people were selecting their luncheon plate from a table set up for the visitors on the Cevo mountaintop, a terrible sound came from above them. It was not the wrong-side-outward sound that I heard on that macabre train ride. It was a cracking sound of something gone terribly wrong, something breaking loose, something coming toward them with unimaginable speed. The sandwiches and salads were hurled to the ground as the pilgrims ran from the sound, fleeing in every direction. They were running from the dark shadow that was coming their way. As the young pilgrim fled, the giant shadow moved rapidly across the sky, before falling directly on him. He was crushed beneath the Cross that was being erected to honor a Pope.

> A 100ft crucifix dedicated to Pope John Paul II collapsed and crushed a young pilgrim to death—just two days before he is declared a saint [the Pope, not the pilgrim]. The curved wooden cross fell on Marco Gusmini who was on a visit with other young Catholics. The 21-year-old had been at a ceremony in the village of Cevo, Italy and was killed instantly. Mayor Silvio Citroni said the accident was "an unexplainable tragedy," reported the *Daily Mail*. "A young life, so many hopes destroyed. The young people were making a snack for lunch, and when they heard the crunching noises coming from the cross they fled in all directions. Unfortunately Marco ran in the wrong direction."[327]

All of us have run in the wrong direction, finding ourselves in the shadow of the Cross of Jesus! All of us have at some point been crushed by life, or by the Cross that offended us so deeply—"How could God allow such evil in the world!"—not seeing our own contribution to the rising tide of depravity. Though God does not crush people with physical crosses, Satan, and bad engineering, do a very good job of this. We trust our engineers, sinners every one, and they

---

[325] John 14:6.

[326] Luke 23:43.

[327] McCann. *Cross Dedicated.*

fail us almost daily. The tragic breakdowns and catastrophic failures take many lives. The terrorists of our age would love to have as good a record with their plots and deadly acts as these engineering miscues.

The Hyatt walkway collapsed, killing those on board. The concrete walkway over a highway fell just a few weeks ago crushing vehicles and people underneath. The Challenger and Columbia Space Shuttles failed due to structural breakdowns and communications failures. The high-speed train was traveling too fast and ran off the curving overpass, killing the people in the cars on the roadway below. The Tay and Tacoma Narrows bridges fell due to static loading, tensile failures, or resonant frequency oscillations that overwhelmed the structures. Software bugs, communication miscues, and fatigue in metals have produced many disasters, with much loss of life. Even the Towers fell because of bad engineering. The burning jet fuel softened the steel, releasing the concrete slabs, killing everyone remaining in the buildings.

When trees fall on houses, that is not God's doing, though we always label it as an, "Act of God." God is in the rescue business, while Satan is in the demolition business. Satan intends to destroy as many as possible with his demonic schemes, while God desires that no one is lost. Our scripts from Oz and Wonderland are packed with the stories of Good and Evil, but we continue to blame God for everything that happens. We deny the existence of evil while we plot evil on our own beds. Beginning with Adam and Eve, our finger points at God! Adam's finger flashed the very first pointer ever placed irreverently in God's face: "You're the One who gave me that woman!" Even Moses cried out in the wilderness, "Where are we going?@#!" He blamed God for taking them on this circular loop in the desert.

Immediately we imagine that God crushed the pilgrim in Cevo Italy, punishing him for some mysterious evil which he had committed. But God loved the young pilgrim as much as He loves the rest of us—beware of the shadow of the Cross! But the truth is, evil is at work in the world, and God is the only Antidote for this evil that has come upon us. God does allow evil to exist, and we cannot fathom why. The Goodness of God trumps the evil schemes of Satan in the world of men. Greater is the God who saves, than the one who is the Prince of the Air.[328]

Has He not lost our attention? Have we not turned away from Him? The great paradox of the Cross is that God has exchanged His own life for you and Myopic Me! Upon His body, all our sins are placed when He calls us out of our sinful lives. The Cross is the symbol of His forgiveness, though we deserved to be crucified for our sins. The Cross is the symbol of Christ's suffering to release us from the yoke of sin. Yes, the Cross is the symbol of punishment and death. But it is the symbol of our deliverance from bondage, removing the dark cloud of evil enveloping our lives. It can become the symbol of the resurrection and the life with God. The Cross contains the judgment, as well as the victory.

---

[328] Romans 5:17.

Every man who has ever lived has to answer for that shadow falling through the sky on his egg salad sandwich and barbecue flavored chips. Every man will have to consider the gratitude and freedom that shadow is offering for those not crushed. The Cross will set many captives free before it lands with a crash at the end of the age. The only way to outrun that shadow is to turn directly into Jesus' open arms—run to the foot of the Cross. Accept His forgiveness and friendship. No good works, human effort, rituals, or obedience, will ever save a man. No religion that depends upon human strength will keep a man from being crushed. Christ Himself will stand above all others on the final day, and no other name in heaven or earth can save a man or a nation.

Many nations have vanished beneath the shadow of His Cross throughout history. Because of the Cross, He has become the Rock that will crush anyone it falls on. Where is the *Union of Soviet Socialist Republics* today, the vast five-thousand mile collection of states where materialism was instituted as the State religion? Christianity was forbidden since Lenin and Trotsky had a better idea, melding Socialism into Communism. That powerful nation during my youth is now gone from the world maps. Where are the Moabites, the Hittites, or the Jebusites today? Their kings are all dead, and their people have been assimilated. Their boundaries have vanished.

"I tell you, the Kingdom of God will be taken away from you and given to a nation that will produce the proper fruit. Anyone who stumbles over that stone will be broken to pieces, and it will crush anyone it falls on." Matthew 21:23-25

According to Jesus, a nation has to bring forth the proper fruit or it will be no more! Nations will rise, and nations will fall according to God's perfect will. You can distinguish a nation which honors God by its fruit. Many nations have rejected the Cross, and they no longer exist. Where is the Roman Empire? Where is the ancient Greek empire? When nations refute through their policies the Word of God, their prosperity is taken from them. Not seeking first His kingdom and righteousness, God's provision is cut off, and the evil one runs rampant through the populace.

"For this is how God loved the world: He gave his one and only Son, so that everyone who believes in him will not perish but have eternal life. God sent his Son into the world not to judge the world, but to save the world through him." John 3:16-17

277

The kings from Persia came to worship Jesus when He was a two-year old toddler in Bethlehem. They came to worship the King of kings though He was a little boy. They had no intention to exploit, but blessed Him with rich gifts. They had no intention to betray Him, warning his parents about King Herod's intention to find Him and kill Him. Though they were kings themselves, they traveled more than a thousand miles, bowing their knees to worship Him as their Lord and Savior.

29.

IT'S ALL ABOUT YOU, JESUS.

That day that I drove my Japanese car home from my German company in the Jewish enclave of Newton (the fig Newton, not Sir Isaac Newton), I could hear God speaking through my American-made *Bose* car stereo. The lyrics of the song shocked me, swept me, consoled me, and assured me that God was with me. The perfection of God's choreography stunned me. He always has his Faith-Time encouragement queued up for the deepest cry of my soul. "Jesus . . . It's all about You, Jesus; and all this is for You, for Your glory and your fame. It's not about me as if You should do things my way. You alone are God, and I surrender to your ways."[329]

I sat in my car, with my boxes of personal items dumped into the back seat. "Jesus" was pure and clean from my CD-player as the Living Word struck my ear when the car started up. I was about to make my final trip home from this parking lot. "Jesus" was the first word I heard as I left a job that paid me six figures and stretched me professionally. His name was held for a full measure because I needed a full measure to measure me in this unexpected change of the course of my life. The lyrics of the song spoke powerfully of what I needed to hear. These perfectly chosen words became my unspoken and edifying prayer.

In my first month working there, my duties took me around the world in ten days, traveling through the UK, Germany, Thailand, and Japan, before crossing the Pacific with my Uncle's wife two seats behind me in the business class seating, before heading back to Boston. The chance encounter with Rutherford's wife resulted when our paths intersected after her visits to art dealers in Korea and Japan to purchase paintings. Before my final morning in Newton, the job had taken me to multiple American states, before riding on top of the double-decker bus through Trafalgar Square in London.

The snow flew that day on my warm new sweatshirt I purchased in Piccadilly Circus before my trip to Buckingham Palace and the Tower of London. I traveled with colleagues on the high-speed trains to points west and east of London, until we were unceremoniously dumped out in East Ham when high winds blew a tree across the power lines and across the tracks. Our stay in the *Tower Hotel* had given us a perfect launching platform for business and tourist ventures.

---

[329] Oakley. *Jesus, Lover of my soul (It's all about you)*.

Before this final ride on *Route 128 with its* breakdown lanes allowing traffic during rush hours, I had traveled the length of Germany and Switzerland in a rented Mercedes. We cruised at 245 kilometers per hour (152 mph) along the surreal north-south extent of the German Autobahn until we arrived again in Goslar, to stay in our apartment that was built inside the five-hundred year old stone walls of the old city. We had rented long pants so that we could walk among the gold plated Temple grounds in Bangkok. We tried to imagine living in the hot humidity of that region, finding it hard to stay away from our cool hotel room high-in-the-sky in the Five-Star Amari Hotel. We jumped a power boat, cooling us in the hot breeze, as I steered the giant canoe down the great Chao Phraya River running between the skyscrapers and the shanties of Bangkok. These strange water taxis were steered and driven by the propeller at the end of an auto engine's extended drive shaft.

I would travel the 185 kilometer journey south to Rayong along the Gulf of Thailand, where the elephants and motorbikes become the primary means of local transport. We ate fried fish on a floating restaurant in the Gulf of Thailand where we imagined we could see Cambodia across the distant waters. Flying over Viet Nam, which God had spared me from flying over in fighter jets during the Viet Nam War, I winged my way to San Francisco. Mexico and Malaysia landed under my feet when America moved its prime manufacturing capabilities to these foreign lands. These Greenfield facilities were often better than our own factories, with standardization of processes and grateful employees eager to learn.

I had sat, moments before, in the Newton office with the hatchet man explaining that my ultimate provision comes from God, including the blessing of working in a very dynamic global German Corporation for the previous five years. His face revealed the great relief hearing my response to his devastating announcement—"It's a business decision. It's not personal. As you know, we have lost nearly two-hundred million dollars of gross revenue during the recent "dot.com" downturn. We have to dramatically reduce our staffing to remain viable." He had been fighting many ugly battles with angry managers all day long, until my peaceful parting stunned him. He had girded his loins when I knocked to enter his office, walking in unprepared for his dreary mission.

The factory had already off-loaded the sodium reduction processing of tantalum and niobium (incredibly toxic and hazardous processes) to that Thailand factory where the elephants walked by on the road every day with young boys riding high on their necks. Fourteen feet up, they used their tiny switches to control these noble beasts, ambling along the side of those Southeast Asian highways near Rayong. In the distant fields, behind that modern factory location, I had peered at the strange red fruit of the Rambutan trees that grew everywhere.

Now, I was standing under the shadow of God's wings, smelling the fine odors emanating from the *Soup Factory* that was seventy-five feet away. I bore the easy yoke of Christ in this unlikely moment on that miraculous morning, for I knew the One who whirled the DNA that made the elephants. His hand easily reached around the earth, as His thumbnail pricked my life in Newton. While His little finger gently rested in the distant Thailand plains, His knuckles dipped into the River Chao, and His Voice spoke through my stereo in the Infinity G35 Sport Coupe when it roared to life.

I was thinking at that very moment, "Where will God lead me next? How will we pay the bills?" I was thankful that the car had been purchased with cash two years before, so I would have no car payment to worry about. How would I tell my wife the news that we had been cut loose from a lot of monthly income and benefits? We had become explicitly dependent upon His mercy to show us the Way? Of course, she handled the trauma better than I did, and we found our way through this financial and spiritual eye of the needle together.

I knew that the Holy Spirit would easily pierce the temporal realm, permeating this interregnum with His wonderful Life. His provision had become very tangible on this surreal day, becoming far too abstract in the months before. This wasn't my first rodeo, for I had suffered this indignity more than once in 40 years—more than once seeing the world change in dramatic ways, when the Bell System divested itself of all the Bell Companies. I had endured the Texas Instruments factory being moved to TI-Taiwan when the law permitted military and space semiconductor manufacture on foreign soil.

Now, I knew that these Newton jobs were being packed up for shipment to Thailand. It all made perfect sense, as this work could be done by workers making less than two dollars an hour in the land of the great elephants. Settling into my bucket seat, I was excited and quietly terrified when I turned this final key, listening to the brand new 280 horsepower engine roar to life. The stereo took its cue from the electrical system, and the CD in the player announced its sounds at the preset volume. It came on loud in that parking lot, set to offset the road noise from *Route 128*. The answer for every one of my questions came directly from my Bose stereo speakers. I was stunned to hear: "Jesus!"

The voice was strong and clear, singing "Jesus, I want you to know, I will follow you all my days." Since He became flesh, dwelling among us, He became the final Word for the Coward, the Tin Man, and the Wicked Witch trying to wreck many lives. His name is spoken to silence the strongholds and powers in heaven and in the earth. He said, "Rise and walk," and the crippled man picked up his mat and walked away. He told us to open our eyes to let in the Light, and we could finally see. He became the all-consuming fire when He looks into our lives to bring us back to the safe way of God. He restores the Scarecrow's right mind, giving him special knowledge that kings and princes have longed to have. Now, He was speaking to me in the most urgent way possible for my present circumstances.

My brokenness never scared Him away, and He continually reminds me to avoid the Wizards and the Mediums, the witches and the naysayers. He spoke to me that morning, telling me that He had my back, that He was for me; therefore, who could be against me? He said that my departure from this good paying position did not come as a surprise to Him. He reminded me that the shepherds were also afraid when the angels spoke to them. "I bring you glad tidings of great joy. Fear not, for this day in Bethlehem is born a Savior, Who is Christ the Lord."[330] The Prince of Peace, the Wonderful Counselor, and the Mighty God is born in the City of David.[331] Therefore, come unto me all of you who are heavy laden with sin and guilt, and I will give you the rest you desperately need."[332]

I grew up in the church, but I did not know God's Words that would permit me to discriminate between the voices that were speaking to me from the world. For a long time, other voices whispered—every god of the age beckoned me, including the political gods of the age which promoted every party spirit to a place far above all rule and authority—even the authority of God. I did not know that Party spirit is a lying spirit founded in human goodness, avarice, and ambition. I did not understand that this spirit was being elevated far above the will of God for millions of Americans who didn't understand the selfish goals and agenda. Everyone who has entered the political world has found this evil underbelly waiting to pounce.[333]

When I understood this, I realized how deeply sin had burrowed into my own life. Sin is not a victimless crime. Its roots and tentacles caused me to say ridiculous things, posting them on the mirror and the windshield of my hot sports car: "God did not really mean . . . that I should drive the speed limit." It was years since my departure from Newton, and I had just returned from clearing a suspension of my driver's license which had occurred during a trip to Maine. I received a warning in the mail, telling me that my Massachusetts license would be suspended if I did not get the state of Maine to clear these speeding violations from my record.

My son and I were traveling in 2004 to visit a Christian internet radio station in Kennebunkport Maine that was named the *Cleft of the Rock*. My son enjoyed their music, and this internet radio technology was fairly new at the time. I intended to give financial encouragement to these young men who were committed to broadcasting Christian music in New England. I thought it was a good thing that he and I could share—a great road trip in my new Infinity G35 Sport Coupe. God had spoken to me when I left the job in Newton for the final time, and I had hidden in the cleft of the rock while God sorted out my life's new direction. The *cleft of the rock* is not something these guys had dreamed up to make their internet radio station sound cool. It was not derived entirely from their imaginations, for they were projecting a powerful parable based on Moses' encounter with God on Mt. Sinai.

---

[330] Luke 2:11.

[331] Isaiah 9:6

[332] Matthew 11:28

[333] Thomas. *My Grandfather's Son.*

For Moses the "cleft of the rock" had come to mean something very potent concerning his own relationship with the Holy God. This experience changed Moses' life during a moment of deep frustration after he had taken more than a million Hebrews from Egypt into the wilderness. They had been freed from slavery in Pharaoh's mud pits, and Moses left them at the base of Mt. Sinai to spend forty days with God on the mountain. God wrote Ten Commandments on two tablets of stone, and told Moses all the history of the world. He explained to Moses that the Israelites would be blessed in a Covenant He was making with them as His chosen people. The Laws would teach them how to relate to God and to each other—the million-plus Hebrews had been living in a realm where thousands of gods were worshiped, and even the Pharaoh was worshiped as a god. They had become an idolatrous people after four-hundred years as slaves.

Moses returned to the camp in the valley to find them embroiled in an orgy, worshiping a golden calf. The new Commandments in his hands forbade them from these same sinful behaviors; therefore, Moses boiled over with anger. He smashed the tablets on the rocks. This was Moses' first experience in the valley, after having a powerful time with God on the mountain. He returned to ask God what to do next. He wanted to know what he should do with them, for he was ostensibly their leader!

Moses found himself in the middle—between the Rock and a hard place. If Moses was ever hysterical, this was it. To answer Moses' tantrum, God ignored his request for a GPS tracking device and a MapQuest printout of where they were going. Rather, He gave him an answer that would address every question he might ever ask. He showed Moses His glory! He permitted Moses to regard Him as a Friend with benefits—a Friend in High Places. To do this, Moses would have to hide in the crevice, or cleft, of the rock. Otherwise, he would die in the powerful presence of God.

> The Lord replied, "I will make all my goodness pass before you, and I will call out my name, Yahweh, before you. For I will show mercy to anyone I choose, and I will show compassion to anyone I choose. But you may not look directly at my face, for no one may see me and live." The Lord continued, "Look, stand near me on this rock. As my glorious presence passes by, I will hide you in the crevice [cleft] of the rock and cover you with my hand until I have passed by. Then I will remove my hand and let you see me from behind. But my face will not be seen." Exodus 33:19-23

> So Moses chiseled out two tablets of stone like the first ones. Early in the morning he climbed Mount Sinai as the Lord had

commanded him, and he carried the two stone tablets in
his hands. Then the Lord came down in a cloud and stood
there with him; and he called out his own name, Yahweh.
The Lord passed in front of Moses, calling out,

"Yahweh! The Lord!
The God of compassion and mercy!
I am slow to anger
and filled with unfailing love and faithfulness.
I lavish unfailing love to a thousand generations.
I forgive iniquity, rebellion, and sin.
But I do not excuse the guilty.
I lay the sins of the parents upon their children and
grandchildren;
the entire family is affected—
even children in the third and fourth generations."
Exodus 34:4-7

On the way to the mobile home, and to the *Cleft of the Rock* "radio station,"
I received two speeding tickets. Adherence to the law would have made this
journey much better. Traveling on I-95, the police were out in search of monthly
quotas. One of my tickets was for driving faster than 80 mph (97) down a long
hill with no cars in sight as far as I could see; the other one came twenty minutes
later in a speed-trap on an unlikely 25 mph zone on the road to Kennebunkport,
where multiple cars were lined up along the side of the road awaiting their tickets
for going 45 in a 25 mph zone. Maine suddenly became known as the "main
source of tickets in my entire life."

The local police had stopped many other drivers that morning—it was a
big revenue day for that small community. The Law was enforced, and these
latter-day orgies of the Israelites ended with a whimper. I was frustrated, but the
Lord allowed me to see His glory as I hid in the cleft of the Rock. The Rock is
Christ Himself—it is friendship with God through the Holy Spirit, whom Christ
sent to live inside of every believer—He said it would be better if I could be
in the cleft of the Rock in this intimate way. He made clear to me that my life
depends upon my doing whatever He tells me to do! He said that friendship
requires us to take each other seriously, honoring, respecting, listening, and
acting accordingly.

"I correct and discipline everyone I love. So be diligent and
turn from your indifference. Look! I stand at the door and
knock. If you hear my voice and open the door, I will come

in, and we will share a meal together as friends. Those who are victorious will sit with me on my throne, just as I was victorious and sat with my Father on his throne. Anyone with ears to hear must listen to the Spirit and understand what he is saying to the churches." Revelation 3:19-22

I paid the expensive fines immediately all those years ago; but just now, the long delayed arm of the law arrived in my mailbox all the way from Maine DOT. This likely happened when I changed auto insurance companies. Though I did not return to Maine once during those fourteen years, I had to be cleared at the Mass DMV in Brockton to avoid the loss of the Mass license to drive. It took twenty minutes from the time I parked my car outside the large building to clear this glitch in the system. I had collected documents from Maine at a cost of about 75 dollars to prove that I was driving properly since those tickets. The officer said, "We wanted you to come into our office, and you came in."

I asked, "You don't need these documents I gathered?" He answered succinctly, "No." Departing with more paper to store away in a file cabinet, I addressed my navigator directly when I got into the car. Speaking as succinctly as the officer has spoken to me, I told my car: "Go Home." I followed my counselor's directions home with no incidents, and Yahweh could be seen in my rearview mirror as I yielded to every speed limit along the way. It was a good day, with my inner ear listening carefully to the voice speaking through the *Faith-Time Continuum*. Materialism, the great snake, had snapped at my heals and missed again. The love of money had tried to combine with the fear of tomorrow, but my anxious heart had enough trouble for a single day. All of these concerns were set aside, when I heard Jesus speak to me clearly.

"All authority in heaven and on earth has been given to me. Therefore go and make disciples of all nations, baptizing them in the name of the Father and the Son and the Holy Spirit, teaching them to obey everything I have commanded you. And remember, I am with you always, to the end of the age."[334]

---

[334] Matthew 28:18-20.

BIBLIOGRAPHY/ REFERENCES

A Hard Day's Night (film). Wikipedia, the Free Encyclopedia. en.wikipedia.org/ wiki/A_Hard_Day%27s_Night_(film). Web. April 21, 2018, 11:25 a.m.

AFI's 100 Years...100 Movies: 10th Anniversary Edition. American Film Institute. afi.com/100years/movies10.aspx. Retrieved 2017-08-09. Web. February 27, 2018, 1:01 p.m.

Alice's Adventures in Wonderland, Wikipedia, the Free Encyclopedia. en.wikipedia.org/wiki/Alice%27s_Adventures_in_Wonderland. Web. March 1, 2018, 10:47 a.m.

Alice in Wonderland (1951). IMDb. imdb.com/title/tt0043274/?ref_=nv_sr_2. Web. March 1, 2018, 12:18 p.m.

Alighieri, Dante. *The Divine Comedy*. Rational Wiki. rationalwiki.org/wiki/The_ Divine_Comedy. Web. August 18, 2018, 1:26 p.m.

And God Created Woman (1956). IMDb. imdb.com/title/tt0049189. Web. March 1, 2018, 12:11 p.m.

Barrett, Laura (March 22, 2006). *From Wonderland to Wasteland: The Wonderful Wizard of Oz, The Great Gatsby, and the New American Fairy Tale*. Papers on Language and Literature. Southern Illinois University Edwardsville. Retrieved 2011-10-28.

Baum, L. Frank. *The Wonderful Wizard of Oz. 1900. New York: Harper Collins Publishers and Book of Wonder. Republished* 1987 by Peter Glassman. *ISBN 0-06-029323-3*.

Bergman, Jerry, Ph.D., May 01, 2005. *Darwin's Passion for Hunting and Killing*. *ICR*. icr.org/article/darwins-passion-for-hunting-killing. Web. February 6, 2018, 12:59 p.m.

Berlinski, David. *The Devil's Delusion—Atheism and Its Scientific Pretensions, 2009.* New York: Basic Books (Random House). ISBN 978-0-465-O1937-3.

Bible, *New International Translation (NIV).* Biblica (formerly the International Bible Society). Zondervan in U.S. and Hodder & Stoughton in UK. Copyright 1978, 1984, 2011.

Bible, *New King James Translation (NKJV).* Bible published: HarperCollins Publishers. Copyright 1979, 1980, 1982. Derived from King James Version. Translations of the New Testament -1979, the Psalms in 1980, and the full Bible in 1982.

Bible, *New Living Translation (NLT).* Revision of The Living Bible. A new English translation from Hebrew and Greek texts. Originally published: 1996. Copyright 1996, 2004, 2015 by Tyndale House Foundation.

Bible, *The Message Translation (MSG).* Translated by Eugene H. Peterson. Copyright 2002 Eugene H. Peterson. Contemporary Language Bible. Published from 1993 to 2002. Idiomatic translation of the original languages of the Bible.

Bishop, Jim. *1957. The Day Christ Died. New York: Harper Collins.*

Black Sunday, April 14, 1935, Norman, Oklahoma. NOAA. crh.noaa.gov/oun/?n=blacksunday. Web. August 7, 2018, 1:12 p.m.

Blood Vessels. The Franklin Institute. fi.edu/heart/blood-vessels. Web. February 26, 2018, 1:27 p.m.

Cast Away. Wikipedia, the Free Encyclopedia. en.wikipedia.org/wiki/Cast_Away. Web. August 19, 2019, 2:51 p.m.

Childe Harold's Pilgrimage. Wikipedia, the Free Encyclopedia. en.wikipedia.org/wiki/Childe_Harold%27s_Pilgrimage. *Web. February 27, 2018, 1:20 p.m.*

Carter, Sidney. *Dear Bet: The Carter Letters, 1861-1863 : The Letters of Lieutenant Sidney Carter, Company A, 14th Regiment, South Carolina Volunteers, Gregg's-McGowan's Brigade, CSA, to Ellen Timmons Carter. Published by the Editor in 1978.* Lane, Bessie Mell, Editor. *Paperback. ASIN: B0006CYYB8.*

Cohen, Elizabeth. *A Consumers' Republic: The Politics of Mass Consumption in Postwar America.* New York: First Vintage Books Edition, Random House Inc, January 2004. ISBN 0-375-70737-9.

Conroy, Pat, 1980. *Lord's of Discipline.* New York: Houghton Mifflin.

Crowther, Bosley (March 13, 1950). *The Screen in Review; 'Black Hand,' With Gene Kelly and J. Carrol Nash in Main Roles, Opens at Capitol.* The New York Times. Retrieved August 15, 2013.

D-Day. History. history.com/topics/world-war-ii/d-day. Web. March 1, 2018, 3:53 p.m.

Defining the Brain Systems of Lust, Romantic Attraction, and Attachment. Helen E. Fisher, Ph,D., Arthur Aron, Ph.D., Debra Mashek, M.A., Haifang Li, Ph.D., and Lucy L. Brown, Ph.D. Archives of Sexual Behavior, Vol 31, No. 5, October, 2002.

Deus ex machina. Wikipedia, the Free Encyclopedia. en.wikipedia.org/wiki/Deus_ex_machina. Web. May 7, 2018, 11:59 a.m.

Ding-Dong! The Witch is Dead. Wikipedia, the Free Encyclopedia. en.wikipedia.org/wiki/Ding-Dong!_The_Witch_Is_Dead. Web. May 15, 2018, 11:36 a.m.

DMZ—Vietnam. United States History. u-s-history.com/pages/h1885.html. Web. September 10, 2018, 10:42 a.m.

Doctor who treated Kennedy relives final moments. Rick Jervis, USA TODAY. Published 5:31 p.m. ET Aug. 7, 2013 | Updated 5:42 p.m. ET Aug. 7, 2013. usatoday.com/story/news/nation/2013/08/07/kennedy-assassination-doctor-parkland/2609969/. Web. May 8, 2018, 10:31 a.m.

Donne, John. *"No Man is an Island." from Meditations XVII, 1624.* Poetry. web. cs.dal.ca/~johnston/poetry/island.html. Web. February 27, 2018, 1:44 p.m.

Dorothy's Ruby Slippers. The National Museum of American History. americanhistory.si.edu/press/fact-sheets/ruby-slippers. Web. May 15, 2018, 11:18 a.m.

D'Souza, Dinesh, January 22, 2009. *The Evolution of Darwin: The scientist's problem with God did not spring from his theory.* CT, Christianity Today. christianitytoday.com/ct/2009/january/24.67.html. Web. February 6, 2018, 12:23 p.m.

Dylan, Bob. *Bob Dylan–Nobel Lecture.* The Nobel Prize in Literature 2016: Bob Dylan. nobelprize.org/nobel_prizes/literature/laureates/2016/dylan-lecture.html. Web. February 28, 2018, 10:57 a.m.

Ebert, Roger (December 22, 1996). *The Wizard of Oz (1939).* rogerebert.com. Retrieved August 30, 2012. Web. February 28, 2018, 5:20 p.m.

Edelman, Julian with Curran, Tom E. *Relentless: A Memoir.* New York, Boston: Hachette Book Group, Inc., 2017. ISBN 978-0-316-47985-1 (hardcover).

Eisenhower warns of military industrial complex, Jan 17, 1961. History. This Day in History. history.com/this-day-in-history/eisenhower-warns-of-military-industrial-complex. Web. May 8, 2018, 10:40 a.m.

English Literature: An Illustrated Record, Vol II, part II. Richard Garnett and Edmund Gosse, Eds. New York: The MacMillan Company, 1904.

Erisman, Fred L. (1968). *L. Frank Baum and the Progressive Dilemma*. American Quarterly. 20(3): Gessel, Michael; Koupal, Nancy Tystad; Erisman, Fred (2001). "The Politics of Oz: a Symposium". South Dakota History. 31 (2): 146–168. ISSN 0361-8676.

Ernest Hemingway. Wikipedia, the Free Encyclopedia. en.wikipedia.org/wiki/Ernest_Hemingway. Web. March 1, 2018, 11:27 a.m.

Fielding, Ben; Brooke Ligertwood. *What a Beautiful Name, Let There Be Light Album*. Hillsong Conference, Sydney, 2016. Hillsong Worship.

Flag Flag Football. Greater Boston's Flag Football League for the LGBTQ and Ally Community. flagflagfootball.com. Web. March 2, 2018, 10:04 a.m.

Fontana Dam. Wikipedia, the Free Encyclopedia. wikipedia.org/wiki/Fontana. Dam. Web Sept. 9, 2018, 9:21 a.m.

Fourth Estate. Wikipedia, the Free Encyclopedia. en.wikipedia.org/wiki/Fourth_Estate. Web. May 14, 2018, 10:34 a.m.

Fox, Justin. *The Economics of Well-Being, January-February 2012*. Harvard Business Review. hbr.org/2012/01/the-economics-of-well-being. Web. April 27, 2018, 9:34 a.m.

Fu, Bob. *God's Double Agent, 2013*. Baker Publishing Group. Grand Rapids, MI. ISBN: 978-0-8010-1590-8.

Fuzzy Boots Corollary. Big Bang Theory transcripts. bigbangtrans.wordpress. com/series-1-episode-3-the-fuzzy-boots-corollary. *"I break up, then I find some cute guy, and then it's just thirty six meaningless of… well, you know." Web. December 2, 2017, 1:32 p.m.*

Galison, Peter Louis (1979). *Minkowski's space-time: From visual thinking to the absolute world*. Historical Studies in the Physical Sciences. 10: 85–121. Web. March 1, 2018, 12:49 p.m.

Gladwell, Malcolm. *Outliers: The Story of Success,*. New York: Little, Brown and Company, *2008*. Hachette Book Group, Inc. ISBN 978-0-316-01792-3.

Grand Unified Theory. Wikipedia, the Free Encyclopedia. en.wikipedia.org/wiki/Grand_Unified_Theory. Web. March 1, 2018, 3:31 p.m.

Gravity. Wikipedia, the Free Encyclopedia. en.wikipedia.org/wiki/Gravity. Web. August 19, 2018, 2:41 p.m.

Griffith, Andy. *A-side: What It Was, Was Football, B-side: Romeo and Juliet*, 45-RPM, Length: 5:40, November 14, 1953.

Griswold, Jerry. *There's No Place But Home: The Wizard of Oz*. The Antioch Review. 45(4): 462–75. doi:10.2307/4611799.

Gross, Rebecca. *Oz and Effect: Baum's book gave Americans otherworldly adventures closer to home*. April 17, 2015. Rebecca Sutton: Features. The Common Reader: A Journal of the Essay. commonreader.wustl.edu/c/oz-and-effect. Web. February 27, 2018, 1:53 p.m.

Grover Cleveland. Wikipedia, the Free Encyclopedia. en.wikipedia.org/wiki/Grover_Cleveland. Web. February 28, 2018, 10:52 a.m.

Groundhog Day. Wikipedia, the Free Encyclopedia. en.wikipedia.org/wiki/Ground_Hog_Day. Web. February 26, 2018, 1:23 p.m.

Gulag. History. history.com/topics/gulag. Web. August 2, 2018, 12:27 p.m.

Hitler, Adolf. *Mein Kampf, July 18, 1925*. Munich: Franz Eher Nachfolger. English translation, vol 1, Thomas Dalton PhD, 2017. CreateSpace Publishing. ISBN-13:9781974502967.

Houlberg, Lauren. *The Wizard of Oz: More Than Just a Children's Story by Lauren Houlberg*. Florida State University Writing Resources. wr.english.fsu.edu/College-Composition. Web. 24 January 2018.

Hughes H-4 Hercules. Wikipedia, the Free Encyclopedia. https://en.wikipedia.org/wiki/Hughes_H-4_Hercules#Specifications_(H-4). Web. May 9, 2018, 11:39 a.m.

Huxley, Aldous. 1936. *Brave New World*. New York: Harcourt & Brace.

Hyperinflation. Wikipedia, the Free Encyclopedia. en.wikipedia.org/wiki Hyperinflation#Germany_(Weimar_Republic). Web. February 26, 2018, 1:44 p.m.

Idi Amin. Wikipedia, the Free Encyclopedia. en.wikipedia.org/wiki/Idi_Amin. Web. August 2, 2018, 1:22 p.m.

I Am Curious Collection: ((I Am Curious Yellow / I Am Curious Blue Set). *amazon.com/Curious-Yellow-Blue-Criterion-Collection/dp/B00007L4I8/*

*ref=sr_1_1?ie=UTF8&qid=1534529022&sr=8-1&keywords=i+am+cur
ious+yellow&dpID=511M33V2Z7L&preST=_SY300_QL70_&dpSrc=srch.*
Web. August 17, 2018, 2:07 p.m.

'*I'm an Atheist:' Stephen Hawking on God and Space Travel.* NBC News.
nbcnews.com/science/space/i-m-atheist-stephen-hawking-god-space-
travel-n210076. Web. April 25, 2018, 10:08.

Invasion of Normandy. Wikipedia, the Free Encyclopedia. en.wikipedia.org/
wiki/Invasion_of_Normandy. Web. February 26, 2018, 1:40 p.m.

*Jaguar escapes zoo habitat, moves from enclosure to enclosure, killing trapped
animals,* Cleve R. Wootson Jr. The Washington Post. washingtonpost.
com/news/animalia/wp/2018/07/14/jaguar-escapes-new-orleans-zoo-
enclosure-killing-4-alpacas-an-emu-and-a-fox/?noredirect=on&utm_
term=.0dbd68889cc9. Web. July 18, 2018, 12:44 p.m.

Jastrow, Robert. Quotes: Robert Jastrow, *God and the Astronomers*. GoodReads.
com. goodreads.com/author/quotes/87585.Robert_Jastrow. Web. December
25, 2017, 3:39 p.m.

Jastrow, Robert, *Creation.* Wikipedia, the Free Encyclopedia. en.wikipedia.org/
wiki/Robert_Jastrow. Web. February 1, 2018, 4:42 p.m.

Jensen, Richard (1971). *The Winning of the Midwest: Social and Political
Conflict, 1888–1896.* Chicago: University of Chicago Press. ISBN 0-226-
39825-0. chapter 10.

Joe Versus the Volcano, directed by John Patrick Shanley (1990; Burbank, CA:
Warner Home Video, 2002), DVD.

Joe versus the Volcano. Roger Ebert. rogerebert.com/reviews/joe-versus-the-
volcano-1990. Web. March 1, 2018, 12:22 p.m.

John C. Calhoun, 7th Vice President (1825-1832). United States Senate. senate.
gov/artandhistory/history/common/generic/VP_John_Calhoun.htm. Web.
May 7, 2018, 11:19 a.m.

John Piper Preaching. The Tragic Cost of Her Cavernous Thirst. U-Tube.com.
youtube.com/watch?v=B9nDLRWdNt4 Web. July 17, 2018, 3:58 p.m.

Johnson, Caitlin. *Cutting through Advertising Clutter, September 17, 2006.* CBS.
cbsnews.com/news/cutting-through-advertising-clutter/. Web. September
8, 2018, 5:12 p.m.

Johnston, Wm. Robert, *Reasons given for having abortions in the United States, January 18, 2016.* johnstonsarchive.net/policy/abortion/abreasons.html#3. Web. September 1, 2018, 9:56 a.m.

Judy Garland. Wikipedia, the Free Encyclopedia. en.wikipedia.org/wiki/Judy_ Garland. Web. February 28, 2018, 10:45 a.m.

Judy Garland as Gay Icon. Wikipedia, the Free Encyclopedia. en.wikipedia. org/wiki/Judy_Garland_as_gay_icon. Web. November 4, 2017, 12:52 p.m.

Karp, Andrew (1998). *Utopian Tension in L. Frank Baum's Oz.* Utopian Studies. Journal Article. Vol. 9, No. 2 (1998), pp. 103-121. Penn State University Press. jstor.org/stable/20719764.

jstor.org/stable/20719764. Retrieved 2011-10-28.

Katz, Jonathan Ned. *Gay American History: Lesbians and Gay Men in the U.S.A.* October 1, 1978. Paperback. New York: Plume, April 1, 1992. ISBN: 0452010926 (ISBN13: 9780452010925).

Khmer Rouge Killing Fields. Wikipedia, the Free Encyclopedia. en.wikipedia. org/wiki/Khmer_Rouge_Killing_Fields. Web. August 2, 2018, 12:23 p.m.

Kruglinski, Susan. *The Man Who Found Quarks and Made Sense of the Universe, Tuesday, March 17, 2009.* Discover Magazine. discovermagazine. com/2009/apr/17-man-who-found-quarks-made-sense-of-universe. Web. May 12, 2018, 10:08 a.m.

Leach, William. *Land of Desire: Merchants, Power, and the Rise of a New American Culture.* First Vintage Books Edition, September 1994. ISBN 0-679-75411-3.

List of military leaders in the American Revolutionary War. Wikipedia, the Free Encyclopedia. en.wikipedia.org/wiki/List_of_military_leaders_in_the_ American_Revolutionary_War. Web. March 2, 2018, 12:05 p.m.

Listwa, Dan. *Hiroshima and Nagasaki: The Long Term Health Effects, August 09, 2012, archived July 23, 2015.* Columbia University Center for nuclear studies: Wayback Machine, updated 7/3/2014. k1project.columbia.edu/ news/hiroshima-and-nagasaki. Web. August 12, 2017, 10:56 a.m.

Liza Minelli [sic], July 3, 1969, p. 117. Arizona Republic from Phoenix, Arizona. A Publisher Extra Newspaper. newspapers.com/newspage/20197722. Web. February 28, 2018, 10:34 a.m.

Liza Minnelli, Wikipedia, the Free Encyclopedia. en.wikipedia.org/wiki/Liza_ Minnelli. Web. May 1, 2018, 11:14 a.m.

Lockheed C-130 Hercules. Wikipedia, the Free Encyclopedia. en.wikipedia.org/ wiki/Lockheed_C-130_Hercules. Web. December 10, 2017, 9:20 a.m.

Lockheed C-5 Galaxy. Wikipedia, the Free Encyclopedia. en.wikipedia.org/wiki/ Lockheed_C-5_Galaxy. Web. December 10, 2017, 9:23 a.m.

Lockheed C-5 Galaxy. Wikipedia, the Free Encyclopedia. en.wikipedia.org/wiki/ Lockheed_C-5_Galaxy. Web. December 10, 2017, 9:23 a.m.

Lockheed SR-71 Blackbird. Wikipedia, the Free Encyclopedia. wikipedia.org/ wiki/Lockheed_SR-71_Blackbird Web. September 10, 2018, 10:08 a.m.

Mamertine Prison. Wikipedia, the Free Encyclopedia. en.wikipedia.org/wiki/ Mamertine_Prison#People_imprisoned_at_the_Tull. Web March 31, 2018, 10:08 a.m.

Mao Zedong. Wikipedia, the Free Encyclopedia. en.wikipedia.org/wiki/Mao_ Zedong. Web. August 2, 2018, 12:25 p.m.

Marinov, Bojidar. *The Fallacy of Materialistic Determinism*, February 1, 2012. The American Vision. americanvision.org/5540/the-fallacy-of-materialistic-determinism. Web. March 8, 2016, 3:32 p.m.

Martinez-Novoa, Lorraine M, Ph.D. *Consumed by Consumption: A Phenomenological Exploration of the Compulsive Clothing Buying Experience (2016), directed by Dr. Nancy Hodges.* libres.uncg.edu/ir/uncg/f/ MartinezNovoa_uncg_0154D_12082.pdf. Web. August 27, 2018, 11:35 a.m.

Mayflower Compact. Wikipedia, the Free Encyclopedia. en.wikipedia.org/wiki/ Mayflower_Compact. Web. May 16, 2018, 9:20 a.m.

McCann, Jaymi, April 25, 2014. *Cross dedicated to Pope John Paul II crushes pilgrim to death.*

Daily Star. dailystar.co.uk/news/latest-news/376055/Cross-dedicated-to-Pope-John-Paul-II-crushes-pilgrim-to-death. Web. February 26, 2018, 11:45 a.m.

McMillan, Graeme. *Real-Life Casualties from "War of the Worlds," March 31, 2008,* 2:40 p.m. io9.gizmodo.com/373869/real-life-casualties-from-war-of-the-worlds. Web. February 28, 2018, 4:56 p.m.

Metaxas, Eric. *Bonhoeffer: Pastor, Martyr, Prophet, Spy, 2010.* Nashville: Thomas Nelson. ISBN 13: 9781595551382.

Metaxas, Eric. *If You Can Keep It: The Forgotten Promise of American Liberty, 2016.* New York: Viking: Penguin Random House. ISBN 9781101979983.

Metaxas, Eric. *Miracles: What They Are, Why They Happen, and How They Can Change Your Life, 2014. New York: Dutton, Penguin. ISBN 978-0-525-95442-2.*

Meyer, Stephen C. *Darwin's Doubt: The Explosive Origin of Animal Life and the Case for Intelligent Design, 2013.* New York: Harper Collins. ISBN-13: 978-0062071484.

Moore's law. Wikipedia, the Free Encyclopedia. en.wikipedia.org/wiki/ Moore%27s_law. Web. March 26, 2018, 11:20 a.m.

Mt. Guyot. Peakware: World Mountain Encyclopedia. peakware.com/peaks. php?pk=948. Web. March 1, 2018, 4:01 p.m.

Myopia: Taking a Closer Look at the Symptoms, Causes and Treatments of Nearsightedness, Rachel Despres, Friday, September 8ᵗʰ. Active Beat. https://www.activebeat.com/your-health/myopia-taking-a-closer-look-at-the-symptoms-causes-and-treatments-of-nearsightedness/. Web. August 22, 2018, 3:22 p.m.

Newton, John. *Amazing Grace, 1779.* Timeless Truths. library.timelesstruths. org/music/Amazing_Grace. Web. August 2, 2018, 10:45 a.m.

1953 Clemson Tigers football team. Wikipedia, the Free Encyclopedia. en.wikipedia.org/wiki/1953_Clemson_Tigers_football_team. Web. March 1, 2018, 1:03 p.m.

Oakley, Paul, *Jesus, Lover of My Soul (It's All about You).* worshiptogether.com/ songs/jesus-lover-of-my-soul-its-all-about-you. Web. February 22, 2018, 1:16 p.m.

Oh Freedom! Negro Spirituals. negrospirituals.com/songs/oh_freedom.htm. Web. March 23, 2018, 11:48 a.m.

Old Yeller (film), 1957. Wikipedia, the Free Encyclopedia. en.wikipedia.org/ wiki/Old_Yeller_(film). Web. February 28, 2018, 5:34 p.m.

On the Origin of Species. Wikipedia, the Free Encyclopedia. en.wikipedia.org/ wiki/On_the_Origin_of_Species#Geological_record. Web. August 13, 2018, 1:13 p.m.

Orton-Gillingham. Wikipedia, the Free Encyclopedia. en.wikipedia.org/wiki/ Orton-Gillingham. Web. March 1, 2018, 12:27 p.m.

Pastor Isaac. *Bereshit and the Depth of Meaning in the First Word of Bible..* Assembly of Called Out Believers. calledoutbelievers.org/

bereshit-and-the-depth-of-meaning-in-the-first-word-of-bible/. Web. August 18, 2018, 4:54 p.m.

Pat Conroy. Wikipedia, the Free Encyclopedia. en.wikipedia.org/wiki/Pat_ Conroy. Web. March 2, 2018, 3:49 p.m.

Peiffer, Frank G. *These Proceedings Are Closed, 70th Anniversary, September 2, 1945, World War II Ends*. ssjohnwbrown.org/blog/2015/8/30/in-their-own-words-musings-on-the-end-of-wwii. Web. February 28, 2018, 11:09 a.m.

Pentagon Papers. Wikipedia, The Free Encyclopedia. en.wikipedia.org/wiki/ Pentagon_Papers. Web. March 9, 2018, 10:56 a.m.

Probability Space. Wikipedia, the Free Encyclopedia. en.wikipedia.org/wiki/ Probability_space. Web. May 12, 2018, 10:24 a.m.

Project Whirlwind begins. Computer History. computerhistory.org/ timeline/1943/#169ebbe2ad45559efbc6eb357200848f. Web. July 24, 2018, 12:32 p.m.

Redd, Nola Taylor. *Einstein's Theory of General Relativity*, Space.com Contributor | November 7, 2017 08:00am ET.

Religious Views of the Beatles. Wikipedia, the Free Encyclopedia. en.wikipedia. org/wiki/Religious_views_of_the_Beatles. Web. July 17, 2018, 11:28 a.m.

Riead, William, Director. *The Letters*, *The Untold Story of Mother Teresa*, *2014*. Big Screen Partners, V. Ltd. foxconnect.com.

Riggs Field. Clemson Wiki. clemsonwiki.com/wiki/Riggs_Field. Web. March 27, 2018, 9:45 a.m.

Science has found the proof of the existence of God!, December 25, 2016. youtube.com/watch?v=Er9D00DXQQs. Fact Reality. Web. November 21, 2017, 1:15 p.m.

Sears Catalogs from the 1900s. google.com/search?q=sears+catalog+1900s&o-q=Sears+Catalogs+from+the+1900s.&aqs=chrome.1.69i57j0.2472j0j4&-sourceid=chrome&ie=UTF-8 Web. August 8, 2018, 6:21 p.m.

Sentinel program, Wikipedia, the Free Encyclopedia. en.wikipedia.org/wiki/ Sentinel_program. Web. February 28, 2018, 10:20 a.m.

Sex, Lies, and Videotape. Wikipedia, the Free Encyclopedia. en.wikipedia.org/ wiki/Sex_Lies_and_Videotape. Web. February 26, 2018, 1:35 p.m.

Shallow Hal. Wikipedia, the Free Encyclopedia. en.wikipedia.org/wiki/Shallow_ Hal. Web. May 16, 2018, 12:05 p.m.

Shane (1953 film). WhatCulture. whatculture.com/film/8-famous-movie-end-ings-people-always-get-totally-wrong?page=5. Web. February 28, 2018, 5:28 p.m.

Sheeran, Ed. *Eraser*. YouTube. youtube.com/watch?v=OjGrcJ4lZCc. Web. July 27, 2018, 1:56 p.m.

Shirvani, Hassan. *The Wizard of Oz as a Monetary Allegory*. Cameron School of Business. blogs.stthom.edu/cameron/the-wizard-of-oz-as-a-monetary-allegory/. Web. August 13, 2018, 11:11 a.m.

Sigmund Freud. Wikipedia, the Free Encyclopedia. en.wikipedia.org/wiki/Sigmund_Freud. Web. May 2, 2018, 11:27 a.m.

Sorley, Lewis. *Westmoreland: The General Who Lost Vietnam. New York: Houghton Mifflin, Harcourt, 2011. ISBN 978-0-547-51826-8.*

Star Trek planet classification. en.wikipedia.org/wiki/Star_Trek_planet_classi-fication. Web. May 1, 2018, 9:55 a.m.

Stuart, Colin; Birch, Hayley; Looi, Mun Keat. *The Big Questions in Science*. Andre Deutsch Ltd, 2015. ISBN: 9780233004488.

The African Queen (film). Bogart, Hepburn. wikipedia.org/wiki/The_African_Queen_(film). Web. January 9, 2018, 1:06 p.m.

The Big Bang Theory. Wikipedia, the Free Encyclopedia. en.wikipedia.org/wiki/The_Big_Bang_Theory. Web. March 1, 2018, 11:32 a.m.

The Circle (2017 movie). Wikipedia, the Free Encyclopedia. en.wikipedia.org/wiki/The_Circle_(2017_film). Web. July 24, 2018, 2:52 p.m.

The Robe. Wikipedia, the Free Encyclopedia. en.wikipedia.org/wiki/The_Robe_(film). Web. March 26, 2018, 10:37 a.m.

The *Sexiest Military Aircraft*. We Are The Mighty. wearethemighty.com/articles/sexiest-military-aircrafts. Web September 11, 2018, 9:21 a.m.

The story of the ultrasecret A-12 Oxcart—father of the SR-71 Blackbird. Gizmodo. gizmodo.com/the-story-of-the-ultrasecret-a-12-oxcart-father-of-the-1684070908. Web. September 11, 2018, 9:42 a.m.

The Ten Commandments (film). Wikipedia, the Free Encyclopedia. en.wikipedia.org/wiki/The_Ten_Commandments_(1956_film). Web. March 26, 2018, 10:43 a.m.

The Theory of Everything (2014 film). Wikipedia, the Free Encyclopedia. en.wikipedia.org/wiki/The_Theory_of_Everything_(2014_film). Web. March 1, 2018, 1:24.

The Vartabedian Conundrum. Big Bang Theory Transcripts. bigbangtrans. wordpress.com/series-2-episode-11-the-vartabedian-conundrum/. Web. September 11, 2018, 10:30 a.m.

The War of the Worlds (1953 movie). Wikipedia, the Free Encyclopedia. en.wikipedia.org/wiki/The_War_of_the_Worlds_(1953_film). Web. February 28, 2018, 3:51 p.m.

The War of the Worlds (1953), Quotes. IMDb. imdb.com/title/tt0046534/quotes. Web. February 28, 2018, 5:07.

The War of the Worlds (2005 film). Wikipedia, the Free Encyclopedia. en.wikipedia.org/wiki/The_War_of_the_Worlds_(2005_film). Web. February 28, 2018, 3:57 p.m.

The Wizard of Oz. British Board of Film Classification. Wikipedia, the Free Encyclopedia. en.wikipedia.org/wiki/The_Wizard_of_Oz_(1939_film) Web. August 25, 2017, 9:09 a.m.

The Wonderful Wizard of Oz. Wikipedia, the Free Encyclopedia. en.wikipedia.org/wiki/The_Wonderful_Wizard_of_Oz. Web. February 28, 2018, 5:43 p.m.

The Yellow Brick Road. A Free Blog about World Events. theyellowbrickroadfreeblog.wordpress.com/the-meaning-of-the-yellow-brick-road. Web. March 1, 2018, 10:58 a.m.

These Proceedings are closed. September 2, 2015. ssjohnwbrown.org/blog/2015/8/30/in-their-own-words-musings-on-the-end-of-wwii. Web. February 28, 2018, 11:06 a.m.

This Day in History. History. history.com/this-day-in-history/john-lennon-sparks-his-first-major-controversy. Web. April 21, 2018, 11:11 a.m.

This 11-year-old girl just beat Einstein on an IQ test. From the Grapevine. fromthegrapevine.com/lifestyle/11-year-old-girl-just-beat-einstein-iq-test. Web. March 1, 2018, 1:45 p.m.

Thomas, Clarence. *My Grandfather's Son*. Harper Collins Publishers: New York, 2008. ISBN 978-0-06-056556-5.

Thomas Green Clemson. Wikipedia, the Free Encyclopedia. en.wikipedia.org/wiki/Thomas_Green_Clemson. Web. February 26, 2018, 1:30 p.m.

Thompson, Lenora. *The Narcissism of The Big Bang Theory's Dr. Sheldon Cooper.* Narcissism Meets Normalcy. blogs.psychcentral.com/narcissism/2016/10/the-narcissism-of-the-big-bang-theorys-dr-sheldon-cooper. Web. December 15, 2017, 12:48 p.m.

To Kill a Mockingbird. Wikipedia, the Free Encyclopedia. en.wikipedia.org/wiki/To_Kill_a_Mockingbird. Web. September 10, 2018, 2:54 p.m.

Turek, Frank. *The Universe had a Beginning, Thursday, December 29, 2011.* Cross-Examined.org. crossexamined.org/the-universe-had-a-beginning. *Web. December 5, 2017, 1:22 p.m.*

20-Best All Time Movies. The Washington Times. washingtontimes.com/multimedia/collection/20-best-american-movies-all-time/?page=3. Web. February 24, 2018, 9:34.

29 Good Bible Sales Statistics, Brandon [Gaille] Marketing Expert & Blog Master. brandongaille.com/27-good-bible-sales-statistics. Web. March 1, 2018, 4:22 p.m.

The Comedy of Errors. Wikipedia, the Free Encyclopedia. en.wikipedia.org/wiki/The_Comedy_of_Errors. Web. May 3, 2018, 3:57.

TV dinner. Wikipedia, the Free Encyclopedia. ten.wikipedia.org/wiki/TV_dinner. Web. July 27, 2018, 11:04 a.m.

UN Offensive, 1950. Wikipedia, the Free Encyclopedia. en.wikipedia.org/wiki/UN_Offensive,_1950. Web. April 20, 2018, 2:03 p.m.

US Suicide Rates by Age Group, 1970–2002: An Examination of Recent Trends. Robert E. McKeown, PhD, Steven P. Cuffe, MD, and Richard M. Schulz, PhD. NCBI. ncbi.nlm.nih.gov/pmc/articles/PMC1586156/. Web. August 18, 2018, 12:57 p.m.

Utopia means nowhere. Google Search. google.com/search?safe=active&ei=Gv-4WuWtGqfQjwT8jJD4Cw&q=utopia+means+nowhere&oq=utopia+means+no&gs_l=psy-ab.1.0.0j0i22i30k1.36273.40160.0.42036.9.9.0.0.0.0.150.891.8j1.9.0....0...1c.1.64.psy-ab..0.9.890...0i67k1j0i131k-1.0.PHyq7NwqSA8. Web. March 26, 2018, 10:14 a.m.

Vittachi, Nury. *Scientists discover that atheists might not exist, and that's not a joke, July 6th 2014 06:03 p.m.* Science 2.0: Join the Revolution. Writer on the Edge. science20.com/writer_on_the_edge/blog/scientists_discover_that_atheists_might_not_exist_and_thats_not_a_joke-139982 Web. *February 28, 2018, 4:11 p.m.*

Washington's Generals, Wikipedia, the Free Encyclopedia. en.wikipedia.org/
wiki/George_Washington. Web. February 28, 2018, 11:22 a.m.

We are just an advanced breed of monkeys. Stephen Hawking Quotes. brainy-
quote.com/authors/stephen_hawking. Web. May 12, 2018, 11:53 a.m.

Webber, Rebecca. *Meet The Real Narcissists (They're Not What You Think).*
Psychology Today Magazine, September 2016. psychologytoday.com/arti-
cles/201609/meet-the-real-narcissists-theyre-not-what-you-think?collec-
tion=1093092. Web. February 28, 2018, 4:23 p.m.

Webster, Richard. *Freud, Satan, and the Serpent.* From *Why Freud Was Wrong:
Sin, Science and Psychoanalysis (1995),* richardwebster.net. Web. December
12, 2017, 11:41 a.m.

Weinstein, Galina. *Max Born, Albert Einstein and Hermann Minkowski's Space-
Time Formalism of Special Relativity.* arXiv. Cornell University Library.
Retrieved 11 July 2017.

Welles, Orson, and Peter Bogdanovich, *This is Orson Welles.* HarperAudio,
September 30, 1992. ISBN 1-55994-680-6 Audiotape 4A 6:25–6:42.

Wells, H. G. *The War of the Worlds.* Serialised in 1897 by Pearson's Magazine in
the UK and by Cosmopolitan magazine in the US. Published 1898. London:
William Heinemann. en.wikipedia.org/wiki/The_War_of_the_Worlds. Web
February 28, 2018, 4:41 p.m.

Who Was the Shulammite Woman? Got Questions. gotquestions.org/Shulammite-
woman.html. Web. February 28, 2018, 4:32 p.m.

William Jennings Bryan. Wikipedia, the Free Encyclopedia. en.wikipedia.org/
wiki/William_Jennings_Bryan. Web. February 26, 2018, 1:34 p.m.

Wonder Woman & Invisible Jet. Amazon. amazon.com/Wonder-Woman-
Invisible-Imaginext-STOCK/dp/B072PWMGTW. Web. March 1:2018,
11:46 a.m.

World War II Casualties. Wikipedia, the Free Encyclopedia. en.wikipedia.org/
wiki/World_War_II_casualties. Web. February 26, 2018, 1:34 p.m.

You're So Vain. Wikipedia, the Free Encyclopedia. en.wikipedia.org/wiki/
You%27re_So_Vain. *Web. March 1. 2018, 3:40 p.m.x*